Praise for Charles Bufe's previous works

"The title of this book will serve as an effective marketing device, but does not do justice to its content that reaches far beyond the two questions it asks. What impressed me most was the author's research, the depth of his insights, and the logical consistency of his conclusions."
—*The Journal of Rational Recovery*
(on *Alcoholics Anonymous: Cult or Cure?*)

"This book is exceptionally well written . . . it is articulate, objective, concise, and complete. . . . This book is an example of honesty and balance, in other words critical thinking."
—Bay Area Skeptics
(on *Alcoholics Anonymous: Cult or Cure?*)

"Such bitterness, such negativity, such unbridled humor, wit and sarcasm."
—*Mensa Bulletin*
(on *The American Heretic's Dictionary*)

"You'll never be at a loss for a droll definition again. Keep this on your desk for that emergency epigram or nicely worded insult."
—*Fact Sheet Five*
(on *The American Heretic's Dictionary*)

"The quirky cartoons by J.R. Swanson nicely complement Bufe' cruel wit. Recommended."
—*Free Inquiry*
(on *The American Heretic's Dictionary*)

"This book is a far-reaching collection of timeless, provocative, politically astute quotations from a wide range of people active in many walks of life. It is fun, informative, and more."
—*Z Magazine*
(on *The Heretic's Handbook of Quotations*)

"[This book] is enormous fun to dip into . . ."
—*Social Anarchism*
(on *The Heretic's Handbook of Quotations*)

"Solidly entertaining . . . reminiscent of early Mick Farren."
—*Publishers Weekly* online
(on *Free Radicals: A novel of utopia and dystopia*)
(under the pseudonym Zeke Teflon)

"The plot holds the reader's interest and should appeal to a fairly broad audience."
—*Booklist* online
(on *Free Radicals: A novel of utopia and dystopia*)

"This book is among the best future-shock reads in years. . . . If we lived in the '60s and '70s—when audience-rattling paperbacks like *Naked Lunch* were cheap, plentiful and available on pharmacy-spinner racks—critics would hail *Free Radicals* as a masterpiece."
—*Tucson Weekly*
(on *Free Radicals: A novel of utopia and dystopia*)

"Geared for rock, pop, and jazz musicians who want to zero in on the theoretical topics most relevant to their chosen styles rather than tackling formal classical theory head-on, this [book] crams a remarkable amount of information into 74 pages."
—*Guitar Player*
(on *An Understandable Guide to Music Theory: The most useful aspects of theory for rock, jazz & blues players*)

"Chaz Bufe has designed a book that does exactly what the title claims it does. This is an excellent way for any musician to tie together any loose ends he or she might have regarding music theory. . . . It's extremely user-friendly without being condescending to the reader. I highly recommend it."
—*Jazz Player*
(on *An Understandable Guide to Music Theory*)

Other Books by Charles Bufe

Alcoholics Anonymous: Cult or Cure?

The American Heretic's Dictionary

Exercises for Individual and Group Development
(with co-author Dale DeNunzio)

Free Radicals: A novel of utopia and dystopia
(as "Zeke Teflon")

Godless: 150 Years of Disbelief

The Heretic's Handbook of Quotations: Cutting Comments on Burning Issues

Resisting 12-Step Coercion: How to fight forced participation in AA, NA, or 12-step treatment
(with co-authors Stanton Peele and Archie Brodsky)

An Understandable Guide to Music Theory: The most useful aspects of theory for rock, jazz, & blues musicians

Translations

Cuban Anarchism: The History of a Movement
by Frank Fernández
(translator/editor)

Dreams of Freedom: A Ricardo Flores Magón Reader
(primary translator, with co-editor Mitch Verter)

Venezuelan Anarchism: The History of a Movement
by Rodolfo Montes de Oca
(translator/editor)

Venezuela: Revolution as Spectacle
by Rafael Uzcátegui
(translator/editor)

24 Reasons to Abandon Christianity

Why Christianity's perverted morality leads to misery and death

by

Charles Bufe

See Sharp Press ◆ Tucson, Arizona

For information contact:

See Sharp Press
P.O. Box 1731
Tucson, AZ 85702

www.seesharppress.com

Bufe, Charles.
24 Reasons to Abandon Christianity / Charles Bufe ; Tucson, Ariz. : See Sharp Press, 2022.
Includes bibliographical references and index.
340 p. ; 23 cm.
ISBN 978-1-947071-42-1

1. Religion. 2. Religion—controversial literature.
I. Title.

200

First Printing

Contents

"Religion is an insult to human dignity. With or without it you would have good people doing good things and evil people doing evil things. But for good people to do evil things, that takes religion."

—Steven Weinberg
winner 1979 Nobel Prize in Physics

Introduction

Becoming a Christian requires no effort, no thought at all. People normally become Christian because of childhood indoctrination, a process that usually begins with the baptism of infants. After baptism, Christian parents and Christian clergy subject children to years of emotional and psychological manipulation that is, ultimately, designed to create a new generation of believers. Those indoctrinated victims then subject others, often their own children, to the same emotional (and all too often physical) abuse they themselves suffered.

But to abandon Christianity, as I argued in *Disbelief 101: A Young Person's Guide to Atheism* (published by See Sharp Press and edited by Chaz), requires thought and courage, and ultimately brings with it a responsibility to help other people free themselves from their destructive beliefs. In other words, atheism in itself is insufficient to the task. It's also necessary to expose the harms caused by religious belief, belief which, in this country, is overwhelmingly Christian. I'd argue that this exposure is a necessary complement to atheism, with a reasonable term for the combination being "anti-theism."

Unfortunately, the canon of antitheistic books remains vastly smaller than the canon of theistic books; in fact, Christian titles often comprise entire sections of bookstores, and sometimes fill entire stores. (No publishing genre in history has ever been so profitable yet so worthless.) But despite the rapid 18th-century spread of atheism among educated Westerners, a true antitheistic book did not appear until Nietzsche's *The Anti-Christ* in 1895. Nietzsche revealed Christianity to be a religion of weakness, whose practitioners turn subservience into a virtue, and who prefer groveling before a nonexistent deity (and its clerical interpreters) to thinking for themselves.

Over three decades passed before English philosopher Bertrand Russell presented, first as a lecture and then as an essay, *Why I am Not a Christian* in 1927. Like Nietzsche, Russell understood that Christianity not only opposes science and free thought, but actively promotes a set of values that can only be described as systematized bigotry, close-mindedness, and hatred of self and others. Following Russell's small book, remarkably few notable atheist and antitheistic works (let alone a powerful atheist movement) appeared prior to the 21st century. (Though the number of atheists is growing, we're still waiting for a movement.)

Historians may one day wonder why the twentieth century never gave rise to a potent antitheistic movement, given what we now know about the Catholic Church, pedophile priests, and the Church's systematic efforts to cover up their crimes. When the pederasts and pederast-enablers in the Church could pull themselves away from altar boys and piling up the loot, it seemed their only focuses were on supporting fascist regimes and opposing gay and women's rights, especially reproductive rights.

The Protestants, as always, were fractured, but it's hard to find a time when a majority of them took a moral stance that was in any real sense moral. There they were, opposing feminism, civil rights, gay rights, and science. Readers might protest, "yes, but there were also Christians who supported those things." Sadly, they were a largely invisible minority, with the only real exceptions being black evangelicals in the civil rights movement. Indeed, it would be difficult to find one person in the twentieth or twenty-first centuries who opposed equal rights for women, minorities, and gay people, or who raised objections to the very well supported theory of evolution, who did so for ethical reasons not rooted in religious belief.

Virtually every single person who justified the oppression of women, and who opposed the integration of African-Americans and the teaching of science, drew their righteous justification from the Bible.

Not until 2004, after the 9/11 attacks, did anti-theism reappear with Sam Harris's *The End of Faith: Religion, Terror, and the Future of Reason*. Harris stated that one could hardly condemn Islam for its nonsensical and bloody teachings without also condemning Christianity, which largely teaches the same things. (Indeed, Islam retains both the Old and New Testaments as scripture, and merely adds additional authoritarian, inhumane "sacred" writings to them.) The same logic that condemns Islam condemns all religion. Two years after publication of *The End of Faith*, the eminent biologist Richard Dawkins published *The God Delusion*, which became a best seller; it prompted the journalist Gary Wolf to coin the phrase "New Atheism" to describe the early 21st-century antitheist intellectual movement.

Shortly thereafter, Dawkins and Harris joined Daniel Dennett and Christopher Hitchens in being deemed the "Four Horsemen" of this so-called new atheism. This label was purely a media construct, though it was useful in spreading the word.

But a close analysis of the "Four Horsemen's" books reveals that Wolf's phrase is misleading. Dawkins, and Dennett produced impressive works of logic, but they wrote like what they were, hyper-educated philosophers, and their works are more properly described as traditional works of atheism. One could enjoy the books of Dawkins and Dennett, as I did, but still come away feeling that they hadn't done enough to reveal the monstrous crimes of Christianity.

In 2007, Christopher Hitchens published *God is Not Great: How Religion Poisons Everything*, a highly entertaining and informative polemic, and began describing himself as not just an atheist but an antitheist. In *God is Not Great*, Hitchens wielded his wit and reason against all religions, even seemingly innocuous Eastern practices, and revealed them all to be diseased branches of the same tree, the tree of illogic, hatred, bigotry, and superstition. Hitchens, with his private-school British diction, celebrity status, and mastery of the facts, seemed capable of carrying the antitheistic movement into a new era all by himself. But the cigarettes and the booze, mostly the cigarettes, got to Hitchens: he died of cancer in 2011, and anti-theism lost its leading voice.

Now, over a decade after the death of Hitchens, Chaz Bufe is reviving anti-theism, and the timing is right given the theofascist threat facing America and much of the rest of the world. To be an atheist is one thing, but to expose the damage done by religion and to call for its end is another. Chaz's book rouses emotions I haven't felt since the heady days of the Four Horsemen; it calls Christianity to task for its hateful philosophy and criminal activities.

As Chaz states, when writing about Christianity's reliance on fear:

> Throughout almost its entire time on Earth, the motor driving Christianity has been—in addition to the fear of death—fear of the devil and fear of hell. One can only imagine how potent these threats seemed prior to the rise of science and rational thinking, which have largely robbed these bogeys of their power to inspire terror.

It's worth remembering, as that mean-spirited gasbag Billy Graham used to point out, that no one in the Bible talked about hell more than Jesus. The evils committed in the name of Christianity aren't the result of misunderstanding: they stem directly from Christianity's basic teachings in both the Old and New Testaments. Christians who emotionally torture children, force a psychological burka on women, bash gay people, and oppose science and rationality are doing exactly what their religion tells them to do.

Becoming a Christian requires no thought, but those who leave Christianity usually need reasons to do so. Chaz Bufe supplies them. To his 24 reasons, I'd add two hopes: that religious readers will abandon their faith after reading this book, and that non-religious readers will abandon their complacency.

—Chris Edwards, author of *Spiritual Snake Oil: Fads and Fallacies in Pop Culture* and (as S.C. Hitchcock) *Disbelief 101: A Young Person's Guide to Atheism*

Preface

While in my early teens, I read Bertrand Russell's *Why I Am Not a Christian and Other Essays*. It was a revelation. I already had grave doubts about the conservative Catholic faith in which I was being raised—due largely to the problem of evil, and to reading and analyzing Aquinas's "proofs" of the existence of God—and Russell's book crystallized those doubts. It showed in clear, direct, if brief, fashion the illogical nature of both Christianity and belief in God; as well, it also touched on some of the reasons why Christianity produces so much misery, both public and private.

Since then, I've read many more books on Christianity. A large number of them retrod familiar ground (the irrational nature of belief in God, for instance), and many others analyzed particular destructive aspects of Christianity (e.g., misogyny), but none of them attempted to deal with all of Christianity's illogical and misery-producing traits. Indeed, that's a near impossible task given the sheer number of such traits, and the most that can be done is to treat the most prominent. Even then, given the sheer magnitude of the task, it would be nearly impossible to do a really thorough job in a reasonable number of pages. Probably the best that can be done is to summarize the most destructive aspects of Christianity, provide brief explanations of why they exist, and provide examples of the harms they produce, as I've done here.

Readers will notice that one of the most prominent reasons to abandon Christianity is missing from this book, the probable nonexistence of God. This matter has been dealt with so well, so often, and at such length elsewhere—see, for instance, Richard Dawkins' *The God Delusion*, Victor Stenger's *God: The Failed Hypothesis*; George H. Smith's *Atheism: The Case Against God*; Sebastien Faure's *Does God Exist?*; and Chris Edwards' (as S.C. Hitchcock) *Disbelief 101*—that I decided to forego dealing with it and instead focus on the damage Christianity has done to individuals and society, both historically and in the here and now, and why Christianity has done so much damage.

Some readers might object, "All of the points you raise here are obvious. Aren't you beating a dead horse into the ground?" Well, no.

Most people (at least in the U.S.) are Christians who still, somehow, consider Christianity a good thing.* A great many of them would contend that the good in Christianity far outweighs its destructive qualities, and some would even contend that Christianity has no destructive qualities. This book is intended as an antidote to such delusions.

Even those under no such misapprehensions, those who know better, often stay silent rather than utter a word about the 800-pound simian on the sofa. I noticed an excellent example of that the evening I started writing this preface. The "Ideas" section of the BBC News site was featuring four short videos, "Prejudice Unpacked," a mini-series of sorts. The videos dealt with misogyny, racism, homophobia, and antisemitism, and they all bore near-identical titles, such as "Why are people anti-Semitic?" and "Why are people sexist?" A subtitle asks, "Why do people hold prejudices—like racism, homophobia and sexism?" and then adds, "We explore some of the root causes."

None of the videos contain a single word about Christianity, one of the root causes of the evils these videos profess to analyze (especially antisemitism which, since the writing of the gospels, is almost entirely due to Christianity). This type of deliberate blindness—less charitably, gutlessness—is routine in the media and in everyday life. It's an all-too-common form of cowardice, and it provided a spur to the writing of *24 Reasons*.

Other spurs included the dishonesty, hypocrisy, irrationality, cruelty, and authoritarianism endemic to Christianity; I've considered all of these things both dangerous and contemptible since I left Catholicism while in high school. So, in the year 2000 I wrote *20 Reasons to Abandon Christianity*, an 8,000-word booklet. In the preface, I said that its purpose was to "list the most outstanding misery-inducing and socially destructive qualities of Christianity in one place." It did the job, but it was short, well under a tenth the size of the present volume.

Over time, I became convinced that the matter deserved more thorough treatment, so several years ago I decided to expand *20 Reasons* to book

---

* An October 2021 Pew Research survey confirms this, with 53% of U.S. adults saying that "churches and other religious organizations" do more good than harm, 21% saying the opposite, and 25% saying they don't make much difference. Large majorities in all Christian denominations said that religion does more good than harm, while only atheists (71% vs. 12%), agnostics (52% vs 24%) and, barely, the general unaffiliated (32% vs. 31%) said it does more harm than good.

length, but a heavy workload and health issues slowed the writing considerably. The year-plus of self-isolation, followed by almost another year of restricted social activity during the Coronavirus pandemic, finally gave me the time to work on the book nearly full time and to finish it.

Twenty-four Reasons to Abandon Christianity turned out considerably different than *20 Reasons to Abandon Christianity*, not only in its greater length, but also in terms of structure: I added several new chapters, combined several others, deleted two I thought were weak, and added a lengthy appendix; the result was a better organized book of over a hundred thousand words.

My motivation when I started writing *24 Reasons to Abandon Christianity* was similar to that when I wrote *20 Reasons*: to point out, but in more compelling form, the many social and personal harms caused by Christianity. During the writing of *24 Reasons*, especially during the pandemic, my motivations expanded beyond that for two reasons.

The first is that Christianity's misery-inducing qualities haven't changed much, if at all, over the past two-plus decades, but the socially and politically destructive aspects of Christianity are becoming ever more apparent. With the ascent of the demagogic Donald Trump on the backs of his theocratic worshipers, it's become apparent that Christianity is even more of a danger than I thought, not only to human happiness and freedom, but to human civilization, and quite possibly to both human and environmental survival. (This is not hyperbole. Christian-supported authoritarian regimes the world over, such as those in Brazil, the Philippines, Poland, Hungary, and the U.S. [while under Trump], have not only attempted to entrench themselves by destroying civil liberties—especially freedom of the press and the right to peacefully protest—but have either done nothing to combat the ongoing and ever more deadly climate change disaster, or have actively worked to worsen it. If these regimes manage to retain power—especially if the Trump cult manages to regain power—they'll continue to push us over the edge of the climate-disaster cliff.)

The second reason is that most people, somehow, still consider Christianity and, more especially, Christian morals as good things. They aren't. All of the harms I catalog here—the misogyny, homophobia, antisemitism, wars of conquest, mass murder of "witches" and heretics, the routine use of the cruelest forms of torture—all of these stem directly from Christianity's perverse moral teachings. My hope now is to alert readers not only to the harm Christianity has done (and is still doing), but also to *why* Christianity has done so much harm.

As regards the title, "abandon," rather than "suppress" or "eliminate," was chosen deliberately. Attempts to coercively suppress beliefs are not only ethically wrong, but in the long run are often ineffective, as the resurgence of Christianity in the former Soviet Union demonstrates. Coercion isn't necessary to achieve a religion-free world. Information, critiques, ridicule, organizing, and outreach are; they're much better tools in the building of a healthier world. Means determine ends, and coercion is not only a very unhealthy means, but one that produces very unhealthy ends.

As regards the subtitle, the phrase "Christianity's perverted morality" was also chosen deliberately. In the United States, when most people hear the word "morality," they automatically assume that the term refers exclusively to Christianity's rules and regulations, without a thought as to whether those rules and regulations are moral in any real sense. If you think morality consists of blindly following the commands of an ancient book and its interpreters, no matter how cruel or nonsensical the commands, then yes, Christian morality is moral. But if you think morality consists of being kind and following what's probably the most enlightened teaching in the entire Bible, the "do unto others" Golden Rule (Matthew 7:12 and Luke 6:31), conventional Christian morality and the teachings in the Bible are, overall, profoundly *im*moral. For instance, what is kind, what is moral about Exodus 22:18, "Thou shalt not suffer a witch to live"? And how moral are the Ten Commandments, the foundation of Christian morality, which prohibit cursing and worshiping graven images, but do not prohibit slavery or torture? (Neither of these horrors are condemned, let alone prohibited, anywhere in the Bible.)

This points to an underappreciated and often overlooked aspect of Christianity: Christians—all of them—are of necessity "cafeteria Christians" who choose those parts of the Bible they want to obey and ignore the rest. Good, kind, live-and-let-live Christians pick the good, kind verses, and cruel, authoritarian Christians pick the cruel, authoritarian verses. It's not a point in the Bible's favor that it contains both types of verse, with the cruel verses predominating. As the website of the notorious Westboro Baptist Church puts it, "For every one verse about God's mercy, love, compassion, etc., there are two verses about His vengeance, hatred, wrath, etc."

Some might object that the New Testament does have some good teachings and that there have been praiseworthy Christian-inspired social movements—the civil rights movement, the sanctuary movement, Dorothy Day's Catholic Workers, and others.

There are three things to remember here. The first is that these movements are a prime example of "cafeteria Christianity." The well-intentioned participants in these movements focus(ed) on the good, kind passages in the Bible, and ignore(d) the hateful, murderous passages. The second point is that the good done by Christians working in the civil rights and other social change movements (and Christians working at food banks, rescue missions, etc.) does nothing to eliminate the Bible's hateful passages, nor the harmful words and deeds of their mean-spirited fellow Christians. The third point is that fear-driven, cruel Christians will continue to self-righteously cite the Bible's cruel, hate-inspiring passages as justification for inflicting harm on others. All too obviously, they enjoy doing that too much to stop, so they'll continue to cause needless suffering as long as they have the power to do so.

Nothing kind, compassionate Christians can do will remove the Bible's brutal passages nor the harms they continue to incite. By continuing to profess Christianity, those doing good in its name are providing cover for their cruel brethren and the evil they do. It would be a huge step forward if kind, compassionate Christians would abandon Christianity. It would remove a smokescreen; it would make it much easier for all to see the harmfulness of that dire religion and those hurting others in its name.

When considered *in toto*, the 24 reasons to abandon Christianity listed here lead to an irresistible conclusion: Christianity must be abandoned for the sake of personal happiness, social progress, and human and environmental survival. And if Christianity is ever to disappear, it will be because individual human beings wake up, abandon their destructive, repressive beliefs, and choose to be here now in the only life we have—and choose to make this life kinder and more humane.

Acknowledgments

I'd like to thank all those who helped in the writing of this book, especially Chris Edwards, who was good enough to write the introduction, and G. Richard Bozarth, Barbara Bailey, Michael Behre, Kristin Eckland, Jack B. Worthy, and Ron and Elaine Jones, all of whom provided useful feedback. I truly appreciate their help.

I'm also indebted to the many writers who have provided insightful critiques of Christianity, and to those who have exposed its long and bloody history. They include Christopher Hitchens, *God Is Not Great*; Sam Harris, *The End of Faith*; Friedrich Nietzsche, *The Anti-Christ*; Chris Mato Nunpa, *The Great Evil*; Chris Edwards, (as "S.C. Hitchcock") *Disbelief 101: A Young Person's Guide to Atheism*; David Stannard, *American Holocaust*; James McDonald, *Beyond Belief: Two thousand years of bad faith in the Christian Church*; Sarah Posner, *Unholy: Why White Evangelicals Worship at the Altar of Donald Trump*; Ryan Cragun, *What You Don't Know About Religion (but should)*; and Steve Wells, *The Skeptic's Annotated Bible*.

Christian sources have also been of help, including Diarmaid MacCulloch's *Christianity: The First Three Thousand Years*, Philip Jenkins' *Laying Down the Sword: Why we can't ignore the Bible's violent verses*, Robert P. Jones' *White Too Long: The Legacy of White Supremacy in American Christianity*, and Bible Gateway (www.biblegateway.com).

Finally, I'd like to thank the critics who will comb through this book looking for errors, no matter how small. I've done my best to make *24 Reasons* airtight, but in a work that's over a hundred thousand words long, and that cites thousands of facts and hundreds of sources, minor errors are bound to creep in. Those who point them out will help to ensure that future printings are even more accurate than this first edition.

Notes: All of the Bible verses quoted in this book were taken from the King James Version (KJV). There are two reasons for this. The first is that it's the most familiar version to English speakers. The second is that while it's not the clearest translation (due mostly to its archaic language, oft-times odd spelling, punctuation, and capitalization, and its frequent use of euphemisms) it has, arguably, the highest literary value of any English translation, and it's always good to present anything you're criticizing in its best light. So, I've used it here. But to avoid confusion, in a few places I've added brief explanatory notes about the KJV passages I quote.

Because I wrote nearly all of this book during the pandemic, and the bulk of it while in self-isolation, I had to rely heavily upon online sources. In order to make it easier for readers of physical copies to access those sources, I've included TinyURLs < within carats > following the full URLs in the endnotes. (TinyURL is a free redirect service.)

Finally, to make the book easier to navigate, the endnotes are used purely to cite sources, while footnotes are reserved for incidental information, parenthetical comments, etc.

"Science flies us to the moon. Religion flies us into buildings."

—Victor Stenger

1

Christianity Harms Children

> To succeed, the theologians invade the cradle, the nursery. In the brains of innocence they plant the seeds of superstition. They pollute the minds and imaginations of children. They frighten the happy with threats of pain—they soothe the wretched with gilded lies. . . . Every Sunday school is a kind of Inquisition where they torture and deform the minds of children.
>
> —Robert Ingersoll, "Truth"

Emotional and Intellectual Abuse

If Christian fear mongering were directed solely at adults, it would be bad enough, but Christians routinely terrorize helpless children through grisly depictions of the endless suffering they'll be subjected to if they don't live obedient Christian lives; Christianity has darkened the early years of generation upon generation of children, who, ironically, victimized following generations in the same manner in which they themselves had been victimized. The nearly two thousand years of Christian terrorizing and indoctrination of children ranks as one of its greatest crimes, and it's one that continues to this day.

As an example of Christianity's cruel brainwashing of the innocent, consider this excerpt from an officially approved 19th-century Catholic children's book:

> Think of a coffin, not made of wood, but of fire, solid fire! And now come into this other room. You see a pit, a deep, almost bottomless, pit. Look down it and you will see something red hot and burning. It is a coffin, a red-hot coffin of fire. . . . It burns him [a sinful child] from beneath. The sides of it

> scorch him. The heavy burning lid on the top presses down close upon him; he pants for breath; he cannot breath; he cannot bear it; he gets furious . . . He tries with all his strength to burst open the coffin. He cannot do it. He has no strength remaining. He gives up and sinks down again. Again the horrible choking. Again he tries; again he sinks down; so he will go on forever and ever.
> —Rev. John Furniss, C.S.S.R.,* *Tracts for Spiritual Reading: Designed for first communions, retreats, missions, &c*

There are many similar passages in this sadistic little book. Commenting on it, William Meagher, Vicar-General of Dublin, states in his Approbation:

> I have carefully read over this Little Volume for Children and have found nothing whatever in it contrary to the doctrines of the Holy Faith; but on the contrary, a great deal to charm, instruct and edify the youthful classes for whose benefit it has been written.

If the purpose of preaching hell to children isn't to terrorize them, it's hard to see what other purpose it could possibly serve. Certainly, Christians have not rushed forth to provide an answer.

As for a more modern exercise in Christian terrorizing of children, the most popular Christian feature film ever produced is Mel Gibson's bloodcurdlingly graphic torture-porn flick, *The Passion of the Christ*, which grossed over $600 million and is the highest earning Christian film of all time. Almost unbelievably, at least some Christian parents deliberately exposed their kids to this nonstop, nauseating exercise in gore, suffering, and sadism. One shudders to think of the emotional damage this inflicted on their innocent children; at the very least, it had to induce nightmares.

Even when indoctrination doesn't include the induction of terror, it's still very unfair to the child. Force feeding children absurdities as absolute truths, and insisting they shouldn't question anything about those absurdities, short circuits their ability to think for themselves, short circuits their ability to think critically. It's an attempt to rob children of the ability to develop a conscience of their own; it's an attempt to rob them of the chance to determine for themselves what's right and what's wrong.

---

* The Reverend Furniss was a popular 19th-century Catholic children's author. He wrote over a dozen more charming, instructive, and edifying books for the young, with titles such as *The House of Death* and *The Terrible Judgment, and The Bad Child*. The abbreviation C.S.S.R. stands for *Congregatio Sanctissimi Redemptoris*, a Catholic religious order commonly called the Redemptorists.

As Mikhail Bakunin put it in *God and the State*, inadvertently pointing out one of the reasons for Christianity's emphasis on indoctrinating children:

> The doctrine taught by the Apostles of Christ, wholly consoling as it may have seemed to the unfortunate, was too revolting, too absurd from the standpoint of reason, ever to have been accepted by enlightened men . . .

So religion—Christianity, Islam, Mormonism, Hinduism, virtually every religion—targets the young. Biologist and author Richard Dawkins explains why children are such easy prey for those who indoctrinate them:

> When a child is young, for good Darwinian reasons, it would be valuable for the child to believe everything it's told. A child needs to learn a language, it needs to learn the social customs of its people, it needs to learn all sorts of rules—like don't put your finger in the fire, and don't pick up snakes, and don't eat red berries. . . . [T]he rule of thumb [is] 'be fantastically gullible, believe everything you're told by your elders and betters.'
>
> That's a good rule, and it works. But any rule that says 'Believe everything you're told' is automatically going to be vulnerable to parasitization. Computers, for example, are vulnerable to parasitization because they believe all they're told. . . .
>
> [T]he survival mechanism that makes children's brains believe what they're told—for good reason—is automatically vulnerable to parasitic codes such as 'You must believe in the great juju in the sky,' or 'You must kneel down and face east and pray five times a day.'[1]

The nominally Christian Mormon Church* provides an excellent if extreme example of how childhood religious indoctrination works. From

---

* Despite the Church of Jesus Christ of Latter-day Saints' title, and despite how vehemently Mormons claim to be Christian, Mormons are no more Christian than Muslims or Moonies (Unification Church). Mormonism, Islam, and the Unification Church are new religions, separate from Christianity, and are distinguished from it by their claims that their "prophets" and ("messiah" as regards the Moonies) received (and, in the case of the Mormons, are still receiving) a new revelation on the level of the Old and New Testaments. As well, Islam, the Moonies, and the Mormons put the revelations from their prophets into the form of holy books that are separate from the Bible and are more revered by the churches' (respective) followers than the Bible. So, it's a huge stretch to say that Mormonism is a form of Christianity. It's more accurate to say that Mormonism, like Islam, is a new religion that incorporates elements of Christianity—just as Christianity incorporates elements of Judaism. But for the purposes of this book, we'll take the Mormons at their word and consider them Christian.

infancy, youngsters subjected to Mormon indoctrination hear day in day out that Mormonism is "true"; they're also forced to say that they "know" that Mormonism is "true," first in front of their families, then in front of an audience at Mormon ceremonies. To further sink in the hook, Mormon children are taught that any positive feelings they experience while praying, singing hymns, participating in Family Home Evening, testifying at worship services, etc., etc. are evidence of the truth of Mormonism. They're also told that doubt is destructive and comes from Satan. So, they're whipsawed between positive and negative emotions, which they're taught to believe come either from God or the devil. The end result is that it's very difficult for those who've been subjected to LDS childhood indoctrination to free themselves from it, especially so since apostates not only have to overcome their own conditioning, but all too often risk shunning by their own families if they're open about leaving Mormonism.*

Childhood religious indoctrination sets children up for a life of obedience to others (who pretend to have a direct line to God), and who often do not have the children's wellbeing at heart. Very often this includes channeling children into a life of fear (of the devil and hell), guilt (about sex), wasted time, and economic exploitation—wasting hours on end on Sundays and sometimes other days of the week, plus tithing to support the very institutions responsible for their indoctrination.

Just how important childhood indoctrination is to Christianity can be seen in the low adult religious conversion rate to Christianity. A 2015 Pew report showed that approximately one in three Americans have switched religious affiliation or abandoned religion entirely, and that over half of them became "nones," with no religious affiliation;** Pew reports that 85.6% of the U.S. population was raised Christian, and 19.2% of Americans have left the various Christian sects; at the same time, converts to the

---

* For a much more thorough description of Mormon indoctrination of children, see Jack B. Worthy's *The Mormon Cult*, pp. 14–27.

** Since the 2015 Pew report, the percentage of "nones" has increased. Only four years later, in 2019, the percentage of the U.S. population that self-identified as Christian had fallen to 65%, down from 78% in 2007, while the number of "nones" had increased to 26%,[2] though in 2020 the number of "nones" had decreased to 23%,[3] which was still significantly higher than the 17% reported in 2009.[4] The 2020 figure, however, turned out to be a statistical blip—a single anomalous data point in an otherwise upward trend. In late 2021, Pew Research reported that the percentage of "nones" had risen to 29%, an all-time high, while at the same time the percentage of Americans who identified as Christian had fallen to 63%, an all-time low.[5]

various branches of Christianity made up only 4.2% of the population, an over 4 to 1 ratio.[6] This means that well over 90% of American Christians are Christian because of childhood religious indoctrination.

As if to underline how fast Americans are fleeing Christianity, Pew Research reports: "Overall, 13% of all U.S. adults are former Catholics—people who were raised in the faith . . . By contrast, 2% of U.S. adults are converts to Catholicism—people who now identify as Catholic after having been raised in another religion (or no religion). This means that there are 6.5 former Catholics in the U.S. for every convert to the faith."[7]

To put this another way, Americans are abandoning Christianity *en masse*. American Christianity is hemorrhaging adherents, with over half of those who leave the faith in which they were raised abandoning Christianity entirely. All of this underscores the importance to American Christian sects of the particular form of child abuse known as childhood religious indoctrination. Without it, they'd wither away.

Beyond its importance in creating religious adherence, childhood religious indoctrination invariably involves the elevation of faith over reason. It teaches children that questioning is bad, and that accepting oft-times absurd assertions at face value—in the complete lack of evidence, or in the face of contrary evidence—is somehow a good thing.

Unfortunately, habits of thought inculcated in childhood tend to carry over into adulthood. If you reject reason, evidence, and a questioning attitude in one fundamental matter, you'll probably reject them in others. As neuroscientist Bobby Azarian puts it:

> It is a combination of the brain's vulnerability to believing unsupported facts and aggressive indoctrination that create the perfect storm for gullibility. Due to the [childhood] brain's neuroplasticity, or ability to be sculpted by lived experiences, evangelicals literally become hardwired to believe far-fetched statements.
>
> This wiring begins when they are first taught to accept Biblical stories not as metaphors for living life practically and purposefully, but as objective truth. Mystical explanations for natural events train young minds to not demand evidence for beliefs. As a result, the neural pathways that promote healthy skepticism and rational thought are not properly developed. This inevitably leads to a greater susceptibility to lying and gaslighting by manipulative politicians, and greater suggestibility in general.[8]

"Manipulative politicians" want to keep it that way. A key portion of the 2012 Texas GOP platform's education section reads as follows:

> Knowledge-Based Education—We oppose the teaching of Higher Order Thinking Skill (HOTS)(values clarification), critical thinking skills and similar programs that are simply a relabeling of Outcome-Based Education (OBE) (mastery learning) which focus on behavior modification and have the purpose of challenging the student's fixed beliefs and undermining parental authority.[9]

So, the evangelical-controlled Texas Republicans oppose teaching students the critical thinking skills they need to "challenge" their "fixed beliefs," and they assert that "the purpose" of teaching critical thinking skills is to "undermin[e] parental authority." (It's highly unlikely that any critical-thinking-skills advocates have ever suggested "undermin[ing] parental authority." If so, this GOP statement is an attempt to pass off a pejorative assumption, or deliberate lie, as fact.) Of course, the Republican platform also expressed opposition to sex education and early childhood education, and support for the teaching of "school subjects with emphasis on the Judeo-Christian principles upon which America was founded."

To cite but one example of the gullibility the Texas GOP seems to prize, a 2015 Pew Research report showed that white evangelicals were the religious group most likely to be climate-change deniers, with only 28% believing that climate change is primarily due to human activity.[10] In contrast, 64% of the religiously unaffiliated accepted the very well supported scientific consensus that human activity is the primary cause of climate change.[11] (That's still a shockingly low figure, but it does show that most "nones," in comparison with most evangelicals, have at least a few functioning brain cells.) So, a large majority of white evangelicals are blind to the greatest long-term threat to their own, and everyone else's, children; they're unwilling to do anything to mitigate this unfolding disaster that is already causing ever-increasing misery and death, and in many cases they even attempt to block efforts to combat this terrible threat to coming generations.

Thus it shouldn't be surprising that data on religious beliefs, educational levels, vocabulary, and critical thinking skills shows that "the more religious individuals are, the lower their IQ and their educational attainment, . . . [and their critical thinking skills]" and that there's a statistically significant difference in vocabulary between fundamentalists, who have the poorest vocabularies, and the nonreligious, who have the best.[12]

Then there's the Bible. The Fifth Commandment (in Exodus 20) orders children to do evil to themselves by honoring their parents, no matter what, no matter how abusive those parents might be. But why on earth should anyone honor an abusive parent, especially a physically or sexually abusive parent? Unfortunately, the Fifth Commandment is a blanket command, so there's no way out for victims: they *must* honor their parents, including abusers. Anyone with an abusive parent who follows this command (or doesn't, and feels guilty about it) will likely end up doing her or himself psychological harm, and will possibly set him or herself up for years of self-blame.

Finally, almost all Christian indoctrination of children involves denigration of sex and the induction of guilt and shame in children over their natural urges. This frequently produces great misery in adolescence, and all too often that misery carries over into adulthood, sometimes for the rest of indoctrinated victims' lives. (More on this in Chapter 12 which covers Christian sexual morbidity.)

Physical Abuse

First consider Proverbs 13:24, "He that spareth his rod hateth his son: but he that loveth him chasteneth him betimes," which admonishes parents to beat their children. As well, consider Proverbs 23:13–14, "Withhold not correction from the child: for if thou beatest him with the rod, he shall not die. Thou shalt beat him with the rod, and shalt deliver his soul from hell."

Even worse, Leviticus 20:9 commands the murder of children who curse their parents: "For every one that curseth his father or his mother shall be surely put to death: he hath cursed his father or his mother; his blood shall be upon him."

Then there's Deuteronomy 21:18–21, which mandates the murder of rebellious children. In 1641, the Massachusetts Bay Colony passed a law that mandated the death penalty for "Stubborn and Rebellious" sons; the law quoted verbatim some of the language in that biblical passage.

To appreciate the full barbarity of Deuteronomy 21:18–21 and the laws it inspired, it's worth quoting that passage in full:

> If a man have a stubborn and rebellious son, which will not obey the voice of his father, or the voice of his mother, and that, when they have chastened him, will not hearken unto them: Then shall his father and his mother lay hold on him, and bring him out unto the elders of his city, and unto the gate of his place; And they shall say unto the elders of his city, This our son is stubborn and rebellious, he will not obey our voice; he is a glutton, and a drunkard. And all the men of his city shall stone him with stones, that he die: so shalt thou put evil away from among you; and all Israel shall hear, and fear.

Yes, these commands are contradicted by Luke 17:2, "But whoso shall offend one of these little ones which believe in me, it were better for him that a millstone were hanged about his neck, and that he were drowned in the depth of the sea," but the Bible is replete with such contradictions. And when all too many Christians get to choose between a verse which gives them license to do evil, and one which enjoins them not to, they'll choose the evil verse. Note also that Luke 17:2 enjoins believers against abusing *only* "those little ones which believe in me."* Nonbelieving children are apparently fair game.

Christians by and large seem to be more enthusiastic about Proverbs 13:24 and the other Old Testament child-beating/murdering verses than the more humane Luke 17:2. There's even a million-selling Christian book on child-rearing, *To Train Up a Child*, by Michael and Debi Pearl, whose title references Proverbs 22:6, and which admonishes Christian parents to beat their children into submission, in line with Proverbs 13:24 and Proverbs 23:13–14. Unfortunately, a number of overzealous readers have taken this sage, Bible-based advice a bit too far and have beaten their children to death.[14] The Pearls, of course, have denied that this was their intent—they just want parents to inflict pain on children, beginning in infancy, in order to control them.

One indication of Christian enthusiasm for inflicting pain on children is that religious believers of all stripes, including religious liberals, are considerably more likely to approve of spanking than nonreligious people. Sociologist Ryan Cragun, citing data from the National Opinion Research Center's General Social Survey, states that, as of 2010, while a majority of people in all groups surveyed approved of the practice, 57% of nonreligious people approved, 67% of both religious moderates and religious liberals approved, and fully 85% of fundamentalists approved of spanking.[15]

---

* Evidently that divine injunction doesn't cover self-promotion after the deaths of "little ones." Ann Retzlaff, QAnon enthusiast and owner of the Christian camp, Annie's Campground, in Gresham, Wisconsin, put up a Facebook post following the drowning death of a five-year-old boy at her camp on July 2, 2021. In the post, she addressed "Lovers of Freedom, who believe in God, who are helpful to others and who are supportive of the Truth." She went on to say, "Know that Little Man is in a much better place filled with the Loving Arms of our Lord, Jesus the Christ. May God's White Light Shine upon the Campground and the many loving families here to appreciate our Freedom that we must still fight to keep. BE the voice and Protector of those innocent ones who can not Protect and Defend themselves" (just like Retzlaff was the "Protector" of the five-year-old "Little Man" who died at her camp). She concluded her post on the death of the boy with the consoling words, "We do have some availability: please stop in the office or call or book online."[13]

So, it seems all but certain that religious parents are more likely to spank their kids than nonreligious parents.

Some fundamentalists are open about what they hope to achieve via corporal punishment. In a Youtube video advocating spanking (transcribed in part by Hemant Mehta), two clergymen at the Verity Baptist Church in Sacramento, pastor Roger Jiménez and deacon Oliver González, after first cautioning parents that "you never want to hit your children with, like a closed fist," they state that the "goal" of spanking children is to "have it hurt." Why would anyone want to deliberately hurt children? ". . . they learn to obey . . . What we're doing is raising adults who will learn to obey their boss at work, learn to obey their pastor at church, learn to obey their husband at home."[16,17]

Another form of "spare the rod" physical abuse—in this case because of supposed demon possession—is the beating and killing of children during exorcisms. Such incidents occur all around the world in Christian lands, but some of the worst recent incidents have occurred in Russia, prompting the Russian Orthodox Church in April 2021 to condemn roll-your-own exorcisms. One particularly gruesome DIY exorcism in Yekaterinburg involved nine-year-old David Kazantsev, who was tortured to death by his Disciples of Christ parents and other members of their congregation during an exorcism. They then tried to resurrect him by praying over his dead body for two days. When David's body was discovered, it was covered with "horrific whip marks," though the cause of death was asphyxiation.[18, 19] Another brutal death involved a young adult, Alexandra Koshimbetova, 25, of Voronezh, who was murdered by her parents during an exorcism. Her parents beat her repeatedly, threw her to the ground, and dragged her around by the hair. They killed her by forcing her to drink five liters of holy water and then jumping on her prone body, rupturing her intestines.[20,21]

There are many further examples of killings during exorcisms, both of adults and children. Run a google search for "exorcism deaths and killings of children," and you'll find well over 100 articles on such killings.* One example of such an exorcism-homicide was that of 13-month-old Amora Carson in Texas in 2008. When investigators found the baby she "had more than 20 bite marks on her body and had been beaten with a hammer." Her parents, Jessica Carson and Blaine Milam, "admitted they thought their daughter was possessed and they tried to beat the demons out of her."[22]

---

* Cult expert Rick Ross's Cult Education Institute has an extensive archive on exorcisms and exorcists. The TinyURL for the archive is < https://tinyurl.com/ywuu3uxs >.

Don't think for a minute that Christian churches (including the Catholic and Russian Orthodox) have given up on the grotesque medieval practice of exorcism. They haven't. They simply want to be exclusive providers. And they're dead serious about it. As evidence, consider the following reality-deficient statement by San Francisco archbishop and exorcist Salvatore Cordileone: "Latin tends to be more effective against the devil because he doesn't like the language of the church."[23]

Returning to institutional maltreatment of children, governments in Christian lands have implemented the "spare the rod" injunction in savage manner, century after century. One egregious episode was the execution of child pickpockets and shoplifters in England during the 1688–1815 "Bloody Code" period. The English colonies in the New World provided other, more colorful examples, including the hanging of Thomas Granger, a 17-year-old Massachusetts youth convicted in 1642 of "buggery" with "a mare, a cow, two goats, five sheep, and a turkey."[24] In line with the passage that inspired the death-penalty law, Leviticus 20:15 ("And if a man lie with a beast, he shall surely be put to death: and ye shall slay the beast"), the Puritan authorities also slaughtered all of the victimized animals. The previous year, Massachusetts executed another youth, 18-year-old William Hackett, who "never saw any beast go before him but he lusted after it." Hackett was hung, despite expressing remorse for "buggering a cow"; of course, the Puritans also slew the poor beast.[25]

A more current example of the apparent joy some Christians take in abusing children was provided by the Rev. Jack Hyles, the early religious-right, segregationist co-founder of Hayes-Anderson College. Hyles said, "When Dr. [Robert] Billings [another founder of the Christian school movement] decides to discipline your child and your child comes home one night and has to stand up while he eats, don't waste your time calling me on the telephone . . . Because, brother, I'm going to be sitting there counting [the blows] as he gives them—Amen one, Amen two, Amen three."[26]

Another example comes from Ewan Whyte, a former student at the high-dollar Anglican boarding school, Grenville Christian College, in Ontario, Canada. Whyte reports that at age 11, in 1980, his devout charismatic Christian mother took him to Grenville, where he met the headmaster, Charles Farnsworth, who would provide him with "child guidance and correction" due to Whyte's "rebellious" desires to wear blue jeans and to sport a hair style longer than a crewcut. Whyte recalls that Farnsworth "proudly [told] us about his experience beating children. He spoke of it with a sense of delight, explaining how he whipped his own sons with a belt, and how good it was for them. . . . About children, he said, 'You have to break their spirit.'"

A few months later, Whyte's mother and his father, an ordained United Church of Christ minister, delivered him to Farnsworth's "care," which consisted of "several years enduring . . . extreme verbal, physical, psychological and sexualized abuse . . . At times, the punishment was in private with one or several adults, who would put their faces an inch away from the child's and scream at them as loudly as possible—condemning, shaming, terrorizing. . . . At Grenville, they used a long wooden paddle resembling a cricket bat. Staff kids and low-status boarders were beaten so hard that they bled, urinated on themselves or could no longer stand."

The victimized children couldn't even take comfort in each other: "The staff created networks of informants: they extorted us to tell on each other for any transgression, supposedly to help our friends 'see the light.' There was a lot of incentive to rat each other out—when we did, we were showered with praise and, best of all, kept out of the hot seat, at least for that day."[27]

In 2020, several former Grenville students won a class action suit against the by-then-shuttered school, the (Anglican) Synod of Toronto, and the estates of two of Grenville's former headmasters. The suit cited "systematic abuse." In her ruling finding Grenville et al. liable, Judge Janet Leiper agreed, stating that "Grenville knowingly created an abusive, authoritarian and rigid culture which exploited and controlled developing adolescents . . ."[28] In 2021, the defendants claimed, in an appeal, that they couldn't have known that the day-in-day-out verbal abuse inflicted on the children in their care—including calling girls "sluts, whores, Jezebels, bitches in heat"—would result in emotional damage. The defendants' attorney, Paul Pape, claimed "It could not be foreseeable to the people who were running the school, during the period of time for the class period . . . [that] calling people these names was a form of emotional abuse."[29]

So much for the joys of training up a child.

At the same time that children are suffering such abuse at the hands of Christian parents, Christian clergy, and Christian schools, six U.S. states still give parents the right to refuse life-saving medical treatment for their children on religious grounds—in other words, they give religious-fanatic parents the right to commit criminally negligent homicide upon their own children. In one of those states, Idaho, a task force set up by its Republican governor concluded in 2015 that the child mortality rate in one sect, the Followers of Christ, was ten times higher than that in Idaho as a whole.[30]

A previous study published in *Pediatrics*, Journal of the American Academy of Pediatrics, found that of "one hundred seventy-two children who died between 1975 and 1995" and whose "parents withheld medical care because of reliance on religious rituals . . . One hundred forty fatalities were from conditions for which survival rates with medical care would have exceeded 90%. Eighteen more had expected survival rates of >50%. All but 3 of the remainder would likely have had some benefit from clinical help."[31] In other words, during those two decades approximately 150 American children suffered preventable deaths because of deliberate medical neglect by their religious parents.

Sexual Abuse

But at present, the most notorious Christian abuse of children is sexual abuse by the Catholic clergy. For decades, probably centuries, such perversion has been very widespread, and the church until relatively recently managed to sweep it under the rug, while at the same time enabling the abusers: once their activities became known, the church hierarchy would routinely transfer the predators to other parishes. This often involved multiple transfers and multiple victims, sometimes dozens, if not hundreds, of them.

One indication of how widespread the problem is came to light in 2021 following a two-year suspension of the statute of limitations on civil suits regarding childhood sexual abuse in New York state. *The Buffalo News* reports that during the two-year period over 600 plaintiffs named 230 priests in the Buffalo area, including priests from nearly every parish. From 1950 on, the Diocese of Buffalo reports that over 2,300 priests were assigned to it, yielding an accused-abuser rate of approximately 10%.[32] Other reported rates are lower. A report prepared for the U.S. Conference of Catholic Bishops put the rate at 4%,[33] and the Royal Commission into Institutional Responses to Child Sexual Abuse reported that 7% of Australian priests were sexual abusers.[34]

In the U.S., the abuse was so widespread that between 2004 and 2021 three Catholic religious orders and twenty-eight American dioceses, including seven archdioceses, filed for bankruptcy protection rather than pay ruinous judgments to the thousands of victims who filed suit against them—and there are countless others who haven't filed. To put this more baldly, Catholic dioceses and religious orders have been filing for bankruptcy protection in order to stiff the victims of pedophile priests.

The number of such bankruptcies seems to be rising. In the first half of 2020 alone, five dioceses filed for bankruptcy protection, and the dioceses that have sought such protection since 2004 aren't small. They include Portland (Oregon), Tucson,* Milwaukee, San Diego, New Orleans, Minneapolis/St. Paul, Buffalo, and Rochester. Even with the partial write-down of settlements due to bankruptcy protection, the church has paid a total of at least $1.3 billion to American victims since 1994.** However, according to a January 2020 *Bloomberg BusinessWeek* report, the various dioceses that had filed for bankruptcy shielded more than $2 billion from victims.[35] With multiple dioceses filing for bankruptcy since the *Bloomberg* article appeared, the total today is undoubtedly much higher.

But as bad as the sexual abuse at regular parochial schools was, the situation at the Catholic-run Indian residential schools was even worse. In the absence of parents, there were almost no moderating influences on the staffs running the schools, staffs that had complete control of the children in their charge 24 hours a day. A survivor of the St. Joseph's Indian School in Chamberlain, South Dakota reports that priests and other staff members would roam the dormitories at night picking out victims, that they treated the children as "a smorgasboard." He added that the sexual abuse at St. Joseph's was so rampant that the school was in effect a "child brothel."[36]

In 2010, "eight plaintiffs [who had been harmed at St. Joseph's] sued the Sioux Falls diocese for alleged rape and sexual abuse they had experienced . . . at the hands of multiple members of the clergy and one staff member." Shortly before the victims "were set to go to court . . . the then Republican governor of South Dakota, Mike Rounds [now a U.S. senator] . . . signed a bill into law prohibiting anyone 40 years of age or older from recovering damages from institutions responsible for their abuse . . . The act crushed the lawsuit, effectively shielding the Catholic Church from any responsibility or accountability." The law was written by attorney Steven Smith, who at

---

* Eight years after declaring bankruptcy in 2004 to avoid paying full damages to those its priests had abused, the Diocese of Tucson went hat in hand to the city council asking for $1.1 million to restore one of its downtown properties, Marist College (which, of course, during its century-plus history never paid a dime of taxes to the city). Fortunately, after atheist activist Don Lacey appeared before the council, reminding it of the diocese' screw-the-victims bankruptcy, the city council refused.

** The Church more than recouped this amount in 2020 when various Catholic entities received $1.4 billion from the federal government under the Paycheck Protection Program, a program designed to keep small businesses and their employees afloat during the Covid pandemic.

the time "was representing the Priests of the Sacred Heart, the founders of St Joseph's Indian school, in several sexual abuse cases . . ."[37]

Of course, the total number of children sexually abused by Catholic clergy is difficult to gauge, but one indication can be found in the number cited by an independent commission of inquiry created in 2018 by the French Catholic Church. In October 2021, the commission estimated that 330,000 children have been sexually abused in French Catholic institutions since 1950, with two-thirds of them abused by clergy.[38,39] Because France has just over 67 million people and the U.S. about 331 million, and the Catholic proportion of the U.S. population is just over half that in France (22% vs. 41%), the extrapolated figure for the U.S. would be over 800,000 child sexual abuse victims (or 535,000 if one restricts the abuse to that perpetrated by clergy). Of course, this is a very rough estimate, but at minimum it's safe to say that American Catholic clergy sexually abused hundreds of thousands of children in the period covered by the French report.

As disgusting as that is, sexual abuse of children by clergy is not a purely Catholic phenomenon. There are news reports seemingly every week about sexual abuse of children by Protestant clergymen, but the amount of sexual abuse in Protestant denominations is more difficult to gauge than in Catholicism, because Protestant churches are largely independent rather than parts of an almost military-style hierarchy that keeps careful records and tracks its clergy.

Still, whistle blowers within American Protestantism have been sounding the alarm. The web site of Godly Response to Abuse in the Christian Environment (GRACE) reports that "Christians protect churches instead of victims." GRACE founder Boz Tchividjian states, "Abusers condemn gossip in their efforts to keep people from reporting abuse. Victims are also told to protect the reputation of Jesus."[40] This fits with what a *New Republic* article reports: "Silence and submission make Christians a ripe target: 'Church people are easy to fool,' boasts one sexual predator."[41]

The biographers of Peoples Temple cult leader and sexual predator, the Reverend Jim Jones, state that Jones shared this assessment of the pliability of "church people": "Jones always said that religious people make the best [cult] members because they were the most easily conditioned to self-sacrifice, devotion and discipline."[42]

Mormons appear to be just as pliable. The authors of *The Mormon Murders* (on the Salamander Letters forgeries and bombings) quote an unnamed Utah reporter: "What you have out here is a bunch of people who are basically educated from birth to unquestioningly believe what they're told, and they do, right up through adulthood. The conditions for fraud are perfect."[43] So are the conditions for sexual abuse and its cover up.

One other thing that's certain in regard to child sexual abuse—beyond the malleability of "church people"—is that Christian denominations' efforts to sweep sex abuse under the rug are widespread. A particularly egregious example is provided by the Jehovah's Witnesses, who appear to cover up instances of abuse in as systematic a manner as the Catholic Church did, in all probability, for centuries. The Witnesses even kept (and are apparently still keeping) a database of accused pedophiles within the church, "created by the Watchtower* headquarters to minimize legal risk"; the list was uncovered by Hollywood producer Aaron Kaufman prior to the release of his 2021 documentary on the Witnesses, *Vice Versa: Crusaders*. The Witnesses have never turned a single name on the list over to the police, no matter how many victims reported being abused by a perpetrator. This is due in part to their two-witness policy, which requires a corroborating witness in every single case, which makes disciplinary action all but impossible in cases of child sexual abuse.[44]

One indication of how serious these abuse and cover-up problems are is that the Watchtower leadership "rack[ed] up $2 million in fines as it refused to hand over its internal documents and database about admitted pedophiles to the state of California."[45] Another indication of the seriousness of these dual problems came to light in 2017 when the Australia Royal Commission on Child Sexual Abuse reported that since 1950 the church in that country was aware of abuse reports by over 1,800 victims, who were abused by in excess of 1,000 perpetrators, and the Witnesses reported not a single one of those incidents to police.[46]

But it gets worse. In 2020, a case came before the Utah Supreme Court that tested the limits of religious privilege in child sexual abuse cases. Starting in 2007, a Utah girl was repeatedly abducted and raped by two acquaintances. When her Jehovah's Witnesses parents learned of the abuse, they took the matter to the Church, which called a Judicial Council. "[W]hen the church learned of it, they decided to investigate not her assailant, but her—for the crime of having sex outside of marriage. . . ."[47]

In 2016, the victim, who had left the church and was then a young adult, sued the Witnesses. According to her complaint, "they [the four-member Witness Judicial Council] questioned her for 45 minutes about the en-

---

* The Watch Tower Bible and Tract Society is the Witnesses' governing body, and *The Watchtower* is one of two official Witnesses publications; the other is *Awake!*

counters, including whether or not they were consensual. . . . With her mother and stepfather present, the four elders began playing a recording that her assailant had made without her knowledge, pausing it at random points to pepper her with questions." Her lawyers stated that "she physically trembled, and pleaded with the elders to stop forcing her to relive the scarring experience. They did not stop. The interrogation lasted over four hours."[48] The church's defense? That this was standard religious practice and was protected by the First Amendment.

The Witnesses have tried this defense in similar sexual abuse cases with mixed success. They've managed to get some suits dismissed through their religious-privilege defense, but in others they've been held responsible for their actions and forced to pay verdicts ranging up into the millions.

The Mormon Church (Church of Jesus Christ of Latter-day Saints) also seems to systematically cover up sexual abuse of children by its members, including ongoing abuse that in some cases extends for years. One example came to light in 2018 in Bisbee, Arizona, a picturesque old mining town 100 miles southeast of Tucson. There, two Mormon bishops were aware of a member, a U.S. Border Patrol agent, sexually abusing his young daughter over a period of seven years, and that he began molesting his infant second daughter after she was born in 2015. Why didn't the bishops report this stomach-churning abuse to police? They were instructed not to by church higher ups.[49]

There's a religious loophole, "clergy-penitent privilege," in Arizona law, and in the laws of 32 other states, that allows clergy to stay silent when they know of child sexual abuse if they believe their silence is "reasonable and necessary within the concepts of the religion." The only reason the awful, ongoing abuse in Bisbee ever came to light was not because of the Mormon Church, it was because the perpetrator videoed himself molesting one of his daughters, posted the videos on child-porn web sites, and was subsequently tracked down by Interpol. After being arrested, the molester hung himself while in jail awaiting trial; his wife pled guilty to child abuse charges in 2018, was sentenced to two years in prison, and was released in October 2020. Their six children were all placed in foster care and subsequently adopted.[50]

In November 2020, a lawsuit filed on behalf of the victims revealed new information. In addition to naming the LDS Church and the two bishops who failed to report the abuse, the suit also stated that the children's Sunday school teacher, a former Border Patrol agent, knew of the abuse and failed to report it. The suit also charged that the perpetrator had raped his infant daughter and had "sexually abused his son, . . . beat him, forced him to watch pornography and witness the abuse of his sisters. This resulted in night terrors and hygiene issues [presumably bed wetting] while he was in foster care."

But the most revealing new information was that the two bishops had contacted the Church's child abuse hotline, run by Salt Lake City law firm Kirton McConkie, and were allegedly told not to report the abuse to civil authorities. The lawsuit states, "the Church implements the Helpline not for the protection and spiritual counseling of sexual abuse victims, as professed in Church doctrine and literature, but for Kirton McConkie attorneys to snuff out complaints and protect the Church from potentially costly lawsuits." John Manly, one of the attorneys for the children, summed up the matter: "What they're really doing is hiding serial criminal conduct under the guise of religion."[51]

In 2021, state senator Victoria Steele introduced a bill to end the religious-privilege loophole in Arizona law; she'd also introduced the bill in the previous two legislative sessions. Even in the wake of the widely reported, horrific abuse in Bisbee, and its cover up by the Mormon Church, the bill didn't even make it out of committee.

There's no way to pinpoint the amount of child sexual predation within Protestant and Mormon churches, but odds are, taking size into account, that it's roughly on par with that in the Catholic Church. And odds are that those churches, like the Catholic Church, will continue to cover it up.

Endnotes

1. Interview with Michael Krasny, *Mother Jones*, March 17, 1997. Quoted by Jack B. Worthy in *The Mormon Cult*. Tucson: See Sharp Press, 2008, p. 21f.

2. "In U.S. Decline of Religion Continues at Rapid Pace." Pew Forum, October 17, 2019. https://www.pewforum.org/2019/10/17/in-u-s-decline-of-christianity-continues-at-rapid-pace/ < https://tinyurl.com/y54m8cjv >

3. "The 2020 Census of American Religion." Public Religion Research Institute, July 8, 2021. https://www.prri.org/research/2020-census-of-american-religion/ < https://tinyurl.com/42rwj86n >

4. Pew Forum, op. cit.

5. "About Three-in-Ten U.S. Adults Are Now Religiously Unaffiliated." Pew Research Center, December 14, 2021. https://www.pewforum.org/2021/12/14/about-three-in-ten-u-s-adults-are-now-religiously-unaffiliated < https://tinyurl.com/327e9yr5 >

6. "America's Changing Religious Landscape, Chapter 2, Religious switching and intermarriage." Pew Research Center, May 12, 2015. https://www.pewforum.org/2015/05/12/chapter-2-religious-switching-and-intermarriage/ < https://tinyurl.com/y2q8z6h3 >

7. "7 facts about American Catholics," by David Masci and Gregory A. Smith. Pew Research: FacTank, October 10, 2018. https://www.pewresearch.org/fact-tank/2018/10/10/7-facts-about-american-catholics/ < https://tinyurl.com/y5hxzcmr >

8. "A neuroscientist explains why Christian evangelicals are wired to believe Donald Trump's gaslighting lies," by Bobby Azarian. *Raw Story*, December 29, 2019. https://www.rawstory.com/2019/12/a-neuroscientist-explains-why-christian-evangelicals-are-wired-to-believe-donald-trumps-gaslighting-lies/ < https://tinyurl.com/5wdzzff8 >

9. "Texas GOP rejects critical thinking skills. Really," by Valerie Strauss. *Washington Post*, July 9, 2012. https://www.washingtonpost.com/blogs/answer-sheet/post/texas-gop-rejects-critical-thinking-skills-really/2012/07/08/gJQAHNpFXW_blog.html < https://tinyurl.com/z92xpr79 >

10. "Religion and Views on Climate and Energy Issues." Pew Research, December 22, 2015. https://www.pewresearch.org/science/2015/10/22/religion-and-views-on-climate-and-energy-issues/ < https://tinyurl.com/yxrym5hs >

11. Ibid.

12. *What You Don't Know About Religion (but should)*, by Ryan Cragun. Durham, NC: Pitchstone Publishing, 2013, pp. 52–54.

13. "Campground owner ignites fury after using young boy's death to seek additional bookings from 'Lovers of Freedom,'" by Sky Palma. *Raw Story*, July 6, 2021. https://www.rawstory.com/annies-campground/ < https://tinyurl.com/w8jyd3pc >

14. "Corpses Don't Rebel: A former follower of Michael Pearl's 'To Train Up A Child' reacts to the death of Hana Williams." No Longer Quivering. https://www.patheos.com/blogs/nolongerquivering/2011/11/corpses-dont-rebel-a-former-follower-of-michael-pearls-to-train-up-a-child-reacts-to-the-death-of-hana-williams/ < https://tinyurl.com/y2cpquhk >

15. Cragun, op. cit., p. 87.

16. "Listen to These Two Horrible Christian Pastors Explain Why They Hit Their Kids," by Hemant Mehta. *Friendly Atheist*, September 26, 2021. https://friendlyatheist.patheos.com/2021/09/26/listen-to-these-two-horrible-christian-pastors-explain-why-they-hit-their-kids/ < https://tinyurl.com/rj5w8fvz >

17. "Landmarks: Spanking Your Children," Episode 2 (Season 2). Verity Baptist Church. https://www.youtube.com/watch?v=MHFu7EyS-_g < https://tinyurl.com/j7zurh54 >

18. "Russian Orthodox Church Clamps Down on DIY Exorcisms After Multiple Deaths," by Brendan Cole. *Newsweek*, April 13, 2021. https://www.newsweek.com/russia-orthodox-church-exorcism-1583176 < https://tinyurl.com/jb43uu4e >

19. "Inside the horrific 'exorcisms' sweeping Russia with sons whipped to death and daughters disembowelled by their parents," by Dan Hall. *The Irish Sun*, April 23, 2021. https://www.thesun.ie/news/6892646/inside-the-horrific-exorcisms-sweeping-russia-with-sons-whipped-to-death-and-daughters-disembowelled-by-their-parents/ < https://tinyurl.com/44cw5akz >

20. Ibid.

21. Cole, op. cit.

22. "Prosecutors: Mother Killed Child During Exorcism Ritual." KTBS, April 5, 2011. https://www.ktbs.com/news/prosecutors-mother-killed-child-during-exorcism-ritual/article_b65fd56d-79f4-5186-a2b3-9b21e53fd5fb.html < https://tinyurl.com/2rz9sx4v >

23. "Exorcism: Increasingly frequent, including after US protests." Associated Press, October 31, 2020. https://wtop.com/national/2020/10/exorcism-increasingly-frequent-including-after-us-protests/ < https://tinyurl.com/27kpkbyx >

24. "The Case of Thomas Granger," by William Bradford. Professor Ben Brown's Law and History Site. http://www.benbrownshistoryandlaw.com/thomas-granger < https://tinyurl.com/svyvcdh9 >

25. "The Cry of Sodom Enquired Into: Bestiality and the Wilderness of Human Nature in Seventeenth-Century New England," by John Canup. *American Antiquarian*, 1988. https://www.americanantiquarian.org/proceedings/44539423.pdf < https://tinyurl.com/4jveec2v >

26. *Unholy: Why White Evangelicals Worship at the Altar of Donald Trump*, by Sarah Posner. New York: Random House, 2020, pp. 112–113.

27. “The Cult That Raised Me,” by Ewan Whyte. *Toronto Life*, January 5, 2021. https://torontolife.com/life/grenville-christian-college-boarding-school-brockville-toronto--cult/ < https://tinyurl.com/y4ydm78d >

28. “Former students win class-action against Grenville Christian College.” CBC News, March 1, 2020. https://www.cbc.ca/news/canada/ottawa/grenville-class-action-ruling-1.5481577 < https://tinyurl.com/2kwjtmnm >

29. “Ontario Christian school tells court it was unaware abuse would cause emotional damage,” by Timothy Sawa. CBC News, May 5, 2021. https://www.cbc.ca/news/canada/toronto/grenville-christian-college-lawsuit-appeal-1.6014135 < https://tinyurl.com/59cf6tt6 >

30. “Letting them die: parents refuse medical help for children in the name of Christ,” by Jason Wilson. *The Guardian*, April 13, 2016. https://www.theguardian.com/us-news/2016/apr/13/followers-of-christ-idaho-religious-sect-child-mortality-refusing-medical-help < https://tinyurl.com/aujsfnez >

31. “Child Fatalities From Religion-motivated Medical Neglect,” by Seth M. Asser and Rita Swan. *Pediatrics*, April 1998, 101 (4) 625-629 https://pediatrics.aappublications.org/content/101/4/625?download=true < https://tinyurl.com/srzc5xhk >

32. “Lawsuits identify 230 priests as molesters, including 8 of WNY’s most-accused abusers,” by Jay Tokasz. *Buffalo News*, August 26, 2021. https://buffalonews.com/news/local/crime-and-courts/lawsuits-identify-230-priests-as-molesters-including-8-of-wnys-most-accused-abusers/article_847e4bee-050c-11ec-82e8-d38af1e219ea.html < https://tinyurl.com/326zscwk >

33. “Catholic child abuse in proportion,” by Andrew Brown. *The Guardian*, March 11, 2010. https://www.theguardian.com/commentisfree/andrewbrown/2010/mar/11/catholic-abuse-priests < https://tinyurl.com/dz3fmrtp >

34. “Highest proportion of Catholic priests accused of child sex abuse were in Diocese of Sale,” by Nicole Asher. ABC News, February 6, 2017. https://www.abc.net.au/news/2017-02-07/highest-proportion-of-priests-accused-of-child-sex-abuse-in-sale/8246928 < https://tinyurl.com/dx5s5tbj >

35. “Catholic Church Shields $2 Billion in Assets to Limit Abuse Payouts,” by Josh Saul. *Bloomberg BusinessWeek*, January 8, 2020. https://www.bloomberg.com/news/features/2020-01-08/the-catholic-church-s-strategy-to-limit-payouts-to-abuse-victims < https://tinyurl.com/2e2v4t9u >

36.“My relatives went to a Catholic school for Native children. It was a place of horrors,” by Nick Estes. *The Guardian*, June 30, 2021. https://www.theguardian.com/commentisfree/2021/jun/30/my-relatives-went-to-a-catholic-school-for-native-children-it-was-a-place-of-horrors < https://tinyurl.com/737vkwwx >

37. Ibid.

38. “French Church abuse: 216,000 children were victims of clergy—inquiry.” BBC News, October 5, 2021. https://www.bbc.com/news/world-europe-58801183 < https://tinyurl.com/t4zzndks >

39. “French report: 330,000 children victims of church sex abuse,” by Sylvie Corbet. Associated Press, October 5, 2021. https://apnews.com/article/europe-france-child-abuse-sexual-abuse-by-clergy-religion-ab5da1ff10f905b1c338a6f3427a1c66 < https://tinyurl.com/kt4pxvs9 >

40. “Evangelicals ‘worse’ than Catholics on sexual abuse,” by Jim Allen. *Christian Century*, October 10, 2013. https://www.christiancentury.org/article/2013-10/evangelicals-worse-catholics-sexual-abuse < https://tinyurl.com/y4ydm78d >

41. “The Silence of the Lambs: Are Protestants concealing a Catholic-size sexual abuse scandal?,” by Kathry Joyce. *New Republic*, June 10, 2017. https://newrepublic.com/article/142999/silence-lambs-protestants-concealing-catholic-size-sexual-abuse-scandal < https://tinyurl.com/y85e9sgf >

42. *Raven: The Untold Story of the Rev. Jim Jones and His People*, by Tim Reiterman with John Jacobs. New York: Penguin, 2008, p. 137.

43. *The Mormon Murders: A True Story of Greed, Forgery, Deceit, and Death*, by Steven Naifeh and Gregory White Smith. New York: Weidenfeld & Nicolson, 1988, p. 27.

44. “‘Vice Versa: Crusaders’ Director Talks Confronting Jehovah’s Witnesses With Child Sexual Abuse, Cover-Up Claims: ‘It’s About Corruption,’” by Etan Vlessing. *Hollywood Reporter*, July 14, 2021. https://www.hollywoodreporter.com/movies/movie-news/vice-versa-crusaders-director-talks-confronting-jehovahs-witnesses-with-child-sexual-abuse-cover-up-claims-its-about-corruption-1234981182/ < https://tinyurl.com/bfv3d9v5 >

45. Ibid.

46. “Reports into Jehovah’s Witnesses released.” Royal Commission into Institutional Responses to Child Sexual Abuse.” Royal Commission into Institutional Responses to Child Sexual Abuse, November 28, 2016. https://www.childabuseroyalcommission.gov.au/media-releases/report-jehovahs-witness-organisations-released < https://tinyurl.com/y3gl37rn >

47. “Will a Church Get Away With Making a Teen Listen to Recording of Her Rape?,” by Emil Sugarman. *The Daily Beast*, November 15, 2020. https://www.thedailybeast.com/will-a-jehovahs-witnesses-church-get-away-with-making-a-teen-listen-to-recording-of-her-rape < https://tinyurl.com/yyxf9ppp >

48. “Bisbee man confesses he’s molesting his daughter. Church tells bishop not to report abuse to authorities,” by Mary Jo Pitzl. *Arizona Republic*/azcentral, April 21, 2020. https://www.azcentral.com/story/news/local/arizona-child-welfare/2020/04/21/bisbee-man-confesses-hes-molesting-his-daughter-church-tells-bishop-not-report-abuse/2876617001/ < https://tinyurl.com/y7aafehk >

49. Ibid.

50. “Lawsuit: LDS Church officials, teacher knew of abuse but kept silent,” by Mary Jo Pitzl. *Arizona Republic*/azcentral, November 30, 2020. https://www.azcentral.com/story/news/local/arizona-child-welfare/2020/11/30/mormon-church-sued-over-not-reporting-fathers-sexual-abuse-his-children/6356979002/ < https://tinyurl.com/yy3glgkn >

51. Ibid.

2

Christian Dishonesty and Hypocrisy

We should always be disposed to believe that which appears white is really black, if the hierarchy of the church so decides.
—St. Ignatius Loyola, *Spiritual Exercises*

Belief means *not wanting* to know what is true.
—Friedrich Nietzsche, *The Anti-Christ*

The Christian appeal to fear—of hell, death, and the devil—and Christianity's reliance on childhood indoctrination is an admission that the evidence supporting Christian beliefs is far from compelling. If the evidence were such that Christianity's truth was immediately apparent to anyone who considered it, Christian churches would be overflowing with converts, and Christians would feel no need to resort to the cheap tactic of using threats to inspire "belief" (more accurately, "lip service"). That most Christian clergy have been more than willing to accept such lip service, plus the money and obedience that go with it, in place of genuine belief, is an indictment of the basic dishonesty of Christianity, dishonesty which has been central to that religion since its beginning.

The Bible, Christianity's foundation, provides an early and extreme example of Christian dishonesty. The Bible is by no means the unitary, inerrant volume many Christians consider it to be, with its 66 books in the Protestant canon and 73 in the Catholic. There were also many other, often incompatible, genuine texts that didn't make it into what we now call the Bible, as well as some outright forgeries that did. In Christianity's first millennium-plus, the church fathers (notably St. Jerome, who outright admitted it), bishops, priests, theologians, abbots, and scribes engaged in a veritable orgy of forgery, alteration, interpolation, and "disappearance" of inconvenient passages and texts (often entire books and documents).

All of this was done in order to bring the supposedly inerrant Word of God into alignment with the viewpoints of those with theological, doctrinal, or historical axes to grind, who made the changes. They included a long line of popes, concerned with buttressing their authority, in part through altering or forging records of apostolic and papal succession. As historian James McDonald notes, "schools of forgers flourished under a long series of popes" until well into the Middle Ages, and the situation in the church, for over a thousand years, was so bad that "it is impossible to be sure that any single surviving Christian document was written by its purported author and is free from amendment." As an example of the extremes to which Christian fabricators went, McDonald cites the Apostolic Constitutions forgery, which "purport[s] to be written in the name of Jesus' apostles, and warn[s] about books falsely claiming to be written in the name of Jesus' apostles."[1]

As we cover the Bible at greater length in the final two chapters of this book, and in its first appendix, and because this chapter is primarily concerned with Christian dishonesty in the modern period, we'll leave Christianity's foundational dishonesty here.*

How deep Christian dishonesty runs can be gauged by one of the most popular arguments for belief in God, Pascal's wager. This "wager" holds that it's safer to "believe" in God (as if belief were volitional!) than not to believe, because God might exist, and if it does, it will save "believers" and condemn nonbelievers to hell after death.

This is an appeal to pure cowardice. It has absolutely nothing to do with the search for truth. Instead, it's an appeal to abandon honesty and intellectual integrity, and to pretend that lip service is the same thing as belief. If the god of Christianity really existed, one wonders how it would judge the hypocrites and cowards who advance and bow to this particularly craven "wager."

Not that the grubbiness of the "wager" stops Christians from advancing it. A brief glimpse at amazon.com reveals several books, both Catholic and Protestant, promoting the wager,[2] with the first book on the list titled

* Those interested in further details regarding biblical forgeries, alterations, interpolations, etc. should consult James McDonald's enlightening *Beyond Belief: Two thousand years of bad faith in the Christian Church*. The entirety of the book is devoted to exposing Christian dishonesty in its myriad and multi-colored forms.

Taking Pascal's Wager: Faith, Evidence and the Abundant Life, which, according to a laudatory review in *Catholic Library World*, explores the "reasonableness of Christianity."[3] So, lip service in place of actual belief is still, somehow, a good thing.

Regarding the absence of actual belief, Nietzsche acerbically noted in *Human, All Too Human*:

> If Christianity were right, with its theories of an avenging God, of general sinfulness, of redemption, and the danger of eternal damnation, it would be a sign of weak intellect and lack of character *not* to become a priest, apostle or hermit, and to work only with fear and trembling for one's own salvation; it would be senseless thus to neglect eternal benefits for temporary comfort. Taking it for granted that there *is belief*, the commonplace Christian is a miserable figure, a man that really cannot add two and two together . . .

Everyday examples of Christian dishonesty include the insistence that abstinence-only sex "education" is effective, or even the most effective form of sex ed. It isn't. Scientific study after scientific study have shown that it's the least effective form.[4] Part of the evidence for that conclusion is that teen pregnancy rates are higher than the U.S. average in politically conservative, religious areas where abstinence-only sex ed is most common.

Another typical form of Christian dishonesty is found in the "pro-life"* movement's insistence that a zygote, a fertilized ovum (two cells, and much smaller than the head of a pin) is somehow a "baby." This is, of course, deliberately disingenuous: a microscope is not normally needed to see "babies." Beyond that, the "pro-life" movement maintains that its attempts to restrict the right to abortion is motivated by concern for women's health and respect for human life, not to make abortion so difficult to obtain that women are forced to carry unwanted pregnancies to term.

---

* One minor but telling form of Christian dishonesty is the use of deliberately misleading labels, with "pro-life" being a prime example. Two other high profile examples are the extreme-right "One Million Moms," which has under five thousand Twitter followers, and "Prager University," which isn't a university in any normal sense of the word. Prager, which claims to "advance Judeo-Christian values," is unaccredited, doesn't issue degrees, has no classroom buildings or dorms, and doesn't even hold classes. It's a media production company that was initially funded by right-wing billionaires, and which produces extreme-right propaganda videos. But Christian verbal dishonesty extends beyond misleading self-labels.

Even the terms Christian "pro-lifers" use are deliberately misleading. Taking their cue from used car salesmen, "pro-lifers" have relabeled zygotes and fetuses as "pre-born children." Even more revealingly, "pro-lifers" use governmental coercion to deny women reproductive choice—and call that coercion "rescuing women from abortion."

"Pro-lifers" also insist that legal abortion is hazardous. This is a jaw-dropping lie—sheer dishonesty, sheer hypocrisy. The "pro-lifers" undoubtedly know that legal abortion is far safer than childbirth, yet they continually lie about it. The NIH reports that the mortality rate for legal abortions was .6 per 100,000 in 2012, while the mortality rate for child birth was 8.8 per 100,000, almost 15 times higher.[5] However, the mortality rate from legal abortions has been falling, while the maternal mortality rate has been rising. CDC figures from 2020 show that the abortion mortality rate had fallen to .3 per 100,000 abortions,[6] while the mortality rate from childbirth had risen to 17.2 per 100,000.[7] In other words giving birth in 2020 was 57 times as dangerous as having an abortion. If "pro-lifers" were really concerned about women's health and lives, they would work to ensure that abortion was legal and readily available to all who want it, because it's far safer than child birth. Instead, to further their efforts to impose their morals on women, they lie about it—as they've done for decades.

As if to underline the hypocrisy of "pro-life," "family values" Christians, in the wake of Joe Biden's victory over Donald Trump, the CEO of the religious-right group Concerned Women for America, Penny Nance, said "Evangelical leaders let down the pro-life movement by not standing firm on the fact that we needed a pro-life president . . . [they let us down] by not understanding or caring that hundreds of millions of dollars were going to be shifted to destroy life if Donald Trump lost."[8]

This is the same Trump who forcibly separated small children from their families, literally ripping babies from their mothers' arms, who locked those kids in cages with no plan for reuniting them with their families, who did his best to strip healthcare coverage from tens of millions of Americans (which would have resulted in untold worry, suffering, and at minimum thousands, and quite possibly tens of thousands, of unnecessary deaths annually), who attempted to increase hunger among the poorest American families by stripping them of SNAP (food stamp) benefits, who returned asylum-seeking migrants to certain death in the countries they fled, who supported the brutal, journalist-murdering Saudi government in its savage military campaign in Yemen, and whose utterly inept response (really, more of a nonresponse) to the Coronavirus pandemic led to well over half-a-million preventable deaths in the U.S.*

---

* Not incidentally, malignant narcissist Trump fulfills almost all 20 of the criteria on the Hare Psycopathy Checklist, a standard diagnostic tool, missing out on a "perfect" score only because he hasn't been to prison (yet—hope springs eternal) due to his privileged back-

All of those killed and harmed were living, feeling, self-aware human beings. Did any of Trump's callousness and cruelty, the death and misery he's caused to thousands of families, matter to the "pro-life," "family values" crowd? Apparently not. They were more concerned with zygotes and fetuses—to be more precise, they were more concerned with imposing their authoritarian morals on the rest of us.

One common form of Christian dishonesty is the pretense that Christians were at the forefront of, if not entirely responsible for, social reform campaigns. Examples of such campaigns include the abolitionist movement (against slavery—an institution that flourished for over 1,500 years in Christian lands) and the women's rights movement. In fact, organized Christianity overwhelmingly opposed these movements; but once they became mainstream, Christians rushed to take credit for them. (We deal with these matters at some length in the chapters on misogyny and slavery, so, for the most part, we'll leave them lie for now.)

One recent example is the civil rights movement, whose most prominent leader was a black Protestant minister, and which was based in large part in black Protestant churches. White Protestants were a different matter. By and large, especially in the South, they opposed the liberatory civil rights movement. But to hear some of them tell it, they were in favor of the civil rights movement and worked for it all along. The prime example here is Jerry Falwell, Sr., who opposed the Civil Rights Act of 1964, claimed Martin Luther King was a Communist (with no evidence of that whatsoever), and called King "the most notorious liar in the country." As Sarah Posner notes, "In her memoir, his [Falwell's] widow Macel" claimed that "when *Roe [v. Wade]* came down, . . . it 'threw Jerry into a dilemma of epic

---

ground and the near impunity that goes with it; the other criterion he seemingly doesn't meet is lack of long-term goals, but only because he does appear to have the goal of destroying American democracy. He more than fulfills the other 18 criteria. The 20 characteristics on the psychopathy checklist are as follows: 1) Glibness/superficial charm; 2) Grandiose sense of self-worth; 3) Need for stimulation/proneness to boredom; 4) Pathological lying; 5) Cunning/manipulative; 6) Lack of remorse or guilt; 7) Shallow affect (limited emotional responses); 8) Callous/lack of empathy; 9) Parasitic lifestyle; 10) Poor behavioral controls; 11) Promiscuous sexual behavior; 12) Early behavioral problems; 13) Lack of realistic long-term goals; 14) Impulsivity; 15) Irresponsibility; 16) Failure to accept responsibility for one's own actions; 17) Many short-term marital relationships; 18) Juvenile delinquency; 19) Revocation of conditional release (from prison); 20) Criminal versatility (commits diverse types of crimes). The checklist is widely available on line, with one place being *Psychology Today*'s site. Steven Hassan has a useful discussion of the checklist and how well Trump's characteristics fit it in his book, *The Cult of Trump*.

proportions, far greater even the struggle against segregation'—implying that he had been involved in the struggle against segregation," rather than fighting to preserve it.[9]

There are also plentiful examples of Christian dishonesty and hypocrisy in the field of science. Fundamentalists insist that creationism (relabeled as "intelligent design") is a scientific theory, when it's anything but. That "theory" has no testable hypotheses, no supporting evidence, and can generate no testable predictions, three of the most basic components of a scientific theory. Yet fundamentalists continue to promote this religious fairy tale as scientific. If they know even the most basic facts about science and the scientific method, they're aware that "intelligent design" is decidedly unscientific; and if that's the case, their promotion of "intelligent design" as a scientific theory is deliberately dishonest. (Much more on this in the chapters on the Christian war on science and reason.) A prime example of this was provided by the recently deceased (from Covid) Dominionist, creationist, anti-vaccination preacher Bob Enyart, whose talk show was titled "Real Science Radio."

Antony Alumkal, in his 2017 book, *Paranoid Science: The Religious Right's War on Reality*, refers to this sort of dishonesty as creation of "a fake scientific discourse to compete with the real one, which they allege to be a conspiracy." This is an immediately noticeable tactic of large swaths of contemporary Christians, and it's both dangerous and dishonest.

But what of the common belief that Christianity, although false, has value because it brings comfort to the afflicted. Max Nordau, in his massive *The Interpretation of History*, disposes of the matter:

> Religion no doubt has brought comfort to many. That this is so is not, however, to its credit. The practical utility of untruth is a cynical defense that all liars bring forward. No doubt the assurance of immortality robs the idea of death of its terrors. The promise of future reunion helps the mother to bear the loss of her child; the thought that eternal justice will be dealt out to good and evil deeds pours balsam in the wounds of the weak, down-trodden, and ill-used who have succumbed before the pride of the mighty. But the means by which these tortured spirits are soothed are unhealthy and immoral in the extreme—invented tales and arbitrary assertions which cannot stand a moment's critical examination. The merit that belongs to the consolation of religion must be granted to every superstition—the amulet that averts the evil eye, spells, the interpretation of cards and dreams, the raising of spirits. All this hocus pocus has lightened dark hours for millions who believed in it, given them confidence and self-reliance, lifted heavy burdens from their souls, and reconciled them to the hardness of their lot. Moreover, physical

> sedatives, like opium, morphine, and alcohol must be assigned an equal value with religion. They, too, console; they, too, bring temporary oblivion of care and suffering; they, too, give an artificial sense of pleasure.

Nordau might have added that the comfort Christianity supposedly offers is all too often elusive. While there are actual believers who derive great comfort from their faith, it seems likely that most "believers" simply *want* to believe, and as death approaches all too many of them are terrified: they've spent their lives attempting to evade the chronic malady known as reality, using plentiful application of scripture and positive thinking as palliatives, and have never come to terms with their own mortality.

As evidence of their lack of real belief, consider how Christians react when a loved one dies. If they really believed the dear departed was "going to a better place," that he or she would sit at the right hand of God forever, experiencing eternal bliss, they'd rejoice—especially since *they'd* be joining the dearly departed when *they* died and went to that "better place." You'd expect the Christian reaction to death to be fist bumps and high fives, followed by "Break out the good shit! *It's party time!*" For some reason, this rarely seems to happen.*

This lack of real belief helps to explain why Christians are often more afraid of death than atheists, who've usually had decades coming to terms with the concept and have little fear of death and no fear of going to hell. (As famed psychologist and outspoken atheist Albert Ellis wryly commented near the end of his life, he had little fear of death, but was "not exactly looking forward to it.") This also explains why so many Christians are extremely hostile to nonbelievers, whose mere existence threatens the illusions to which they so desperately cling. It also explains why the more devout believers are, the more often they think of death: 28% of those who consider religion very important often think of death, versus only 10% of those who consider religion unimportant, an almost three to one ratio.[10]

---

* Apologies to Jimmy Kimmel and Adam Carolla who did a routine based on this premise on an episode of "The Man Show." Comedian Doug Stanhope also does a routine based on this premise.

The Ends Justify the Means
(A Foundation Stone of Christianity)

> It is the profound, suspicious fear, an incurable pessimism, which compels whole centuries to fasten their teeth into a religious interpretation of existence … Piety, the 'Life in God,' regarded in this light, would appear as the most elaborate and ultimate product of the *fear* of truth … as the will to inversion of truth, to the lie at any price.
> —Friedrich Nietzsche, *Beyond Good and Evil*

> Until I had read religious papers, I did not know what malicious and slimy falsehoods could be constructed from ordinary words. The ingenuity with which the real and apparent meaning can be tortured out of language is simply amazing. —Robert Ingersoll

In the instances cited above, as in so many others, Christians lie and deliberately twist the facts in the service of their "higher truth," their "higher morality." They very evidently believe that the ends justify the means, no matter how dishonest, no matter how dishonorable those means. They don't seem to realize that means determine ends. So they lie. *Anything* is justified in pursuit of their supposed greater good.*

This ends-justify-the-means mentality has been on lurid display in the Trump personality cult, with Trump's largely evangelical and conservative Catholic worshipers prostrating themselves before their golden idol, even though, by their own lights, he's a moral cesspool: a pathological liar who consistently bears "false witness," a malignant narcissist, a bully, sadist, con man, glutton, philandering husband, and boastful sexual predator. As baseball writer Grant Brisbee put it a few years ago, Trump is the "wriggling embodiment of the seven deadly sins, all of them competing against the others for supremacy at all times."[11]**

---

* As St. Paul put it in Romans 3:7–8, "For if the truth of God hath more abounded through my lie unto his glory; why yet am I also judged as a sinner? And not rather, (as we be slanderously reported, and as some affirm that we say,) Let us do evil, that good may come? whose damnation is just." Here, Paul is carefully distinguishing between lies that merely support the Church and lies that directly inspire evil deeds; in other words, lies are fine as long as they just shore up "the truth of God."

** The "seven deadly sins" are lust, gluttony, greed, sloth, wrath, envy, and pride. The list was devised by Pope Gregory the Great in the 6th century.

If the admonition "Know them by the company they keep" is sound, what does this say about the members of the Trump personality cult? They worship him because they see him as the means to their ends: ensuring their "freedom" to discriminate against gay people, their "freedom" to use public monies to fund religious charter schools, their "freedom" to avoid paying taxes on church properties, their "freedom" to restrict the reproductive rights of others, and their "freedom" to inflict pain and injury on those they hate (largely those Trump has scapegoated: Mexicans, immigrants, Muslims, atheists, anarchists, black people, gay people, journalists, reproductive rights advocates, and anti-racism protesters).

That admonition also holds regarding the relationship of evangelicals and other conservative Christians to the Unification Church ("Moonies"—now called the Unification Movement), a straight-up religious cult notorious for brainwashing and exploiting its members, and for its mass weddings involving thousands, often strangers picked for each other by Church higher-ups. The Church, founded by the Reverend Sun Myung Moon, who served time in federal prison in the 1980s for tax evasion and obstruction of justice, holds—in a similar manner to the LDS Church and its Book of Mormon—that their "sacred" text, *Divine Principle*, authored by the Church's founder, is a revelation on par with the Bible—in fact, greater than the Bible; according to cult expert and former high-ranking Unification Church official, Steven Hassan, Moon repeatedly described himself as "ten times greater than Jesus."[12] The Church also wants to eliminate the cross as the symbol of Christianity; in 2004 it held a "Moonification" tour, with one goal being "to remove Christian crosses from almost 300 churches in poor neighborhoods."[13] The tour culminated in a bizarre coronation ceremony in the U.S. Senate's Dirksen Office Building in which Moon was crowned as the "King of Peace" (thus pulling rank on the "Prince of Peace"), and which over a dozen members of Congress attended.[14]

None of this apparently bothers conservative Christians and the politicians they support. Why? Sex, politics, and money. Moon held "views somewhere to the right of the Taliban's Mullah Omar." He advocated abstention outside of marriage and abstinence-only sex "education," and preached that "gays are 'dung-eating dogs,' Jews brought on the Holocaust by betraying Jesus, and the U.S. Constitution should be scrapped in favor of a system he call[ed] 'Godism'—with him in charge," in other words, theocracy.[15]

All of this has been well known for years, and in some particulars for decades, yet evangelical and Catholic Republicans have been happy to take the Moonies' political and monetary support ever since the time of Reagan. One conduit for that support is the extreme-right, Moonie-owned newspaper, *The Washington Times*, into which the Moonies have poured an estimated $2 to $4 billion since its founding in 1982. They've also been regular and major contributors to right-wing institutions, including the Nicaraguan Freedom Fund (which supported the terrorist Nicaraguan "contras") and Jerry Falwell's Liberty University.[16] Indeed, in May 2021, the painfully devout Mike Pence and the rapture-awaiting Mike Pompeo, along with Catholic grifter Newt Gingrich,* spoke at the Moonies' "Rally of Hope" in Washington, DC, in what was billed as a kickoff for a Moonie think tank, the Universal Peace Federation, Think Tank 2022. The Reverend Jonathan Falwell of the Thomas Road Baptist Church, one of Jerry Falwell's sons, also spoke. (Pompeo and Pence refused to say whether the Moonies paid them to attend and speak.)[17]

Of course, Donald Trump also loves the Moonies. A headline on the *Business Insider* site put the matter succinctly: "Trump spoke at a 9/11 'Moonies' conference organized by the widow of the Rev. Sun Myung Moon, praising the controversial Unification Church." On September 11, 2021—while he bypassed the official memorial ceremony in New York honoring the 9/11 victims and heroes—Trump spoke via video to the attendees at the Moonie event (as did Newt Gingrich) and said, "I want to thank the Universal Peace Federation and in particular Dr. Hak Ja Han Moon [Moon's widow], a tremendous person, for her incredible work on behalf of peace all over the world. What they have achieved on the [Korean] peninsula is just amazing. In just a few decades, the inspiration that they have caused for the entire planet is unbelievable, and I congratulate you again and again."[18]

So, rather than attending the official event honoring the 9/11 heroes and victims on the 20th anniversary of the tragedy, that's how Christian favorite Donald Trump commemorated the day. (There was no mention of whether the Moonies paid him to speak, but given Trump's mercenary nature it seems likely that they did.) That evening, he and his son, Don Jr., once again honored the 9/11 dead by charging Trump's worshipers $49.99 for commentary on a pay-per-view fight involving two aging has-beens,

---

* Money has seemingly always been a lodestar for Gingrich. As one example, in the early 2000s, he created the "Entrepreneur of the Year" award, which he would apparently give to anyone who ponied up the necessary $5,000. Award recipients included Dawn Rizos, owner of the The Lodge, a Texas strip club, and Allison Vivas of the porn-production company Visual Pink.[19]

44-year-old UFC fighter Vitor Belfort and 58-year-old Alexander Holyfield, who hadn't fought in a decade. (Belfort won.)

One rarely sees a more inspiring expression of patriotism. (To all appearances, not a single one of Trump's even slightly prominent sycophants and accomplices uttered a word of criticism of either his presumably paid appearance lauding the Moonies nor his crass grifting that evening.)

Back in the Middle Ages, Christians would have launched a crusade to the death against the extremely heretical Moon sect, and they would have burned its founder at the stake. Literally—no question about it. Today, evangelical and Catholic politicians take the Moonies' money and work with them to destroy reproductive and gay rights, and to turn the United States into a theocracy. Their only apparent major disagreement with the Moonies is over who they want as God-ordained dictator.

Yet again, the devout ends justify the sacrilegious means.

One of the ultimate confirmations of the destructiveness of the ends-justify-the-means belief (and the inevitable dishonesty and hypocrisy that go with it) that is so common among the religious is that "the ends justify the means" was a frequently spoken article of faith in the Peoples Temple, a belief advanced in exactly those words in both worship services and less formal settings by the Reverend Jim Jones and his blindly obedient followers. They not only believed the ends justify the means, they acted on it. In Jonestown, they staked their lives (and those of hundreds of children) on that premise, in the form of "revolutionary suicide" (which was more mass murder, carried out by Jones's goon squad, than suicide), a supposedly courageous means to hasten the desired end, "the revolution."

Another religious con man, L. Ron Hubbard, founder of the Church of Scientology, "claimed that [in a previous life] he was a contemporary of Machiavelli's, and he was still upset that the author of *The Prince* stole his line, 'The ends justify the means.'"[20]

This "line," this article of faith, extends to all authoritarian movements. Authoritarian political cultists share this belief with their religious brethren. One of the slogans of Mao's fanatical Red Guards during the violent, convulsive Chinese Cultural Revolution of the 1960s and 1970s, that resulted in millions of deaths, put the matter succinctly: "So long as it is revolutionary, no action is a crime."[21] In other words, the ends justify the means.

Unsurprisingly, the nominally Christian LDS Church, despite its unstinting efforts to project a squeaky clean image, also subscribes to this belief. At a time when the Church hierarchy was clamping down on historians and other academic researchers within its own ranks, firing, demoting, or otherwise silencing those revealing uncomfortable truths, Elder Boyd Packer, president of the Church's Quorum of the 12 Apostles, spelled out the Church's ends-justify-the-means position in a speech on August 22, 1981:

> I have come to believe that it is the tendency for many members of the Church who spend a great deal of time in academic research to begin to judge the Church, its doctrines, organization, and leadership, present and past, by the principles of their own profession. . . . In my mind it ought to be the other way around. . . . There is a temptation for the writer or the teacher of Church history to want to tell everything, whether it is worthy [befitting a good, obedient Mormon] or faith promoting, or no. . . . Some things are true that are not very useful [to the Church].[22]

In other words, the truth doesn't matter: the ends justify the means, no matter how dishonest the means.

If you use foul, authoritarian means, you'll end up with foul, authoritarian ends, as has happened throughout the ages, as in Mao's China and the Peoples Temple, to cite but two among countless examples. The ends-justify-the-means proposition is dishonesty raised to a guiding principle, a guiding principle that leads to disastrous results. It's simply wrong, both ethically and practically, and inevitably leads to the grossest types of immoral behavior and human suffering, yet it's perhaps the most outstanding feature of contemporary Christianity.

The Pro-Life Death Cult

> Life, n. According to pro-lifers, the most beautiful, precious thing in the world, from the moment of conception to the moment of execution.
> —*The American Heretic's Dictionary*

For all its moral posturing and endless talk about the "sacredness of life," the "pro-life" movement is a death cult, as can be seen in its political and social positions, and in its actions; its hypocritical cant aside, the "pro-life" movement has remarkably little respect for the lives and rights of living human beings; the only type of life "pro-life" Christians seem to value is that of zygotes and fetuses.

Let's briefly look at just a few of the ways all too many Christians show their disdain for the lives of their fellow sentient, suffering human beings while they fixate on fetuses. (Because there are so many biblical passages commanding both mass and individual murder, we're listing the relevant passages in the following footnote rather than in the text in the interest of readability.)*

Death penalty. The Bible has a great many commands ordering both individual and mass murder. The mass-murder commands occur in Old Testament passages in which the Almighty orders its chosen people to commit slaughter as part of their land-stealing campaigns.

As for divinely ordered individual murders, the Bible orders execution of those guilty of adultery; fornication; homosexual acts; being a rape victim but not crying out; being unable to prove (female) virginity; having sex with one's wife and mother-in-law; blasphemy; cursing one's father or mother; witchcraft; bestiality; having sex with one's "father's wife"; having sex with one's daughter-in-law; rebelliousness against one's parents; worshiping other gods; working on the sabbath; and being an enemy of Christ who refuses to submit to him.

Given the abundance of such commands, it's not surprising that Christian governments the world over, since the time of the first Christian rulers, have put the death penalty into law and have carried it out, often capriciously, often for political purposes, and often for shockingly picayune reasons (frequently those enumerated in the Bible). The first abolition of capital punishment in Christian lands didn't occur until well into the 20th century. The UK didn't abolish capital punishment until 1965, France didn't abolish it until 1981, and it's still in force in the United States at the federal level and in most of the states.

Given that human judgment is fallible, it's certain that vast numbers of innocent people have been judicially murdered over the ages, and this

---

* **Death Penalty** (mass murder): Deuteronomy 7:1–2, 5–6; Deuteronomy 20:10–17; Numbers 31:3–18; Joshua 11:10–14; and 1 Samuel 15:3.

Death Penalty (individual murder): (adultery) (Leviticus 20:10, Deuteronomy 22:22, Ezekiel 23:45–47); (fornication) (Leviticus 21:9, Ezekiel 16:35–40); homosexual acts (Leviticus 20:13); being a rape victim but not crying out (Deuteronomy 22:23–24); inability to prove (female) virginity (Deuteronomy 22:13–21); sex with wife and mother-in-law (Leviticus 20:14); blasphemy (Leviticus 24:16); cursing one's father or mother (Leviticus 20:9); witchcraft (Exodus 22:18, Leviticus 24:14–16); bestiality (Exodus 22:19, Leviticus 20:15–16); having sex with one's "father's wife" (Leviticus 20:11); having sex with one's daughter-in-law (Leviticus 20:12); rebelliousness against parents (Deuteronomy 21:18–23); worshiping other gods (Deuteronomy 13:6–9, 17:2–5); working on the sabbath (Exodus 35:1–2, 31:14–15); being an enemy of Christ who refuses to submit to him (Luke 19:27) horrifying practice continues to this day. The National Academy of Science (NAS) estimated in 2014 that 4.1% of those that have been sentenced to death in the United States were innocent, saying that was a "conservative estimate."[23]*

But apparently this doesn't matter a whit to many Christians and many Christian churches. A great number of Protestant churches still support capital punishment, as does the Mormon Church. Only the Catholic Church (after close to two millennia of supporting it) now officially opposes the death penalty—though it seems to spend much more time, money, and effort on its opposition to reproductive rights. Sadly, the more literal minded the individual believer in the Christian religion of love, the more likely he or she is to support the death penalty.

Death from unwanted pregnancies. Childbirth is hazardous. It's less so in modern times thanks to scientific and medical advances, but it's still hazardous. As mentioned above, in 2020 the maternal mortality rate stood at 17.2 per 100,000.[24] In contrast, the mortality rate from legal abortions was only .3 per 100,000. So, the mortality rate from childbirth was 57 times that of the mortality rate from abortion complications. The CDC reports that in 2017, with 619,591 abortions performed, only two women died from abortion complications.[25] Given the 57 to 1 mortality rate, over 100 of the women who had abortions would have died if forced to give birth, in comparison with the two who died from complications from legal abortions. But if "pro-life" policies were put into law nationally, the death toll would be higher because some women would resort to more hazardous

---

* One of the reasons for these false convictions is false confessions, which are more common that you might think. In his book *Pre-Suasion*, the sequel to his very popular *Influence*, psychologist Robert Cialdini outlines at length (pp. 58–65) the means by which police interrogators extract confessions, both true and false, using techniques common to the Salem Witch Trials, the Chinese Cultural Revolution of the 1960s and 1970s, and American policing today. (He could have added Stalin's purges and show trials.) These means include wearing people down through sleep deprivation and hour after hour of relentless, repetitious leading questions, leaving those under questioning confused and exhausted, desperate for their ordeal to end. In one case Cialdini highlights, an innocent 18-year-old boy confessed to murdering his mother after 16 hours of continual questioning, with the interrogators supplying all of the details of the boy's alleged crime. Add to this the fact that all too many prosecutors (often those with political ambitions) are perfectly willing to use such extracted confessions, and in an alarming number of cases are also willing to use incriminating evidence planted by dirty cops and/or to suppress exculpatory evidence—as was the case with the falsely convicted 18-year-old Cialdini cites—and it's little surprise that the NAS considers its estimate of 4.1% "conservative."

back-alley abortions. (More on this in Chapter 21 which covers Christian opposition to reproductive rights.)

"Pro-life" Christians value zygotes and fetuses over the lives of women. "Pro-lifers" want to go back to involuntary pregnancy, unwanted babies, stunted lives, back-alley abortions, and hundreds, perhaps thousands, of preventable deaths annually. Their assertion that they're concerned about women's health and lives is transparently false, transparently hypocritical.

When you consider that "pro-life" politicians routinely oppose measures that would make the lives of single mothers and their children more bearable—universal healthcare, early childhood education, publicly funded daycare, increased nutritional benefits, equalized school funding, a livable minimum wage, and affordable housing programs—the level of "pro-life" hypocrisy jumps off the charts.

Death from lack of access to healthcare. Every year in the United States tens of thousands of people die because of lack of healthcare access. Roughly a quarter of the U.S. population is in this position because they have no or inadequate health insurance. In 2009, Harvard Medical School put the number of preventable deaths due to inadequate medical care at 45,000 annually among the uninsured and under-insured.[26] It's no mystery why so many of them die, and why so many are poor and working class. When people have no medical insurance, or have insurance with high deductibles, they tend to have no preventive care, no or inadequate prenatal care, and they tend to put off going to the doctor as long as they possibly can, with sometimes fatal results, especially when they've put off having medical problems diagnosed. Oftentimes, this means preventable deaths—deaths due to diseases or other conditions which would have been treatable had they been diagnosed earlier.

The "pro-life" crowd is fine with all of this misery and death. They have to be. Otherwise they wouldn't keep electing the "pro-life" politicians responsible for it, politicians who place insurance industry and pharmaceutical company profits (and campaign contributions) above human life.

Death from hunger and starvation. Here in the U.S., "pro-life" politicians work relentlessly to strip SNAP benefits (food stamps) from the poor, and reduce those already inadequate benefits. Feeding America estimates that in pre-pandemic 2019, 13 million children, more than one in six, "lived in a food-insecure household," with the USDA defining "food insecurity" as "the lack of access, at times, to enough food for all household members."[27]

To put this another way, tens of millions of Americans don't know where their next meal is coming from at some time during any given year. The result is that while starvation is rare in the United States, hunger isn't; it's a source of misery, worry, psychological problems, and preventable (with adequate nutrition) illness.

The situation abroad is worse. According to figures from the United Nations, over 9,000,000 people die annually worldwide, about 25,000 per day, from starvation.[28] You would think that terrible death toll would be of concern to "pro-life" lawmakers. But you'd be wrong. They (at least a good majority of them) seem to be indifferent to all this preventable death and suffering, as evidenced by their actions. A great many "pro-lifers" and "pro-life" politicians oppose foreign aid, including food aid. Because of such opposition, U.S. foreign aid amounts to only about 1% of the federal budget, with a third of that in the form of military aid, as death from starvation kills nine million of the world's poorest and most vulnerable every year.

This already bad situation is certain to worsen in coming decades due to climate change-induced drought, increasing temperatures and decreasing rainfall in crop-producing areas, torrential rainfall and flooding in other areas, and sea level rise causing loss of farm lands in low-lying coastal regions. All of this has been obvious for decades, yet most "pro-life" politicians and most "pro-lifers" do nothing to combat the deadly climate-change threat, and in fact resist attempts to mitigate this unfolding disaster which is already causing large-scale death, destruction, and misery.

Death from deliberate medical neglect. In comparison with the above, this is a minor problem, and one seemingly unique to the United States in the developed world. In six states, religious parents have the right to deny life-saving medical care to their own children, and members of sects such as the Christian Scientists and Jehovah's Witnesses sometimes do this. The *Pediatrics* study cited in the previous chapter estimated that the number of American children who died because "parents withheld medical care because of reliance on religious rituals" was approximately 150 in the 1975–1995 period.[29] These were preventable deaths, deaths directly attributable to Christian religious belief overriding the right of children simply to live. Such tragic, avoidable deaths of children will continue until the states stop giving religious nut job parents the right to commit negligent homicide by withholding life-saving medical care from their own kids.

Death from science denial. The most pertinent example is the massive and largely avoidable death toll in the United States from Covid-19. Due to the "pro-life" Trump regime's inaction and refusal to institute nationwide public health measures (mass testing, contact tracing, quarantining, mask wearing, and social distancing), hundreds of thousands of Americans died from Covid unnecessarily. "Pro-life" Republican governors and legislatures went even further, not only refusing to implement those public health measures, but banning counties, cities, and school districts from implementing them, and in some cases banning private employers from mandating them. Some "pro-life" state governments even banned vaccination mandates by private employers. Tens, probably hundreds, of thousands of people died because of these policies.

To cite but one example of this, the Covid death rate in Arizona—where its "pro-life" Catholic governor Doug Ducey, and the GOP-controlled state legislature, aggressively blocked public health measures and vaccination mandates—was over twice as high as in two comparable Western states (Colorado and Washington) that implemented basic public health measures; because of Ducey's and the Republican legislators' death-dealing policies, over 10,000 Arizonans died unnecessarily from Covid infections in the 19-plus months from March 17, 2020 to October 24, 2021.[30] (We'll keep this short here, because we cover the topic at much greater length in Chapter 11 on the deadly effects of Christian science denial.)

There are many other ways in which "pro-lifers" and other Christians demonstrate their hypocrisy, their lack of concern and contempt for the lives and rights of others. But these examples should be enough to show that hypocrisy is endemic to Christianity, and especially so among the "pro-life" crowd.

Endnotes

1. *Beyond Belief: Two thousand years of bad faith in the Christian Church*, by James McDonald. Reading, England: Garnet Publishing, 2011, pp. 259, 260.

2. https://www.amazon.com/s?k=pascal%27s+wager&i=stripbooks&qid=1600323125&ref=sr_pg_1 < https://tinyurl.com/y3fkj6mf >

3. Cited at https://www.amazon.com/Taking-Pascals-Wager-Evidence-Abundant/dp/0830851364/ref=sr_1_2?dchild=1&keywords=pascal%27s+wager&qid=1600323137&s=books&sr=1-2 < https://tinyurl.com/y3q8juug >

4. "Abstinence-Only Education Is Ineffective And Unethical," by Sarah McCammon. National Public Radio, August 23, 2017. https://www.npr.org/sections/health-shots/2017/08/23/545289168/abstinence-education-is--ineffective-and-unethical-report-argues < https://tinyurl.com/y36sxbjy >

5. "The comparative safety of legal induced abortion and childbirth in the United States." National Library of Medicine/NIH, February 2012. https://pubmed.ncbi.nlm.nih.gov/22270271/ < https://tinyurl.com/yxo8lqsp >

6. "Abortion Surveillance—United States, 2018," by Katherine Kortsmit, et al. Centers for Disease Control and Prevention, Morbidity and Mortality Weekly Report, November 27, 2020. https://www.cdc.gov/mmwr/volumes/69/ss/ss6907a1.htm < https://tinyurl.com/ejfxcr2z >

7. "US Ranks Worst in Maternal Care, Mortality Compared With 10 Other Developed Nations," by Gianna Melillo. *American Journal of Managed Care*, December 3, 2020. https://www.ajmc.com/view/us-ranks-worst-in-maternal-care-mortality-compared-with-10-other-developed-nations < https://tinyurl.com/2hfsbmpa >

8. "Russell Moore, John Piper 'let down the pro-life movement' by opposing Trump, Penny Nance says," by Ryan Foley. *Christian Post*, February 16, 2021. https://www.christianpost.com/news/anti-trump-evangelicals-let-pro-life-movement-down-activist-says.html < https://tinyurl.com/1xnquqbq >

9. *Unholy: Why White Evangelicals Worship at the Altar of Donald Trump*, by Sarah Posner. New York: Random House, 2020, p. 107.

10. *What You Don't Know About Religion (but should)*, by Ryan Cragun. Durham, NC: Pitchstone Publishing, 2013, p. 167.

11. "Donald Trump wanted to buy the San Francisco Giants," by Grant Brisbee. *McCovey Chronicles*, August 4, 2017. https://www.mccoveychronicles.com/2017/8/4/16097944/donald-trump-san-francisco-giants < https://tinyurl.com/y2tmtr5z >

12. *The Cult of Trump: A Leading Cult Expert Explains How the President Uses Mind Control*, by Steven Hassan. New York: Free Press, 2019, p. xiv.

13. "Hail to the Moon King," by John Gorenfeld. *Salon*, June 22, 2004. https://www.salon.com/2004/06/21/moon_7/ < https://tinyurl.com/3wea7xfh >

14. Ibid.

15. "Pence and Pompeo Headlined an Event Mounted by a Group That Says the 'Christian Era Has Ended,'" by David Corn. *Mother Jones*, May 20, 2021. https://www.motherjones.com/politics/2021/05/pence-pompeo-headlined-event-mounted-by-unification-church/ < https://tinyurl.com/ws8af6k6 >

16. Ibid.

17. "Trump spoke at a 9/11 'Moonies' conference organized by the widow of the Rev. Sun Myung Moon, praising the controversial Unification Church," by Alia Shoaib. *Business Insider*, September 13, 2021. https://www.businessinsider.in/politics/world/news/donald-trump-spoke-at-a-9/11-moonies-conference-organized-by-the-widow-of-reverend-sun-myung-moon-praising-the-controversial-unification-church/articleshow/86142099.cms < https://tinyurl.com/3eu39smu >

18. "Strip club owner: Gingrich group pulled award." Associated Press, October 1, 2009. https://www.nbcnews.com/id/wbna33130841 < https://tinyurl.com/ewrthjb4 >

19. *Going Clear: Scientology, Hollywood, & the Prison of Belief*, by Lawrence Wright. New York: Alfred A. Knopf, 2013, p. 100.

20. *Losing Reality: On Cults, Cultism, and the Mindset of Political and Religious Zealotry*, by Robert Jay Lifton. New York: New Press, 2019, p. 35.

21. *The Mormon Murders: A True Story of Greed, Forgery, Deceit, and Death*, by Steven Naifeh and Gregory White Smith. New York: Weidenfeld & Nicolson, 1988, p. 121.

22. "Every Execution in U.S. History in a Single Chart," by Chris Wilson. *Time*, April 15, 2017. https://time.com/82375/every-execution-in-u-s-history-in-a-single-chart/ < https://tinyurl.com/4z583b97 >

23. "Rate of false conviction of criminal defendants who are sentenced to death," by Samuel R. Gross, et al. *Proceedings of the National Academy of Sciences*, May 20, 2014. https://www.pnas.org/content/111/20/7230 < https://tinyurl.com/5fe9uw42 >

24. Melillo, op. cit.

25. "Abortion Surveillance—United States, 2018," by Katherine Kortsmit, et al. Centers for Disease Control and Prevention, Morbidity and Mortality Weekly Report, November 27, 2020. https://www.cdc.gov/mmwr/volumes/69/ss/ss6907a1.htm < https://tinyurl.com/ejfxcr2z >

26. " New study finds 45,000 deaths annually linked to lack of health coverage," by David Cecere. *The Harvard Gazette*, September 17, 2009. https://news.harvard.edu/gazette/story/2009/09/new-study-finds-45000-deaths-annually-linked-to-lack-of-health-coverage/ < https://tinyurl.com/y3kmh26j >

27. "The Impact of the Coronavirus on Food Insecuritiy in 2020 & 2021." Feeding America. https://www.feedingamerica.org/sites/default/files/2021-03/National%20Projections%20Brief_3.9.2021_0.pdf < https://tinyurl.com/45fnfm5e >

28. "Losing 25,000 to Hunger Every Day," by John Holmes. *UN Chronicle*. https://www.un.org/en/chronicle/article/losing-25000-hunger-every-day < https://tinyurl.com/2xe3abct >

29. "Child Fatalities From Religion-motivated Medical Neglect," by Seth M. Asser and Rita Swan. *Pediatrics*, April 1998, 101 (4) 625-629 https://pediatrics.aappublications.org/content/101/4/625?download=true < https://tinyurl.com/srzc5xhk >

30. "Covid-19 as the leading cause of death in Arizona during the pandemic: An evidence review," by Alan N. Williams and Will Humble. Arizona Public Health Association, October 20, 2021. http://azpha.wildapricot.org/resources/Documents/2020-2021%20Leading%20Causes%20of%20Death%20October%2020%202021%20Final%20Final.pdf < https://tinyurl.com/j8d67ejk >

3

Christianity Is Based on Fear

> Religion is based primarily and mainly upon fear. It is partly the terror of the unknown and partly the wish to feel that you have a kind of elder brother who will stand by you in all your troubles and disputes. Fear is the basis of the whole thing—fear of the mysterious, fear of defeat, fear of death. Fear is the parent of cruelty, and therefore it is no wonder if cruelty and religion have gone hand in hand. It is because fear is at the basis of those two things.
> —Bertrand Russell, *Why I Am Not a Christian*

While today there are liberal clergy who preach a gospel of love, they ignore the bulk of Christian scripture, not to mention the bulk of Christian history. Throughout almost its entire time on Earth, the motor driving Christianity has been, in addition to the fear of death, fear of the devil and fear of hell. One can only imagine how potent these threats seemed prior to the rise of science and rational thinking, which have largely robbed these bogeys of their power to inspire terror. But the fear of death is all but inescapable, and even today the existence of the devil and hell are cardinal doctrinal tenets of almost all Christian creeds.

Nowadays, Catholics and liberal Protestants tend to downplay the fear-inducing doctrines of their faith, but many fundamentalist preachers still openly resort to terrorizing their followers—and, worse, their followers' children—with lurid, sadistic portraits of the suffering of nonbelievers and sinners after death. This is not an attempt to convince through logic and reason; it is not an attempt to appeal to the better nature of individuals; rather, it's an attempt to whip the herd into line through threats, through appeals to a base part of human nature, fear and cowardice.

A few quotations from the devout illustrate just how heavily Christianity relies on fear. First, a passage from a sermon by Jonathan Edwards (1703–1758), America's leading Congregationalist preacher and theologian of the 18th century:

> That world of misery, that lake of burning brimstone, is extended abroad under you. There is the dreadful pit of the glowing flames of the wrath of God; there is hell's wide gaping mouth open; and you have nothing to stand upon, nor any thing to take hold of; there is nothing between you and hell but the air; it is only the power and mere pleasure of God that holds you up.
> —"Sinners in the Hands of an Angry God"[1]

Then consider this passage from the previously mentioned 19th-century Catholic children's book, *Tracts for Spiritual Reading*, which illustrates in stark form the Christian appeal to fear, to the fear of hell in its grossest form—fear mongering aimed at children:

> Look into this little prison. In the middle of it there is a boy, a young man. He is silent; despair is on him . . . His eyes are burning like two burning coals. Two long flames come out of his ears. His breathing is difficult. Sometimes he opens his mouth and breath of blazing fire rolls out of it. But listen! There is a sound just like that of a kettle boiling. Is it really a kettle which is boiling? No; then what is it? Hear what it is. The blood is boiling in the scalding veins of that boy. The brain is boiling and bubbling in his head. The marrow is boiling in his bones. Ask him why he is thus tormented. His answer is that when he was alive, his blood boiled to do very wicked things.

It's difficult to think of a reason for this skin-crawling passage other than to inspire terror. Reverend Furniss's officially approved book for young people told kids that they'll be tortured forever if they don't follow the Church's dictates. Worse, it told them that if they simply *think* about violating even the most ridiculous Church commands—such as avoiding meat on Fridays or during Lent—they'll be condemned to eternal torment. The unwritten part of this, which Catholic children have drilled into their heads, is that the only way to avoid eternal torment for committing any mortal sin is to to "make a good confession," or to make a "sincere act of contrition" immediately before death.

But why such a drastic punishment—eternal torture—for such a trivial offense as eating meat on Friday (or during Lent)? One Catholic web site gives the game away: ". . . if you eat meat on a Friday the sinful thing is not the eating of the meat itself, but the disobedience to what the Church is asking us to do as a matter of discipline."[2] (Notice the euphemism "asking," used in place of the more accurate "commanding.") To put this another way, the purpose of this and other ridiculous "mortal sins" is to terrorize Catholics, children and adults, into obedience to the Church on even the pettiest matters. As a result, generation after generation of Catholic kids (myself among them) lived in dire fear of going to hell if they ate meat on Friday or—horrors!—had "impure thoughts" and died before going to confession. (If you were run down and killed by a speeding truck on your way to confession after eating some forbidden bacon, you'd be s.o.l. unless you had time to make a "sincere act of contrition" before dying.)

To reiterate, the purposes of the loathsome doctrine of hell and eternal torture are clear: to rule through fear and to induce dependence on the church and its clergy.

Unfortunately, the Reverend Furniss's fear-mongering, with its sadistic undertones, while unusually lurid, is far from being out of the Christian mainstream. Other religious leaders, including the early Christian fathers, are also guilty of making such threats. One example:

> Ah! The broad magnificence of that scene! How shall I laugh and be glad and exult when I see these wise philosophers, who teach that the gods are indifferent and men soulless, roasting and browning before their own disciples in hell. —Tertullian (155–240), *De Spectaculis* ("On Spectacles")

In addition to relying upon fear of hell and the devil, Christianity also relies on the fear of death. Reverend Furniss's words to children are a case in point: "Never forget that you must die; that death will come sooner than you expect . . . God has written the letters of death upon your hands. In the inside of your hands you will see the letters M.M. It means *Memento Mori*—remember you must die."

Protestants are equally guilty of fear mongering. It's still very common among evangelicals, with fire-and-brimstone preachers providing almost endless examples month after month, year after year, century after century. Consider the following from the previously mentioned 18th-century Congregationalist theologian and preacher, Jonathan Edwards:

> Reprobate infants are vipers of vengeance, which Jehovah will hold over hell in the tongs of his wrath until they turn and spit venom in his face.
> —"The Eternity of Hell's Torments"

One wonders what kind of a god would declare infants "reprobate" (prenatally damned), but the intent of this passage is clear: to terrify believers.

In another sermon, the previously cited "Sinners in the Hands of an Angry God," Edwards doubled down on the fear of death and hell: "God may cast wicked men into hell at any given moment"; and "Simply because there are not visible means of death before them at any given moment, the wicked should not feel secure." In the same sermon, Edwards threatened believers with another favorite Christian bogey, Satan: "At any moment God shall permit him, Satan stands ready to fall upon the wicked and seize them as his own." In these beliefs, Edwards typified his Puritan brethren. It would be easy enough to cite additional blood curdling passages (and we will cite more, particularly in the chapters on Christian cruelty), but for now the above provide good illustrations of the Christian reliance on fear and threats.

Hate, the offspring of fear

> The doctrine of eternal punishment is in perfect harmony with the savagery of the men who made the orthodox creeds. It is in harmony with torture, with flaying alive and with burnings. The men who burned their fellow-men for a moment, believed that God would burn his enemies forever.
> —Robert Ingersoll, "Crumbling Creeds"

Hate is often the result of fear, so it's not terribly surprising that it's a prominent feature of Christianity. The Old Testament is filled with hateful, sadistic passages designed to inspire terror, so it's only natural that a great many of those who claim to adhere to everything in the Bible (they don't) reflect those hateful, sadistic passages in their words and deeds.

It's rare for American Christians to acknowledge the threatening nature and hatefulness of much of the Bible, but at least a few do. The Westboro Baptist Church—the church founded by the Reverend Fred Phelps, and whose members routinely picket the funerals of AIDS victims and soldiers killed in America's foreign wars with signs reading, "God Hates Fags" and "God Hates Dead Soldiers"—offers some refreshing honesty on its web site: "Why do you preach hate? Because the Bible preaches hate. For every one verse about God's mercy, love, compassion, etc., there are two verses about His vengeance, hatred, wrath, etc."[3] Say what you will about the Westboro Baptist Church, at least it's honest about this. Most Christians and most Christian churches aren't.

As you might expect, Phelps, who died in 2014, practiced the hate he preached. In addition to picketing funerals, he and members of his church have harassed the grieving relatives of AIDS victims. As one example, they sent a letter to the parents of AIDS victim Kevin Oldham, calling their son "a filthy dead sodomite," before picketing his funeral; they also sent AIDS victim Nicholas Rango's grieving mother a flyer that called her son a "filthy piece of human garbage who checked into hell."[4] Victims have also reported telephone harassment following funerals, something Phelps and his church have denied.

It's hard to compete with such hatred and cruelty, but that hasn't stopped other Christian preachers and "pro-life" activists from trying. The stridently anti-mask, anti-vaccine Reverend Bob Enyart, of the Denver Bible Church, on his now-defunct TV show, *Bob Enyart Live*, "would gleefully read obituaries of AIDS sufferers while cranking 'Another One Bites the Dust' by Queen in the background."[5]

Making his (and his group's) embrace of hate even more explicit, Randall Terry, founder of the extreme anti-choice group Operation Rescue, once said: "I want you to just let a wave of intolerance wash over [you]. I want you to let a wave of hatred wash over you. Yes, hate is good . . ."[6]

For some reason, many Christians have a problem with such sentiments, and try to ignore both hate mongers such as Terry and the vicious Bible passages (and in Terry's case, Catholic dogma) that inspire them.*

Hence virtually all American Christians are "cafeteria Christians" who pick and choose which parts of the Bible they "believe" in. Kind, considerate Christians—such as the reverends Martin Luther King, Jr. and William J. Barber II (president of the Poor People's Campaign)—tend to focus on the "nice parts" of the Bible, especially the New Testament (love thy neighbor—Matthew 22:39; treating strangers and foreigners well—Leviticus 19:33–34, among other passages; God is love—1 John 4:8 and 4:16; "Judge not, that ye be not judged"—Matthew 7:1; and the Golden Rule—Matthew 7:12 and Luke 6:31, etc.).

Conversely, hateful, malicious Christians—such as the reverends Jerry Falwell and Billy Graham—tend to ignore those "nice parts" and instead focus on the cruel, authoritarian passages, though they almost invariably focus only on those passages they themselves do not routinely and visibly violate, or which are so shocking they'd repel all but the most fanatical Christians—for example, the passages in which Jehovah commands believers to murder those who work on the sabbath, Exodus 31:14–15 and

---

* Though they're in a decided minority, some Christian authors deal honestly with the dark sides of Christianity. Two notable recent examples are Philip Jenkins' book *Layng Down the Sword: Why we can't ignore the Bible's violent verses* and Robert P. Jones' *White Too Long: The Legacy of White Supremacy in American Christianity.*

Exodus 35:1–2. (As well, Numbers 15:32–36 approvingly relates a tale about God ordering Moses to command the Israelites to murder by stoning a man caught "gathering sticks" on the sabbath, which presumably violated the work-on-the-sabbath ban.)

That both types of Christians, the kind, considerate ones and the hateful, sadistic ones,* ignore inconvenient portions of the Bible, tells you all you need to know about the Bible's consistency, its "inerrancy," and its usefulness as a moral guide. It also tells you that even though both kind and hateful passages can be found in the Bible, hate and terror are integral parts of Christian scripture, that they continue to be a prominent part of contemporary Christianity, and that the more humane Christians almost invariably turn a blind eye toward the vicious passages.**

But even the cruelest Christians, those intent on using the government to control and harm others, or intent on doing it directly, realize how disreputable it is to acknowledge their hatefulness and bloodlust. They'll cite passages such as Leviticus 18:22 ("Thou shalt not lie with mankind as with womankind: it is abomination") as justification for passing and enforcing draconian legislation designed to destroy people's lives—and in the same breath they'll insist that they're acting out of love.

The Reverend Jonathan Shelley of the Stedfast (sic) Baptist Church in Hurst, Texas provided a recent and stark example of hate masquerading as love. Following the accidental death of a marcher, hit by a truck in a Pride parade in Fort Lauderdale, Shelley rejoiced in the death:

> [I]t's great when when trucks accidentally go through those . . . parades . . . I think only one person died, so hopefully we can hope for more in the future. . . . the Bible says that they're worthy of death!** . . . I think it's great! I hope they all die! I would love it every fag would die right now. . . . I really mean it!"[7]

In a following sermon, after receiving considerable blowback for his hateful words, Shelley attacked critics who "take things out of context and

* All four of the clergymen mentioned on the previous page, the reverends King, Barber, Falwell, and Graham, were or are Baptists. This might seem odd, but there's no hierarchy enforcing doctrinal orthodoxy among Baptists—a denomination, not a hierarchically organized church—so individual Baptist preachers and their churches are free to interpret the Bible any way they like, which accounts for the extremely disparate interpretations of scripture by these four clergymen.

** Although he didn't specifically cite it by chapter and verse, Shelley was almost certainly referring to Leviticus 20:13, "If a man also lie with mankind, as he lieth with a woman, both of them have committed an abomination: they shall surely be put to death; their blood shall be upon them" try to make it appear we don't love people." In the same sermon, he stated that all gay men are pedophiles and called for their murder: ". . . all these sodomites . . . they just simply are attracted to children . . . anybody who loves children, who loves their family, would want this person [sic] executed . . ."[8] (Shelley also argues that, somehow, these murders wouldn't be murders if carried out by the state, thus sidestepping the Sixth Commandment.)

Even though most Christians and most preachers aren't as cruel and ghoulish as Shelley, Phelps, and Enyart, it's undeniable that all too many Christians find plentiful and explicit justification for their hatefulness in the Bible. It's also undeniable that kind, considerate Christians, doing good in the name of Christianity, are providing a smokescreen for their vicious brethren.

As "Friendly Atheist" Hemant Mehta says, "There's no hate like Christian love."

Endnotes

1. "Sinners in the Hands of an Angry God," by Jonathan Edwards. Blue Letter Bible. https://www.blueletterbible.org/Comm/edwards_jonathan/Sermons/Sinners.cfm < https://tinyurl.com/22acxjte >

2. "I ate meat on Friday… am I going to Hell?!," by Deacon Matthew Newsome. WCU Catholic Ministry. http://wcucatholic.org/i-ate-meat-on-friday-am-i-going-to-hell/ < https://tinyurl.com/yyqztwvr >

3. "Frequently Asked Questions." Westboro Baptist Church. www.godhatesfags.com/faq.html

4. "Dancing on Your Grave," by Donna Minkowitz. POZ, December 1, 1994. https://www.poz.com/article/Dancing-On-Your-Grave-Donna-Minkowitz-Gets-Close-To-Fred-Phelps-AIDS-Funeral-Picketer-13378-8060 < https://tinyurl.com/yuwb9wjs >

5. "Covid Hits Pastor /Podcaster Who Sued Over Masks in Church," by Michael Roberts. *Westword*, September 1, 2021. https://www.westword.com/news/bob-enyart-denver-pastor-catches-covid-12233423 < https://tinyurl.com/kbhmrc5t >

6. Quoted in the *Fort Wayne News Sentinel* on August 16, 1993. Quoted in turn by David Irish in *America's Taliban: In Its Own Words*. Tucson, See Sharp Press, 2003, p. 23.

7. "Hate-Preacher Celebrates Death of Gay Man at Pride Parade: 'I hope they all die,'" by Hemant Mehta. *Friendly Atheist*, June 21, 2021. https://friendlyatheist.patheos.com/2021/06/21/hate-preacher-celebrates-death-of-gay-man-at-pride-parade-i-hope-they-all-die/ < https://tinyurl.com/yesj6hkd >

8. "Christian Hate Preacher Reiterates Desire to See Gay People Executed," by Hemant Mehta. *Friendly Atheist*, June 30, 2021. https://friendlyatheist.patheos.com/2021/06/30/christian-hate-preacher-reiterates-desire-to-see-gay-people-executed/ < https://tinyurl.com/jv7d67xf >

4

Christianity Encourages Cruelty to Oneself

> If we survey the moral demands of the earliest times of Christianity, it will everywhere be found that the requirements are exaggerated in order that man *cannot* satisfy them; the intention is not that he should become more moral, but that he should feel himself as *sinful as possible.*
> —Friedrich Nietzsche, *Human, All Too Human*

Throughout its history, cruelty—both to self and others—has been a hallmark of Christianity. From its very start, Christianity, with its bleak view of life, its emphasis upon sexual sin, and its almost impossible-to-meet demands for sexual "purity," encouraged guilt, penance, and self-torture. This was no aberration. Taking their cue from Luke 6:25, "Woe unto you that are full! for ye shall hunger. Woe unto you that laugh now! for ye shall mourn and weep," Christian clerics "taught that laughter was evil and sinful. . . . As they pointed out, there is not a single example of Jesus laughing or even smiling in the Bible."[1] So the Christian clergy taught that mirth was meretricious and suffering saintly, and they encouraged self-torment. Today, this self-torture is primarily psychological, in the form of guilt arising from following (or denying, and thus obsessing over) one's natural sexual desires. In earlier centuries, the self-torment was often physical. W.E.H. Lecky, in *The History of European Morals*, relates:

> There is, perhaps no phase in the moral history of mankind of a deeper or more painful interest than this ascetic outbreak [starting in the 3rd century

> CE]. A hideous, sordid, and emaciated maniac, without knowledge, without patriotism, without natural affection, passing his life in a long routine of useless and atrocious self-torture, and quailing before the ghastly phantoms of his delirious brain, had become the ideal of the nations which had known the writings of Plato and Cicero and the lives of Socrates and Cato. For about two centuries, the hideous maceration of the body was regarded as the highest proof of excellence. St. Jerome declares, with a thrill of admiration, how he had seen a monk, who for thirty years had lived exclusively on a small portion of barley bread and of muddy water; another who lived in a hole and never ate more than five figs for his daily repast; a third, who cut his hair only on Easter Sunday, who never washed his clothes, who never changed his tunic till it fell to pieces, who starved himself till his eyes grew dim, and his skin 'like a pumice stone' . . .
>
> The cleanliness of the body was regarded as a pollution of the soul, and the saints who were most admired had become one hideous mass of clotted filth. St. Athanasius relates with enthusiasm how St. Antony, the patriarch of monachism [monasticism], had never to extreme old age, been guilty of washing his feet.
>
> The occasional decadence of the monks into habits of decency was a subject of much reproach. 'Our fathers,' said the abbot Alexander, looking mournfully back to the past, 'never washed their faces, but we frequent public baths.'

Lecky goes on:

> But of all the evidences of the loathsome excesses to which this spirit was carried, the life of St. Simeon Stylites is probably the most remarkable. . . . He had bound a rope around him so that it became embedded in his flesh, which putrefied around it. A horrible stench, intolerable to the bystanders, exhaled from his body, and worms dropped from him whenever he moved, and they filled his bed. . . . For a whole year, we are told, St. Simeon stood upon one leg, the other being covered with hideous ulcers, while his biographer [St. Anthony] was commissioned to stand by his side, to pick up the worms that fell from his body, and to replace them in the sores, the saint saying to the worms, 'Eat what God has given you.' From every quarter pilgrims of every degree thronged to do him homage. A crowd of prelates followed him to the grave. A brilliant star is said to have shone miraculously over his pillar; the general voice of mankind pronounced him to be the highest model of a Christian saint; and several other anchorites [Christian hermits] imitated or emulated his penances.

The words of a Catholic saint are equally revealing. In his "charming" 19th-century Catholic children's book, *Tracts for Spiritual Reading*, the Reverend John Furniss quotes a church father, St. John Climacus:

> I saw there [an Egyptian monastery] such sights as the eye of slothful man never saw, the ear of the idle never heard of, and the heart of the coward never thought.
>
> In that monastery they always fasted on bread and water for their sins. Some of them stood upright all night in the open air. When sleep tempted them they drove it away and reproached themselves for their cowardice. Some, with their eyes lifted up to heaven, and with a sorrowful voice, called upon God to have mercy on them. Others stood with their hands tied behind their backs, as if they were great criminals. . . . Others placed on sack-cloth and ashes, hid their heads betwixt their knees or beat their foreheads against the ground. . . . No laughter was ever heard amongst them. . . . There was no care about their body, what they should eat or drink, or what was pleasant to the taste. Even the desire of these things was no longer in their heart. They thought about nothing but their sins and death. . . .
>
> As for me, when I had seen and heard all these things, I was near falling into despair, for I remembered how little my own penance had been.[2]

Self-mortification, self-torture if you will, has been a part of Christianity almost since its inception, when the self-tormenting hermits, the Anchorites, so vividly described by Lecky and St. John Climacus, were commonly regarded as exemplars of the Christian spirit. They flourished (if that's the proper word) in the Egyptian and Syrian deserts for centuries.

The next well known and considerably more widespread exhibition of public self-mortification came with the (self-) flagellant frenzy during the Middle Ages, especially during the Black Death in the 14th century, when processions of flagellants marched from town to town, whipping themselves bloody in an attempt to appease God and ward off the plague. This approach was not notably successful: the flagellants sometimes *brought* the plague to uninfected towns.

During the centuries following the adoption of Christianity as Rome's state religion, Christians seemed to concentrate more on tormenting others than themselves, but contrary to popular belief Christian physical self-torment didn't die out in the Middle Ages. It lives on, and while not as common today as in centuries past, it's still a notable feature of Christianity.

Perhaps the most gruesome current example of self-mortification surfaces every Good Friday in the form of "penitentes," primarily in the Philippines, men who willingly suffer crucifixion, with some enduring nails being driven through their limbs in imitation of the crucifixion of Christ. Other penitentes don't go quite that far, and settle for flagellating themselves bloody and crawling near naked across concrete. There are also penitentes in New Mexico and Southern Colorado who follow similar practices, and whose numbers, according to an estimate in the *Albuquerque Journal* in 2007, run to between 800 and 1,200 members.[3]

The other more prominent and more widespread example of organized self-torment is provided by the secretive, ultra-conservative, extremely wealthy Catholic organization Opus Dei ("The Work of God"), which was founded by the recently canonized (2002) saint, Josemaría Escrivá de Balaguer y Albás, in 1928 in Spain, which currently has approximately 85,000 to 100,000 members worldwide, and has an estimated $2.8 billion in assets.[4] As evidence of the group's extreme-right orientation, a number of Opus Dei members served as ministers in Spanish dictator/mass murderer Francisco Franco's cabinet. In the United States, extreme-right Catholics tied to Opus Dei include the deceased Supreme Court Justice Antonin Scalia, defeated Supreme Court nominee Robert Bork, former U.S. senators Rick Santorum and Sam Brownback,[5] and Donald Trump's attorney general Bill Barr, who served on the board of directors of Opus Dei's bookstore/chapel, the Catholic Information Center, in Washington, DC., from 2014 to 2017.[6]

Opus Dei's founder, Escrivá de Balaguer, was an enthusiastic devotee of self-torment. In his book, *Camino* ("The Way"), Escrivá de Balaguer wrote, "Blessed be pain! Beloved be pain! Sanctified be pain!" Given such enthusiasm, it's not surprising that pain, in the form of self-mortification, is an integral part of Opus Dei. Members of the group flagellate themselves weekly, but their most infamous form of self-torture is the cilice (featured in *The Da Vinci Code*), a spiked metal chain worn around the upper thigh so that the spikes dig into the flesh. *Vice* estimates that 30% of Opus Dei members wear this self-lacerating device.[7]

Other Christian, especially Catholic, sects apparently still practice physical self-abuse. The late Frank K. Flinn (1939–2015) was a former Franciscan monk who held a degree from Harvard Divinity School and was an emeritus professor of religious studies at Washington University; he testified many times as a witness for the Church of Scientology in court cases. In his testimony, he repeatedly said, with considerable justification, that the abuses suffered by Scientologists (especially in Scientology's Rehabilitation Project Force) were no worse than the abuses suffered by members of Christian mendicant orders, such as the Franciscans and Dominicans.*

* These two Catholic mendicant orders were more than willing to torment others, as well as themselves. They provided the Inquisition with its interrogators and torturers.

Flinn stated that as a Franciscan he "willingly submitted to the religious practice of flagellation on Fridays, whipping his legs and back in emulation of the suffering of Jesus before his crucifixion."[8]

Such physical self-mortification was, and apparently still is, also a feature of Mother Teresa's Missionaries of Charity. Former members of the order describe it as a cult-like group having "an obsession with chastity so intense that any physical human contact or friendship was prohibited; according to [former member Mary] Johnson, Mother Teresa even told them [members of her order] not to touch the babies they cared for more than necessary. They were expected to flog themselves regularly—a practice called 'the discipline'—and were allowed to leave to visit their families only once every 10 years."[9] According to the *Irish Times*, former members described the order as a "hive of psychological abuse and coercion."[10]

Today, though, most Christian self-mortification is either psychological or takes the form of token physical mortification, as has been institutionalized in Catholic churches through the use of padded "kneelers" attached to the backs of pews, which allow worshipers to abase themselves in comfort. The petty self-denials practiced by Catholics during Lent are another example. (I had a devout Catholic uncle, a former monk, for whom lenten penance wasn't enough: he routinely drove around Phoenix in the summertime, with temperatures well above 100 degrees, and would sit in traffic and sweat rather than use his car's AC, offering up his suffering as a gift to "the poor souls in purgatory.")

But the more serious and more common forms of self-mortification are psychological, usually in the form of self-loathing due to failure to "live up to" (more fittingly, live down to) impossible-to-meet Christian sexual prohibitions. We cover this in some detail in the chapter on Christian sexual morbidity, so we'll keep this short here. For now, suffice it to say that Christianity's obsessive focus on and denigration of sex leads to great, in part self-inflicted, suffering by those who follow Christian moral teachings.

Endnotes

1. *Beyond Belief: Two thousand years of bad faith in the Christian Church*, by James McDonald. Reading, England: Garnet Publishing, 2011, pp. 294–295.

2. "Venerable John Climacus of Sinai, Author of 'The Ladder.'" Orthodox Church in America. https://www.oca.org/saints/lives/2013/03/30/100943-venerable-john-climacus-of-sinai-author-of-the-ladder < https://tinyurl.com/y5hlteex >

3. "Penitentes are not a Secret Society," by Polly Summar. *Albuquerque Journal*, April 5, 2007. https://www.abqjournal.com/news/metro/552250metro04-05-07.htm < https://tinyurl.com/y4vs6bso >

4. *The Cult of Trump: A Leading Cult Expert Explains How the President Uses Mind Control*, by Steven Hassan. New York: Free Press, 2019, p. 164.

5. "The Opus Dei Code." *Time*, April 20, 2006. http://content.time.com/time/europe/mediakit/pr/article/0,18181,1185287,00.html < https://tinyurl.com/y4vpp3vd >

6. "William Barr Is Neck-Deep in Extremist Catholic Institutions," by Joan Walsh. *The Nation*, October 15, 2019. https://www.thenation.com/article/archive/william-barr-notre-dame-secularism/ < https://tinyurl.com/y5pdrqgw >

7. "The Opus Dei Look." *Vice*, September 30, 2010. https://www.vice.com/en_us/article/kwnebz/the-opus-dei-look < https://tinyurl.com/y4nc45nt >

8. *Going Clear: Scientology, Hollywood, and the Prison of Belief*, by Lawrence Wright. New York: Alfred A. Knopf, 2013, pp. 227–228.

9. "Children tied to beds, nuns who flogged themselves, filthy homes: Was Mother Teresa a cult leader?," by Michelle Goldberg. *Irish Times*, May 24, 2021. https://www.irishtimes.com/life-and-style/people/children-tied-to-beds-nuns-who-flogged-themselves-filthy-homes-was-mother-teresa-a-cult-leader-1.4573449 < https://tinyurl.com/scuyz2v6 >

10. Ibid.

5

Christianity Encourages Cruelty to Others

> Religiosity . . . by setting up absolute standards of godly or proper conduct, makes you intolerant of yourself and others when you or they slightly dishonor these standards. Born of this kind of piety-inspired intolerance of self and others, come some of the most serious of emotional disorders—such as extreme anxiety, depression, self-hatred, and rage.
> —Albert Ellis, *The Case Against Religiosity*

> Infinite punishment is infinite cruelty, endless injustice, immortal meanness. To worship an eternal jailer hardens, debases, and pollutes even the vilest soul. —Robert Ingersoll, "Origin of God and the Devil"

Given that the Bible nowhere condemns torture and sometimes prescribes shockingly cruel punishments (especially, and repeatedly, stoning and burning alive), and that Christians have so wholeheartedly approved of and engaged in self-torture, it's not surprising that many of the devout have been quite willing, in fact eager, to torture others.

Today, believers routinely dismiss the shocking barbarities committed by their Christian forebears in the medieval, Renaissance, and early modern periods—witch burnings, heretic burnings, the crusades, the routine use of torture, widespread pogroms, the appallingly brutal treatment, mass murder, and enslavement of indigenous peoples by Christian conquerors—as being irrelevant because they happened centuries ago. At first glance, this seems reasonable. But it's not. This excuse is anything *but* reasonable. All of these *routine* exercises in mass murder and almost unbelievable cruelty were carried out by European Christians at the absolute zenith of Christianity's power and influence, at a time when, but for persecuted Jews, virtually the entire population of Europe was Christian.

If, as Christians almost invariably assert, Christian beliefs lead to good moral behavior, why was Christian behavior in centuries past so abominable? Clearly, something has changed. Christian doctrine is the same now as it was in the Middle Ages—the supposedly inerrant Word of God, the Bible, doesn't change—and as late as 1893, Pope Leo XIII, in *Providentissimus Deus* ("The God of All Providence"), insisted that the entirety of the Bible was divinely inspired.

So, what changed? Why are morals, overall, so much better now than they were during the millennium-plus that Christianity was Europe's undisputed moral guide?

What caused that improvement wasn't Christianity, it was the rise of science, rationality, and humanism. These powerful forces have been gradually eroding religious dogmatism and cruelty, at what seems like an agonizingly slow pace, for the last several centuries. Christianity, which for the most part isn't as barbaric as it was a few hundred years ago, reacted to the rise of science and humanism by becoming less cruel and less dogmatic, gradually giving ground, but fighting every inch of the way. Sam Francis, a religious right founder, Christian Identity adherent, and white supremacist confirms this, at least in one specific, saying that the Enlightenment resulted in "a bastardized form of Christian ethics that condemns slavery."[1]

So, the horrors of Christianity's past are highly relevant when evaluating Christianity as a moral system and moral force.

In 1252, Pope Innocent IV issued his papal bull, *Ad extirpanda* ("To Extirpate"). It ordered the imprisonment and torture of heretics, specifying in some detail who was to do it and under what circumstances. The bull also ordered the seizure of heretics' property, the destruction of their houses, and the "investigation" of the sons and grandsons of accused heretics.[2]

This set the stage for the mass witch and heretic burnings to come. As an indication of how many people the church brutally murdered—it had state authorities carry out the murders so it could pretend its hands were clean—consider a single inquisitor, the Dominican Bernard Gui, Bishop of Tul, France and later Bishop of Lodeve, France. In only 15 years, this monster condemned 633 heretics, both male and female, including 17 on a single day, April 5, 1310.[3] As if to illustrate the phrase, "the banality of evil," the church kept detailed records of the expenses incurred in the burning of heretics, such as Gui's victims.

As for witches, historian Susannah Lipscomb places the total number of those accused of witchcraft at approximately 100,000, and those executed at 40,000 to 50,000, with 70%–80% of the victims being female.[4] Similarly, historian Diarmaid MacCulloch estimates that "maybe between forty or fifty thousand people [accused of witchcraft] died in Europe and colonial North America between 1400 and 1800."[5]

Other estimates of the number of victims are higher than Lipscomb's and MacCulloch's. Historians Alan C. Kors and Edward Peters state in their introduction to *Witchcraft in Europe 1100–1700: A Documentary History*:

> It was not uncommon for scores, and occasionally hundreds of witches, contemporaries claimed, to be executed in a single city or region during a period of terror lasting several years. It is impossible to calculate accurately the total number of convicted witches who were burned at the stake or hanged between the fourteenth and seventeenth centuries, but few [students of the period estimate] below fifty to one hundred thousand, and some would double or triple that figure.[6]

As to why church and state engaged in this orgy of sadism and brutality, historian Lipscomb notes that the authorities believed, in line with the Bible and well into the modern period, that witchcraft existed and was a dire threat: "[Britain's] Lord chief justice Anderson noted in 1602: 'The land is full of witches . . . they abound in all places—not as a symbol or figure of fun, but as a deadly threat to life, livelihood and divine order.'"[7]

In 1484, Pope Innocent VIII followed up on Innocent IV's heretic-burning manual with a witch-burning manual, his bull *Summis Desiderantes* ("Desiring with Complete Ardor"). Andrew Dickson White, in his massive *The History of the Warfare of Science with Theology*, describes how torture was endorsed by the pope and then used against the tens, possibly hundreds, of thousands of women and men accused of witchcraft.

> On the 7th of December, 1484, Pope Innocent VIII sent forth his bull *Summis Desiderates*. Of all the documents ever issued from Rome, imperial or papal, this has doubtless, first and last, cost greatest shedding of innocent blood. . . . Inspired by the scriptural command, "Thou shalt not suffer a witch to live," [Ex. 22:18] Pope Innocent exhorted the clergy of Germany to leave no means untried to detect sorcerers, and especially those who by evil weather destroy vineyards, gardens, meadows, and growing crops. These precepts were based upon various texts of Scripture . . . and to carry them out, witch-finding inquisitors were authorized by the Pope to scour Europe, especially Germany, and a manual was prepared for their use—The Witch-Hammer, *Malleus Maleficarum*.

> With the application of torture to thousands of women, in accordance with the precepts laid down in the Malleus, it was not difficult to extract masses of proof for this sacred theory of meteorology. The poor creatures writhing on the rack, held in horror by those who had been nearest and dearest to them, anxious only for death to relieve their sufferings, confessed to anything and everything that would satisfy the inquisitors and judges. . . . the prisoners, to shorten their suffering, were sure sooner or later to give the answer required, even though they knew that this would send them to the stake or scaffold. Under the doctrine of 'excepted cases,' there was no limit to torture for persons accused of heresy or witchcraft [because the Church posited that Satan would give heretics and witches exceptional ability to endure torture]; . . .

As for the torture itself, consider George E. MacDonald's description of some of the torture instruments used at the height of Christianity's dominance of Europe:

> [Thumbscrews] may be used on the wrists, legs, or to prize the offender's teeth apart so that the 'blasphemous' tongue may be torn out with pincers . . . The larger ones crush the shinbones or the bones of the wrist. . . . Here again appears the deadly thumbscrew, which runs through the whole system of religious torture as the cross runs through the system of worship. A comparison of the one and of the other upon the growth of Christianity might be decided in favor of the screw.[8]

He goes on:

> [L]et the women gaze on this horrible piece of ingenuity, the spider [also known as the breast ripper]. It is a cluster of steel hooks pointed like needles. It is designed to be spread over the breast of the woman; the hand of the torturer grasps the central ring, drawing the points together, and then the flesh is torn away.[9]

Inquisitors routinely used such horrific instruments, along with the rack (designed to pull limbs out of their sockets and stretch connective tissues past the breaking point), red hot pokers, thumbscrews, and other astonishingly cruel devices. While torture had been common since ancient times, the cruelty of the torture and the inventiveness of the torturers likely reached an all-time high in the 16th century following the Reformation and the "need" of both Catholics and Protestants to root out heretics and witches.

Perhaps the most sadistic torture device was the Judas Cradle, a pyramid-like device on which the victim would be placed, with the apex in the anus, perineum, or vagina. Weights would then be placed on the legs of the victim to draw them down more heavily onto the sharp point in order to increase their agony. When death didn't result, genital or anal mutilation often did.

Another horrid device was "the boots," iron boots into which a victim's feet would be placed, and then heated to the point of anguish, to the point where the victim's feet were destroyed. During the conquest of the Americas, the conquistadors in their lust for gold reportedly employed a variation on this form of torture: "If a certain Indian was not giving the Conquistadores gold or 'not enough' they would burn his/her feet, until the marrow began to drip out."[10]

Still another inquisitorial device was "the chair," whose seat, back, and arms were covered with upward- and outward-pointing sharp spikes. The victim would be forced down into the chair, where the spikes pierced their flesh, leaving them bleeding, in agony, and with no hope of a quick death.

Yet another common form of torture was "strappado," in which a victim's arms would be bound behind them, and they would be hauled into the air, then dropped, but with the drop stopping short of the victim's feet hitting the floor, dislocating their shoulders and causing agonizing pain; they'd be left hanging until the torturers decided to lower their broken bodies back to earth. To increase the pain, weights were sometimes attached to victims' legs. Centuries later, the Nazis would follow the lead of the Inquisition in use of this ultra-sadistic form of torture against those who resisted them.

The ingenuity of the torturers didn't end with the devices just described; there were a great many others just as horrifying,[11] which we'll bypass here in the interest of conciseness.

One thing that all of these forms of torture had in common was that they were designed to prolong the victim's suffering, often for hours, sometimes for days, before death.

All of these loathsome, extremely cruel types of torture were employed by the church (both Catholic and Protestant) at the height of its power and influence, while it was the undisputed moral arbiter of Europe.

While the torture and murder of heretics and "witches" is now largely a thing of the past—murder of "witches" still occurs in some parts of Africa—Christian cruelty continues. To cite one near-contemporary example of Christian cruelty, the recently minted saint (and anti-contraception/anti-abortion zealot, and sycophantic supporter of dictators),[12] Mother Teresa (Anjezë Gonxhe Bojaxhiu), forbade even the most minimal comforts to the destitute sick in her homes for the dying. This cruelty included, as an institutional norm, denying analgesics beyond aspirin to those dying horrible deaths from cancer and other painful diseases. She considered the agony of these poor folk a good thing, and in fact made sure that those under her control suffered by denying them pain medication. Her former secretary, Rathy Sreedhar, quotes her as saying: "I think it is very beautiful for the poor to accept their lot, to share it with the passion of Christ. I think the world is being much helped by the suffering of the poor people."[13*]

Another fan of human suffering, colonial-era Congregationalist theologian and clergyman Jonathan Edwards, preached that just punishment for sinners is perpetual pain: "They *deserve* to be cast into hell; . . . justice calls aloud for an infinite punishment of their sins."[14] (italics added)

But all of this cruelty should not be surprising coming from members of a religion that teaches that eternal torture is not only justified, but that the saved will enjoy seeing the torture of others. In the 13th century, St. Thomas Aquinas (1225–1274), put it like this in his magnum opus, *Summa Theologica*:

> In order that the happiness of the saints may be more delightful and that they may give to God more copious thanks for it, they are permitted perfectly to behold the sufferings of the damned . . . The saints will rejoice in the punishment of the damned.[15]

Thus the vision of heaven of Christianity's greatest theologian is a vision of the sadistic enjoyment of endless torture.

The vision of 19th-century America's greatest freethinker, Civil War veteran, and Illinois Attorney General, Colonel Robert Ingersoll, stands in sharp contrast:

> It is far better to have no heaven than to have heaven and hell: better to have no God than God and devil: better to rest in eternal sleep than to be an angel and know that the ones you love are suffering eternal pain: better to live a free and loving life—a life that ends forever at the grave—than to be an eternal slave. —"Some Reasons Why"

---

* Of course, this canonized saint went to Europe and the United States for treatment of her own ailments. As one example of this, in December 1991 she went to the renowned Scripps Clinic and Research Foundation (now Scripps Research) in La Jolla, California for treatment.[16]

Legislative Cruelty

Our Christian neighbors know better than we what is good for us, and their judgment being infallible, they legislate for us accordingly.
—W.S. Byrne

A shipwrecked sailor, landing on a lonely beach, observed a gallows. 'Thank God,' he exclaimed, 'I'm in a Christian country!'
—Anonymous

Christian legislative cruelty dates back to antiquity, to the time when Christian rulers were first able to impose murderous penalties for violation of petty offenses (and for the exercise of free speech), and has continued uninterrupted ever since then. The sheer number of capital offenses likely reached an all-time high in the period 1688–1815 in Britain, where the "Bloody Code" listed over 200 death-penalty crimes, some shockingly trivial, such as shoplifting and pickpocketing; other Bloody Code capital offenses included burglary, larceny, embezzlement, forgery, cutting down trees, stealing from a rabbit warren, being an unwed mother with a stillborn infant, stealing from a shipwreck, and being caught at night with a blackened face.[17,18]

Enthusiasm for capital punishment was also a notable feature in Catholic and Catholic-controlled lands. To cite but one example, the third Duke of Alba, Fernando Álavarez de Toledo y Pimentel, executed over a thousand people as governor of the Netherlands in only six years between 1567 and 1573 during the reign of Philip II of Spain (which at the time controlled the Netherlands).[19]

Today, Christian cruelty is still largely inflicted by the state. In the U.S., roughly 90% of legislators are Christians, and the situation in the U.S. Senate is fairly typical: in 2020, of the 100 senators, 82 were Christians; 4 were Mormons; 8 were Jewish; 1 was Buddhist; and only 5 were unaffiliated. The percentage of Christians in the House of Representatives is even higher. Indeed, 91% of lawmakers are Christians, and Christians make up 100% of the delegations from 28 states.[20]

Given their near-complete domination of legislative bodies at both the state and federal levels, Christian lawmakers are responsible for a huge amount of unnecessary cruelty and suffering. (Not coincidentally, almost all U.S. presidents have been at least nominally Christian, including every single one in the 20th and 21st centuries.)

One grievous example of Christian legislative cruelty (and authoritarianism) is prohibition of suicide and assisted suicide, no matter what the circumstances. Christian-inspired laws against suicide date back to fourth-century Rome, when the Council of Arles prohibited slaves from killing themselves on the grounds that suicide was both immoral and deprived slave owners of their property.[21] This was not only an expression of the belief that individuals' lives are not their own, but rather the property of the Christian Church (and the owners of slaves), but also an indication of just how deeply slavery was embedded in Christian society of the time.

Today, in the United States, this cruel, authoritarian attitude, that individuals should not control their own lives, lives on in the form of laws prohibiting assisted suicide. A great many Christians routinely assert that *their* morality overrides the must fundamental human right, the right to control one's own life. As a result, Christians routinely treat pet animals more kindly than they do their fellow human beings. If a beloved pet is suffering, with no hope of recovery, many Christians will take that pet to the vet to end its misery, and will hold the pet in their arms as it dies. Yet they deny that mercy to incurably ill, pain-wracked human beings, on the grounds that assisting the suffering to die is somehow immoral—even though the suffering *want* to die. They've even made it a felony to be in the same room as a dying person during a suicide or an assisted suicide. They've made offering comfort to the dying a crime. Only eight states have statutes guaranteeing death with dignity.[22] In the others (minus Montana where it's legal because of court rulings), unnecessary suffering abounds, and those who help others escape intolerable pain, or simply comfort them, can be, and sometimes are, prosecuted for murder.

Even worse, Christians, especially white Protestants, disproportionately support the death penalty (the premeditated killing of individuals by the state), with white evangelicals having the highest level of support for capital punishment of any religious group.[23] This would be bad enough if all of those executed were guilty. But they're not. As mentioned in Chapter 2, the National Academy of Science (NAS) states "that if all death-sentenced defendants remained under sentence of death indefinitely at least 4.1% would be exonerated. . . . We conclude that this is a conservative estimate of the proportion of false conviction among death sentences in the United States."[24] In other words, if the wrongly condemned had adequate time and resources (competent attorneys, private investigators, expert witnesses, etc.) to prove their innocence, over one in 25 would likely have their convictions overturned or would never have been convicted in the first place.

Time reports that since the year 1700 nearly 16,000 people have been executed in the United States (and the colonies preceding independence), and that since 1973 over 1,500 have been executed.[25] Taking the National Academy of Science's estimate that at least 4.1% were wrongfully convicted and executed, that means that the American "justice" system has murdered at least 650 innocent people since the colonial period, and over 60 in the last half century.

Why such large numbers? Neglecting such things as deliberate framings (e.g., the Haymarket anarchists and Sacco & Vanzetti), perjury by the police and jailhouse informers, and planted or fabricated evidence, a large majority of the wrongfully convicted didn't (and don't) have the time and resources to adequately defend themselves, and ended up being judicially murdered. It's impossible to know the exact number, but one single innocent person executed is one too many, and it's certain that the real number of victims is far higher. Please think for a moment about how horrible it would be to be one of them, knowing that you're innocent, sitting in a cell suffering mental torture, usually for years, knowing that agents of the state will murder you on a given date. Unfortunately, this basic exercise in empathy is apparently beyond most American Christians.

A majority of them are fine with judicial murder including, unavoidably—while human judgment remains fallible—murder of the innocent. The Public Religion Research Institute reported in 2015 that 59% of white evangelicals, 52% of white mainline Protestants, and 45% of white Catholics supported capital punishment (despite the Catholic Church officially opposing it).[26] (Unsurprisingly—with the death penalty falling disproportionately on the poor, blacks, and hispanics—more black and hispanic Christians tend to oppose the death penalty than white Christians.)[27] A 2021 poll by Pew Research showed even stronger support for capital punishment, with 75% of evangelicals, 73% of mainline Protestants, and 56% of white Catholics supporting the death penalty; surprisingly, the poll also showed that 50% of black Protestants and 61% of hispanic Catholics supported it. Of all the groups Pew surveyed, atheists and agnostics were the only groups who, overall, opposed capital punishment, with 65% of atheists and 57% of agnostics opposing it.[28]

Other Christian-inspired, cruel legislative impositions are so obvious and so numerous that they need little elucidation. Current and relatively recent examples include prohibition of contraceptives; prohibition of abortion; prohibition of paid sex work; prohibition of gay sex ("sodomy"); prohibition of adultery; prohibition of fornication; prohibition of blasphemy; prohibition of "obscene" books and pictures (including even the description of contraceptive devices); and prohibition of drug use and possession.* All of these prohibitions have come with draconian penalties, up to and including execution. Christians, as is obvious, are across the board the most enthusiastic proponents of all of these prohibitions and the cruel, destructive penalties imposed upon those who violate them.

To cite but one individual example of the cruelty inherent in the state's enforcement of Christian morality, consider the treatment of civil libertarian and writer Peter McWilliams, author of *Ain't Nobody's Business If You Do: The Absurdity of Consensual Crimes in a Free Society,* which was published in 1996. In that same year, McWilliams was diagnosed with AIDS, and then began suffering severe nausea from his AIDS medications. The prescription meds prescribed to reduce the nausea didn't do the job, so he turned to marijuana, which did. As a result of his high profile (*Ain't Nobody's Business* was selling well), McWilliams was targeted by the DEA and arrested for cultivation of medically necessary marijuana. At his 1998 trial, the judge refused to allow a "medical necessity" defense, and thus refused to hear both scientific evidence of marijuana's efficacy in combating nausea and any mention of California's 1996 medical marijuana law. McWilliams was convicted, and after his family put up their homes to raise his bail (higher than for most rapists and armed robbers), he was released on bail, but on the condition that he not use marijuana to combat his nausea. In 2000, while his case was still on appeal, and he was still under the restriction prohibiting his use of marijuana, he died as a result of choking on his own vomit.

That cruel, intrusive laws against victimless crimes do more harm than good is obvious, but our purpose here is to merely list the most blatant and arrogant types of religious intrusion into individuals' lives, so we'll restrict ourselves to this single example. There are countless other victims beyond McWilliams, most pointedly the thousands upon thousands of American women who died from back alley abortions before *Roe v. Wade,* and the victims of the "war on drugs," which has resulted in mass incarceration.

---

* One indication of Christian cruelty and authoritarianism in this area is that fundamentalists are the religious group most opposed to legalization of marijuana. As of 2010, only 39% of them favored legalizing pot, as opposed to 42% of religious moderates, 48% of religious liberals, and a full 73% of the nonreligious.[29] Those numbers all rose over the next decade, and in 2021 Pew reported that 44% of white evangelicals and 76% of the unaffiliated supported legalization. Of all the groups Pew surveyed, atheists, at 88%, were the most likely to favor it.[30]

As of 2018, there were nearly half-a-million Americans in prison on drug charges, and since drug prohibition was established last century, it has resulted in literally tens of millions of damaged or ruined lives, all at a cost in 2015 alone of $7 billion just for incarceration (not including the cost of drug cops, prosecutors, judges, courts, etc.), and a total cumulative cost over the decades exceeding $1 trillion.[31]

Christian approval, and in all likelihood enjoyment, of this pervasive cruelty is all too plain: if Christians, who comprise 63% of the U.S. population, didn't approve of this appalling viciousness, they wouldn't support the Christian legislators directly responsible for it.

Even worse, the more literal minded Christians are, the more likely they are to approve of torture. According to a 2009 Pew poll, 62% of evangelicals approve of torture. And *all* Christian groups are more approving of torture than the religiously unaffiliated. Of all the groups surveyed, the unaffiliated were the only ones in which a majority opposed torture.[32] Unsurprisingly, these results mirror those regarding political leanings. A 2017 Pew poll reported that a full 79% of conservative Republicans favor torture; in contrast, only 25% of liberal Democrats approve of this appalling form of cruelty.[33]

But perhaps the final word on Christian callousness and cruelty to others was delivered in 2020 by one of their own, the Reverend Douglas Wilson, pastor of Christ Church in Moscow, Idaho. The Christian Reconstructionist pastor has a talk show on Amazon Prime, "Man Rampant." The first episode of Wilson's show was titled "The Sin of Empathy."[34]

Endnotes

1. *Unholy: Why White Evangelicals Worship at the Altar of Donald Trump*, by Sarah Posner. New York: Random House, 2020, p. 107.

2. "Ad extirpanda, Bull of Pope Innocent IV, 15 May 1252." http://www.cathar.info/121295_ad_extirpanda.htm < https://tinyurl.com/y2a7c5ww >

3. "Torturer's Apprentice," by Cullen Murphy. *The Atlantic*, January-February 2012. https://www.theatlantic.com/magazine/archive/2012/01/torturers-apprentice/308838/ < https://tinyurl.com/y27hvcxv >

4. "A very brief history of witches," by Susannah Lipscomb. HistoryExtra (BBC). https://www.historyextra.com/period/tudor/history-witches-facts-burned-hanged/ < https://tinyurl.com/y2cd2k7c >

5. *Christianity: The First Three Thousand Years*, by Diarmaid MacCulloch. London: Penguin, 2009, p. 686.

6. *Thumbscrew and Rack*, by George E. MacDonald. Tucson: See Sharp Press, 1998, p. 6.

7. Lipscomb, op. cit.

8. *Witchcraft in Europe 1100–1700: A Documentary History*, edited by Alan C. Kors and Edwin Peters. Philadelphia: University of Pennsylvania Press, 1972, 1992, p. 13.

9. MacDonald, op. cit., p. 18.

10. "El Conquistador: El infierno en los lagos." University of Michigan. http://umich.edu/~ltpao/conqui.html < https://tinyurl.com/y6q9cp8e >

11. "Medieval Torture and Punishment." *Medieval Life and Times*. http://www.medieval-life-and-times.info/medieval-torture-and-punishment/ < https://tinyurl.com/o7rpyoq >

12. "Without Walls, Hell's Angel: Mother Teresa of Calcutta," Jenny Morgan, director. Channel 4, November 8, 1994. https://www.youtube.com/watch?v=76_qL6fiyDw < https://tinyurl.com/3zy2ad6s >

13. Quoted by Christopher Hitchens in *The Missionary Position: Mother Teresa in Theory and Practice*. London: Verso, 1995, p. 11.

14. "ILLNESS: Mother Teresa's Illness Is Termed Life-Threatening," by Tom Gorman and Sebastian Rotella. *Los Angeles Times*, January 1, 1992. https://www.latimes.com/archives/la-xpm-1992-01-01-me-1185-story.html < https://tinyurl.com/3au6hwex >

15. "Question 94: The relations of the saints toward the damned." *New Advent*. https://www.newadvent.org/summa/5094.htm < https://tinyurl.com/yyl5p98v >

16. "Sinners in the Hands of an Angry God," by Jonathan Edwards. Blue Letter Bible. https://www.blueletterbible.org/Comm/edwards_jonathan/Sermons/Sinners.cfm < https://tinyurl.com/22acxjte >

17. "A brief history of capital punishment in Britain." HistoryExtra (BBC). https://www.historyextra.com/period/modern/a-brief-history-of-capital-punishment-in-britain/ < https://tinyurl.com/yxsbdpup >

18. "The 'Bloody Code.'" National Justice Museum. https://www.nationaljusticemuseum.org.uk/museum/news/what-was-the-bloody-code < https://tinyurl.com/wb4e4df7 >

19. MacCulloch, op. cit. Caption of illustration facing p. 197.

20. "Mostly Catholic but 100% Christian: What is Pa.'s Congressional delegation?," by Ivey De Jesus. *PennLive/Patriot News*, May 22, 2019. https://www.pennlive.com/news/2017/04/congressional_christian_delega.html < https://tinyurl.com/y64fofem >

21. "A Brief History of Anglo-Western Suicide: From Legal Wrong to Civil Right," by Helen Y. Chang. *Southern Law Review* Vol. 46.1, 2018, p. 159. https://digitalcommons.law.ggu.edu/cgi/viewcontent.cgi?article=1854&context=pubs < https://tinyurl.com/y63t9z3x >

22. "Death with Dignity Acts." Death With Dignity. https://www.deathwithdignity.org/learn/death-with-dignity-acts/ < https://tinyurl.com/y822ntz9 >

23. "Support for the Death Penalty by Religious Affiliation," by Joanna Placenza. Public Religion Research Institute, April 9, 2015. https://www.prri.org/spotlight/support-for-death-penalty-by-religious-affiliation/#.VaMS__lViko < https://tinyurl.com/47pd2rzz >

24. "Rate of false conviction of criminal defendants who are sentenced to death," by Samuel R. Gross, et al. *Proceedings of the National Academy of Sciences*, May 20, 2014. https://www.pnas.org/content/111/20/7230 < https://tinyurl.com/5fe9uw42 >

25. Placenza, op. cit.

26. Ibid.

27. "Unlike other U.S. religious groups, most atheists and agnostics oppose the death penalty," by Stephanie Kramer. Pew Research Center, June 15, 2021. https://www.pewresearch.org/fact-tank/2021/06/15/unlike-other-u-s-religious-groups-most-atheists-and-agnostics-oppose-the-death-penalty/ < https://tinyurl.com/2nwt78j4 >

28. "Ending the War on Drugs: By the Numbers," by Betsy Pearl. Center for American Progress, June 27, 2018. https://www.americanprogress.org/issues/criminal-justice/reports/2018/06/27/452819/ending-war-drugs-numbers/ < https://tinyurl.com/ycemrmn9 >

29. *What You Don't Know About Religion (but should)*, by Ryan Cragun. Durham, NC: Pitchstone Publishing, 2013, p. 136.

30. "Religious Americans are less likely to endorse legal marijuana for recreational use," by Stephanie Kramer. Pew Research Center, May 26, 2021. https://www.pewresearch.org/fact-tank/2021/05/26/religious-americans-are-less-likely-to-endorse-legal-marijuana-for-recreational-use/ < https://tinyurl.com/dj2ju3p9 >

31. “The Religious Dimensions of the Torture Debate.” Pew Research Center, May 7, 2009. https://www.pewforum.org/2009/04/29/the-religious-dimensions-of-the-torture-debate/ < https://tinyurl.com/y4efbgdr >

32. “Americans divided in views of use of torture in U.S. anti-terror effort.” Pew Research Center, January 26, 2017. https://www.pewresearch.org/fact-tank/2017/01/26/americans-divided-in-views-of-use-of-torture-in-u-s-anti-terror-efforts/ < https://tinyurl.com/y4eaukxm >

33. “In Moscow, Idaho, conservative ‘Christian Reconstructionists’ are thriving amid evangelical turmoil,” by Crawford Gribben. *Yahoo!life*, August 9, 2021. https://www.yahoo.com/lifestyle/moscow-idaho-conservative-christian-reconstructionists-122836348.html < https://tinyurl.com/36ru8hw7 >

34. “The Sin of Empathy,” by Reverend Douglas Wilson. Man Rampant. (On Amazon Prime; the opening monologue is also on Youtube.) Youtube, March 31, 2020. https://www.youtube.com/watch?v=ZDtIRMGrrNA < https://tinyurl.com/th9mm7hx >

6

The Christian Persecution Complex

> Just like what Nazi Germany did to the Jews, so liberal America is now doing to the Christians. It's no different. It is the same thing. It is happening all over again. It is the Democratic Congress, the liberal-based media and the homosexuals who want to destroy the Christians. Wholesale abuse and discrimination and the worst bigotry directed toward any group in America today. More terrible than anything suffered by any minority in history.
> —Rev. Pat Robertson, 1993 interview with Molly Ivins

Feelings of persecution, what one might term the Christian Persecution Complex, have been a notable feature of Christianity since its inception. Today, the Reverend Eric McKiddie's comments in his "5 Promises for the Persecuted" are typical: "We should be surprised when we *don't* face persecution, not when we do, because God's word promises us that at times we will."[1] Feelings of persecution are so much a part of Christianity that one Christian web site even features a collection of "10 Persecutions of Early Church" flashcards.[2]

As the title of the cards indicates, the Persecution Complex dates back to the very beginnings of Christianity. There are literally dozens of New Testament verses lamenting persecution, three of the clearest passages being:

> Yea, and all that will live godly in Christ Jesus shall suffer persecution.
> —2 Timothy 3:12)

> Blessed are they which are persecuted for righteousness' sake: for theirs is the kingdom of heaven. Blessed are ye, when men shall revile you, and persecute you, and shall say all manner of evil against you falsely, for my sake. Rejoice, and be exceeding glad: for great is your reward in heaven: for so persecuted they the prophets which were before you.
> —Matthew 5:10–12

> If the world hate you, ye know that it hated me before it hated you. If ye were of the world, the world would love his own: but because ye are not of the world, but I have chosen you out of the world, therefore the world hateth you. Remember the word that I said unto you, The servant is not greater than his lord. If they have persecuted me, they will also persecute you; . . ."
> —John 15:18–20*

While there was some persecution of Christians under the Romans, all reason for the Persecution Complex vanished with the adoption of Christianity in 312 by the emperor Constantine (reign 306 to 337 CE), who following his conversion became head of the church—not the pope—as were succeeding emperors until well into the fifth century.

While the Catholic Church (fallaciously) traces the papacy back to Peter, this is more than a bit self-serving. The title "pope" was used for leading clerics in other places, including Alexandria and Carthage, and it wasn't until the time of Leo the Great in the mid-5th century that the title was routinely used to refer to the Bishop of Rome.

So, Constantine predated the popes (in the modern sense of the word), and as emperor he was the head of the Roman state religion, as were his successors for over a century; he was considered infallible, was honored by church bodies as both holy man and king, was bestowed with honorifics such as "Pontiff Emperor," and shortly began granting favors to his chosen religion. Following his conversion, he lifted all legal sanctions against Christianity and began giving the church both financial and land grants.

While Christians had been subject to sporadic persecution prior to Constantine's conversion, they were largely tolerated in the polytheistic Roman world before the coming of the first Christian emperor, as long as they conformed outwardly. As Gibbon put it in *The Decline and Fall of the Roman Empire*, "The various modes of worship which prevailed in the

---

* Other pertinent passages include Matthew 10:22; Mark 10:29–30; Luke 6:22; John 2:13; Revelation 2:10 and 6:9–11; and 2 Corinthians 4:8–10

Roman world were all considered by the people as equally true, by the philosopher as equally false, and by the magistrate as equally useful."*

So, while there were occasional persecutions and executions of Christians prior to Constantine, they tended to be intermittent and localized (as in Rome, in 64 CE, when Nero used Christians as scapegoats for the great fire), and the number of martyrs was almost certainly nowhere near as high as posited in Christian mythology. Unfortunately, record keeping in the Roman Empire was woefully inadequate, so it's difficult to accurately gauge the number of victims. Estimates typically range from several hundred to several thousand, but no one really knows the total—the evidence is too scanty.

As historian Garrett G. Fagan points out in his lecture series, "The History of Ancient Rome," persecutions of Christians (and adherents of other religions), when they took place, occurred for social and political reasons, not because of the beliefs of the persecuted, but because of their actions. As regards the Christians, what bothered the Roman authorities was that they refused to take part in public pagan ceremonies, sometimes met in secret, and that there were "rumors of cannibalism," which is understandable given the ritual cannibalism of the eucharist.

While there were sporadic persecutions under several emperors, the only generalized persecution of Christians across the Roman Empire was the Decian Persecution, which occurred under the emperor Decius (reign 249–251 CE); the more serious, that is, more bloody, Diocletian Persecution ran from 299 to 311 CE, though it was less systematic than the Decian Persecution. Both were triggered by Christian refusal to take part in public pagan ceremonies, which was essentially a refusal to honor and acknowledge the gods providing the divine authority of the emperor.

While the number of Christians martyred by the Romans is unclear, what is clear is that the number of victims murdered by Christians during the centuries-long witch hysteria in the Middle Ages and Renaissance far

---

* While persecution of Christians was out of the norm, educated Romans tended to look down on Christianity, regarding it as absurd. The words of the Roman historian Tacitus (56–120 CE) nicely illustrate this contempt:

"The [Christians] derived their name and origin from Christ, who in the reign of Tiberius had suffered death by the sentence of the procurator Pontius Pilate. For a while, this dire superstition was checked, but it again burst forth; and not only spread itself over Judea, the first seat of this mischievous sect, but was even introduced into Rome, the common asylum which receives and protects whatever is impure, whatever is atrocious."
—quoted by Gibbon in *The Decline and Fall of the Roman Empire*

surpassed the number of Christians martyred by the Romans. The same can be said of the perhaps even higher number of Jews murdered by Christian mobs in pogroms. If you include the approximately six million Jews murdered by Christians during the Holocaust, the ratio of Jews murdered by Christians to Christians murdered during pagan persecutions rises to approximately 1,000 to 1.

One indication of the much higher number of victims killed by Christians versus the number of Christians killed by the Romans is that it was common for the Romans to give Christians an opportunity to abjure Christianity before sentencing; if they did, the Romans would let them go. This stands in sharp contrast to the routine Christian practice of torturing "witches" and "heretics" in order to *extract* confessions, which in part explains the much greater number of people killed in persecutions by Christians than in persecutions by the Roman pagans.

Following the conversion of Constantine in 312,* Christianity dominated the Roman Empire and later all of Europe plus much of North Africa and the western part of the Middle East, and persecution of pagans by Christians, and persecution of Christians *by Christians*, became routine. In 314, Constantine called the Council of Arles, which declared Donatism (a North African Christian sect centered around Carthage) heretical, and he launched a persecution of the Donatists that lasted until 321. Constantine's son, Constantius II (reign 337 to 361), went further, enacting laws outlawing idol worship and pagan sacrifices under penalty of death. The anti-pagan persecution picked up further steam under Theodosius I (Theodosius the Great, emperor 379–395), with destruction of pagan temples and construction of Christian churches at state expense being hallmarks of his reign.

However, much of the day-to-day persecution of pagans (and Christians holding differing doctrinal beliefs) was carried out by rank-and-file Christians. One example was the destruction in 391 by a Christian mob in Alexandria of the temple to the Egyptian god Serapis, the Serapeum, which held many of the surviving books from the Great Library of Alexandria. That was followed by the brutal murder in 415 in the same city of the female mathematician Hypatia, who was killed after being abducted by a Christian mob, followers of the local bishop, Cyril (now St. Cyril), who

---

* Constantine's conversion apparently didn't do much for his morals. He ordered—he had others do the dirty work—a large number of murders, including that of his eldest son and his second wife, who he had "boiled alive in her bath."[3]

seized her, stripped her naked, dragged her through the streets, and then slashed her to death in a Christian church. Why would the mob do such a horrible thing? The Christian authorities considered mathematics a form of sorcery, and the mob was following the divine command to murder sorcerers spelled out in Leviticus 20:27: "A man also or woman that hath a familiar spirit, or that is a wizard, shall surely be put to death: they shall stone them with stones: their blood shall be upon them."

As for Christian persecution of Christians, W.E.H. Lecky, in his *History of European Morals*, reports:

> If, indeed, we . . . consider the actual history of the Church since Constantine, we shall find no justification for the popular theory that beneath its influence the narrow spirit of patriotism faded into a wide and cosmopolitan philanthropy . . . The eighty or ninety sects (St. Augustine estimated 89), into which Christianity speedily divided, hated one another with an intensity that extorted the wonder of [the Roman emperor] Julian and the ridicule of the Pagans of Alexandria . . . There is, indeed, something at once grotesque and ghastly in the spectacle. The Donatists, having separated from the orthodox simply on the question of the validity of the consecration of a certain bishop, declared that all who adopted the orthodox view must be damned . . . [they] beat multitudes to death with clubs, blinded others by anointing their eyes with lime . . . The Catholics tell how an Arian [another heretical Christian sect] Emperor caused eighty orthodox priests to be drowned on a single occasion . . . the Arian bishop of Alexandria caused the widows of the [orthodox] Athanasian party to be scourged on the soles of their feet, the holy virgins to be stripped naked, to be flogged with the prickly branches of palm trees or to be slowly scorched over fires till they abjured their creed . . . In the contested election that resulted in the election of St. Damasus as Pope of Rome, though no theological question appears to have been at issue, the riots were so fierce that one hundred and thirty-seven corpses were found in one of the churches.

During the millennium and a half that Christianity entirely dominated the Western world, Christians were doing virtually all of the persecuting, and the Persecution Complex nearly vanished, but for widespread conspiracy theories about "Christ killer" Jews murdering Christian children to use their blood in rituals (the pogrom-inspiring "blood libel"—more on that in Chapter 22), and also conspiracy theories about witchcraft, and the consequent widespread torture and murder of those accused of it (more on this in chapters 5 and 20).

In the centuries immediately following the Enlightenment (basically the rise of science and rationality among an educated few) in the 17th and 18th centuries, Christianity still completely dominated Europe, and except for conspiracy theories about Jews and witchcraft the Christian Persecution Complex continued to be at a low ebb. Christianity was still firmly in the saddle, and it wasn't until the mid-20th century in the United States that the Persecution Complex resurfaced in virulent form, spurred by fears of rising secularism and, especially, Supreme Court decisions protecting individual rights, decisions that struck down Christian-inspired intrusions into both public life and the private lives of individuals. Significant decisions involved the banning of mandatory prayers and Bible reading, and the banning of segregation, in public schools. (Voluntary private prayer and Bible reading were never banned in any U.S. schools.) Other court decisions that outraged right-wing Christians included the striking down of laws that outlawed contraception, abortion, "obscene" books and films, and gay sex.

Since the first of these decisions came down, a great many Christians, especially evangelicals and conservative Catholics, have been weeping and moaning about being persecuted—which apparently means they're not "free" to use taxpayer money (in the form of public facilities) to spread their religious beliefs; they're not "free" to outlaw contraception; they're not free to intrude into women's most intimate healthcare decisions; they're not "free" to control what others see, hear, read, and say; and they're not "free" to discriminate against or imprison gay people.

If you have any doubts about how hypocritical those with the Persecution Complex are, just consider their constant whining about "imposition" of the "gay agenda," and then consider that they, "persecuted" Christians, passed laws criminalizing gay sex, laws that mandated sending people to prison for years for sex acts between consenting adults—and in centuries past Christians brutally executed people for such acts, often burning them alive. Then remember that gays have not even proposed laws criminalizing the practice of Christianity, and it's highly unlikely that any but a tiny minority (if even that) would ever do so. So, who exactly is persecuting whom?

But why do so many Christians feel that they're being persecuted? Writer John Stoehr puts it like this: most white evangelicals (and, though Stoehr doesn't mention them, Mormons, and most white American Catholics) have "a worldview in which power is ordered. First God, then man, then woman, then child. White over nonwhite. Heterosexual over LGBTQ. Christian over non-Christian. When you believe with your whole being that power is ordered according to God's will, 'giving freedoms to gay people and members of minority groups' is not political equality . . . It's knocking you out of the order of power. It's taking something away. Equality is literally theft [to evangelicals]. When political equality is theft, you cannot apply the Golden Rule universally and unconditionally. . . . The Golden Rule demands white people share power with nonwhite people. It demands husbands share power with their wives. Neither can ever be done."[4]

Lending support to Stoehr's analysis, a decades-spanning study of perceived bias against LGBT+ people, published in 2021 in the *Journal for Personality and Social Psychology*, revealed that Christians, especially fundamentalists, regard gay rights gains as a loss for themselves, a zero sum game. The study reported that in 1950 approximately 85% of Christians perceived discrimination against gay people (which they undoubtedly approved of) while only about 30% perceived discrimination against Christians. Over the decades, especially since 1980, the numbers have converged. In 2020, the percentage of Christians perceiving bias against gay people had dropped to approximately 50%, while the percentage of Christians who perceived bias against themselves had risen to the same figure.[5]

Today, the Christian great white wail about "persecution" continues unabated, despite, as mentioned previously, Christians constituting 63% of the U.S. population and approximately 90% of state and federal legislators, with the congressional delegations from 28 states being 100% Christian.[6] Unsurprisingly, as regards government services, they're getting a free ride at the expense of the rest of us. Properties (churches, schools, hospitals, rectories, parsonages, etc.) owned by religious groups are completely exempt from paying property and income taxes. Religious organizations are, in addition, exempt from paying capital gains taxes; they're also exempt from paying sales taxes on anything they buy. Religious groups "also pay no income taxes for businesses that they own, if they can show that the businesses further the objectives of the religion."[7] These income tax-free businesses can include such things as radio stations, television stations, television networks, magazine publishers, book publishers, and bookstores. Even beyond that, clergy are partially exempt from paying individual federal income taxes because of a deduction unique to clerics called the "parsonage allowance"—unlike the rest of us, they can deduct the cost of their housing when filing their individual income taxes.

The avoided capital gains taxes are at the federal level, the avoided sales taxes at the state and local levels, the avoided property taxes at the local level, and the avoided income taxes at all levels. But there's more: donations to religious institutions above a certain amount are tax deductible for both individuals and corporations.[8]

And the avoided taxes aren't chump change. Ryan Cragun, professor of sociology at the University of Tampa, estimated in 2012 that religious institutions avoided $71 billion annually in taxes,[9] which adjusted for inflation equalled $84 billion in 2021. (To state the obvious, there is no clearer evidence that you're being persecuted than receiving tens of billions of dollars of tax exemptions annually.)

To further underline the hypocrisy of Christians whining about "persecution" in the U.S., during the Coronavirus outbreak in 2020 and 2021 churches in all parts of the country (including New York, New Jersey, Michigan, Tennessee, and Louisiana) were exempted from prohibitions against gatherings of more than, variously, 10 or 50 people, with some states, including Florida, going so far as to declare church meetings an essential service.[10,11] A significant number of churches, especially Protestant megachurches, took advantage of these exemptions, irresponsibly placing their selfish desires above the lives and wellbeing of others. During the pandemic, medical experts in three Kansas hospital systems ranked the Covid-19 risk level of 50 common activities, and indoor church attendance with over 30 participants was tied for third riskiest behavior, with only hanging around in bars and attending indoor concerts being more of a threat to individual and public health.[12] As a result, churches became Covid-19 hot spots.

If those infected and dying as a result of these immoral, irresponsible gatherings were only those attending the services, it'd be highly tempting to say "you reap what you sow" or "Darwin takes his own." But the religious plague carriers went out into their communities and infected innocent people, including first responders, doctors, nurses, EMTs, grocery store workers, pharmacy workers, and restaurant workers, with many undoubtedly dying as a result. One indication of the extent that conservative Christians and Republicans have spread a deadly disease is that 83 of the 100 U.S. counties with the highest Covid death rates in March 2021 had voted for Trump, and in the full 100 counties Trump's average margin of victory was 18%. The 83 counties that voted for Trump were almost all rural and heavily white and, of course, also heavily Republican and evangelical.[13]

Another indication that there is some justice in life (albeit far from enough) is that in December 2021 an NPR News study of 3,000 American counties showed that the Covid death rate in the counties that had voted most heavily for Trump (with Trump getting over 60% of the vote) was 5.5 times as high as in the counties that had voted most heavily for Biden. This difference was twice what it was in May 2021, and was due primarily to disinformation in the right-wing echo chamber and consequent refusal to be vaccinated among Trump's supporters.[14] So, at least some of those responsible for exposing others to a deadly disease paid the price.

Perhaps the final word on Christian callousness, denial of reality, and entitlement—masquerading as resistance to persecution—was delivered by the Arkansas legislature in February 2021. In that month, the legislature passed HB 1211, which forbids the Arkansas state government from ordering the shutdown of church services during future pandemics,[15] all but ensuring further church-enabled death and disease in the years to come.

Still, American Christians continue to lament being "persecuted." A complaint from Megan Bailey, Social Media Specialist and Content Producer for belief.net, exemplifies this paranoid, self-pitying attitude. Bailey asserts that there is "persecution happening right at home," and it consists of "hostility as a result of identification with Christ."[16] In other words, people are saying things about Christianity that she doesn't like. How *could* they! She seems to think that this verbal "persecution" is on par with the physical persecution Christians suffer overseas. Indeed, she all but equates the "persecution" of U.S. Christians—with nary a qualifying word—to the rape, murder, torture, and sexual enslavement suffered by the Yazidi Christians at the hands of ISIS, the mass murder of Christians in Nigeria by Boko Haram, and the imprisonment of Christians under brutal conditions in North Korea. To Bailey, these horrors are apparently on par with verbal criticism.

A more amusing example of the Persecution Complex was provided in February 2020 by the far-right National Association of Christian Lawmakers (NACL), whose board of advisors includes former Baptist preacher, Fox News bloviater, and GOP presidential candidate Mike Huckabee, Tony Perkins, head of the virulently anti-gay, anti-choice Family Research Council, and faith-healing preacher Andrew Wommack, who in May 2021 said, "It's a very destructive lifestyle. . . . homosexuality is three times worse than smoking."[17]

This group of geniuses decided to run a poll on Twitter, asking, "Do you believe America would be better off if more Christians served in elected office?" As you've probably guessed, the poll didn't turn out quite the way they wanted: 95.8% of the 16,000 respondents answered "No," they didn't want more Christian lawmakers in office.

How did the NACL react to this minor, in part self-inflicted, humiliation? You guessed it—they started whining about "religious persecution," which they blamed on "atheists and Satanists."[18]

As amusing as this is, Christians' paranoid delusions about persecution have three undesirable consequences: 1) They trivialize the very real persecution that Christians, Jews, Muslims, and nonbelievers face in other parts of the world; 2) They spur on "persecuted" Christians to embrace authoritarian demagogues who support their "freedom" to discriminate against and imprison anyone who violates their perverse morals; and 3) They stir up fear, hatred, and occasional violent lashing out against LGBT+ people, secularists, defenders of reproductive rights, and Muslims, Hindus, and Sikhs. (Here in the U.S., idiot zealots have murdered Sikhs and Hindus because they thought their victims were Muslims.)

There are many examples of such lashing out, and many victims of it, with most of the worst acts carried out by extremist anti-choice and Christian Identity groups. (Christian Identity groups posit that, somehow, white Anglo-Saxons comprise the ten lost tribes of Israel.) For examples, look no further than the murders of abortion providers, such as Dr. George Tiller in 2009; the bombings of abortion clinics (including one that killed Birmingham, Alabama police officer Robert Sanderson in 1998 in a bombing by Christian terrorist Eric Rudolph); the 2015 attack on a Planned Parenthood Clinic in Colorado, which left five dead, by the "very evangelical" (as described by his wife) terrorist Robert Deer; the 1984 murder of Denver talk show host Alan Berg, plus other acts of domestic terrorism, by The Order, a racist, antisemitic, Christian Identity group; and the plague of lynchings and other acts of racist violence decade after decade in the U.S.—especially in the South, the most religiously conservative part of the country—by the Ku Klux Klan, a self-identified Christian group dedicated to "defending" the white race (note the implied persecution), whose symbol is a burning cross, and which features the singing of "The Old Rugged Cross" at its ceremonies.

During the Coronavirus pandemic, racist violence by Christians extended to violence against Asians, very probably inspired by anti-Asian rhetoric from the self-described "Presbyterian Protestant" Donald Trump and Christian politicians such as Senator Tom Cotton and House minority leader Kevin McCarthy: these politicians and many others blamed China for the outbreak and routinely referred to the Coronavirus as the "Wuhan virus" or the "China virus." These remarks played into the Persecution Complex mentality—in this case presenting Americans as victims of

China, which in turn fueled anti-Asian racism. (Violent racists, not being the sharpest tacks on the board, attacked Asians indiscriminately, regardless of ethnicity.)

So, it's probably no coincidence that there was a huge uptick in anti-Asian violence and other hate crimes during the pandemic, with anti-Asian hate crimes in 2020 increasing 150% over pre-pandemic levels, and approximately 3,000 anti-Asian incidents occurring in the U.S. during that year.[19] The hateful incidents continued in 2021, with another thousand anti-Asian incidents occurring in just the first two-and-a-half months, with two-thirds of the victims being women. In August 2021, Stop AAPI (American Asian and Pacific Islander) Hate reported that over 9,000 anti-Asian incidents had taken place in the U.S. since the start of the pandemic, including over 1,200 violent incidents.[20]

One of the worst incidents, involving 21-year-old born-again Christian Robert Aaron Long, happened on March 16, 2021. On that date Long, a member of the Crabapple First Baptist Church, murdered eight people in a rampage across the Atlanta area targeting Asian spas, with six of his victims being Asian women. Prior to his killing spree, Long wrote in an Instagram post, "Pizza, guns, drums, music, family, and God. This pretty much sums up my life." A high school classmate stated that Long "wouldn't even cuss . . . He was big into religion."[21] Correlation isn't causation, but it's fair to say that Long's devout Christian beliefs did nothing to stop him from committing mass murder—although they did stop him from "cussing." (Bizarrely, Long denied that he was a racist, blaming his rampage on "sex addiction.")

But perhaps the ultimate expression of the Christian Persecution Complex, and its concomitant self-pity and shirking of personal responsibility, was uttered by poster-boy Christian hypocrite Seth Welch, who was convicted in January 2020 of murdering his 10-month-old daughter Mary by starving her to death. (Welch's wife, Tatiana Fusari, was convicted of the same crime in a separate trial.) Welch said he was "stunned" when he was charged with murder, and added, "I believe I am being unfairly charged, being made an example of for my very strong faith." He added, "The Lord giveth, the Lord taketh . . . It was something that was just out of our hands . . . In the Bible, it says that good food is our medicine. We fed her. We were feeding her chicken, potatoes, apples, cheese. We were giving her the good stuff." Which is why the baby weighed one pound more when she died at 10 months than she did at birth.[22,23,24]

There have been many other instances of Christianity-inspired murder and terrorism in this country in recent years, undoubtedly spurred on by delusions of persecution. In contrast, there have been *no* religiously motivated murderous acts (at least none that I'm aware of) directed against Christians by secular humanists, atheists, and gays, the groups that evangelicals and right-wing Catholics claim are persecuting *them*.

In the end, the Christian Persecution Complex boils down to a massive sense of entitlement: American Christians want to be "free" to discriminate against (or imprison) gay folks; they want their church properties to skate on the backs of those of us who pay taxes; they want to be "free" to use tax-free church income to back political candidates; they want to be "free" to use the public schools to teach their creation myth; they want to be "free" to dictate morality and intrude into the most intimate aspects of the lives of others; they want to be "free" to dictate what others can read, hear, see, and say; and, of course, they want to be "free" of criticism ("persecution," to use their term). In short, a hell of a lot of American Christians, probably most, believe that they're the new chosen people, want the power and privilege that go with it, and want their inferiors—every non-Christian in the country—to meekly acquiesce with nary a word of protest.

Endnotes

1. "5 Promises for the Persecuted," by Eric McKiddie. Crosswalk.com, June 5, 2015. https://www.crosswalk.com/faith/spiritual-life/5-promises-for-the-persecuted.html < https://tinyurl.com/y54o-nat5 >

2. "10 Persecutions of Early Church." Quizlet. https://quizlet.com/20636670/10-persecutions-of-early-church-flash-cards / < https://tinyurl.com/6h5kcnjx >

3. *Beyond Belief: Two thousand years of bad faith in the Christian Church*, by James McDonald. Reading, England: Garnet Publishing, 2011, p. 265f.

4. "Trump and white Evangelical Christians are bonded by sadism," by Eric Stoehr. *Raw Story*, August 18, 2020. https://www.rawstory.com/2020/08/trump-and-white--christians-are-bonded-by-sadism/ < https://tinyurl.com/y36loenl >

5. "Research documents how fundamentalists view LGBTQ inclusion as a zero-sum game they are losing," by Mark Wingfield. *Baptist News*, September 7, 2021. https://baptistnews.com/article/research-documents-how-fundamentalists-view-LGBT+q-inclusion-as-a-zero-sum-game-they-are-losing/ < https://tinyurl.com/72868m25 >

6. "Majority of states have all-Christian congressional delegations," by Aleksandra Sandstrom. Pew Research Center, March 21, 2017. https://www.pewresearch.org/fact-tank/2017/03/21/majority-of-states-have-all-christian-congressional-delegations/ < https://tinyurl.com/5r8rxhwz >

7. "Amid calls to #TaxTheChurches—what and how much do US religious organizations not pay?," by Ryan Cragun. *Raw Story*, August 12, 2021. https://www.rawstory.com/amid-calls-to-taxthe-churches-what-and-how-much-do-us-religious-organizations-not-pay-the-taxman/ < https://tinyurl.com/9z8es69d >

8. Ibid.

9. Ibid.

10. "Religious Exemptions During the Coronavirus Pandemic Will Only Worsen the Crisis," by Maggie Saddiqi et al. Center for American Progress, March 27, 2020. https://www.americanprogress.org/issues/religion/news/2020/03/27/482359/religious-exemptions-coronavirus-pandemic-will-worsen-crisis/ < https://tinyurl.com/vs559wg >

11. "As states crack down on gatherings, some religious exemptions could keep pews full," by Liz Alesse. ABC News, March 29, 2020. https://abcnews.go.com/Health/states-crack-gatherings-due-coronavirus-exemptions-religious-groups/story?id=69847021 < https://tinyurl.com/y4umv5qe >

12. "Kansas doctors rank activities based on Covid risk," by Alex Flippin. WIBW, July 24, 2020 https://www.wibw.com/2020/07/28/kansas-doctors-rank-activities-based-on-covid-risk/?utm_source=fark&utm_medium=website&utm_content=link&ICID=ref_fark < https://tinyurl.com/yy6ujpwj >

13. "Weekly Update: Which Counties have the highest per capita rates of COVID19 cases and deaths?" ACASignups.net ("Obamacare" signup site), March 6, 2021. https://acasignups.net/21/03/06/weekly-update-which-counties-have-highest-capita-rates-covid19-cases-and-deaths < https://tinyurl.com/y5k78mr5 >

14. "Pro-Trump counties now have far higher COVID death rates. Misinformation is to blame," by Daniel Wood and Geoff Brumfiel. NPR, December 5, 2021. https://www.npr.org/sections/health-shots/2021/12/05/1059828993/data-vaccine-misinformation-trump-counties-covid-death-rate < https://tinyurl.com/4dubhznm >

15. "AR Senate Passes Bill to Let Churches Hold Super-Spreader Events in a Pandemic," by Hemant Mehta. *Friendly Atheist*, February 4, 2021. https://friendlyatheist.patheos.com/2021/02/04/ar-senate-passes-bill-to-let-churches-hold-super-spreader-events-in-a-pandemic/ < tinyurl.com/rohmb1ze >

16. "Is there Christian Persecution in America?," by Megan Bailey. Beliefnet. https://www.beliefnet.com/news/is-there-christian-persecution-in-america.aspx < https://tinyurl.com/y3mgvams >

17. "Pastor wants LGBTQ warning label on foreheads—and is asking his followers to take over a town," by Bob Brigham. *Raw Story*, May 22, 2021. https://www.rawstory.com/andrew-wommack-woodland-park-colorado/ < https://tinyurl.com/5xmka56n >

18. "Christian Lawmakers Group Blames Satanists After Twitter Poll Goes Badly Awry," by Ed Mazza, *Huffington Post*, February 18, 2020. https://www.huffpost.com/entry/christian-lawmakers-poll-satanists_n_5e4b7a2bc5b65f25da4e4ca4 < https://tinyurl.com/wkmc6rn >

19. "'Stop killing us': Attacks on Asian Americans highlight rise in hate incidents amid COVID-19," by N'dea Yancey- Bragg. *USA Today*, February 11, 2021. https://www.usatoday.com/story/news/nation/2021/02/12/asian-hate-incidents-covid-19-lunar-new-year/4447037001/ < https://tinyurl.com/jtjrs72b >

20. "More than 9,000 anti-Asian incidents reported in US since pandemic started," by Maya Young. *The Guardian*, August 12, 2021. https://www.theguardian.com/world/2021/aug/12/anti-asian-stop-aapi-hate-covid-report < https://tinyurl.com/p2wsccn4 >

21. "Massage Parlor Massacres Suspect Said He Loved Guns & God," by Blake Montgomery, et al. *Daily Beast*, March 17, 2021. https://www.thedailybeast.com/seven-killed-in-shootings-at-atlanta-spas?ref=home < https://tinyurl.com/xpjtpv4a >

22. "Dad: Charges in baby's death 'unfair,' about faith." WoodTV8, August 9, 2018. https://www.wishtv.com/news/dad-charges-in-babys-death-unfair-about-faith/ < https://tinyurl.com/emcssmh3 >

23. "Michigan Woman Found Guilty of Murdering Infant Daughter Whose Face Police Described as 'Sunken Into Her Head,'" by Jerry Lambe. Law & Crime, October 15, 2021. https://lawandcrime.com/crime/michigan-woman-found-guilty-of-murdering-infant-daughter-whose-face-police-described-as-sunken-into-her-head/ < https://tinyurl.com/7n5c24t8 >

24. "'Mary got justice,' prosecutor says after woman's conviction in baby's starvation death," by John Tunison. Mlive, October 14, 2021. https://www.mlive.com/news/grand-rapids/2021/10/mary-got-justice-prosecutor-says-after-womans-conviction-in-babys-starvation-death.html < https://tinyurl.com/4rp833tu >

7

Christian Egocentrism

The cosmos is a gigantic fly wheel making 1,000 revolutions a minute. Man is a sick fly taking a dizzy ride on it. Religion is the theory that the wheel was designed and set spinning to give him the ride.*

—H.L. Mencken, *A Mencken Chrestomathy*

Perhaps Christianity's strongest appeal is its promise of eternal life. While there is absolutely no evidence to support this claim, most people are so terrified of death that they cling to this treacly promise insisting, like frightened children, that it must be true. Nietzsche put the matter well in *The Anti-Christ*: "*salvation of the soul*—in plain words, the world revolves around *me*." It's difficult to see anything spiritual in this desperate grasping at straws, this desperate grasping at the illusion of personal immortality.

Another manifestation of the egocentricity of Christians is the belief that God is intimately concerned with picayune aspects of, and directly intervenes in, their lives. If God, the creator and controller of the universe, is vitally concerned with the most trivial aspects of your existence, you must be pretty damn important.

Many Christians take this particular form of egotism, their "personal relationship with God," much further and actually imagine that the deity does *favors* for them. Several years ago a friend told me, "My moronic

---

* Years ago I picked up a Bible published by The Way International, which used this quotation as the epigraph (quote on the first page of the book). Rather, they used *two-thirds* of it. They omitted the final sentence, thus providing a near perfect example of the Christian ends-justify-the-dishonest-means mentality at the very beginning of their holiest book.

sister-in-law once told me that God found her parking spots near the front door of WalMart! Years later, when she developed a brain tumor, I concluded that God must have gotten tired of finding parking places for her and gave her the tumor so that she could get handicapped plates." (Luther scholar Phillip Cary relates a similar story, sans the brain tumor and sarcasm, in his lecture series, "The History of Christian Theology.")

Some Christians even believe that God has a plan for them, talks to them, or directs their actions. This belief in divine guidance has deep religious roots, dating back to the pietist movement within Lutheranism in 17th- and 18th-century Germany. This belief in "guidance" spread across Northern Europe in the 18th and 19th centuries, and is now common among American evangelicals, many of whom believe God speaks directly to them.

If one ignored the frequent and glaring contradictions in this supposed divine guidance, its often trivial or nonsensical nature, and the dead bodies sometimes left in its wake, one could almost believe that the individuals making such claims are guided by God. But one can't ignore the oftentimes grisly results of following such "guidance." Check the news on almost any given day, and odds are reasonably good that you'll find at least one report of a Christian murdering others because "God told him (or her) to do it." As "Agent Mulder" put it (perhaps paraphrasing Thomas Szasz) in a 1998 "X-Files" episode, "When you talk to God it's prayer, but when God talks to you it's schizophrenia. . . . God may have his reasons, but he sure seems to employ a lot of psychotics to carry out his job orders."

An apparent member of that group, 31-year-old Nadejda Reilly of Drums, Pennsylvania put an unusually egocentric spin on her personal relationship with God. On January 7, 2020, Reilly was arrested for aggravated assault, and following her arrest told Pennsylvania State Trooper Bruce Balliet that she had been driving for hours waiting for a message from God, and then decided to test her faith by driving head on *through* another vehicle. The vehicle's occupants were injured in the crash and had to be hospitalized, while Reilly was unhurt, and said that "God took care of her. . . . Reilly also stated she did not care if the other people were injured because God would have taken care of them."[1]*

---

* While it's easy to dismiss Reilly as crazy, it certainly doesn't help that a great many Christians including, obviously, Reilly, believe that God does talk to them; that belief is promoted ceaselessly from pulpits, podcasts, TV broadcasts, and even at 12-step meetings—AA was originally part of the evangelical Oxford Group Movement, one of whose slogans was "When man listens, God speaks." This belief is still thoroughly embedded in AA and all of the 12-step groups cloned from it.

One particularly grisly divine job order was carried out by deluded Christian Dena Laettner Schlosser, who, on November 22, 2004, in Plano, Texas, cut off both of her infant daughter's arms, killing the baby: "With a calm and dispassionate voice and a hymn playing in the background, Dena Schlosser confessed to the unthinkable, telling a 911 operator she'd cut off the arms of her baby girl."[2]

Why did she commit such a cruel, terrible act? Schlosser said God told her to do it.

Unfortunately, that's an all-too-common excuse for murder. Another example of such murder took place within a pentecostal cult* in Knutby, Sweden in 2004. That particular murder was so lurid that it was the subject of an aptly titled HBO mini-series, *Pray. Obey. Kill.*[3]

More recently, God has apparently gotten fed up with the modern bent of the hits he's ordered, and decided to go old school. In September 2021, devout Christian and serial killer Jason Thornburg, of Euless, Texas, admitted to five killings. According to Dallas-Forth Worth CBS 11/21, residents of the motel where Thornburg was staying said that "Thornburg was often seen outside reading his Bible, and talk[ing] about God."[4] Thornburg himself said that he had "in depth knowledge of the Bible and believe[d] he was called to commit human sacrifices."[5] A member of a Fort Worth church Thornburg had attended said the members of the church told the admitted murderer, prior to his arrest, "Oh Jason, God must have a great plan for you."[6] Boy, did he ever.

When I googled the words "God told me to do it murders," there were millions of results. Of course, the bulk of these were not reports of actual God-inspired murders, but a lot of them were. I looked through the first 200 results (20 pages), and a great majority of the results did in fact deal with religious belief-inspired murders. As an example, the top result on the twentieth page, the final Google page I viewed, was awkwardly titled, "Killer husband says 'God told me' to behead his ex-wife."[7] (I didn't know that God had an ex-wife.) In 2019, a Florida man provided another example of delusional religious mania. Stanley Mossburg, who killed three people, said, "I'm doing what God tells me to do" and "I'm a prophet, not a serial killer."[8] Widening the playing field even further, in 2019 God ordered Seattle resident Buckley Wolfe to kill his brother James, because, in Buckley's words, "God told me he was a lizard." In a motion to deny bail to the

---

* Pentecostals are distinguished from other evangelicals in that they "speak in tongues" in observance of 1 Corinthians 14.

killer, prosecutor Scott O'Toole wrote, "The defendant's actions—jamming the tang end of a four-foot long sharpened metal-bladed sword-like instrument completely through the victim's head and killing him—demonstrate the danger he poses."[9]

But God has apparently expanded the scope of its criminal activities beyond murder and human sacrifice. In February 2021, a Washington County, Utah man, Gabriel Newland Dutson, was charged with rape, object rape, aggravated assault, and assault with substantial bodily injury. The probable-cause affidavit stated: "The victim described the pain as that it felt like Gabriel Dutson was ripping flesh off of the victim's body . . ." What was Dutson's motivation? "God told him to do [it] and [he] was frustrated because he failed. . . . Dutson also stated that he knew of a way to solve the issue and that he needed to 'shoot' the victim with an arrow."[10]

More worryingly, God has also been giving orders to terrorists, both Islamic and Christian. As for the Christians, God has been giving anti-choice zealots their marching orders for decades, and of late has apparently broadened its scope of operations to include political terrorism. Citing recordings, prosecutors said that Barry Croft, Jr., leader of the far-right vigilante/"militia" group the 3 Percenters, "expounds in an excited tone about his intent to commit acts of terrorism, and claims God has granted him permission to violate His (God's) commandments [in all probability, the sixth being one of them]. In one passage, Croft explicitly states his intent to kidnap Gov. [Gretchen] Whitmer."[11] Croft's reason? The Michigan governor ordered the implementation of basic public health measures during the Covid pandemic.

On a somewhat lighter note, in May 2021 God told Kansas state Republican representative and substitute teacher Mark Samsel to physically attack three unruly high school students, including one who stated that Samsel "kick[ed] him in the balls." As a result, police arrested Samsel on three misdemeanor battery charges. His justification? Samsel told investigators that he was following God's orders. But why would God command such a thing? Samsel apparently doesn't know: he told police, "God moves in mysterious ways."[12,13] After pleading guilty, Samsel escaped going to jail, and even kept his seat in the state legislature.

Such are God's job orders. As Hemant Mehta observed on his *Friendly Atheist* blog, "God never tells these people to go volunteer at a homeless shelter."[14]

One can't help but wonder whether the common beliefs that God exists and that it talks to people contribute to all of the violent crimes committed in its name. If public health authorities and religious leaders made it plain that voices in the head are a sign of mental illness and nothing else, one suspects that the number of God-ordered violent incidents would fall. There would still be violent nut jobs, but at the very least they'd have one less excuse for their actions.

An example of how social acceptance enables murderous religious craziness came to light in 2021 with "devout Christian" Matthew Coleman's horrific spear-gun murder of his ten-month-old baby and two-year-old toddler. Coleman, whose "Christian faith was central to everything he did," told FBI agents—it was a federal case because he killed his children in Mexico—that he "was enlightened by QAnon and Illuminati conspiracy theories and was receiving visions and signs revealing that his wife possessed serpent DNA and had passed it on to his children."[15]

Helen Rose, who was raised in the same household as Coleman, said, "I believe that Matt has an undiagnosed mental illness . . . but [in] the community he was an integral part of, the fundamentalist Christian evangelical community, seeing 'signs and interpreting messages from God' is accepted and encouraged." An unnamed person who knew Coleman added, "if someone says they are receiving visions or revelations . . . people might think it was odd or concerning, but in [the] narcissistic privileged bubble he has always lived in—Santa Barbara—it made him unique and interesting."[16]

In cases less extreme than God-ordered murder, the insistence that one is receiving divine guidance or special treatment from God is usually the attempt of those who feel worthless—or helpless, adrift in an uncaring universe—to feel important or cared for. This less sinister form of egotism is commonly found in the statements of disaster survivors that the supposedly omnipotent, omniscient deity who caused the disaster "must have had a reason for saving me" (in contrast to their less-worthy-of-life fellow disaster victims, whom God—who controls all things—killed). Again, it's very difficult to see anything spiritual in such egocentricity.

The Prosperity Gospel

> That little hypocrites and half-crazed people dare to imagine that on their account the laws of nature are constantly *broken*—such an enhancement of every kind of selfishness to infinity, to *impudence*, cannot be branded with sufficient contempt. And yet Christianity owes its *triumph* to this pitiable flattery of personal vanity." —Friedrich Nietzsche, *The Anti-Christ*

In contrast to the "God told me to do it" mentality, with its implied license to commit mayhem, another manifestation of Christian egocentrism, the Prosperity Gospel, is almost amusing. Because the promise of a nonexistent reward in "the next life" is wearing thin—as witnessed by the increasing number of Americans abandoning Christianity—many preachers have turned to promising both heaven in the next life *and* riches in this life.

As with virtually every other belief system or movement within Christianity, the Prosperity Gospel is based upon a pick-and-choose reading of scripture. Prosperity Gospel hucksters and their marks are particularly fond of Philippians 4:19: "My God shall supply all your need according to his riches in glory by Christ Jesus" and 3 John 1:2: "Beloved, I wish above all things that thou mayest prosper and be in health, even as thy soul prospereth."

To use the apt "cafeteria Christian" analogy once more, Prosperity Gospel preachers and believers are reaching for the sugary treats while ignoring the healthy entrees and vegetables, verses such as Matthew 19:24, "And again I say unto you, It is easier for a camel to go through the eye of a needle, than for a rich man to enter into the kingdom of God," and Luke 6:31, "And as ye would that men should do to you, do ye also to them likewise."

The Prosperity Gospel posits that God will provide wealth to its faithful followers, God's chosen people, as long as they're steadfast in their faith and exhibit the proper positive attitude in thought, speech, and deed, especially the deed of giving money to the Prosperity Gospel hustler selling them the promise of coming wealth. Prosperity Gospel peddlers often refer to these self-interested gifts as "seed money," assuring their avaricious (and oft-times financially desperate) marks that God will multiply the money they give tenfold. To put this another way, Prosperity Gospel preachers posit that you will become rich if you believe and give, give, give. In other words, you create your own reality, in this case, prosperity.

If you don't have the cash on hand for the gift, they'll tell you that you can get it by taking out a payday or auto-title loan, or by putting the gift on a credit card. And, yes, many Prosperity Gospel hustlers actually do this. As the Reverend John Osborne, a televangelist I was watching ages ago, put it, "Give until it hurts. And then give until it starts feeling good."

To drive home just how well the Prosperity Gospel supposedly works, Prosperity Gospel televangelists routinely flaunt their wealth before their willing victims, and the gaudier the display the better. Former Prosperity Gospel preacher Costi Hinn, niece of prominent televangelist Benny Hinn, describes the lifestyle her uncle Benny, Kenneth Copeland (with his fleet of private jets), and other Prosperity Gospel preachers enjoy:

> Life in the prosperity gospel is the good life. No, let me go further. It's the great life. At least on the surface. Our houses were multimillion-dollar homes in the best ZIP codes in the country. Our annual salaries were more than some people make in a lifetime. I drove a BMW, Hummer (H2), Ferrari F430, Mercedes-Benz SL500. On a run-of-the-mill weekend, we could easily make upwards of $100,000 (take home) from offerings in our services for barely three days of work.[17]

The message to the dupes is that the Prosperity Gospel works: You too can have all this if you believe and continue to give, give, give. (Somehow, the marks never seem to notice that the preachers became rich by receiving rather than by giving.)

The other problems with the Prosperity Gospel are almost equally plain; they're so obvious that, to borrow a phrase from H.L. Mencken, even journalists and clergymen sometimes notice them.

The most blatant is that if Prosperity Gospel believers can become wealthy by simply choosing to be wealthy (and giving to Prosperity Gospel con artists), everyone else must be choosing not to become wealthy: the poor must choose to be poor (and remain poor because they choose not to give to the hustlers), so they're responsible for their own poverty.

This type of egocentrism and magical thinking primarily serves the interests of Prosperity Gospel preachers and their accomplices, but it also serves the interests of those at the top of the socio-economic food chain in several ways: it divorces individual wellbeing from social context; it allows the few Prosperity Gospel believers who somehow manage to become rich to feel smug about it and brag about it (thus reinforcing the preachers' message); it very probably induces self-loathing in at least some of the much larger number of believers who don't become wealthy—they simply weren't strong enough in their faith, or they just didn't give enough "seed money"; and so it discourages poor and oppressed believers from taking political or social action to improve their own lives.

But the situation is even worse than that. As Ryan Cragun points out in *What You Don't Know About Religion (but should)*, the willing evangelical victims of Prosperity Gospel hustlers tend to be poor because they are, overall, less educated than average, evangelical women are less likely to work (and thus add to family income), and they tend to give relatively large amounts of money to their churches, money they can often ill afford.

Their multi-millionaire Prosperity Gospel preachers tell them they should give, give, give, with some urging tithing a full 10% of income, and others going so far as to ask for congregants' first month's income *plus* 10% of what they earn the rest of the year. The preachers are essentially urging their economically drowning flocks to grasp at straws—promises of coming wealth—as they sink further into the economic abyss. And as they sink they become more desperate, grasping ever more frantically at those straws.

The Prosperity Gospel, with its appeal to egocentrism, magical thinking, selfishness, and grubby materialism (dressed in gaudy spiritual garb), helps only Prosperity Gospel preachers, those at the top of the economic pyramid and, arguably, the few believers who manage to claw their way up that pyramid over the backs of others (which gives them license to feel self-righteous about their wealth and to look down on the poor). It doesn't serve the vast majority of the hustlers' terminally gullible marks nor anyone else.*

Endnotes

1. "Police: Pennsylvania Woman Drives Into Path Of Oncoming Vehicle While Waiting For Calling From God." CBSPhilly, January 7, 2020. https://philadelphia.cbslocal.com/2020/01/17/police-pennsylvania-woman-drives-into-path-of-oncoming-vehicle-while-waiting-for-calling-from-god/ < https://tinyurl.com/7722d7xs >

2. "Mother confesses to severing baby's arms." NBC News/Associated Press, November 22, 2004. https://www.nbcnews.com/id/wbna6561617 < https://tinyurl.com/yxut652s >

3. "HBO Documentary Films' Five-Part Series 'Pray, Obey, Kill' Debuts April 12." The Futon Critic, April 1, 2021. http://www.thefutoncritic.com/news/2021/04/01/hbo-documentary-films-five-part-series-pray-obey-kill-debuts-april-12-248114/20210401hbo01/ < https://tinyurl.com/4shfwtpr >

4. "'Pure Evil', Accused Killer Jason Thornburg Spoke At Alleged Victim's Funeral," by Jason Allen. CBSDFW, September 28, 2021. https://dfw.cbslocal.com/2021/09/28/pure-evil-accused-killer-jason-thornburg-spoke-at-alleged-victims-funeral/ < https://tinyurl.com/w78xu7np >

5. "Affidavit: Accused Killer Jason Thornburg Says Slayings Were Human Sacrifices," by CBSDFW staff. CBSDFW, September 28, 2021. https://dfw.cbslocal.com/2021/09/28/affidavit-accused-serial-killer-jason-thornburg-says-slayings-were-human-sacrifices/ < https://tinyurl.com/ydx82w4h >

6. Allen, op. cit.

---

* Fittingly enough, political con artist Donald Trump's multi-millionaire "spiritual adviser" is religious con artist Paula White, a Prosperity Gospel hustler. Trump's first exposure to religious services was courtesy of his slumlord dad, who repeatedly took him to see the spiritual ancestor of all Prosperity Gospel con men, Rev. Norman Vincent Peale. Trump reportedly loved Peale's "positive thinking" message, probably because it strongly implied that he deserved the $200,000 a year allowance he began to receive at age three, and the subsequent $400+ million his dad eventually gave him.[18] Trump maintained friendly relations with Peale well into his adulthood, and even had Peale officiate at his first wedding.

7. "Killer husband says 'God told me' to behead his ex-wife," by Alexander Fulbright. *Times of Israel*, March 30, 2017. https://www.timesofisrael.com/suspected-beheader-god-told-me-to-chop-off-ex-wifes-head/ < https://tinyurl.com/y2m93qdp >

8. "'I'm a prophet, not a serial killer': Florida murder suspect says God told him to do it." KCET News, October 17, 2019. https://www.wect.com/2019/10/17/im-prophet-not-serial-killer-florida-murder-suspect-says-god-told-him-do-it/ < https://tinyurl.com/yxqedjyr >

9. "'God told me he was a lizard': Seattle man accused of killing his brother with a sword," by Sara Jean Green. *Seattle Times*, January 8, 2019. https://www.seattletimes.com/seattle-news/crime/god-told-me-he-was-a-lizard-seattle-man-accused-of-killing-his-brother-with-a-sword/?utm_source=fark&utm_medium=website&utm_content=link&ICID=ref_fark < https://tinyurl.com/28vyw536 >

10. "Police: Utah man raped woman, said God told him to," by McKenzie Stauffer. KUTV, February 15, 2021. https://kutv.com/news/local/police-utah-man-raped-woman-said-god-told-him-to < https://tinyurl.com/yhjcdhl2 >

11. "Man charged in alleged plot to kidnap Michigan governor says God gave him permission to kill," by Tribune News Service. *Los Angeles Times*, January 14, 2021. https://www.latimes.com/world-nation/story/2021-01-14/man-charged-in-alleged-plot-to-kidnap-michigan-governor-says-god-gave-him-permission-to-kill < https://tinyurl.com/bv5dapsn >

12. "Police: Kansas Rep. Mark Samsel left student with bruise, kicked him in testicles," by Jonathan Shoreman, et al. *Kansas City Star*, May 25, 2021. https://www.kansascity.com/article251666688.html < https://tinyurl.com/ydc929ds>

13. "Kansas GOP lawmaker kicked student in the testicles on 'instructions from God': police," by Brad Reed. *Raw Story*, March 25, 2021 https://www.rawstory.com/mark-samsel/ < https://tinyurl.com/9b2t54t4 >

14. "Utah Man Charged with Rape: God 'Told' Me to Do It," by Hemant Mehta. *Friendly Atheist*, February 17, 2021. https://friendlyatheist.patheos.com/2021/02/17/utah-man-charged-with-rape-god-told-me-to-do-it/ < https://tinyurl.com/1d7rvmpx >

15. "QAnon Surfer Who Allegedly Killed His Kids With a Spear Gun Could Face Death Penalty," by David Gilbert. *Vice*, September 10, 2021. https://www.vice.com/en/article/qj897p/qanon-surfer-who-allegedly-killed-his-kids-with-a-spear-gun-could-face-death-penalty?utm_source=fark&utm_medium=website&utm_content=link&ICID=ref_fark < https://tinyurl.com/yetztex8 >

16. Ibid.

17. "Why I used to believe in the Prosperity Gospel like Kenneth Copeland," by Costi W. Hinn. *Religion News*, June 6, 2019. https://religionnews.com/2019/06/06/why-i-used-to-believe-in-the-prosperity-gospel-like-kenneth-copeland-believes/ < https://tinyurl.com/yyabqkhk >

18. "Trump was reportedly earning $200,000 in today's dollars by the time he was 3 years old. And he was a millionaire by age 8," by Allan Smith. *Business Insider*, October 2, 2018. https://www.businessinsider.com/trump-tax-fraud-fred-inheritance-millionaire-by-age-8-2018-10 < https://tinyurl.com/y7hhllau >

8

Christian Authoritarianism

> Let every soul be subject unto the higher powers. For there is no power but of God: the powers that be are ordained of God. Whosoever therefore resisteth the power, resisteth the ordinance of God: and they that resist shall receive to themselves damnation. —Romans 13:1–2

> The more important religion is to someone, the more likely he or she is to say that governments need strong leaders, that governments should emphasize order over freedom, that having the army rule at times is a good thing, that crime should be severely punished, and that it is justifiable to beat one's wife.
> —Ryan Cragun, *What You Don't Know About Religion (but should)**

Christian authoritarianism starts with the Bible, with the story of Adam and Eve. The real sin of those two was disobedience; acquiring knowledge was a distinctly secondary offense. The whole point of that story is to threaten believers, to tell them *don't think! obey!* In this case, obey God. Later, the New Testament extended this command to obeying secular authorities and slave masters.

---

* One indication of Christian authoritarianism cited by Cragun, in turn citing World Values Survey data, is that 30% of those to whom religion is very important agree that it is "very or fairly good having army rule"; 19% of those to whom religion was rather important agreed, as did 14% of those who considered religion not very important, and 12% of those to whom religion is not at all important. While the other indicators of authoritarianism cited by Cragun aren't as stark as the differences in attitudes toward military rule, they all show a steady decline in authoritarianism from the most religious group (to whom religion is very important) to the least religious (to whom it's not at all important).[1]

Several passages in the New Testament leave little doubt on the matter: they explicitly command believers to submit to coercive authority, *all* coercive authority. Here, we'll mention only two such commands from the New Testament, Romans 13:1–2, quoted above, and 1 Peter 2:13–14: "Submit yourselves to every ordinance of man for the Lord's sake: whether it be to the king, as supreme; Or unto governors . . ." There are many similar passages. (See Appendix A for additional verses.)

During the millennium-plus following the writing of the New Testament, Christians doubled down on this authoritarian biblical message, with theologian Thomas Aquinas, in his masterwork, *Summa Theologica*, justifying the murder of dissenters:

> Yet if heretics be altogether uprooted by death, this is not contrary to Our Lord's command [in Matthew 13:30], which is to be understood as referring to the case when the cockle [weeds] cannot be plucked up without plucking up the wheat . . . when treating of unbelievers in general. . . . If forgers and malefactors are put to death by the secular power, there is much more reason for excommunicating and even putting to death one convicted of heresy.

This attitude was par for the course well up into the 17th century. *Obey or die!* was the motto of the day, from the writing of the New Testament until well into the Enlightenment period, and simply *Obey!* until well into the 20th century. In 1929, Pope Pius XI, in his *Divini illius Magistri* ("That Divine Teacher"), could still write, "Indeed a good Catholic, precisely because of his Catholic principles, makes the better citizen, attached to his country, and loyally submissive to constituted civil authority in every legitimate form of government."[2] Even in the wake of World War II and the Nuremberg trials (where the most infamous defense advanced by Nazi war criminals was "I was just following orders"), most Christian churches still teach that unquestioning obedience is a virtue, and as a result progress toward greater human freedom has been painfully slow, resisted every step of the way by the church.

Virtually all Christian denominations have long histories of authoritarian preachings and practices, but of late the most prominent exponents of Christian authoritarianism are American fundamentalists, as illustrated by the following quotations from three prominent 20th- and 21st-century evangelicals:

> Should Christians govern and are Christians the only ones who are truly qualified to govern, and the answer is, of course, Yes.
> —Rev. Bob Enyart (pastor Denver Bible Church, www.enyart.com)

> The long-term goal of Christians in politics should be to gain exclusive control over the franchise. Those who refuse to submit publicly to the eternal sanctions of God by submitting to His Church's public marks of the covenant—baptism and holy communion—must be denied citizenship.
> —Gary North,* *Political Polytheism: The Myth of Pluralism*

> The significance of Jesus Christ as the 'faithful and true witness' is that He not only witnesses against those who are at war against God, but he also executes them. —R.J. Rushdoony, *The Institutes of Biblical Law*

Given that Christians claim to have the one true faith, to have a book that is the Word of God, and in many cases to receive guidance directly from God, they feel little or no compunction about using force and coercion to impose "God's Will" (which they, of course, interpret and understand) upon others. Given that they believe, or pretend to believe, that they're receiving orders from the Almighty, who would cast them into a lake of fire should they disobey, it's little wonder that they feel no reluctance, and in fact are often eager, to intrude into the most intimate aspects of the lives of others, and to do it through violence or the threat of violence, either direct or institutional (via the state).

This is most obvious today in the area of sex, with Christians attempting to deny women the right to abortion, to outlaw gay sex, and, ignoring overwhelming scientific evidence, to mandate ineffective abstinence-only sex "education" in the public schools. (More on this in chapters 1, 13, and 20.)

It's also obvious in other areas of education, with Christians attempting to force biology teachers to teach their creation myth (but not those of Hindus, Native Americans, et al.) in place of, or as being equally valid as, the very well established theory of evolution.

---

* North is the son-in-law of the "father of Christian Reconstructionism," R.J. Rushdoony. Reconstructionism is the most extreme strand in the Christian Dominionist movement, which derives its name from Genesis 1:28: "And God blessed them, and God said unto them, Be fruitful, and multiply, and replenish the earth, and subdue it: and have dominion over the fish of the sea, and over the fowl of the air, and over every living thing that moveth upon the earth." Reconstructionist leaders have called for imposition of a theocracy, execution of gay people, atheists, and adulterers, and reimposition of slavery—in other words, "reconstruction" of society based on the most atrocious Old Testament commands, prohibitions, and practices.

But the authoritarian tendencies of Christianity reach much further than this.

Christianity models hierarchical, authoritarian organization

> How could men who lived free and equal . . . ever have found in their experience the idea of a mighty God whose frequent anger had to be propitiated by currish fawning, supplication, flattery, and sacrifice . . . ?—an idea quite natural to a pack of slaves, who imagined their God in the image of the despotic ruler who cracked the whip above their heads.
> —Max Nordau, *The Interpretation of History*

> We declare, we say, we defend and pronounce that to every human creature it is absolutely necessary to salvation to be subject to the Roman Pontiff.
> —Pope Boniface VIII, *Unam Sanctam* ("One Holiness," issued in 1302)

As surprising as it seems today, Christianity was not always organized hierarchically, with the first monarchical bishop of Rome appearing only in 154. As Catholic writer Juicio Brennan notes, "In these early centuries [of the church], the nominations and elections of bishops were done solely by a popular vote of all the faithful," including women until at least the middle of the third century.[3] (The dates when women were first excluded from voting for bishops undoubtedly varied from place to place.) In fact, bishops of Rome were elected by that city's Christian community until 769. Well before then, however, the popes had begun maneuvering relentlessly to increase their own power—essentially trying to set themselves up as dictators, temporal and spiritual—through ever-more-grandiose claims buttressed by almost innumerable forged and altered documents, and often by violence. This gradual process culminated in the last few centuries of the Middle Ages with complete papal control of the church, and with the (Roman Catholic) hierarchy in the form with which we're familiar today.*

The result is that Christianity is perhaps the ultimate top-down enterprise. In its simplest (post-Reformation) form, it consists of God on top, its "servants," the clergy, next down, and the great unwashed masses at the bottom, with those above issuing thou-shalts and thou-shalt-nots backed

---

* For a thorough discussion of all of these matters, see James McDonald's *Beyond Belief: Two thousand years of bad faith in the Christian Church.*

by the threat of eternal damnation. This is still the norm in many Protestant churches, with unquestioning obedience by the laity to the clergy being all too common.

But some Christian sects go far beyond this, having several layers of management and bureaucracy. Catholicism is perhaps the most extreme example, with its laity, deacons, monks, nuns, mothers superior, abbots, priests, monsignors, bishops, archbishops, vicars general, cardinals, and pope, all giving and taking orders in an almost military manner. The nominally Christian LDS (Mormon) Church is almost equally hierarchical and every bit as, perhaps more, authoritarian, with, in ascending order, its deacons (young male members), priests (male members), bishops (lay members, not equivalent to Catholic bishops), stake presidents, presiding bishoprics, general authorities (the 70), presidency of the 70, quorum of the 12 apostles, first presidency, and at the very top the prophet, who according to LDS dogma has a direct line to God and can speak in his—always "his"—name. (Mormon organization is even more byzantine than this—e.g., there are two types of priesthood, Aaronic and Melchizedek—but in broad strokes this is accurate.)

As regards Mormon women, Elaine Jones notes, "The female hierarchy in the church is the Relief Society. That's it. No decision-making power. Absolutely no admittance to any of the priesthood levels. And a woman can't attain the highest level of exaltation unless she is married to a man in the LDS temple. Single men don't have that problem."[4]

These types of organizations cannot but accustom those in their sway—especially those who have been indoctrinated and attending religious ceremonies since birth—into accepting hierarchical, authoritarian organization as the natural, if not the only, form of organization. Those who find such organization normal will see nothing wrong with hierarchical, authoritarian organization in other social structures, be they corporations, with their multiple layers of brown-nosing, back-stabbing management, or governments, with their judges, legislators, presidents, and politburos. The indoctrination by example that Christianity provides in the area of organization is almost surely a powerful influence against social change, a powerful influence against freer, more egalitarian forms of organization based on mutual aid and voluntary cooperation.

Christian Support for Authoritarian Regimes

Whoever can make you believe absurdities can
make you commit atrocities.
—Voltaire, *On the Question of Miracles*

It's no accident that Christianity has been a bulwark of authoritarian regimes almost since its inception. The characteristics of Christianity and such regimes are surprisingly similar. In his illuminating *How Fascism Works: The Politics of Us and Them*, historian Jason Stanley, in the book's table of contents (plus subtitle), lists what he considers the essential features of fascism* (this list is significantly paraphrased and somewhat elaborated): 1) enshrinement of a mystic past; 2) propaganda—deliberately lying and misleading people; 3) anti-intellectualism; 4) "unreality"—rejection of reality and attempts to replace it psychologically with myths that conform to dogma; 5) hierarchy; 6) victimhood (feelings of persecution, no matter how unmoored from reality); 7) a law and order mentality; 8) sexual anxiety; 9) puritanism (a Sodom and Gomorrah view of sex); 10) an "us vs. them" view of others, with "us" being superior and deserving, and "them" being inferior and undeserving.

Within the body of the book, Stanley mentions other characteristics of fascism, including antisemitism, misogyny, homophobia, and authoritarianism—about all he missed was militarism, bullying/domineering behavior, and a willingness, often eagerness, to engage in violence. Almost all of these characteristics of fascism are also typical of white American evangelicals and conservative Catholics, and all Christian sects, no matter how liberal, share some of them.

So it's no surprise that for the better part of two millennia, almost since it adopted formal, hierarchical organization, Christianity has been closely tied to, and a major support of, the formal, hierarchical organizations known as nation states. Since Christianity first received state support in Armenia (followed shortly by Rome, Georgia, and Ethiopia) in the early

* There's still occasional debate about the definition of fascism, with some holding that Mussolini's "corporate state" ideology—basically that capital and labor should be partners with the state—is essential to fascism. However, that ideology all but disappeared with the end of World War II, and today it's more common to define fascism by its characteristics, with there being broad agreement that the characteristics listed above are its primary components.

fourth century, Christianity has been entwined with the state. During the Middle Ages, Christian and state hierarchies were all but identical. Historian James McDonald reports that bishops and abbots swore allegiance to the king "like any other feudal tenant" and served as royal functionaries, including as tax collectors, diplomats, and judges. He adds that "in many respects kings were senior churchmen, often having total control over the Church" in the areas they controlled.[5]

Christianity has received support from many regimes, has been the state religion of others, or has been the state church in still others. Even today, a few such state-church arrangements, where the church receives financial support from the state (e.g., the Church of England and the Evangelical Lutheran Church of Denmark), live on, although mostly in vitiated form, as in the UK and Denmark.

The results of the close intertwining of church and state have, century after century, been catastrophic. Consider just a few religion-induced disasters: the crusades; the massacre of the Albigensians; the persecution of the Huguenots; the Thirty Years War; the Hundred Years War; the English Civil War; the Inquisition; witch and heretic burnings; the near-extermination of Native Americans; the mass murders during and after the Spanish Civil War; the Rwandan genocide.

All of these atrocities were carried out by Christians and the governments they controlled. The number of victims will never be known, though Christian armies and Christian-backed authoritarian regimes have very probably killed tens of millions, which could be a low estimate. To cite but one of the above exercises in mass murder, near the beginning of the 21-year crusade against the Albigensian gnostics (Cathar "heretics"), the 1209 Beziers massacre took approximately 20,000 lives, and it's only the most notorious atrocity in that shameful chapter in Christian history—the notoriety owing in large part to the widely reported remark of the commanding papal legate, Arnaud Amalric, prior to the massacre: "Kill them all. God will recognize His own" ("*Caedite eos. Novit enim Dominus qui sunt eius*"). (There's some dispute about whether Amalric actually said this, and about the number of victims; there's no dispute that the papal forces massacred thousands of townspeople, Cathars and non-Cathars alike.) The total number killed during the Albigensian Crusade (1208–1229) was at least 100,000, and perhaps considerably higher than that.

In more contemporary times, there have been many instances of Christians and Christian churches backing authoritarian regimes, backing which helped those regimes perpetrate mass murder. One example is the

Catholic Church's support of Francisco Franco's falangists (fascists) during and after the Spanish Civil War (1936–1939). Franco's troops committed countless atrocities during the war and in its aftermath, and executed (a more palatable word than the more accurate "murdered") an estimated 100,000 to 200,000+ political prisoners (estimates vary), with what's likely the most accurate estimate being 200,000 murdered during the war and another 20,000 murdered in its aftermath.[6] Mass graves of Franco's victims are still being discovered and exhumed all over Spain.[7] (While both sides committed atrocities during the exceptionally brutal civil war, the thousands upon thousands of murders of political prisoners following the war's end were, of course, committed by the victorious Catholic fascists.)

In return for Catholic support during the civil war, following its end Franco made Catholicism the state religion of Spain, mandated Catholic religious instruction at all educational levels, and paid the salaries of priests and the costs of constructing church buildings. (Not incidentally, Franco is still popular with right-wing Catholics. In his 1997 autobiography, *Right from the Start*, Pat Buchanan described Franco as a "Catholic savior,"[8] and in his syndicated column on September 17, 1989, Buchanan described both Franco and Chilean dictator/torturer/mass murderer Augusto Pinochet as "soldier-patriots.")

In Italy, the relationship with Mussolini was similarly cozy. Following the signing of the Lateran Pact in 1929,[9] Mussolini recognized the Vatican as a sovereign state and gave the Vatican financial compensation for its loss of the Papal States to the Italian republic in the 19th century. During his reign, Mussolini also provided financial support to the Catholic clergy, in part by paying the salaries of Catholic chaplains in all of the fascist youth groups, and he also mandated that Catholic religious instruction be a part of all primary and secondary education. In return, the Church gave Mussolini its moral backing, with, among other things, priests often celebrating mass at the start of fascist rallies.

Here in the U.S., during the 1920s and 1930s, rank-and-file Catholics, the Catholic clergy, especially those at the top of the Church hierarchy, and the editors of the most influential Catholic periodicals were largely in favor of Mussolini and fascism, which they saw as bulwarks against Bolshevism and (horrors!) secular humanism. Catholic allies of Mussolini included Archbishop Hayes in New York, Archbishop O'Connell in Boston, Bishop (later archbishop) Fulton Sheen, host of "The Catholic Hour" on NBC radio, and the notorious antisemitic "radio priest" Charles Coughlin. The most influential Catholic publications almost uniformly supported Il

Duce: *Commonweal*; the Jesuits' *America*; and, during the first few years of the Mussolini dictatorship, *Catholic World*.[10]

In Germany, things were a bit more complicated. In March 1933, immediately after Hitler became chancellor, the Catholic Center Party supported the "enabling act" that gave Hitler dictatorial powers, but it's important to note that there was significant grassroots opposition to Hitler among both laity and clergy prior to his rise to power. However, in the immediate wake of Hitler's ascension, Cardinal Eugenio Pacelli (later Pope Pius XII), the Vatican's secretary of state and papal nuncio to Germany, instructed the German bishops to drop opposition to Hitler. In July 1933, the Vatican and the Reich signed the *Reichskonkordat*, in which the Catholic Church capitulated to Hitler, agreed to the disbanding of the Catholic Center Party, the forbidding of Catholic engagement in any political activity proscribed by the Reich, and ordered Catholic bishops to swear an oath of allegiance to the German state. In return, Hitler agreed to the Church's unrestricted control over Catholic education and the free practice of the Catholic religion.

The German Protestant churches were almost as supine as the Vatican, which had paved the way for their accommodation. This acquiescence was predictable: Christian historian Diarmaid MacCulloch cites estimates that in the aftermath of World War I "80 per cent of [Germany's] Protestant clergy . . . were monarchist and angrily nationalistic."[11] While defenders of Christianity are quick to point out the courageous moral stands against Hitler of Lutheran pastors Dietrich Bonhoeffer and Martin Niemoller, they so often mention these two upright men because they have so little else they can point to: Bonhoeffer and Niemoller were very much the exceptions to the Protestant acquiescence to Hitler.

Upon his accession to the papacy, as Pius XII in 1939, after six years of ever-worsening persecution and murder of Germany's Jews, gays, Romani, and political dissidents, and the murderous military intervention in Spain, Pacelli almost immediately sent a letter to Hitler. Dated March 6, 1939, it began, "To the illustrious Herr Adolf Hitler, Fuhrer and Chancellor of the German Reich! Here at the beginning of Our Pontificate We wish to assure you that We remain devoted to the spiritual welfare of the German people entrusted to your leadership."[12] In the same year, following Pacelli's elevation, the German Catholic hierarchy instituted an annual celebration of Hitler's birthday, April 20th.

As well, it's beyond dispute that during the war the Vatican was well aware of the atrocities taking place in Germany and the lands it occupied.

For instance, it would have been impossible for the Vatican not to know what was taking place in Slovakia during the war, because the Nazi puppet government there "was led between 1939 and 1945 by Monsignor Josef Tiso, who continued to act as a Catholic parish priest during his presidency, and was responsible for implementing deportation of approximately 100,000 Jews and Roma (gypsies)" to the Nazis' concentration camps.[13] It's simply impossible that Tiso's superiors in the Catholic hierarchy—who, of course, reported to the Vatican—were unaware of his atrocious activities. The evidence is even more direct that the Vatican ignored the atrocities, including mass murder, committed by the "self-consciously Catholic regime" of Ante Pavlevic in Croatia. Historian MacCulloch states, "A significant number of Catholics in neighbouring Slovenia were sickened by the Croatian atrocities and drew up a protest demanding public condemnation from the Pope; it reached the Vatican in 1942 and had no public result."[14]

During the entirety of Hitler's reign, including the Holocaust, neither Pius XI nor Pius XII denounced Nazi war crimes or genocide, nor did they threaten Catholic supporters of Hitler with excommunication—not even the active participants in Hitler's military aggression and operation of the death camps.

Would such a threat have had an impact? Sad to say, we'll never know. However, at the time of Hitler's rise to power in 1933, approximately 67% of Germans were Protestants and 33% Catholics, with Jews comprising under 1% of the population. (The vast bulk of the Jews the Nazis murdered were from other European countries.) Thus essentially *all* of the SS torturers, concentration camp guards, and war criminals were at least nominal Christians, a third were Catholics, and some of them might have been swayed by the threat of excommunication.

Following the war, Catholic clergy, allegedly with the support of Pius XII, organized two separate "rat lines" to spirit Nazi war criminals to safety in Argentina, Brazil, Chile, and other South American countries.[15] Those aided by the "rat lines" included Dr. Josef Mengele, infamous for his grotesque and sadistic experiments upon concentration camp prisoners, and Adolf Eichmann, a major architect of the Holocaust.

But don't think that Christian backing for extreme right regimes ended in the wake of World War II.

At present, the Russian Orthodox Church is a bulwark of dictator Vladimir Putin's murderous regime, a regime which does the Orthodox Church's misogynistic, homophobic dirty work for it. The Catholic Church is likewise a bulwark of the authoritarian Duda and Orban regimes in Poland and Hungary, both of which do the Catholic Church's moral (anti-gay, anti-choice, anti-free speech) dirty work, just as Putin does the Russian Orthodox Church's. Not incidentally, all three regimes receive backing from not only the Catholic or Russian Orthodox churches, but also from American evangelicals.

But the worst current example of Christian-backed authoritarian regimes is probably that of Jair Bolsonaro, the extreme right Brazilian president, "Brazil's Trump," who has endorsed police and paramilitary death squads, has enabled the accelerating destruction of the Amazon rain forest by agribusiness, logging, and mining interests, and who did nothing to stop the Coronavirus pandemic in his country; in fact, Bolsonaro not only refused to mount a federal-level response to the pandemic, he impeded mayors and state governors who attempted to take basic public health measures to slow the virus's spread. Prior to that, while president-elect in 2018, Bolsonaro had threatened to cut diplomatic ties with Cuba and had demanded a renegotiation of the agreement between Cuba, Brazil, and the World Health Organization under which Cuba supplied doctors to poor, often rural, Brazilian communities in the "*Mais Medicos*" (more doctors) program. In response to Bolsonaro's threats and demands, in 2019, on the eve of the Covid pandemic, the Cuban government withdrew over 8,000 doctors from Brazil, leaving many rural areas with no doctors at all.[16] As a result of this "pro-life" president's callousness, ineptitude, and obstructionism, at the time of this writing, over 600,000 Brazilians have died from the virus, and the count is still rising.

Perhaps the most heartbreaking incidents in that tormented country have occurred in the Amazon rain forest: Protestant missionaries have been spreading the virus to the region's isolated indigenous peoples—who because of their isolation have little or no resistance to many diseases, including Covid—*and* the missionaries have been using scare tactics to frighten local people out of getting vaccinated. As a result, some villagers have threatened and driven off public health workers, who were there to save lives. According to Claudemir da Silva, a leader of the Apuriña people, "It's not happening in all villages, just in those that have missionaries or chapels where pastors are convincing the people not to receive the vaccine, [telling them] that they will turn into an alligator and other crazy ideas."[17]

Not surprisingly, Brazil's evangelicals love Bolsonaro. A key component of Bolsonaro's backing in the 2018 presidential election, in which he ran on a "traditional values"/anti-LGBT platform, came from Brazil's pentecostals and other evangelicals, an estimated 30% of the population. Bolsonaro carried them by 11.5 million votes.[18]

Naturally, American evangelicals also love Bolsonaro. In 2019, after Bolsonaro met with Trump in Washington, DC, he met with a group of American backers, including Rev. Pat Robertson and the soon-to-be-disgraced Rev. Jerry Falwell, Jr., with Robertson saying of the murderous would-be dictator, "Lord, uphold him. Protect him from evil. And use him mightily in years to come."[19]

Here in the U.S., evangelicals and conservative Catholics formed the base of the Trump regime. It's easy to see why. There's considerable overlap between the extreme right and conservative Christians: 1) Both groups are authoritarian; 2) Both are dogmatic; 3) Both groups believe that the ends justify the means, including violent means; 4) Both long for simple answers; 5) Both take their marching orders from their leaders and the sacred texts that supply those answers (the Bible on one hand, *Mein Kampf* and *The Turner Diaries* on the other); 6) Both groups long for an imagined, idyllic past; 7) Both groups maintain that they're being persecuted (on the one hand by secular humanists and LGBT+ people imposing a satanic "gay agenda," and on the other by immigrants and "mud people" "displacing" or "replacing" them); 8) Both groups are seething with fear and anger toward their scapegoats; and 9) Both groups long for a messiah (or fuehrer) who will save them from their imagined persecutors. So they're easy prey for manipulators and demagogues. They're essentially weaponized puppets eager to do the bidding of their masters—and the more sadistic that bidding is, the better. (Separating parents from small children and locking the kids in cages? The botched response to Covid-19 with nearly a million agonizing, largely preventable deaths? They're fine with it.)

In 2016 and 2020, Donald Trump tailored his campaign to appeal to both conservative Christians and white supremacists with his not even barely concealed racism (e.g., calling Mexican immigrants rapists and criminals and demonizing anti-racism protesters). His slogan, "Make America Great Again," encapsulates his appeal to his fearful, angry followers who felt that "their" country had been "stolen" from *them* (never mind the country's original inhabitants); they wanted to go back to an imaginary greater time and place, perhaps the 19th century with millions enslaved and the near-extermination of indigenous peoples an ongoing atrocity. But more likely they want to go back to a Disneyland version of 1950s America with the ugly reality hidden behind a cloyingly wholesome facade.

Of course, the real 1950s America was far from the Disney ideal. The real 1950s America had Jim Crow laws; segregation; lynchings; ever-present police harassment, beatings, murders, and framings of gay, black, and hispanic people (and to a lesser extent poor whites); laws prohibiting inter-racial marriage; prison terms for gay sex between consenting adults; psychiatric classification of gay people as mentally ill; "treatment" of their "disorder" with electro-shock "therapy," castration, and lobotomy; prohibition of contraceptives; back-alley abortions; unquestioned female subservience; persecution and imprisonment of supposed communists; blacklisting; the gagging of comics and writers via obscenity laws; censorship of movies under the Hays Code; and the propping up of dictatorships and the overthrow of democratically elected governments by U.S. intelligence agencies—all with the ever-present threat of nuclear annihilation lurking in the background.

This is what Trump's religious supporters find so appealing. *This* is what they consider "great."

As a result of Trump's racist, regressive agenda, and his talent for enraging and inciting the absolute worst in his followers, 77% of white evangelicals and 64% of white Catholics voted for him in 2016.[20] In 2020, after nearly four years of cruel, authoritarian thuggery (family separations, kids in cages, secret police abduction of peaceful protesters,* Trump's encouragement of violence against protesters and reporters), his support of the journalist-murdering, barbaric Saudi regime, his subservience to Russian dictator Vladimir Putin, and a grotesquely inept response to a pandemic that had already killed hundred of thousands, Trump's support in the 2020 election among the religious had barely budged. The percentage of evangelicals supporting the sadistic would-be dictator *increased* from that in 2016, rising from 77% to 84%.[21] At the same time, Trump's support among white Catholic voters declined slightly, dropping from 64% to 57%.[22] (Even after Trump's coup attempt on January 6, 2021, 62% of white evangelicals continued to support him, as did 41% of white mainline Protestants and 39% of white Catholics; in contrast, Trump's support among religiously unaffiliated whites was 26% following the failed insurrection.)[23]

---

* Several abductions by DHS agents showing no identification on their uniforms or vehicles occurred in Portland, Oregon during anti-racist demonstrations in 2020—evidently a test run before rolling out secret-police abductions nationwide. This was met with such outrage—even sovereign-citizen leader Ammon Bundy reportedly denounced it—that Trump abandoned it.

As if to underline the importance to conservative Christians of culture war wedge issues, hispanic support for Trump increased from 28% in 2016 to 32% in 2020.[24] Why? Despite Trump's overt, racist attacks against latinos during his four years in office, his monstrous family separation policy directed almost entirely against latino asylum seekers and would-be immigrants, and his callous, inept response to the Coronavirus pandemic, which disproportionately affected hispanic families, those things were quite obviously of secondary importance to the 32% of latinos who voted for Trump. His opposition to reproductive and gay rights was more important to them than his racism, deliberate infliction of severe harm upon hispanic immigrant families, and the tens of thousands of unnecessary deaths in hispanic communities caused by his botched response to the pandemic. Even the health and wellbeing of their own families was less important to Trump's hispanic (and black) supporters than his anti-gay, anti-choice moral posturing (plus, in some cases, the stupid belief that Trump's continued rule would, somehow, benefit them economically).

Given the length and breadth of Christian support for repressive regimes, and the willingness of many of those regimes to impose Christian "moral values," it would be surprising if Christian backing for Trump and other authoritarian demagogues doesn't continue.

A final and somewhat amusing note on Christian authoritarianism: Fox News reports that since its founding in 1971 by the Reverend Jerry Falwell, Sr., far-right Liberty University has had a policy in place banning the use of alcohol, a policy "so severe that students are subjected to random breath, blood and urine tests."[25]

Liberty indeed.

Endnotes

1. *What You Don't Know About Religion (but should)*, by Ryan Cragun. Durham, NC: Pitchstone Publishing, 2013, p. 150.

2. *Divini illius Magistri*, by Pope Pius XI. Papal Encyclicals Online. https://www.papalencyclicals.net/pius11/p11rappi.htm < https://tinyurl.com/6terh54 >

3. "An Intriguing History: Election of Bishops in the Catholic Church," by Juicio Brennan. https://juiciobrennan.com/files/bishopselection/bishopSelectionFlier.pdf < https://tinyurl.com/sccsnfwp >

4. Elaine Jones, personal correspondence December 28, 2020.

5. *Beyond Belief: Two thousand years of bad faith in the Christian Church*, by James McDonald. Reading, England: Garnet Publishing, 2011, p. 206.

6. "What Is the Association for the Recovery of Historical Memory (ARMH)." Asociación para la Recuperación de la Memória Historica. https://memoriahistorica.org.es/who-are-we/ < https://tinyurl.com/ydrbhbrt >

7. “Franco’s Forgotten Crimes,” by Noah Hahn. *Jacobin*. https://www.jacobinmag.com/2019/01/auschwitz-holocaust-madrid-franco-civil-war < https://tinyurl.com/24cu9yt5 >

8. Quoted by David Irish in *America’s Taliban: In its own words*. Tucson: See Sharp Press, 2003, p. 9.

9. “Lateran Pacts of 1929” (full text). http://www.uniset.ca/nold/lateran.htm < https://tinyurl.com/yxpky9fz >

10. *Mussolini and Fascism: The View from America*, by John P. Diggins. Princeton, NJ: Princeton University Press, 1972, pp. 182–197.

11. *Christianity: The First Three Thousand Years*, by Diarmaid MacCulloch. New York: Penguin, 2011, p. 941.

12. “Letter from Pius XII to Adolf Hitler.” Covenant Protestant Reformed Church. https://cprc.co.uk/articles/popepiusxiilettertohitler/ < https://tinyurl.com/y6z24equ >

13. MacCulloch, op. cit., p. 945.

14. Ibid.

15. “The ratlines: What did the Vatican know about Nazi escape routes?” *Deutsche Welle*. https://www.dw.com/en/the-ratlines-what-did-the-vatican-know-about-nazi-escape-routes/a-52555068 < https://tinyurl.com/yx59qxsp >

16. “Thousands of Cuban doctors leave Brazil after Bolsonaro’s win,” by Don Phillips and Ed Agustin. *The Guardian*, November 23, 2018. https://www.theguardian.com/global-development/2018/nov/23/brazil-fears-it-cant-fill-abrupt-vacancies-after-cuban-doctors-withdraw < https://tinyurl.com/ha5z-prta >

17. “Brazil: missionaries ‘turning tribes against coronavirus vaccine.’” *The Guardian*, February 11, 2021. https://www.theguardian.com/world/2021/feb/11/brazil-missionaries-turning-tribes-against-coronavirus-vaccine < https://tinyurl.com/2mdtbrdx >

18. “Brazil’s Evangelicals Take Over While Bolsonaro’s Allies Jump Ship,” by Simone Preissler Iglesias and Samy Adghirni. *Bloomberg*, June 5, 2020. https://www.bloomberg.com/news/articles/2020-06-05/evangelicals-take-over-while-bolsonaro-s-allies-jump-ship < https://tinyurl.com/y3dqfpe4 >

19. “US leaders met, prayed with Brazil’s conservative President Bolsonaro,” by Samuel Smith. *The Christian Post*, March 21, 2019. https://www.christianpost.com/news/us-leaders-met-prayed-with-brazils-conservative-president-bolsonaro.html < https://tinyurl.com/yyh2jmy6 >

20. “An examination of the 2020 electorate, based on validated voters,” by Ruth Igielnik, et. al. Pew Research Center, June 30, 2021. https://www.pewresearch.org/politics/2021/06/30/behind-bidens-2020-victory/ < https://tinyurl.com/yp7rk56w >

21. Ibid.

22. Ibid.

23. “A Majority of Americans View Biden Favorably as Trump Hits Historic Low.” PRRI, January 20, 2021. https://www.prri.org/research/more-than-half-of-americans-view-biden-favorably-as-trump-hits-historic-lows/ < https://tinyurl.com/yyj2vncc >

24. “How Trump Increased His Support Among Latinos,” by Geraldo L. Cadava. *The Atlantic*, November 9, 2020. https://www.theatlantic.com/ideas/archive/2020/11/how-trump-grew-his-support-among-latinos/617033/ < https://tinyurl.com/yxtlrtn3 >

25. “911 call from Falwell house reveals ex-Liberty president was drinking, fell down, lost ‘a lot of blood’ after resigning,” by Barmini Chakraborty. Fox News, September 18, 2020.https://www.foxnews.com/us/jerry-falwell-liberty-drinking-fell-911-call < https://tinyurl.com/y3me2uwy >

9

Christian Opposition to Free Speech

> From the polluted fountain of indifferentism flows that absurd and erroneous doctrine, or rather raving, which claims and defends liberty of conscience for everyone. From this comes, in a word, the worst plague of all, namely unrestrained liberty of opinion and freedom of speech.
> —Pope Gregory XVI, *Mirari Vos* ("To Wonder at You," 1832)

From its very beginnings, Judeo-Christianity opposed freedom of speech, especially freedom of religious speech. This dates back to the first books of the Old Testament. Leviticus 24:16 commands, "And he that blasphemeth the name of the Lord, he shall surely be put to death."

Condemnation of heresy came later. As Christian religious scholar Phillip Cary notes in his lecture series, "The History of Christian Theology," heresy is largely a Christian invention. Christians and Christian churches have always been obsessed with doctrine (perhaps more accurately, dogma), while the preceding pagan religions (and the rulers to whom they lent legitimacy) were obsessed with ceremony and outward conformity. As long as people conformed publicly, honoring the local gods, attending ceremonies, etc., what they actually thought didn't matter much to the authorities.

Things changed drastically when Christianity became the Roman state religion in the fourth century: doctrine became paramount, and deviation from it (heresy) became a deadly offense. To put this another way, dogma-obsessed Christians *invented* a reason to burn people alive.

Over two millennia after the writing of Leviticus, and nine hundred years after Christianity became Rome's state religion, Thomas Aquinas made this change in emphasis (from outward conformity to dogmatic belief) explicit. In his *Summa Theologica*, Aquinas reasoned, "If forgers and malefactors are put to death by the secular power, there is much more reason for excommunicating and even putting to death one convicted of heresy."

Almost simultaneous with Aquinas's writing of the *Summa*, and two years after the end of the Albigensian Crusade in 1231, Pope Gregory IX established the Inquisition and loosed it upon the church's perceived enemies. According to writer Michael Newton, "the sole appropriate means of execution for heretics" was fire.[1]

But despite advocating and employing that terrible form of torture and murder, at least the Church has been consistent: it has always opposed freedom of speech (especially "heresy," "blasphemy," and lately "obscenity"), and hasn't been shy about using force to suppress it. Two cases in point being the Catholic Church's treatment of Galileo Galilei, forced by the Inquisition, under threat of torture and execution, to recant the heresy that the Earth revolves around the sun, and Giordano Bruno, who was burnt alive for saying there was a multiplicity of worlds.

That was all too common a fate for heretics and blasphemers during the Middle Ages and Renaissance. Church and state, inextricably entwined during those eras, routinely used horrific torture to suppress free speech, to satisfy the sadistic lusts of the torturers and to terrify dissenters into silence. The following two examples of tortures and torture devices show just how far our Christian forebears were willing to go to suppress dissent.

As for the tools used by Christian enemies of free speech, the pear of anguish was a device with four sections, shaped somewhat like a pear, that the torturer would force into the victim's heretical mouth. The torturer would then turn the screw at the base of the implement forcing the victim's jaws apart. Depending on the degree of the torturer's sadism, this could result in dislocation of the victim's jaws. (There's some debate about how often this torture device was used; for a description of some of the other horrors used by inquisitors, see Chapter 5.) Torturers also commonly flogged blasphemers and then burned their tongues with a red hot poker, bored a hole through their tongues, or slit their tongues with a knife.

But with the advent of movable type and printing, and the increasing availability of books, the church also became quite interested in suppressing dissent in print media. Pope Gelasius I had issued a decree in the late fifth century banning certain books, but it wasn't until the mid-16th century that the first list with a title including "index" appeared, and with it the best known example of the Christian tendency toward censorship, the Catholic Church's *Index Librorum Prohibitorum*, its Index of Prohibited Books. The Index remained in place for over 400 years, but was never uniformly enforced—that was too big a job even for the Inquisition. The Church finally abandoned the Index in 1966, not because the Church recognized it as a crime against human freedom, but because there was no plausible way to enforce it and it had become an embarrassment.

Another prong of the Christian attempt to suppress free speech, in addition to the Index and Inquisition, consisted of blasphemy laws in both Catholic and Protestant lands.

Blasphemy Laws

In England, until the early 20th century, atheists who had the temerity to openly advocate their beliefs were sometimes jailed. In 1842, the prominent atheist editor and lecturer George Jacob Holyoake was convicted of blasphemy for a lecture he gave at the Mechanics Institute* in Cheltenham, and was jailed for six months. Holyoake's offense? Saying "I flee the Bible as a viper, and revolt at the touch of a Christian."[2]

Holyoake was relatively fortunate. In earlier centuries he might have been burned alive. From the late 14th century on, blasphemy and heresy were outlawed in England, bishops could order the arrest of heretics and blasphemers, and at least dozens—no one knows the exact count—were burned at the stake prior to the establishment of the Church of England under Henry VIII. If you include those executed for heresy during the internecine struggles between Catholics and Protestants in the 16th and 17th centuries, the total number of "heretic" victims in Britain was in the hundreds. The death penalty for blasphemy was abolished only in 1676.

The last person imprisoned for blasphemy in England was the pamphleteer John William Gott. The British government imprisoned him four times for exercising his right to free, anti-religious speech. In one instance, referencing Matthew 21:5, which states that Christ entered Jerusalem riding an ass and a foal simultaneously, he said that Christ entered the city "like a circus clown on the back of two donkeys." Gott's final imprisonment, doing hard labor, took place in 1921. It broke Gott's health, and he died at 56 in 1922. Sporadic prosecutions continued through the end of the

---

* Mechanics institutes were educational establishments that served in lieu of colleges for the working class.

1970s, and it wasn't until 2008 that the blasphemy laws were repealed in England and Wales, with Scotland following suit only in 2021.

In the United States, things were no better. The Puritans and most other Christian sects—who, but for the Quakers, did *not* flee England in pursuit of religious liberty, but rather to be free to impose their own religious beliefs in the areas they controlled—passed blasphemy laws early in the colonial period. Puritan Massachusetts passed an anti-blasphemy law in 1697, and Catholic Maryland followed suit in 1723. The wording of the statutes was similar, as were the penalties. The Massachusetts statute, which incredibly is still on the books, though not enforced, reads in part, "Whoever willfully blasphemes the holy name of God by denying, cursing or contumeliously reproaching God, His creation, government or final judging of the world, or by cursing or contumeliously reproaching Jesus Christ or the Holy Ghost, or by cursing or contumeliously reproaching or exposing to contempt and ridicule, the holy word of God contained in the holy scriptures shall be punished by imprisonment in jail for not more than one year or by a fine of not more than three hundred dollars . . ." (Previously in Massachusetts the death penalty could be applied, as could the searing of a blasphemer's tongue with a red hot iron.)[3] The Maryland law prescribed a punishment of up to six months in jail and a fine of one hundred dollars.

Similar statutes were put in place in the other colonies, and additional anti-blasphemy statutes were enacted in almost every state following the revolution. The last anti-blasphemy law in the United States was passed by the state legislature in Pennsylvania in 1977 (yes, really), and it wasn't struck down until 2010. (Ironically, William Penn, the founder of Pennsylvania, spent eight months in the Tower of London in 1668 after being charged with blasphemy.)

Anti-blasphemy laws are still on the books in several states. In addition to Massachusetts, they still exist in South Carolina, Michigan, and Oklahoma.[4]

There were at least sporadic attempts to enforce these laws until well into the 20th century. The last person jailed for blasphemy in the United States was Abner Kneeland, who was convicted of the offense in Massachusetts in 1838 and served 60 days. Still, as late as 1928 Charles Lee Smith was charged with blasphemy in Little Rock, Arkansas for giving away atheist pamphlets at a storefront he'd rented. The blasphemy charge didn't stick, but Smith was convicted of distributing "obscene" material, pamphlets with titles such as "The Bible in the Balance" and "Godless Evolution." He was sentenced to 26 days confinement and jailed. Even in 2007, film maker

George Kalman's application to register his company as a corporation in Pennsylvania was rejected because its name violated the state's still-on-the-books blasphemy law. The name Kalman applied for? "I Choose Hell LLC."[5]

As justification for these laws, the best that Christians can come up with is that blasphemy "rends the moral fabric of society," whatever that might mean. They also argue that anti-religious speech is so dangerous, so upsetting (to them) that it cannot be tolerated. What they really mean is that they don't like what "blasphemers" are saying, have no respect for the free speech rights of others, and are eager to use institutional violence (the state) to silence them. They're also tacitly admitting that their religious beliefs can't stand up to scrutiny, and that their omniscient, omnipotent deity needs *their* help to defend itself. Such humility.

As Robert Ingersoll said in 1877, while defending one C.B. Reynolds against a blasphemy charge in New Jersey, "By making a statute and by defining blasphemy, the church sought to prevent discussion—sought to prevent argument—sought to prevent a man giving his honest opinion. Certainly a tenet, a dogma, a doctrine, is safe when hedged about by a statute that prevents your speaking against it."[6]

Even today in the United States, many Christians want to reintroduce blasphemy laws, as the following words from a prominent Christian Reconstructionist demonstrate:

> The question eventually must be raised: Is it a criminal offense to take the name of the Lord in vain? When people curse their parents, it is unquestionably a capital crime (Ex. 21:17). The son or daughter is under the lawful jurisdiction of the family. The integrity of the family must be maintained by the threat of death. Clearly, cursing God (blasphemy) is a comparable crime, and is therefore a capital crime (Lev. 24:16).
> —Gary North, *The Sinai Strategy*[7]

Obscenity Laws

As the case of Charles Lee Smith demonstrates, blasphemy laws are only one component of Christian attempts to suppress free speech via legislation. The other is anti-obscenity laws.

In the United States, these laws date from the 1873 Comstock Act which outlawed the possession, distribution, and importation of birth control devices; it also outlawed the description of such devices and instructions on how to use them. Following the passage of the Comstock Act, a great many states followed suit and passed similar prohibitions (the Comstock acts), which remained in effect until struck down in 1965 by the Supreme Court in *Griswold v. Connecticut*. In the near century between passage of the Comstock Act and *Griswold* there were innumerable legislative and judicial violations of free speech via anti-obscenity laws.

These laws, and the threat of their enforcement, resulted in the wholesale bowdlerization of American movies, radio, and television, to a lesser extent the bowdlerization of American books, the banning of "obscene" books published abroad (e.g., *Lady Chatterley's Lover* and *Tropic of Cancer*), and the persecution and imprisonment of those with the courage to defy the censors, notably comic Lenny Bruce, who was hounded to death by police and prosecutors.

During the ferment of the 1960s, ever-increasing numbers of people began to resist the Christian-generated laws against free speech, and in 1973, in *Miller v. California*, the Supreme Court almost entirely gutted the anti-obscenity laws by ruling that material was obscene only if it had no redeeming social value. That opened the floodgates: it allowed people to express themselves without fear of police and prisons. Today, one of the last vestiges of the Christian assault on free speech is the FCC's ban on the use of the "seven words" on broadcast radio and television stations.

As with other laws against victimless crimes (e.g., smoking pot), the blasphemy and obscenity laws were a great convenience to authoritarians: those laws allowed them to inflict terrible punishments on entirely specious grounds; those laws relieved them of the burden of proving any tangible harm to anyone before tossing their victims into jail. Even today, as rationales for both obscenity and blasphemy laws, which many Christians still pine for, they'll invariably cite abstractions such as "undermining morality" or "rending the social fabric," and when challenged to cite any concrete harm to anyone, they invariably can't do it: they'll either retreat back into abstractions or they'll cite hypothetical absurdities, never any harm to real people directly attributable to blasphemy or "obscene" speech or writings.

If you have the temerity to speak out against Christianity, if your words are not in accord with Christian morality and its dictates, you can bet that all too many Christians will feel completely justified—not to mention righteous—in attacking you physically or in using the institutional violence of the state to silence you.

As evidence that this is so, the National Opinion Research Center (NORC) reported in 2010 that the more religious people are, the more likely they are to oppose freedom of speech. NORC's General Social Survey revealed that the more conservative their religious beliefs, the more likely it was that respondents "would not allow atheists, communists, homosexuals, or racists to speak in their local community"; among its other findings, the survey revealed that 38% of fundamentalists would deny atheists the right to speak, and a full 50% of them would deny that right to communists.[8]

Endnotes

1. *Holy Homicide*, by Michael Newton. Port Townsend, WA: Loompanics, 1998, p. 117.

2. "George Jacob Holyoake," by Bob Forder. National Secular Society. https://www.secularism.org.uk/george-jacob-holyoake.html < https://tinyurl.com/yy5cldyf >

3. "We swear, blasphemy laws still on the books," by Andrew Seidel. *Freethought Today*, April 2014. https://ffrf.org/outreach/item/20813-we-swear-blasphemy-laws-still-on-the-books < https://tinyurl.com/y34g7bo3 >

4. Ibid.

5. "Anti-blasphemy laws have a history in America." WHYY, October 9, 2012. https://whyy.org/articles/anti-blasphemy-laws-have-a-history-in-america/ < https://tinyurl.com/y54cefuk >

6. "Trial of C.B. Reynolds for Blasphemy." Project Gutenberg. https://www.gutenberg.org/files/38103/38103-h/38103-h.htm < https://tinyurl.com/yxueyfpf >

7. Quoted by David Irish in *America's Taliban: In its own words*. Tucson: See Sharp Press, 2003, p. 12.

8. *What You Don't Know About Religion (but should)*, by Ryan Cragun. Durham, NC: Pitchstone Publishing, 2013, p. 120.

10

Christianity's Anti-Scientific Attitude

> Being led . . . to prefer the Christian doctrine, I felt that her proceeding was more unassuming and honest in that she required to be believed things not demonstrated . . . —St. Augustine, *Confessions*

> There is on earth among all dangers no more dangerous thing than a richly endowed and adroit reason. Reason must be deluded, blinded, and destroyed. —Martin Luther, *Table Talk*[1]

For over a millennium, Christianity arrested the development of science and scientific thinking. In Christendom, from the time of Augustine (354–430) until the Renaissance, investigation of the natural world was restricted to the realm of theology—the interpretation of biblical passages, the conjectures of the various church fathers, deciphering clues from the lives of the saints, etc.—and to the writings of Aristotle, who was considered, along with the Bible and church authorities, the final word on nature; there was no direct observation and analysis of natural processes, because that was considered a useless pursuit, as all knowledge resided in scripture, the pronouncements of church authorities, and the conjectures of the Greek philosopher. The results of this are well known. In Europe, scientific knowledge advanced hardly an inch in the over one thousand years from the rise of orthodox Christianity in the fourth century to the 1500s, and the populace was mired in the deepest squalor and ignorance, living in desperate fear of the supernatural, believing in paranormal explanations for the most ordinary natural events.

That ignorance had tragic results. It made the populace more than ready to accept witchcraft as an explanation for everything from illness to thunderstorms, and tens of thousands of women (and some men) paid for that ignorance with their lives. One of the commonest charges against witches was that they had raised hailstorms or other weather disturbances to damage their neighbors' crops. In an era when supernatural explanations were readily accepted, such charges held weight, and countless innocent people died horrible deaths as a result. Another result was that the fearful populace remained very dependent upon the Christian church and its clerical wise men for protection against the supernatural evils which they believed surrounded and constantly menaced them. For men and women of the Middle Ages, the walls and ceilings veritably crawled with demons and devils, and their only defense against those evils was the church.

Medieval believers found ample justification for their superstitious beliefs in scripture, most notably in what could well be the most pernicious verse in the entire Bible, "Thou shalt not suffer a witch to live," Exodus 22:18. There are many other biblical references to witches, wizards, and familiar spirits, including a typically bloodthirsty passage in Leviticus: "A man also or woman that hath a familiar spirit, or that is a wizard, shall surely be put to death: they shall stone them with stones: their blood shall be upon them." (Leviticus 20:27)

Such passages led in a straight line to the persecution and murder of thousands upon thousands of innocent people in Christianity-soaked medieval and Renaissance Europe.

There are also dozens of references to demons in the Bible, including in the New Testament. To cite but three examples:

> The demons begged Jesus, 'If you drive us out, send us into the herd of pigs.' —Matthew 8:31

> You believe that there is one God. Good! Even the demons believe that and shudder. —James 2:19

> Jesus asked him, 'What is your name?' 'Legion,' he replied, because many demons had gone into him. —Luke 8:30

Christianity's great medieval theologian, Thomas Aquinas, shared this belief in demons. In *Summa Theologica* he stated, "It is a dogma of faith that the demons can produce wind, storms, and rain of fire from heaven." Three centuries after Aquinas, Martin Luther, in his *Table Talk*, wrote,

"Many demons are in woods, in waters, in wildernesses, and in dark poolly places ready to hurt and prejudice people; some are also in the thick black clouds, which cause hail, lightning and thunder, and poison the air, the pastures and grounds."

This was the background when the scientific revolution began. It's little wonder that Copernicus delayed, until he lay on his death bed, publication of *De revolutionibus orbium coelestium* ("On the revolutions of the celestial spheres"), his book advocating the heliocentric theory, that the Earth and other planets revolve around the sun.

When scientific investigation into the natural world resumed in the Renaissance, after a thousand-year-plus hiatus, organized Christianity opposed it—all of it—because it saw rational inquiry as threatening to Christian dogma. (For the sake of brevity, we'll deal only with astronomy here, but it's important to understand that the Church opposed scientific investigation across the board.)

The cases of Copernicus and Galileo are relevant, because when the Catholic Church banned the Copernican theory (heliocentrism) and forbade Galileo from teaching it (under threat of torture and execution), it did not consider the evidence for that theory; it was enough that it contradicted scripture. Given that the Copernican theory directly contradicted the Word of God, the Catholic hierarchy reasoned that it *must* be false. As St. Augustine put it in his *De Genesi* ("On Genesis"), "Nothing is to be accepted save on the authority of Scripture, since greater is that authority than all the powers of the human mind."

The Inquisition's findings against Galileo spell this out even further:

> The first proposition that the sun is the center and does not revolve about the earth, is foolish, absurd, false in theology, and heretical, because it is expressly contrary to Holy Scripture. The second proposition, that the earth is not the center but revolves about the sun, is absurd, false in philosophy, and, from a theological point of view at least opposed to the true faith.
> —Roman Inquisition, judgment on the writings of Galileo, 1615

As well as in scripture, the Church found justification for its views in the words of Aquinas:

> If . . . the motion of the earth were circular, it would be violent and contrary to nature, and could not be eternal, since . . . nothing violent is eternal . . . It follows, therefore, that the earth is not moved with a circular motion.
> —*Commentaria in libros Aristotelis de caelo et mundo* ("Commentaries in the books of Aristotle on heaven and earth")

As you might expect, the works of Copernicus (*On the Revolution of the Celestial Spheres*, which outlined the heliocentric theory), Johannes Kepler (*The New Astronomy*, which for all intents and purposes proved the heliocentric theory mathematically), and Galileo (*Dialogue Concerning the Two Chief World Systems* [the ptolemaic and heliocentric], which presented observational evidence supporting the heliocentric theory) were all placed on the Catholic Church's Index of Prohibited Books.

The Protestants shared the Catholics' rejection of science. John Calvin stated:

> We will see some who are so deranged, not only in religion but who in all things reveal their monstrous nature, that they will say that the sun does not move, and that it is the earth which shifts and turns. When we see such minds we must indeed confess that the devil possesses them, . . .[2]
> —Sermon on 1 Corinthians 10:19–24

Martin Luther's view of science was equally benighted:

> People gave ear to an upstart astrologer [Copernicus] who strove to show that the earth revolves, not the heavens or the firmament, the sun and the moon. Whoever wishes to appear clever must devise some new system, which of all systems is of course the very best. This fool [Copernicus] wishes to reverse the entire science of astronomy; but sacred scripture tells us that Joshua commanded the sun to stand still, and not the earth.
> —*Table Talk*

More recently, the Catholic Church and the more liberal Protestant churches have realized that fighting against science is a losing battle, and they've taken to claiming that there is no contradiction between science and religion. This is more than a bit disingenuous. As long as Christian sects continue to claim as fact—without offering a shred of evidence beyond the anecdotal—that physically impossible events ("miracles") occurred or are still occurring, the conflict between science and religion will remain. That many churchmen and many scientists seem content to let this conflict lie doesn't mean that it doesn't exist.

Today, in the United States, the conflict between religion and science is largely being played out in the area of public school biology education, with Christian fundamentalists demanding that their creation myth be taught in place of (or alongside) the theory of evolution in public schools. Their tactics rely heavily on public misunderstanding of science. Creationists nitpick the fossil record for its gaps (hardly surprising on a geologically and meteorologically active planet), while offering absurd assertions which we're supposed to accept at face value—such as that dinosaur fossils were placed in the earth by Satan to confuse humankind, or that Noah took baby dinosaurs on the ark (hence the kiddie-ride saddled dinosaur at the Creation Museum in Petersburg, Kentucky).

They also attempt to take advantage of public ignorance of the nature of scientific theories. In popular use, "theory" is employed as a synonym for "hypothesis," "conjecture," or even "wild guess," that is, it signifies an idea with no special merit. The use of the term in science is very different. There, "theory" refers to a testable, logically consistent explanation of a phenomenon, an explanation that is consistent with observed facts, that has withstood repeated testing, and that can generate accurate predictions, as in "the theory of gravity" or "the theory of relativity." This is very different from a wild guess. But Christian fundamentalists deliberately confuse the two uses of the term in an attempt to make their creation myth appear as valid as a well supported scientific theory.

They also attempt to confuse the issue by claiming that those nonspecialists who accept the theory of evolution have no more reason to do so than they have in accepting their myth, or even that those who accept evolution do so on faith. Again, this is more than a bit dishonest.

Thanks to scientific investigation, human knowledge has advanced to the point where no one can know more than a tiny fraction of the whole. Even the most accomplished scientists often know little beyond their specialty areas. But because of the structure of science, they (and everyone else) can feel reasonably secure in accepting the theories developed by scientists in other disciplines as the best possible current explanations of the areas of nature those disciplines cover.

They (and we) can feel secure doing this because of the structure of science and, more particularly, because of the scientific method. That method basically consists of gathering as much information about a phenomenon as possible, both in nature and in the laboratory, then developing explanations for it (hypotheses), then testing the hypotheses to see how well they explain the observed facts and whether or not any of those observed facts are inconsistent with the hypotheses, and finally seeing if the hypotheses can generate accurate predictions. Those hypotheses that are inconsistent with observed facts are discarded or modified, while those that are consistent are investigated further, and those that survive years of repeated testing and generate accurate predictions are often labeled "theories," as in "the theory of gravity" and "the theory of evolution."

This is the reason that both scientists and nonscientists are justified in accepting scientific theories outside their own areas of expertise as the best current explanations of the physical world: those who developed the theories were following standard scientific practice and reasoning, and if they deviated from that, other scientists would have quickly called them to task.

No matter how much Christians might protest to the contrary, there is a world of difference between "faith" in scientific theories produced using the scientific method and subject to testing and scrutiny, and faith in the unsupported myths recorded thousands of years ago by slave-holding goat herders.

Nearly five hundred years ago Martin Luther, in his *Table Talk*, stated, "Reason is the greatest enemy that faith has."

The opposite is also true.

Christian Dogmatism vs. Science

> If today there are persons to be found who do not know how *indecent* it is to be a 'believer'—or in how far it is a sign of *decadence*, of a broken will to live—they will know it tomorrow. . . . Faith, indeed, has up to the present not been able to move real mountains. But it can put mountains where there are none.
>
> —Friedrich Nietzsche, *The Anti-Christ*

There are a great many reasons why accepting reality rather than burying your head in religion is of importance, often life-or-death importance. Here are some of them:

A. The scientific method is the only reliable way to arrive at the most probably correct explanation of almost anything. Once you abandon logic, science, and reality (accepting facts even if you don't like them), you have no even remotely reliable means of reaching conclusions, and when you act on faulty conclusions, the results are often bad, sometimes catastrophic.

In contrast to accepting religious myths, scientists reach conclusions by formulating hypotheses regarding observed phenomena, checking the hypotheses for internal consistency, devising experiments to test them, and checking to see if the hypotheses can generate accurate predictions. Then doing all this over and over again, with different scientists repeatedly testing the hypotheses ("theories" if they consistently pass all these tests over a prolonged period of time) through experiment, observation, and analysis. (Even today, you'll still see occasional reports of scientists testing Einstein's theory of relativity, well over a hundred years after he devised it.)

That's a bit different than pointing to a hoary book written by Iron Age slaveholders and asserting, "This is true! It's a fact! It says so here!"

Tertullian, an influential church father, took this absurd assertion even further in his *De Carne Christi* ("Of the Body of Christ"), saying in regard to the resurrection, "It is certain because it is impossible" ("*Certum est quia impossibile est*").

To that, all one can say is "all rightee, then. Thirty-foot-tall methane-breathing spiders roaming the surface of Mars? It's certain."

(Christian apologists often attempt to discount Tertullian's "impossible" remark saying that it's out of step with the tenor of his other writings. Unfortunately for them, it's undeniably there in *De Carne Christi*.)

B. Science is self-correcting. Religion isn't. Science continually tests and refines hypotheses and theories to arrive at more accurate explanations. Religion doesn't.

A good example of this is provided by scientific exploration of racial differences between humans. In the 19th century, some scientists asserted that whites were superior to other races. By the middle of the 20th century, other scientists had definitively debunked those assertions through observation, experiment, and analysis. (Yes, there are still a few racist scientists, but their assertions are knocked down almost as soon as they make them, and the vast majority of scientists now accept, in line with scientific evidence and research, that assertions of racial superiority or inferiority are baseless.)

The overt racism of the Book of Mormon (1830—published two months prior to Andrew Jackson's signing the Indian Removal Act) slightly predates the racist assertions of some 19th-century scientists, with the Book of Mormon itself referring to caucasians as "white and exceedingly fair and delightsome" (2 Nephi 5:20–21); earlier in that ineptly written fantasy novel—"chloroform in print," according to Mark Twain—its author, LDS founder and fraudster Joseph Smith, referred to Native Americans, "Lamanites," as "a dark and loathsome and a filthy people, full of idleness, and all manner of abominations" (1 Nephi 12:23). And as late as 1935, Mormon Prophet Joseph Fielding Smith asserted that "because of [Cain's] wickedness he became the father of an inferior race."[3]

Finally, in 1978, in response to widespread social condemnation (and undoubtedly a desire to increase the number of potential converts), then-prophet Spencer W. Kimball announced a new revelation: that the church should abandon its racial restrictions on the priesthood. But he didn't, and couldn't, abandon the "revealed" racist passages in 1 Nephi and 2 Nephi, nor the "inspired" racist statements of previous prophets; rather, he simply didn't address them.

That's a bit different than the way science handled the matter, eh?

C. Science improves daily life. Christianity doesn't (nor does any religion). One clear example of this is in the field of medicine, where scientists discovered the microbial nature of disease. That discovery led to the use of antiseptics and the later development of antibiotics, which have saved the lives of untold millions.

The list of scientific discoveries and subsequent technologies that have made life better and longer for a good majority of human beings is almost endless. To cite but a few examples, electricity, vaccines, radio, railroads, refrigeration of food, sewage disposal, computers, optics, anesthesia, telephones—the list goes on and on.

The list of physical improvements to daily life and human wellbeing created by religion? . . . . (crickets)

Religion has led to no developments that improve daily life. Not a single one.

(Please don't start talking about the power of prayer and the peace it supposedly brings—we're speaking here of demonstrable physical improvement. As Chris Edwards observed in *Disbelief 101*, no one has ever invented a prayer-powered car.)

D. Science leads. Religion lags. A good example of this is our understanding of the universe beyond the Earth. Early scientists (Copernicus, Galileo, et al.) led the way to accurate description of the physical universe.

At the same time, the church was insisting that the sun revolves around the Earth, and hauling scientists who dared to state the opposite before the Inquisition.

Another example is the scientific versus religious attitude toward women. Science has established that while there are obvious and not-so-obvious differences between men and women, their intellectual abilities are almost identical, with a few end-of-the-bell-curve differences in a few specific areas.

In contrast, from its inception Christianity has insisted on the inferiority and subordination of women. To cite but two of a great many Bible verses denigrating women, "How then can man be justified with God? or how can he be clean that is born of a woman?" (Job 25:4) and "These [redeemed] are they which were not defiled with women." (Revelation 14:4)

Today, some sects have acknowledged reality and accept the equality of men and women. Others have dug in their heels and still insist upon female subordination, though most are now wary of openly claiming that women are inferior. And it's safe to say that the more conservative the religion—that is, the more literally its members take their scripture—the more likely they are to insist upon the inferiority and subjugation of women

E. **Finally**, as Neil deGrasse Tyson famously remarked, science opens doors and religion closes them. Science not only leads to improvements in daily life, but to broader intellectual horizons; it encourages people to think for themselves, to question everything; it leads to one question after another.

Religion insists that all the answers are contained in ancient holy books and the words of popes, preachers, and prophets. Religion insists that it's wrong, dangerous to question those "revealed" answers, that you have a brain, but you shouldn't use it.

It's hard to conceive of anything more stultifying.

Endnotes

1. *Table Talk*, by Martin Luther. Christian Classics Ethereal Library. http://www.ccel.org/ccel/luther/tabletalk.html < https://tinyurl.com/wk6cxrxw >

2. "John Calvin on Nicolaus Copernicus and Heliocentrism," by Wyatt Houtz. *Biologos*, June 8, 2014. https://biologos.org/articles/john-calvin-on-nicolaus-copernicus-and-heliocentrism/ < https://tinyurl.com/kbzzv29n >

3. *The Way to Perfection*, by Joseph Fielding Smith. Salt Lake City: Genealogical Society of the Church of Jesus Christ of Latter-Day Saints, 1951, p. 101.

11

The Deadly Results of Christian Science Denial

> A religion like Christianity, which is not in touch with reality on any point, which immediately falls down as soon as reality gets its right even in a single point, must, of course, be mortally hostile to the 'wisdom of the world,' i.e., to *science*—it will approve of all expedients by which discipline of intellect, the noble coolness and freedom of intellect, can be poisoned, calumniated, and defamed. 'Belief,' as an imperative, is the veto against *science*—in practice, the lie at any price . . . —Friedrich Nietzsche, *The Anti-Christ*

> In the case of an unexplained matter [those ignorant of science and logic] become heated for the first idea that comes into their heads which has any resemblance to an explanation—a course from which the worst results constantly follow, especially in the field of politics.
> —Nietzsche, *Human, All Too Human*

Rejection of reality and rejection of science have always been fashionable among the religious. Many Christians insist that assertions contained in an ancient book are every bit as valid as carefully arrived at, repeatedly tested scientific theories and conclusions. In a striking bit of irony, some go even further and unconsciously mimic academic postmodernists, who insist that all "opinions" (including scientific conclusions) are equally valid. Thus willful ignorance among the least educated mirrors willful ignorance among the most educated.

Isaac Asimov, who could have been talking about postmodernists, anti-vaxxers, fundamentalist Christians, conspiracy theorists, or the (largely overlapping) Trump cult, put the position of the wrong-headed like this:

"My ignorance is just as good as your knowledge"—an attitude held by a good third of the American public.

Given this widespread embrace of willful ignorance, it's good to remind ourselves of the real-world damage caused by rejection of science and reality. To cite a trivial example, if you believe you're invulnerable, you can test your hypothesis by stepping in front of a speeding truck. If anyone actually did this, it would bear more than a passing similarity to the 19th- and 20th-century revolts in which religious believers thought they were invulnerable to gunfire because of divine protection, and acted accordingly. One sad and pertinent example is the Maji Maji Rebellion (1905–1907) in what is now a part of Tanzania, which at the time was occupied by Germany. The rebels believed they were invulnerable to the Germans' bullets because of supernatural protection, with predictable results. Estimates of the number slaughtered by the Germans range from the tens of thousands to a quarter of a million—though far from all were rebels; a great many were innocent civilians*—while casualties among the very well armed Germans were almost nonexistent.[1] The rebels were probably doomed in any event, but it certainly didn't help that they believed themselves impervious to gunfire.

To cite a broader, all-too-real example of why acceptance of scientific investigation and conclusions matter—as opposed to religious belief—science has established that the similarities between human beings vastly outweigh the differences, and that there's no basis for assertions that any race is superior to any other. So, are the opinions of racists just as valid as the scientific conclusion that the differences between racial groups are trivial? If you say "no," but reject science, you're left with nothing but your own assertion in the face of the racist assertion.

As well, as previously mentioned, in medieval Europe with science at a standstill—with no scientific investigation of nearly anything—many believed that illness and bad weather were caused by witchcraft. End result? Tens, possibly hundreds, of thousands of "witches" were brutally murdered for supposedly causing storms and disease. Science put an end to this madness, but if we were still mired in gross ignorance compounded by religious zealotry, such horrors might still exist.

Today, anti-vaccination hysteria is common in the U.S., despite the fact that it was given birth by a tiny, poorly designed study (only eight sub-

* The Germans weren't picky about who they killed. In a near-simultaneous rebellion (1904–1908) in Namibia, another of their African colonies, they killed an estimated 75,000 to 100,000 people, deliberately targeted and murdered unarmed civilians, and tossed many of the survivors into concentration camps.

jects with no control group) published in 1998 in *Lancet*. The study, whose lead author was Dr. Andrew Wakefield, purported to show a link between MMR (measles, mumps, rubella) vaccinations and autism. Unfortunately for Wakefield, other investigators were unable to replicate his results, and many subsequent, better designed and larger studies have shown no connection between vaccination and autism.

In 2010, Wakefield was struck from the medical registry (banned from practicing medicine in the UK) amidst allegations of outright fraud by, among others, the *British Medical Journal*, which cited "clear evidence of falsification of data."[2] Another investigator revealed that Wakefield had planned to profit from the anti-vaccination panic he'd set off by forming a corporation that would engage in "litigation-driven testing."[3]

But despite these revelations of falsified data and planned profiteering, the damage was done—to public health, not to Wakefield. Since being revealed as a fraud, Wakefield has made a career of the anti-vax movement. In 2010, he published a book on the topic, and he was the director of a 2016 "documentary" which was dropped from the Tribeca film festival because it was misleading. Wakefield has also drawn six-figure salaries from Texas-based anti-vax charities and businesses.

While Wakefield was profiting from anti-vax fears, measles outbreaks skyrocketed. In 1998, the year of Wakefield's deeply flawed study in *Lancet*, there were only 100 cases of measles in the U.S. By 2019, the number had reached 1,250. Meanwhile in Europe, measles cases doubled from 40,000 in 2000 to 83,000 in 2017. Worldwide, there were 140,000 measles *deaths* in 2018;[4] most of these were in countries with poor healthcare systems, but the huge number of deaths is indicative of the seriousness of the disease, which leads to pneumonia in up to 5% of cases, and more rarely to encephalitis. And it's not just anti-vaxxers' children who fall victim to this entirely preventable disease: measles also strikes infants too young to be vaccinated and those with compromised immune systems.

Anti-vaxxers might also consider the number of measles cases and deaths in the United States prior to the measles vaccine. The CDC reports that "In the decade before 1963 when a vaccine became available, nearly all children got measles by the time they were 15 years of age. It is estimated 3 to 4 million people in the United States were infected each year. Among reported cases, an estimated 400 to 500 people died, 48,000 were hospitalized, and 1,000 suffered encephalitis (swelling of the brain) from measles."[5] Compare these facts with anti-vaxxer propaganda citing a nonexistent link between vaccination and autism.

Perhaps the most maddening things about all this are that measles was on the road to eradication before the anti-vax movement (at least in the U.S. and other developed countries), and that vaccines are safe. On average, there are serious complications in only about one in a million cases as regards measles vaccinations, according to the WHO.[6]

The Covid-19 Disaster

As bad as all this is, it became even worse with the coming of the Covid pandemic. There's now significant overlap between anti-vaxxers, Trump supporters, and QAnon, which is a toxic waste dump of conspiracy theories that draws deep from the cesspit of earlier conspiracy theories, including the "blood libel" against Jews (see Chapter 22), and posits that Trump is fighting a "deep state" cabal running a cannibalistic pedophile ring involving the Obamas, Clintons, Bushes, satanists, and (yes) Tom Hanks and other Hollywood stars.

What do these three things—the anti-vax movement, the Trump personality cult, and QAnon—have in common? Their membership is disproportionately made up of conservative Christians; unsurprisingly, during the pandemic, QAnon rapidly gained followers in Christian churches across the country.[7]

This fits. Only a mind that never learned to think critically could embrace the deranged anti-vax and QAnon conspiracy theories, and, to point out the blindingly obvious, conservative Christianity discourages critical thinking. As journalist Adrienne LeFrance, who has done extensive research on QAnon and is also editor of *The Atlantic*, put it in an interview with "Fresh Air," "This was one of the more mind-melting aspects of my reporting—is in talking to Q believers, it [facts] didn't matter. Facts just don't matter [to them]."[8]

One example of this willful ignorance is the insistence of plague-enthusiast Christians that "Jesus is my vaccine." (A number of online sellers, including several on Amazon, are still selling T-shirts emblazoned with that slogan.) Even after more than three quarters of a million Covid deaths, some evangelical preachers continued to peddle the insane idea that faith in Jesus somehow shields believers from Covid infection. Unfortunately, the irresponsible behavior associated with that belief (rejection of basic public health measures such as mask-wearing and social distancing, and refusal to be vaccinated) endangered the health of everyone, not just the health of the deluded.

An indication of how anti-vax delusions sometimes work out in real life was provided in June 2021 by the Manatee County, Florida IT Department, a month after the county commissioners repealed Covid safety requirements. Of six employees in the IT Department, only one was vaccinated. The other five caught Covid and two of them died, while the vaccinated employee went unscathed.[9]

Unfortunately, the irresponsibility of the victims (and the county commissioners) not only caused them and their loved ones grief, but it affected unrelated others: the County had to shut down its central administrative building because of the outbreak, and it's quite likely that the unvaccinated Covid victims infected others, both at work and at home. That led Manatee County Administrator Scott Hopes to express his sadness and frustration at the unnecessary death, suffering, and disruption: "It's been devastating to staff and it's been difficult for the organization. The SARS virus* is still in our community and the vaccine protects people."[10]

That June outbreak, and especially the resultant deaths, was entirely preventable. In May 2021, with vaccination readily available to all American adults who wanted it, over 99% of Covid infections and Covid deaths in the U.S. (about 18,000 that month) were among the unvaccinated.[11] What makes this even worse is that the Covid vaccines used in the U.S. were remarkably effective; as well, serious side effects were rare, and deaths due to vaccination were all but nonexistent.** Yet nearly 30% of Americans said they'd refuse vaccination, choosing to risk contraction of a deadly, highly contagious disease and spreading it to their families, friends, and other members of the community, either because of conspiracy theories or because of fear of hypothetical after-effects years in the future.

By August 2021, almost all new cases in the United States were caused by the highly infectious delta variant, which is estimated to be two to three times as infectious as the original Covid strain. Because of its infectiousness, the delta variant spread to fully inoculated people in so-called "breakthrough infections," and the percentage of new cases among the unvaccinated had fallen to 93%, with the rest being breakthrough cases. As if to illustrate just how infectious the delta variant was, a single unvaccinat-

---

* SARS, more properly SARS-CoV-2, "severe acute respiratory syndrome coronovirus 2," is another name for the Covid virus.

** There were a few fatalities in Europe and Australia from blood clots due to the AstraZeneca vaccine, with a rate of about one fatality per million shots; there were also a few deaths in the United States due to the J&J vaccine, with a rate of about one fatality per two million shots, but no fatalities from the more commonly used Pfizer and Moderna vaccines.

ed, infected Oregon healthcare worker spread the infection to 64 nursing home patients, five of whom died.[12]

An even starker example of the results of ignoring scientific reality came later in the same month as the Manatee and Oregon outbreaks. A "super spreader" birthday party in Sydney, Australia resulted in every single unvaccinated participant contracting Covid. Of the 30 people attending, 24 came down with Covid's highly infectious delta variant. All of the infected were unvaccinated. The six who didn't come down with Covid were all vaccinated. The unvaccinated, infected partiers then went on to infect "many of their household contacts," who presumably then infected still others.[13]

Those infected partiers weren't totally to blame for this. Half a year after vaccines became available, and three months after they became widely available in most other industrialized countries, a large majority of Australians who wanted to be vaccinated still couldn't get a shot because of the Australian government's slow vaccine rollout. At the time of the Sydney outbreak near the end of June, fewer than 5% of the population were fully vaccinated. So, the outbreak was a result of both the irresponsibility of the attendees—refusing to follow scientific advice on containing the virus—and the irresponsibility of Australian Prime Minister Scott Morrison, who failed to follow the advice of public health experts regarding the urgency of mass vaccination. As a sign said in the window of a shuttered antiques shop in Sydney during one of the city's periodic Covid lockdowns, "Dear customers, we will be closed for the foreseeable future because Scott Morrison is a useless dickhead who only ordered enough vaccine to vaccinate 4% of the population 18 months into a pandemic."

The Cost of Bad Leadership, Magical Thinking, and Disinformation

Then there's Donald Trump, who was quite possibly the worst person on earth to lead America's response to the pandemic. While he was still in office, he repeatedly rejected advice from public health experts, refused to acknowledge the seriousness of the Coronavirus pandemic, and repeatedly said the Coronavirus would magically go away. In large part because of Trump's rejection of reality, precious time was lost and the U.S. was woefully unprepared for the pandemic. Despite being repeatedly warned of the seriousness of the problem by U.S. Intelligence agencies and public health officials, Trump sat on his hands for months before weakly responding.

Trump refused to authorize the government to use the most powerful and easily applied tools for containing the virus, nationally mandated mask wearing and social distancing, and nationally coordinated Covid testing and contact tracing; he even refused to use his powers under the Defense Production Act to order the production of personal protective equipment (PPE) for doctors, nurses, and others on the Covid front lines—a failure which directly led to the deaths of nearly three thousand American medical workers in 2020,[14] with many of the deaths occurring during the first months of the pandemic, when PPE was in short supply and some doctors and nurses were wearing garbage bags and scuba masks in place of necessary PPE. By the end of March 2021, one year into the pandemic, the number of medical-worker Covid deaths had increased to 3,600.[15]

As a result of Trump's wishful thinking, callousness, rejection of science, refusal to admit mistakes, and his consequent abdication of responsibility, hundreds of thousands of Americans died horrible, unnecessary deaths. A Brookings Institute study estimates that if "pro-life" Donald Trump hadn't sat on his hands and had instead, on May 1, 2020 instituted proven-effective public health measures—mask wearing, social distancing, mass testing, and contact tracing—the U.S. death toll would have been 292,000,[16] not the well over 900,000 it eventually reached.

Trump had been warned repeatedly of the deadliness of the Coronavirus months before he instituted his half-hearted lockdown in March 2020, and even then did nothing with the time he'd bought. If he'd simultaneously instituted the public health measures mentioned above, along with the lockdown, the U.S. death toll would have been lower than even the 292,000 figure, in all likelihood far lower.

For evidence of this, look no further than South Korea, which had its first diagnosed Covid-19 case on the same day as the United States, January 19, 2020 (across the International Dateline in Korea, January 20). In contrast to the inept American response, South Korea instituted all of the public health measures recommended by experts, and very effectively contained the virus. As of March 2021, South Korea, a country of approximately 50 million people, had suffered only an estimated 2,750 Covid deaths (with some estimates lower, in the 2,000 range); in contrast, in the Christianity- and conspiracy-soaked United States, over 550,000 people had died in the same period—a 200:1 ratio. Adjusting for the difference in population, the ratio falls to "only" 30:1. So, if Trump had instituted the same public health measures as South Korea, and at the same time, the U.S. likely would have been spared well over half a million deaths.

Amazingly enough, despite all of this unnecessary misery and death—due directly to Trump's callousness, incompetence, and irresponsibility—many members of Trump's personality cult, and the overlapping anti-vax and QAnon movements, *admired* (and still admire) Trump because of his rejection of science, because of his refusal to act on scientific advice. They're proud of their deadly willful ignorance (though one suspects they're even prouder of their ability to deeply and lovingly kiss Trump's ample ass).

Of course, Trump is also proud of his ignorance. On March 25, 2021, on the disinformation-spewing Laura Ingraham show on Fox, he bragged that he had deliberately ignored the advice of the nation's leading infectious disease expert, Dr. Anthony Fauci. Trump boasted, "I didn't really listen to him too much because I was doing the opposite of what he was saying." Of course, Ingraham didn't call him on this admission of weapons-grade stupidity by a self-described "genius" who, but for massive financial gifts and bailouts from his Klan rally-attending father,[17] would have done well to end up as an assistant manager at a Circle K.

How did Trump's and his minions' willful ignorance affect the public's willingness to adopt public health measures during the Covid pandemic? In June 2020, as the U.S. death toll was already above 100,000 and rapidly climbing, fully half of the American public said they wouldn't take a Covid vaccine.[18] In October 2020, the number who said they would get vaccinated once a vaccine was available stood at only 58%, considerably short of the number necessary for herd immunity.[19] In December, following announcement that the Pfizer vaccine had successfully passed its phase 3 trial and would receive FDA emergency approval, that figure increased, but only to 61%, with another 10% saying they were unsure about being vaccinated, and 29% saying they'd refuse it.[20] Nine months later, in August/September 2021, that figure had dropped, but only to 24%, with a large majority of the refusers being right-wing Republicans.[21]

The Mayo Clinic says that a 94% vaccination rate is necessary to achieve herd immunity for measles,[22] but since the initial strain of Coronavirus was less transmissible than measles, the percentage necessary for Covid herd immunity was lower, with Mayo putting it 70%.[23] In June 2021, the delta variant exploded across the country, and by July 2021 it had become the dominant strain, with infections skyrocketing in areas with low vaccination rates, and with the vast majority of new cases among the unvaccinated. By September, the delta variant accounted for more than 99% of cases in the U.S. And in September 2021, CNN, citing a number of public health experts, reported that a "rough target of 80–90% of fully vaccinated citizens . . . is required to drop restrictions" such as mask wearing and social distancing.[24] In the same month, as mentioned above, with over 650,000 dead from Covid and life-saving vaccines free, effective, and readily available, 24% of those polled still said they'd refuse to get vaccinated[25]—even though the contagiousness of the delta variant meant that getting Covid was more a matter of when, rather than if, for the unvaccinated.

How did this play out? With vaccination free and readily available to all American adults since April, and to kids 12 and up since mid-May, vaccine refusal from June on led directly to at least another 100,000 deaths in the following months. In early October, Dr. David Dowdy, an epidemiologist at Johns Hopkins, stated, "it's safe to say at least 70,000 of the last 100,000 deaths were in unvaccinated people. And of those vaccinated people who died with breakthrough infections, most caught the virus from an unvaccinated person . . . If we had been more effective in our vaccination, then I think it's fair to say we could have prevented 90% of those deaths."[26]

By November, due to the delta variant, estimates of the vaccination rate necessary to achieve herd immunity were in the 90% to 95% range. In other words, Covid-19 was approaching the infectiousness of measles.[27]

Mule-headed vaccine refusal makes it almost certain that we'll never achieve herd immunity in the U.S. Other factors are at play, of course, including the slow vaccine rollout in most of the rest of the world and the consequent development of more easily transmissible strains there. Still, the determination of many American right-wingers to remain ambulatory disease vectors didn't help children too young to be vaccinated or the nine million immuno-compromised Americans; rather, it caused parents of young children unnecessary stress, and it led to unnecessary exposure of their children to a dangerous disease. It also caused the immuno-compromised unnecessary stress, unnecessary social restriction, and unnecessary exposure to an oft-times serious, sometimes fatal illness. The selfishness, callousness, and willful ignorance of those refusing vaccination essentially made the immuno-compromised prisoners in their own homes, and undoubtedly caused some to become infected and die. It also led to hundreds of thousands of Covid cases in children too young to be vaccinated.

Doctor Thanh Neville expressed ICU workers' frustration with this almost entirely avoidable situation: "My experiences in the ICU these past weeks have left me surprised, disheartened, but most of all, angry" because of the vaccine-refusers' "decision to not protect themselves or their families, to fill a precious ICU bed, to let new variants flourish, and to endanger the health care workers and immunosuppressed people around them.

Their inaction is a decision to let this pandemic continue to rage. I have no way to comfort my rightfully outraged transplant patients who contracted COVID-19 after isolating for over a year and getting fully vaccinated as soon as they could. With angry tears, these patients tell me it's not fair that there are people who are choosing to endanger both themselves and the vulnerable people around them. They feel betrayed by their fellow citizens and they are bitter and angry. I cannot blame them."[28]

One affected, non-Covid patient, Betsy Phillips, a columnist for the *Nashville Scene*, expressed her anger and frustration after her pulmonary surgery was canceled because of the surge of unvaccinated Covid patients overwhelming hospitals and ICUs. In her September 7, 2021 column she wrote that the unvaccinated were "selfish assholes" and also said, "I did my part to get COVID over with as quickly as possible. And all these people who did not do their part are clogging up the hospitals. Fuck them. I'm so pissed. . . . At this point, refusing to get vaccinated when you can looks, from the outside, like a kind of self-harm that quickly spreads to harming others. Refusing to wear a mask makes you look selfish and myopic. Keeping masks off your kids looks like you're trying to get your kids and other people's kids sick. . . . [The anti-maskers and unvaccinated] will harm others to get their way. I have evidence, based on my own experience, that this is true. I have been harmed now by people refusing to get vaccinated. I will be very wary of them for the rest of my days. Maybe they don't see it as wishing me harm, but they have harmed me, and I would be a fool to give them the benefit of the doubt . . ."[29]

One of the others they harmed was 12-year-old Seth Osborn. In a late July day in 2021 he began showing signs of appendicitis, and his parents took him to the emergency room at Florida's Cleveland Clinic Martin Health North Hospital, arriving at 1:00 pm. The hospital was clogged with unvaccinated Covid patients, and he wasn't diagnosed with appendicitis until six hours after he arrived. Because the hospital was so overwhelmed, they didn't operate on him immediately and instead, at midnight, sent him to another hospital. By the time he arrived, his appendix had burst. Fortunately, the 12-year-old survived.[30]

Other victims of the unvaccinated didn't. Bellville, Texas resident, U.S. Army veteran and Purple Heart recipient Daniel Wilkinson began feeling ill in late August 2021, and his mother took him to the emergency room at the Bellville Medical Center where he was diagnosed with gallstone pancreatitis, an extremely painful and potentially deadly condition demanding immediate treatment. The Bellville Center wasn't equipped to operate on Wilkinson, and he needed immediate transfer to a facility that was equipped to do it, a facility with an ICU. Wilkinson's attending physician, Dr. Hasan Kakli, said, "I do labs on him, I get labs, and the labs come back, and I'm at the computer, and I have one of those 'Oh, crap' moments. If that stone doesn't spontaneously come out and doesn't resolve itself, that fluid just builds up, backs up into the liver, backs up into the pancreas, and starts to shut down those organs. His bloodwork even showed that his kidneys were shutting down." It took seven hours of frantic searching before Kakli found an ICU that would accept Wilkinson. But by that time it was too late. His internal organs had shut down, and he died at age 46.[31]

Wilkinson wasn't alone. Others died too, because of the irresponsibility and callousness of the unvaccinated. In early September 2021, Ray Martin DeMonia, of Cullman, Alabama died from a cardiac event in a hospital in Meridian Mississippi—200 miles from his home—after being refused admittance to ICUs at 43 hospitals across three states, because they were filled with unvaccinated Covid patients. In his obituary, his family asked, "In honor of Ray, please get vaccinated if you have not, in an effort to free up resources for non-COVID related emergencies. He would not want any other family to go through what his did."[32]

To make matters even worse (though darkly amusing), in the summer of 2021 many rural Trump worshipers, rather than getting vaccinated, turned to a new miracle cure for Covid, animal-grade ivermectin, a livestock de-wormer meant for horses and cattle. The result? There was a wave of ivermectin poisonings across the country, especially in white rural areas. Tractor Supply stores and feed stores in many areas reported that ivermectin paste was selling so fast they couldn't keep it on the shelves. Other stores put up signs warning customers that humans shouldn't take animal-grade ivermectin, and still others demanded proof of horse ownership before they would sell the paste to customers.

But why were those foolish enough to take a livestock de-wormer ODing on it? A lot of the dumbasses took doses intended for horses (which typically weigh a thousand pounds or more), with the result that they showed up at emergency rooms suffering from nausea, vomiting, temporary vision loss, and other side effects, including diarrhea, low blood pressure, and dizziness; those who poisoned themselves also risked the more serious side effects of seizures, liver damage, comas, and death.* On August 26,

---

* In Peru, where the ivermectin craze first broke out in May 2020, use of an injectible form of the livestock-grade drug led to another side effect: necrotic skin lesions.[33]

the CDC reported that "poison control centers across the U.S. received a three-fold increase in the number of calls about human exposures to ivermectin in January 2021 compared to the pre-pandemic baseline. In July 2021, ivermectin calls have continued to increase, to a five-fold increase above baseline. These reports are also associated with increased frequency of adverse effects and emergency department/hospital visits."[34]

This is more than a bit ironic in that many of the people poisoning themselves with ivermectin undoubtedly refer to those who follow the advice of public health experts as "sheeple"—while they swallowed whole the advice of right-wing bullshit artists and consumed a dangerous, ineffective (against Covid) drug intended for livestock.

On August 21, the FDA issued a warning on Twitter, in language ivermectin fans could presumably understand: "You are not a horse. You are not a cow. Seriously, y'all. Stop it." Of course, the warning had no discernible effect.

The next miracle cure, which surfaced in September, was betadine, a topical antibacterial iodine solution. *Rolling Stone* quoted New York City emergency room physician Kenneth Weinberg as saying, after being informed that anti-vaxxers were gargling with the disinfectant, "Fuck me! Of course they are."[35]

As if to illustrate the vaccine-refusers' weapons-grade ignorance, an August 2021 Ipsos poll revealed that, with the unvaccinated accounting for well over 90% of Covid hospitalizations and deaths, 27% of the unvaccinated blamed the "mainstream media" for "rising Covid-19 cases and the spread of new variants in the U.S." At the same time, a large majority of the unvaccinated refused to take personal responsibility for that rise in infections and variants: only 10% of them said that they, the unvaccinated, bore any responsibility for the rise in cases and new variants.[36]

Worse, some of the unvaccinated who contracted Covid abused the medical workers trying to help them. Dr. Wing Province, director of the Park City (Utah) Hospital, said in late September 2021 that "many" unvaccinated Covid patients were antogonistic toward medical personnel. He cited one Covid patient brought in to his hospital's emergency room:

> She, being COVID positive, spit in our nurse's face, kicked our nurse in the chest with her foot, and scratched all the technicians and everyone else that were coming in to try and put in an IV, tried to resuscitate her, calling them every name in the book. We had to close the door cause there were children in the emergency department that shouldn't be hearing the kinds of words she was using to describe our care-givers. And that was just one, who then

> gets admitted up to the ICU where we had three other patients like that, where the nurses and the technicians and the physicians that are here, literally trying to save their lives . . . are being treated like this.[37]

Dr. Province added that "family or friends of those patients have the same attitude, which means they don't want to wear masks in the hospital or observe visitor limits in hospital rooms."[38]

In the same month, on September 11, Michigan pulmonologist Matthew Trunsky posted on Facebook that he had treated eight "aggressive and combative" unvaccinated Covid patients in the previous two days. In a September 24 interview in *The Washington Post* he revealed that six of the eight had died.[39]

As bad as vaccine refusal, failure to follow public health measures, abuse of medical providers, and quack cures are, the most attention grabbing feature of the refusal to accept reality among Trump's evangelical followers was the insistence of many large churches on continuing to hold indoor services with little if any social distancing and little if any mask wearing—two effective and easy-to-implement measures—while the pandemic was raging and prior to vaccine availability.

Institutionally, the Catholic Church, mainline Protestants, the Mormon Church, and some evangelical churches acted responsibly during the pandemic. The problem was that bad-actor evangelical churches and pastors had a disproportionate impact in spreading the virus.

Let's consider one such bad actor. Chris Bartlett, the pastor of the Boaz, Alabama, Church of God, was quite explicit about his rejection of reality, his rejection of advice by public health professionals near the start of the pandemic. In a since-deleted Facebook post in mid-March 2020, a time when public health scientists had been warning for weeks against large gatherings, the Reverend Bartlett said:

> Our top priority is not primarily the safety and health of our members, but that they advance in faith and godliness even on occasions at the expense of their safety and wellbeing. Yes I believe that Jesus Christ gave up the safety and comfort of heaven . . . In light of His example we will not disassemble ourselves due to any threat to our physical bodies or status in the world.
>
> So with boldness of faith if you have the coronavirus or feel threatened by such, you are most welcome at Boaz Church of God Sunday morning at 10 AM. We will gladly anoint the sick with oil and pray the prayer of faith over you! . . . Perhaps we have the greatest opportunity in years to show forth [the] Greatness of our God!![40]

As if not to be outdone, Reverend Tony Spell of the Life Tabernacle Church in Central, Louisiana, ignored warnings against both mass gatherings and close contact, and on March 22, 2020, with 40,000 Coronavirus infections already diagnosed in the U.S., probably ten times that many undiagnosed, and with Louisiana being one of the hardest hit states, Spell had 26 buses pick up 1,825 worshipers for his megachurch's Sunday services. That works out to 70 people per bus—they were packed in like sardines.[41]

Said the Reverend Spell, "I feel the Covid-19 scare is politically motivated"; he added, "Keep going to church! Keep on worshiping God! . . . The church is a hospital for the sick!"[42] Referencing Mark 16:18, the same verse that advises believers to "take up serpents," Spell said that if any of his congregants fell ill with Coronavirus he would "address that by laying hands on them and praying for them and depending on God to heal their body."[43]

The following Sunday, March 29, Spell's megachurch held another mass meeting as did megachurches in other states, including Ohio and Florida; on the following Palm Sunday and on Easter, Spell's and many other megachurches again held services. Spell then kicked it up a notch, using Twitter to urge his marks to give him their $1200 pandemic relief checks under the hashtag #PastorSpellStimulusChallenge. In 2021, he revealed that over 200 of his dupes had done so.

Some Republican governors, notably Florida governor Ron DeSantis, went so far as to classify religious events as an essential service—and this at a time when church membership had been plummeting for decades; in 1998 about 70% of the U.S. population were church members, but by 2018 that percentage had fallen to 50%, according to Pew Research.[44] Gallup's figures align with Pew's. Gallup reports that as of 2018 only 45% of Protestants and 39% of Catholics attended their weekly "essential" services.[45] Still, given that DeSantis classified professional wrestling (the WWE) as an essential service, it's hardly surprising that he'd give similar preferential treatment to the religious extremists who comprise such an important part of the Republican base. (To be fair, Democrats have also been guilty of pandering to religious believers at the expense of public health. Like Republican-ruled states such as Florida, Texas, and Ohio, Democratic states including California and New York either classified religious worship as "essential" or issued exemptions for religious services.)

And this despite the fact that Americans strongly rejected such special treatment. Pew Research reported in August 2020 that "U.S. adults overwhelmingly say houses of worship should be required to follow the same rules about social distancing and large gatherings as other organizations or businesses in their local area. About eight-in-ten Americans (79%) take that position, four times the share who think houses of worship should be allowed more flexibility than other kinds of establishments when it comes to rules about social distancing (19%)."[46]

As depressing as all this is, there are a few bright spots. Decades ago, Frank Zappa opined, "it's too bad stupidity isn't painful." Well, now it is—in fact, it's deadly. In June 2021, the Associated Press reported that over 99% of those who died of Covid in the U.S. in May 2021 were unvaccinated.[47] With Covid vaccination readily available to any American adult or teen who wanted it, the stupidity chickens had come home to roost. (Unfortunately, they also roosted upon the innocent: with the delta variant exploding across the country during the summer of 2021, thanks to the unvaccinated, "breakthrough" cases among the fully vaccinated, though relatively rare, increased considerably. In mid-September, the CDC reported that "breakthrough" cases amounted to 18% of observed cases.)[48] But the unvaccinated still faced an inordinate risk of death. In November, the Texas Department of State Health Services reported that "Unvaccinated Texans died from COVID-19 at 40 times the rate of vaccinated Texans."[49]

As regards Covid deaths due to Christian willful ignorance, a number of pastors and, undoubtedly, many members of their flocks died after attending church services during the pandemic. They included Bishop Gerald O. Glenn of Richmond, Virginia's New Deliverance Evangelistic Church, who stated, "I firmly believe that God is larger than this dreaded virus. You can quote me on that, you can quote me on that. I am essential, I'm a preacher—I talk to God!" It was evidently a one-way conversation: on April 13, 2020 Glenn died of a Coronavirus infection.[50] Similarly, pastor and musician Landon Spradlin, who had denounced the response to the pandemic as "mass hysteria" designed to hurt Donald Trump, died of the Coronavirus after deliberately exposing himself to it by attending Mardi Gras and publicly performing at it in Coronavirus hot spot New Orleans.[51]

Such deaths continued throughout the pandemic. On September 13, 2021 the stridently anti-vaccination, anti-public health measures, and himself unvaccinated Reconstructionist preacher, podcaster, and broadcaster Bob Enyart, of the Denver Bible Church, died after contracting Covid from his likewise unvaccinated wife.

In June 2021, the Crossing Church, a megachurch with branches in three states, provided still another example of Christian willful ignorance and irresponsibility. The church holds an annual youth summer camp,

Crossing Camp, in Rushville, Illinois. Even though almost all of the campers and counselors were eligible to be vaccinated, only "a handful" were, according to the Illinois Department of Public Health.[52] The church camp, of course, didn't check for vaccination status, didn't test campers, didn't require indoor mask wearing, and didn't require social distancing. The camp apparently instituted no Covid safety measures whatsoever. The result? "At least 50 confirmed cases," later updated to "at least 85 confirmed cases." And this was the *second* Covid outbreak linked to the church that sponsored the camp.[53]

A week after the Crossing Camp outbreak, a Christian summer camp in Texas, Galveston's Clear Creek Community Church youth ministry camp, saw another mass Covid outbreak among its largely unvaccinated preteen and teenage campers and its presumably at least partially unvaccinated staff. The church's press release about the incident reads in part, "Our recent Student Ministry Camp was a wonderful experience with many of our students placing their faith in Jesus and growing in their faith. . . . Unfortunately, upon return from camp, 125+ campers and adults reported to us that they tested positive for COVID-19. Additionally, hundreds more were exposed to COVID-19 at camp. And hundreds of others were likely exposed when infected people returned home from camp."[54]

Christian mistreatment of children during the pandemic went well beyond the negligence displayed by the camps. It extended to deliberate, life-endangering mistreatment. Notwithstanding all of their hypocritical rhetoric about local control, in the spring and summer of 2021 Republican governors (all Christians) in nine states, pandering to Donald Trump's idiot base, either issued executive orders or signed laws passed by Republican legislatures banning mask mandates in schools, with some even banning private businesses from requiring customers to wear masks. Such mandates were one of the most effective means of limiting Covid transmission among the immuno-compromised and the unvaccinated, which at the time the bans were instituted included all children under 12; almost worse, these bans were instituted at a time when the more infectious delta variant was ripping through the country, sending infection rates, hospitalizations, and deaths through the roof. Not incidentally, the delta variant was also much more likely to infect children and people under 50, and to make them sicker than previous strains of the virus.

In most of the states with mask-mandate and vaccine-requirement bans, including Florida, Arizona, and Texas, these were blanket bans; the "pro-lifers" in control of state governments even prohibited local school boards from protecting children. In mid-August, months after the delta variant began to wreak havoc, with Covid cases skyrocketing nationwide, up tenfold from the low point in June and early July,[55] with a record high 1,900 children hospitalized with Covid infections,[56] and over 100,000 kids per week becoming infected, the Republican governors and legislators refused to relent. They refused to institute (or reinstitute) necessary public health measures to safeguard children's lives, and they even blocked local school districts from taking those measures. Why? The only even remotely plausible explanation is that they were playing politics with children's health and lives in order to pander to Donald Trump's proudly irrational base.

Because of the actions of these disease-enthusiast Republican governors and legislatures, tens of millions of children were exposed to Covid and millions became infected. On September 13, 2021 the CDC and American Academy of Pediatrics reported that the number of infected children had skyrocketed over the summer, and that there had been 500,000 child Covid infections in the previous two weeks. The CDC also reported that there had been almost 5.3 million child infections, and that children made up 28.9% of the infected as of early September,[57] a rate approximately 30 times higher than in June and early July due to exponential growth in childhood cases. The CDC also said that as of September 8 there had been 486 child Covid deaths in the U.S.[58] And of course the infected children infected others, including the immuno-compromised, causing additional, needless suffering and death.

How did the virus affect the children who contracted it? A large majority of them had no symptoms or mild symptoms, but most doesn't equal all, and "mild" is a relative term. UK physician Dr. Amir Khan describes what happened to his 11-year-old niece, who became only "mildly tired and had a blocked nose," and his 9-year-old nephew, Ben, who also had a mild case (not requiring hospitalization): "he had come home from school in tears, complaining of a headache and pain in his legs. While the latter symptom dissipated, the headache continued and kept him awake at night. He became overwhelmed by fatigue and was struggling to get out of bed. This lasted for a week and was accompanied by frantic phone calls from my sister . . . It was nearly two weeks before he began to feel better, and during that time not only was he missing school and vital education, he was also suffering. It made me think about all the children who were contracting COVID in school and for whom the illness was not a mild one."[59]

Much of the suffering endured by children was unnecessary: there's direct evidence that basic public health measures are effective in reducing transmission. A CDC study in September 2021 showed that following the opening of the school year, counties without school mask mandates saw over twice as many new Covid cases as counties that had universal school mask mandates.[60]* Another CDC study of nearly 1,000 schools in Maricopa County and Pima County in Arizona (basically the Phoenix and Tucson metro areas) revealed that "the odds of a school associated COVID-19 outbreak in schools with no mask requirement . . . were 3.5 times higher than those in schools with an early mask requirement."[61]

Victims of QAnon/Republican anti-vax, anti-public health lunacy who don't die often face long-term health problems. Penn State Medical College researchers analyzed data on over 250,000 unvaccinated children and adults who had been diagnosed with Covid (and survived), with most of them having been hospitalized. The researchers concluded that "More than half of the 236 million people who have been diagnosed with COVID-19 worldwide since December 2019 will experience post-COVID symptoms—more commonly known as 'long COVID' . . . Overall, one in two survivors experienced long-term COVID manifestations. The rates remained largely constant from one month through six or more months after their initial illness." The researchers reported that common symptoms of "long Covid" include weight loss, fatigue, fever, chest pain, decreased mobility, difficulty concentrating, difficulty breathing, hair loss, rashes, vomiting, and diarrhea.[62] (Of course, not all "long Covid" sufferers experience all or even most of these symptoms, but experiencing any of them for months, perhaps years, on end is a frightening prospect.)

The Penn state conclusions were in line with the results of other studies. A September 2021 UK study published in the journal *PLOS Medicine* showed that the incidence of long Covid symptoms among nearly 274,000 nonhospitalized patients was 57% during the entire six-month study period, and 36.5% in the three-to-six-months period.[63] A much smaller study showed that 52% of 247 nonhospitalized Norwegian Covid patients had long-Covid symptoms six months after diagnosis.[64] And a longer-term study of 2,433 hospitalized patients in Wuhan, China, the site of the initial outbreak, showed that 45% were suffering from at least one long-Covid symptom a year after discharge.[65]

---

* Near the end of that month, the number of Covid deaths in the U.S. exceeded 2,000 per day over a period of most of a week, a more than tenfold increase over the low point of an average of 186 per day in early July. To put this in perspective, the 2,000+ deaths per day in the U.S. in late September 2021 nearly equaled all of the Covid deaths in South Korea over the entirety of the pandemic to that point. The difference? South Korea instituted and followed basic public health measures nationwide during the entire pandemic.

To make matters even worse, 16 Republican-controlled states, overlapping those with bans on mask mandates, also banned schools and universities from requiring that students be vaccinated. One of those states, Tennessee, passed a law prohibiting the state's health commissioner from adding Covid-19 vaccination to the list of required vaccinations for school children. Two Republican-controlled states, Montana and Texas, even banned privately owned businesses from instituting vaccine mandates for their employees, despite decades of hypocritical Republican rhetoric about private property owners' rights.

To cite but one instance of how these dangerous, irresponsible policies played out, consider the case of Arizona. Under its stridently anti-public-health Republican governor, Doug Ducey, during the first 19 months of the pandemic (3/17/20 to 10/24/21) Covid was the leading cause of death in Arizona, beating out cancer and heart disease. In comparison with two comparable-size Western states, the number of Covid deaths was far higher in Arizona (20,500) than in Colorado (7,917) or Washington (8,234), where state governments implemented standard public health measures. An analysis of CDC data by the Arizona Public Health Association showed that over 10,000 of the Covid deaths in Arizona were preventable; over 10,000 people died because of the malfeasance of Arizona's "pro-life" governor. Adjusted for population differences, the Covid death rate in Arizona was over twice as high as in Colorado, and over two-and-a-half times higher than in Washington.[66]

What was the Republican excuse for the dangerous and deadly policies that directly led to these unnecessary deaths? "Freedom," which is an abbreviated version of their slogan, "Freedom to expose others to a deadly disease!" And these people crying "freedom!" were and are, by and large, the same intrusive, authoritarian jerks who want to throw people in jail for smoking pot, throw gay people in jail for having sex, and who want the state to dictate women's most personal healthcare decisions. (Ironically, cops, who make a career of forcing others to follow government mandates—laws—were among the biggest whiners; they were among the most mask- and vaccine-resistant segments of the public.)

While the mask-mandate and vaccine-requirement bans were among the most egregious of the willful ignorance-created, avoidable horrors during the Covid pandemic, they hardly appeared in a vacuum: some evangelical Christians, including prominent preachers, encouraged this idiocy.

And some of them paid the price. Reports of science-denying pastors dying from the Coronavirus appeared almost from the start of the outbreak. In November 2020, the Reverend Irving Baxter, founder of Endtimes Ministries, died from Covid. In March of that year Baxter had appeared on televangelist (and convicted felon and fraudster) Jim Bakker's show to explain why America was being afflicted with the Coronavirus pandemic: fornication! "Fifteen million people . . . are living together unmarried. And that's increased over the last 10 years by 138%. Now, in addition to that—I hope this research is not correct, but I got it straight from the encyclopedia—it says that 5% of new brides in America now are virgins. That means 95% have already committed fornication!"[67] Well, that explains everything including, perhaps, Baxter's subsequent demise from Covid-19—one possible explanation for his infection and death being that the Almighty was displeased with Baxter's undisclosed past behavior and decided that judgment is a dish best served cold.

If Covid-19 deaths were limited to plague enthusiasts such as Baxter—and the above-mentioned reverends Enyart, Glenn, and Spradlin—one would have little sympathy; but their irresponsibility led to the unnecessary exposure of innocent people (children, grocery store workers, doctors, nurses, first responders, et al.), and has undoubtedly led to much unnecessary infection, suffering, and death. Almost worse, while Trump voters (largely made up of evangelicals, conservative Catholics, and Mormons) are relatively well off and overwhelmingly white, the death toll from the virus fell predominantly upon the poor, a disproportionate number of whom are black, brown, and indigenous, with the Mayo Clinic reporting that the Covid death rate among black and hispanic Americans was 4.7 times higher than among white Americans.[68*]

Much of this death and suffering was unnecessary. Many outbreaks have been linked to super-spreader church services, not only in the U.S., but in other countries as well. An early example occurred in South Korea in February 2020, when a majority of the country's cases were among members of the secretive Shincheonji Church of Jesus; over 5,000 Covid cases have been linked to that church.[69] Since then, at least some South Korean

---

* There are several reasons for this disparity. One is that black, indigenous, and hispanic people tend to be poorer than white people, tend to have poorer nutrition, less and worse access to healthcare, and so tend to have poorer health than whites. They (especially hispanics) also tend to live in larger households than whites, and so have more household routes to infection than whites. Another reason for the disparity is that minorities tend to work in low paying jobs where there's a lot of public contact (e.g., restaurant, grocery store, clerk, and cashier jobs). A third reason is that their vaccine hesitancy is due, at least in part, to a history of neglect and condescension by the medical community, and (especially among black Americans) occasionally being the subjects of horrific medical experimentation.

Christians have kept up their irresponsible behavior. According to a January 2021 piece in the *South China Morning Post*, "Fringe Protestant groups have been linked to major outbreaks."[70]

One of those outbreaks was in a "tiny rural church" in the village of Cheonan: of the town's 427 residents, "at least 241 people linked to the religious community had tested positive for Coronavirus."[71] Such outbreaks make South Korea's "fringe Protestants" a distinct outlier in that country, where the Covid-19 response has been exemplary, in large part because of the responsible behavior of the nation's people, who by and large have followed public health mandates.

But, as you'd expect, the worst problems regarding Christian irresponsibility, entitlement, and threats to public health have been in the United States. In mid-March 2020, when the pandemic was spreading rapidly in the U.S., with the death toll already ramping up—and governors and public health officials already urging, and in some cases ordering, social distancing, avoidance of social gatherings, and self-isolation—"nearly a fifth of religious Americans said they were still attending in-person services."[72] That percentage likely held steady or increased in the following months: in August 2020, Pew Research reported that 63% of regular churchgoers (those going to church at least once a month) said they were either confident (29%) or very confident (34%) "they could safely attend religious services in person . . . without spreading or catching the coronavirus."[73] This was months before the first Covid vaccine was available.

As for actual behavior, evangelicals were more irresponsible than other Christians. In May 2020, 1% of mainline Protestants were attending "in person at least weekly" services, as were 5% of Catholics, and 11% of evangelicals. In December 2021, with the super-infectious omicron variant sweeping the country, the numbers were even worse: 14% of mainline Protestants, 26% of Catholics, and 37% of evangelicals were attending weekly services.[74]

Displaying yet another aspect of Christian denial of reality, Reverend Jeffrey Whittaker, of Michiana Christian Embassy in Niles Michigan, blamed 71-year-old church member Les Tom, who died of Covid in mid-December 2020, for his own death. Did he blame him for being reckless enough to attend dangerous indoor religious services during a pandemic? No. Whittaker said of Tom, "he died of COVID because he's weak, because he has no faith."[75]

As of summer 2021, the pandemic was still raging and over 600,000 Americans were already dead, but many churches and megachurches continued to hold indoor services, with attendance at some churches well up into the thousands. Perhaps even worse, a fair number of pastors discouraged their flocks from being vaccinated.

One example was the previously mentioned Reverend Spell, who continued doing the Lord's work by discouraging congregants from getting vaccinated or wearing protective masks, and saying, "if being anti-mask and anti-vaccine is anti-government, then I'm proud to be anti-government."[76] In June 2021, Spell did more work for the Lord by poaching an alligator out of season. He was dumb enough to post a video of himself with the dead 'gator on Instagram, and was subsequently cited for poaching by officers of the Louisiana Department of Wildlife and Fisheries, who confiscated the carcass from Spell behind his church.[77,78]

To be fair, a good majority of evangelical pastors aren't as benighted as Spell—at least as regards Covid vaccination and, presumably, shooting 'gators out of season—but there's plenty of motivation for the bad actors: University of Oklahoma sociologist Samuel Perry states that fearmongers such as Spell "have an incentive to keep stoking that fear [of vaccination] because people keep clicking, and people keep listening."[79] He could have added, "and keep giving money."

So, it should be no surprise that of all American religious groups, white evangelicals are the most resistant to Coronavirus vaccination. In early April 2021, 40% of them said they were hesitant, would be vaccinated only if required to do so, or, in most cases, would outright refuse.[80] In the following three months, that number didn't budge an inch,[81] despite mounting evidence that the vaccines available in the U.S. are highly effective, that there have been almost no reports of serious adverse reactions, that more infectious Covid variants were emerging, and that vaccination was effective against them, too. (The partially vaccine resistant omicron variant which surfaced in November 2021 was approximately three times as infectious as the already highly infectious delta variant, though somewhat less severe.)

How have evangelical clergymen, who had to be aware of all this, reacted? Some acted in a responsible manner, but others didn't. According to a *Politico* report, "Biden administration and state officials hoped that pastors would play an outsized role in promoting Covid-19 vaccines, but many are wary of alienating their congregants and are declining requests to be more outspoken." Why? Some pastors have simply given up, and others "said they have already lost congregants to fights over coronavirus restrictions and fear risking further desertions by promoting vaccinations."[81] So, these clergymen chose their careers and pocketbooks over the health and wellbeing of their congregants and the public.

An October 2021 Pew Research poll reported that by a three-to-two margin churchgoers in all denominations said their pastors had either discouraged vaccination (5%) or hadn't "said much about the vaccines either way"(54%). Black evangelicals were the only religious group where most pastors (62%) had encouraged vaccination, while white evangelical pastors were the least likely (21%) to encourage it, with 4% discouraging vaccination, and a whopping 75% saying little (or, one suspects, nothing) about it. A majority of the pastors in *all* American Christian churches, with the sole exception of black evangelicals, kept silent about the deadly Covid threat to their congregations and the rest of their communities.[83]

Meanwhile, snake oil salesmen such as Tony Spell continued to rail against vaccination, in effect encouraging their flocks to expose themselves and others to a deadly disease, and to have an outsize role in spreading it. Unfortunately, that outsize role is almost certain to persist. Natural immunity following infection wanes with time, and as of fall 2021 reinfection, due largely to the highly infectious delta variant, was skyrocketing. There were self-reports from previously infected, unvaccinated individuals of "catching Sars-CoV-2 for a second or even third time." Analysis of the reinfection data "suggested that unvaccinated individuals should expect to be reinfected with Covid-19 every 16 months, on average."[84] And of course, they'll spread the disease to others. This terrible situation became even worse with the appearance of the omicron variant in late November 2021, which is as infectious as measles, so for the unvaccinated it's become a matter of when and how often, not if, they'll become reinfected—and then infect others.

As if to underline the deep sense of entitlement many Christians have, and their disregard for the health and wellbeing of others, many churches held packed indoor Christmas Eve services in 2020, sans masks or social distancing, and prior to the national vaccine rollout. Unsurprisingly, there was a huge post-Christmas spike in Covid infections and deaths.

Two megachurches in Albuquerque, Legacy Church and Calvary Church, held such services and even had the brass balls to put videos of them up on Instagram. This prompted New Mexico Governor Michelle Grisham's spokesperson, Tripp Stelnicki, to comment, "They endangered the lives, livelihoods and health of not only their parishioners but their entire communities—and given how quickly this virus can spread, potentially our state as a whole."[85]

One rarely sees a clearer example of the awesome good done in the name of Jesus.

Endnotes

1. "The Maji Maji Rebellion." Emory University. https://scholarblogs.emory.edu/violenceinafrica/sample-page/the-maji-maji-rebellion-2/ < https://tinyurl.com/y5o2ho7l >

2. "Wakefield's aticle linking MMR vaccine and autism was fraudulent," by Fione Godley et al. *British Medical Journal* 342, January 6, 2011. https://www.bmj.com/content/342/bmj.c7452 < https://tinyurl.com/ybntmdzd >

3. "How the vaccine crisis was meant to make money," by Brian Deer. *British Medical Journal* 342, January 11, 2911. https://www.bmj.com/content/342/bmj.c5258 < https://tinyurl.com/y65naxz6 >

4. "More than 140,000 die from measles as cases surge worldwide." World Health Organization. https://www.who.int/news/item/05-12-2019-more-than-140-000-die-from-measles-as-cases-surge-worldwide < https://tinyurl.com/y4x6dfka >

5. "Measles History: Pre-vaccine Era." Centers for Disease Control. https://www.cdc.gov/measles/about/history.html < https://tinyurl.com/y58a22lp >

6. "Vaccine Safety Basics: Rates of Adverse Vaccine Reactions, Module 3." World Health Organization. https://vaccine-safety-training.org/rates-of-adverse-vaccine-reactions.html < https://tinyurl.com/9sabva6b >

7. "How QAnon Conspiracy Is Spreading In Christian Communities Across The U.S." National Public Radio, August 21, 2020. https://www.npr.org/2020/08/21/904798097/how-QAnon-conspiracy-is-spreading-in-christian-communities-across-the-u-s < https://tinyurl.com/y3n5ta4q >

8. "Journalist Enters The World Of QAnon: 'It's Almost Like A Bad Spy Novel'," by Dave Davies. WUNC, North Carolina Public Radio, August 20, 2020. https://www.wunc.org/post/journalist-enters-world-QAnon-its-almost-bad-spy-novel < https://tinyurl.com/y66pzxyx >

9. "COVID-19 outbreak forces closure of Manatee government headquarters. 2 people have died," by Jessica de Leon and Ryan Callahan. *Bradenton Herald*, June 18, 2021. https://www.bradenton.com/news/coronavirus/article252212853.html?utm_source=fark&utm_medium=website&utm_content=link&ICID=ref_fark < https://tinyurl.com/8ex4phry >

10. Ibid.

11. "Nearly all COVID deaths in US are now among the unvaccinated," by Carla K. Johnson and Mike Stobbe. Associated Press, June 29, 2021. https://apnews.com/article/coronavirus-pandemic-health-941fcf43d9731c76c16e7354f5d5e187 < https://tinyurl.com/kyzr53fn >

12. "Vaccinated health workers at West Hoxton birthday party didn't contract COVID-19, NSW Health reveals," by Kevin Nguyen. Australian Broadcasting Corporation, June 26, 2021. https://www.abc.net.au/news/2021-06-28/vaccinated-attendees-west-hoxton-birthday-party-avoid-covid-19/100249612?utm_source=fark&utm_medium=website&utm_content=link&ICID=ref_fark < https://tinyurl.com/dj7p9nf5 >

13. "Oregon counties request trucks for bodies as Covid overwhelms morgues," by Dani Anguiano. *The Guardian*, August 30, 2021. https://www.theguardian.com/us-news/2021/aug/30/oregon-corona-virus-deaths-hospitals-morgues < https://tinyurl.com/ys2pcz3v >

14. "Revealed: Guardian/KHN find nearly 3,000 US health workers died of Covid," by Christina Jewett, et al. *The Guardian*, December 23, 2020. https://www.theguardian.com/us-news/2020/dec/23/us-healthcare-worker-deaths-covid-19-pandemic < https://tinyurl.com/y8hgtet7 >

15. "Our key findings about US healthcare worker deaths in the pandemic's first year." *The Guardian*, April 8, 2021. https://www.theguardian.com/us-news/ng-interactive/2020/dec/22/lost-on-the-front-line-our-findings-to-date < https://tinyurl.com/46ek8jd8 >

16. "Behavior and the dynamics of epidemics," by Andrew G. Atkenson. Brookings Institute, March 24, 2001. https://www.brookings.edu/bpea-articles/behavior-and-the-dynamic-of-epidemics/ < https://tinyurl.com/nrj6v6en >

17. "Trump reveals he did the 'opposite' of what Dr. Fauci recommended during pandemic," by Bob Bingham. *Raw Story*, March 25, 2021. https://www.rawstory.com/donald-trump-dr-fauci/ < https://tinyurl.com/n63s85sc >

18. "Just 50% of Americans plan to take a Covid-19 vaccine," by Warren Cornwall. *Science,* June 30, 2020. https://www.sciencemag.org/news/2020/06/just-50-americans-plan-get-covid-19-vaccine-here-s-how-win-over-rest < https://tinyurl.com/ybangbqv >

19. "STAT-Harris Poll: The share of Americans interested in getting Covid-19 vaccine as soon as possible is dropping," by Ed Silverman. *Stat News*, October 19, 2020. https://www.statnews.com/pharmalot/2020/10/19/covid19-coronavirus-pandemic-vaccine-racial-disparities/ < https://tinyurl.com/y6ngaslw >

20. "Poll shows 61 percent of Americans likely to take COVID-19 vaccine," by David Beard. *National Geographic.* https://www.nationalgeographic.com/science/2020/12/poll-shows-61-percent-americans-likely-to-take-coronavirus-vaccine/ < https://tinyurl.com/yx92o7tt >

21. "CNBC poll shows very little will persuade unvaccinated Americans to get Covid shots," by Robert Towey. CNBC, September 10, 2021. https://www.cnbc.com/2021/09/10/cnbc-poll-shows-very-little-will-persuade-unvaccinated-americans-to-get-covid-shots.html?utm_source=fark&utm_medium=website&utm_content=link&ICID=ref_fark < https://tinyurl.com/7w8zm63b >

22. "Herd immunity and COVID-19 (coronavirus): What you need to know." Mayo Clinic. https://www.mayoclinic.org/diseases-conditions/coronavirus/in-depth/herd-immunity-and-coronavirus/art-20486808 < https://tinyurl.com/yca5fyun >

23. Ibid.

24. "Vaccine slowdowns in the wealthy West could incubate the next disaster in the Covid crisis," by Luke McGee. CNN Health, September 4, 2021. https://edition.cnn.com/2021/09/04/health/vaccine-rollout-slowdown-intl-cmd/index.html < https://tinyurl.com/6scsxnz2 >

25. Towey, op. cit.

24. "KFF COVID-19 Vaccine Monitor: March 2021," by Liz Hamel et al. Kaiser Family Foundation. https://www.kff.org/coronavirus-covid-19/poll-finding/kff-covid-19-vaccine-monitor-march-2021/ < https://tinyurl.com/6u2uratz >

25. "Tennessee Vaccine Messaging Study." https://www.tn.gov/content/dam/tn/health/documents/Vaccine-Messaging-Market-Survey-Executive-Summary-Reports.pdf < https://tinyurl.com/2frbyu9y >

26. "COVID-19 deaths eclipse 700,000 in US as delta variant rages," by Tammy Webber and Heather Hollingsworth. Associated Press, October 2, 2021. https://apnews.com/article/coronavirus-pandemic-dead-us-milestone-80209c66802902e42adfbe075ff5272b < https://tinyurl.com/4sn55tj3 >

27. "Covid cases are surging in Europe. America is in denial about what lies in store for it," by Eric Topol. *The Guardian*, November 12, 2021. https://www.theguardian.com/commentisfree/2021/nov/12/covid-cases-surging-europe-america-denial < https://tinyurl.com/4j9kn8rc >

28. "I'm An ICU Doctor And I Cannot Believe The Things Unvaccinated Patients Are Telling Me," by Thamh Neville, MD. *Huffington Post*, August 1, 2021. https://www.huffpost.com/entry/icu-doctor-health-care-workers-unvaccinated-patients_n_6102ad2ae4b000b997df1f17 < https://tinyurl.com/y7sjkfsw >

29. "Hospitals Are Full of Unvaccinated COVID Patients, and It's Hurting Others," by Betsy Phillips. *Nashville Scene*, September 7, 2021. https://www.nashvillescene.com/news/pithinthewind/hospitals-are-full-of-unvaccinated-covid-patients-and-its-hurting-others/article_b2e91460-0f33-11ec-919c-638d85f0904a.html < https://tinyurl.com/3ku3hcb4 >

30. "A Boy Went to a COVID-Swamped ER. He Waited for Hours. Then His Appendix Burst," by Jenny Deam. *ProPublica*, September 15, 2021. https://www.propublica.org/article/a-boy-went-to-a-covid-swamped-er-he-waited-for-hours-then-his-appendix-burst?utm_source=fark&utm_medium=website&utm_content=link&ICID=ref_fark < https://tinyurl.com/48hktac5 >

31. "Veteran dies of treatable illness as COVID fills hospital beds, leaving doctors 'playing musical chairs.'" CBS News, August 27, 2021. https://www.cbsnews.com/news/covid-us-hospital-icu-bed-shortage-veteran-dies-treatable-illness/ < https://tinyurl.com/76shphjt >

32. "Alabama man dies of cardiac event after 43 hospitals with full ICUs turned him away," by Hadley Hitson. *USA Today/Montgomery Advertiser*, September 10, 2021. https://www.usatoday.com/story/news/health/2021/09/10/cullman-al-man-dies-hospitals-full-icus-turn-away-covid/8281712002/ < https://tinyurl.com/ru95ke9e >

33. "Rapid Increase in Ivermectin Prescriptions and Reports of Severe Illness Associated with Use of Products Containing Ivermectin to Prevent or Treat COVID-19." Centers for Disease Control and Prevention, Health Alert Network, August 26, 2021. https://emergency.cdc.gov/han/2021/han00449.asp < https://tinyurl.com/5cy59yh5 >

34. "Desperation, misinformation: how the ivermectin craze spread across the world," by Nick Robins-Early. *The Guardian*, September 25, 2021. https://www.theguardian.com/world/2021/sep/24/ivermectin-covid-peru-misinformation < https://tinyurl.com/49hcdnjy >

35. "Anti-vaxxers Are Now Gargling Iodine to Prevent Covid-19," by E.J. Erickson. *Rolling Stone*, September 13, 2021. https://www.rollingstone.com/culture/culture-news/betadine-anti-vaxxer-covid-treatment-iodine-1225438/ < https://tinyurl.com/37n6hhj6 >

36. "As Delta surges, poll data suggests that unvaccinated America's opposition to the shots is declining." Ipsos, August 3, 2021. https://www.ipsos.com/en-us/news-polls/axios-ipsos-coronavirus-index?utm_source=newsletter&utm_medium=email&utm_campaign=newsletter_axiosam&stream=top < https://tinyurl.com/3w7b6xan >

37. "Park City Hospital Dr. Reports That Unvaccinated COVID Patients Can Be Abusive," by Rick Brough. KPCW, September 14, 2021. https://www.kpcw.org/post/park-city-hospital-dr-reports-unvaccinated-covid-patients-can-be-abusive#stream/0 < https://tinyurl.com/5us69dc7 >

38. Ibid.

39. "After a Michigan doctor wrote about combative COVID-19 patients, most of them died," by Joseph Choi. *The Hill*, September 26, 2021. https://thehill.com/homenews/state-watch/574000-michigan-doctor-says-some-patients-denying-covid-19-diagnosis-dismissing < https://tinyurl.com/3chcn2r7 >

40. "Boaz, AL Pastor Invites Coronavirus Infected To Service," by Brent Wilson. *Bama Politics*, March 17, 2020. https://www.bamapolitics.com/51007/boaz-al-pastor-invites-coronavirus-infected-to-service/ < https://tinyurl.com/s96px2o >

41. "Central church hosts more than 1,800 people amid covid-19 outbreak," by Abbi Rocha. *brproud*, March 22, 2020. https://www.brproud.com/health/coronavirus/central-church-hosts-1800-people-amid-covid-19-outbreak/?utm_source=fark&utm_medium=website&utm_content=link&ICID=ref_fark < https://tinyurl.com/y4le9lal >

42. "A Louisiana pastor defies a state order and holds a church service with hundreds of people." WTVA/CNN, March 19, 2020. https://www.wtva.com/content/news/568926132.html < https://tinyurl.com/yxfvhez5 >

43. Rocha, op. cit.

44. "In U.S., Decline of Christianity Continues at Rapid Pace." Pew Research Center, October 10, 2017. https://www.pewforum.org/2019/10/17/in-u-s-decline-of-christianity-continues-at-rapid-pace/ < https://tinyurl.com/y54m8cjv >

45. "Catholics' Church Attendance Resumes Downward Slide." Gallup, April 9, 2018. https://news.gallup.com/poll/232226/church-attendance-among-catholics-resumes-downward-slide.aspx < https://tinyurl.com/yarasec6 >

46. "Americans Oppose Religious Exemptions From Coronavirus-Related Restrictions." Pew Research Center, August 7, 2020. https://www.pewforum.org/2020/08/07/americans-oppose-religious-exemptions-from-coronavirus-related-restrictions/ < https://tinyurl.com/yyczo3ly >

47. "Nearly all COVID deaths in US are now among unvaccinated," by Carla K. Johnson and Mike Stobbe. Associated Press, June 24, 2021. https://apnews.com/article/coronavirus-pandemic-health-941fcf43d9731c76c16e7354f5d5e187 < https://tinyurl.com/9488ned3 >

48. "Unvaccinated people 11 times more likely to die from COVID-19, CDC study shows," by Alexander Tin. CBS News, September 11, 2021. https://www.cbsnews.com/news/covid-19-vaccine-deaths-unvaccinated-cdc-study/ < https://tinyurl.com/48thxnp5 >

49. "Unvaccinated Texans 45x more likely to test positive for COVID, 40x more likely to die, according to new health department study," by William Joy. WFAA, November 8, 2021. https://www.wfaa.com/article/news/health/coronavirus/vaccine/covid-texas-unvaccinated-more-likely-test-positive-die/287-b701299a-1796-463f-855a-7c3ac27e46b2?utm_source=fark&utm_medium=website&utm_content=link&ICID=ref_fark < https://tinyurl.com/drau5w62 >

50. "Virginia pastor who defiantly held church service dies of coronavirus," by Lee Brown. *New York Post*, April 4, 2013. https://nypost.com/2020/04/13/virginia-pastor-who-held-packed-church-service-dies-of-coronavirus/?utm_source=twitter_sitebuttons&utm_medium=site+buttons&utm_campaign=-site+buttons&fbclid=IwAR1n5Hoz76UEZz3GRac5WbE8PtD0dAWIUaiwj-w2BaCWWgzqpgQvqZ9w5YA < https://tinyurl.com/yxyvl2mg >

51. "Virginia Pastor Dies From Coronavirus After Previously Saying 'Media Is Pumping Out Fear' About Pandemic," by Ewan Palmer. *Newsweek*, March 27, 2020. https://www.newsweek.com/virginia-pastor-dies-coronavirus-after-previously-saying-media-pumping-out-fear-about-pandemic-1494702 < https://tinyurl.com/yxya8ucw >

52. "At least 85 COVID cases now linked to central Illinois summer camp," by Angie Leventis Lourgos. *Chicago Tribune/Peoria Journal Star*, June 29, 2021. https://amp.pjstar.com/amp/5358386001 < https://tinyurl.com/2bjfsum9 >

53. Ibid.

54. "A people, not a place: Covid Updates and Response." Clear Creek Community Church, July 3, 2021. https://www.clearcreek.org/covid19/ < https://tinyurl.com/f97d4pey >

55. "Trends in Number of COVID-19 Cases and Deaths in the US Reported to CDC, by State/Territory." Covid Data Tracker, Centers for Disease Control and Prevention, August 14, 2021. https://covid.cdc.gov/covid-data-tracker/#trends_dailytrendscases < https://tinyurl.com/34emtp2x >

56. "Children hospitalized with COVID-19 in U.S. hits record," by Gabriella Borter. Associated Press, August 14, 2021. https://www.reuters.com/world/us/children-hospitalized-with-covid-19-us-hits-record-number-2021-08-14/ < https://tinyurl.com/5b935y7c >

57. "Children and COVID-19: State-Level Data Report." American Academy of Pediatrics, September 13, 2021. https://www.aap.org/en/pages/2019-novel-coronavirus-covid-19-infections/children-and-covid-19-state-level-data-report/ < https://tinyurl.com/c4zs47vz >

58. "Provisional COVID-19 Deaths: Focus on Ages 0-18." Centers for Disease Control, September 8, 2021. https://data.cdc.gov/NCHS/Provisional-COVID-19-Deaths-Focus-on-Ages-0-18-Yea/nr4s-juj3 < https://tinyurl.com/4u2hhbx4 >

59. "Do COVID vaccines prevent transmission of the virus?," by Dr. Amir Khan. *Al Jazeera*, October 13, 2021. https://www.aljazeera.com/features/2021/10/13/do-coronavirus-vaccines-prevent-transmission-of-the-virus < https://tinyurl.com/y82h3eyc >

60. "Pediatric COVID-19 Cases in Counties With and Without School Mask Requirements—United States, July 1–September 4, 2021," by Samantha E. Budzyn, MPH, et al. CDC Morbidity and Mortality Weekly Report, September 24, 2021. https://www.cdc.gov/mmwr/volumes/70/wr/mm7039e3.htm?s_cid=mm7039e3_w < https://tinyurl.com/by7r5kxt >

61. "Association Between K–12 School Mask Policies and School-Associated COVID-19 Outbreaks—Maricopa and Pima Counties, Arizona, July–August 2021," by Megan Jehn, PhD, et al. CDC Morbidity and Mortality Weekly Report, September 24, 2021. https://www.cdc.gov/mmwr/volumes/70/wr/mm7039e1.htm?s_cid=mm7039e1_w < https://tinyurl.com/5a2ycaae >

62. "How many people get 'long COVID?' More than half, researchers find," University of Pennsylvania, Medical Xpress, October 13, 2021. https://medicalxpress.com/news/2021-10-people-covid.html?utm_source=fark&utm_medium=website&utm_content=link&ICID=ref_fark < https://tinyurl.com/wkuv4err >

63. "Incidence, co-occurrence, and evolution of long-COVID features: A 6-month retrospective cohort study of 273,618 survivors of COVID-19," by MaximeTaquet, et al. *PLOS Medicine*, September 28, 2021. https://journals.plos.org/plosmedicine/article?id=10.1371/journal.pmed.1003773#pmed.1003773.s003 < https://tinyurl.com/9hutc66y >

64. "Long COVID in a prospective cohort of home-isolated patients," by Bjorn Blomberg, et al. *Nature Medicine*, June 23, 2021. https://www.nature.com/articles/s41591-021-01433-3?utm_medium=affiliate&utm_source=commission_junction&utm_campaign=3_nsn6445_deeplink_PID100017430&utm_content=deeplink < https://tinyurl.com/zdjy5zx8 >

65. "Symptoms and Health Outcomes Among Survivors of COVID-19 Infection 1 Year After Discharge From Hospitals in Wuhan, China," by Xue Zhang, et al. JAMA Network. https://jamanetwork.com/journals/jamanetworkopen/fullarticle/2784558 < https://tinyurl.com/4ckx7adt >

66. "Covid-19 as the leading cause of death in Arizona during the pandemic: An evidence review," by Alan N. Williams and Will Humble. Arizona Public Health Association, October 20, 2021. http://azpha.wildapricot.org/resources/Documents/2020-2021%20Leading%20Causes%20of%20Death%20October%2020%202021%20Final%20Final.pdf < https://tinyurl.com/j8d67ejk >

67. "Pastor Who Blamed COVID on People Who 'Committed Fornication' Dies of COVID," by Hemant Mehta. *Friendly Atheist*, November 5, 2020. https://friendlyatheist.patheos.com/2020/11/05/pastor-who-blamed-covid-on-people-who-committed-fornication-dies-of-covid/?utm_source=dlvr.it&utm_medium=twitter < https://tinyurl.com/y66dmdmz >

68. "Coronavirus infection by race: What's behind the health disparities?," by Dr. William F. Marshall, III. Mayo Clinic. https://www.mayoclinic.org/diseases-conditions/coronavirus/expert-answers/coronavirus-infection-by-race/faq-20488802 < https://tinyurl.com/23js6f44 >

69. "Religious cult at center of South Korea's new Covid outbreak; daily cases hit record high." Reuters/CNBC, November 24, 2021. https://www.cnbc.com/2021/11/24/south-korea-covid-latest-updates.html < https://tinyurl.com/e9dzrc >

70. "Coronavirus hotspots: anger in South Korea as fringe church schools drop masks, put faith in God," by Park Chan-kyong. *South China Morning Post*, January 29, 2021. https://www.scmp.com/week-asia/health-environment/article/3119633/coronavirus-hotspots-anger-south-korea-fringe-church < https://tinyurl.com/qhhemuz6 >

71. Reuters/CNBC, op. cit.

72. "'My President Is Not My God': Some Churches Are Planning To Host Hundreds For Easter Sunday Services Despite The Coronavirus," by Ema O'Connor and Kadia Goba. *Buzzfeed News*, April 11, 2020. https://www.buzzfeednews.com/article/emaoconnor/churches-easter-services-coronavirus-outbreak < https://tinyurl.com/y6rhdqte >

73. Pew Research Center, August 7, 2020, op. cit.

74. "Across US, houses of worship struggle to rebuild attendance," by David Crary. ABC News, December 19, 2021. https://abcnews.go.com/Health/wireStory/us-houses-worship-struggle-rebuild-attendance-81843150?utm_source=fark&utm_medium=website&utm_content=link&ICID=ref_fark < https://tinyurl.com/bdhsjafe >

75. "Pastor Mocked Follower's COVID Death in Sermon," by Hemant Mehta. *Friendly Atheist*, December 31, 2020. https://friendlyatheist.patheos.com/2020/12/31/pastor-mocked-followers-covid-death-in-sermon-hes-weak-he-has-no-faith/ < https://tinyurl.com/y6h64yao >

76. "Many Evangelicals say they won't be vaccinated against Covid-19. Some experts say distrust and misinformation have played a role," by Elle Reeve, et al. CNN, April 14, 2021. https://www.cnn.com/2021/04/14/us/covid-vaccine-evangelicals/index.html < https://tinyurl.com/s8nwu4sc >

77. "Pastor Tony Spell, known for flouting COVID rules, cited for illegal alligator hunting," by Jennifer Wadsworth and James Finn. *The Advocate*, June 11, 2021. https://www.theadvocate.com/baton_rouge/news/article_1ba36974-cadd-11eb-a4ea-13587bf53024.html < https://tinyurl.com/4rpp5ncd >

78. "Pastor Tony Spell: We Won a Major Legal Battle '100%'," by Hemant Mehta. *Friendly Atheist*, June 12, 2021. https://friendlyatheist.patheos.com/2021/06/12/pastor-tony-spell-we-won-a-major-legal-battle-100-the-court-says-otherwise/ < https://tinyurl.com/3enk76n3 >

79. Reeve et al., op. cit.

80. "Survey: 'Faith-Based Approaches' Could Help Convince Millions of Americans to Get COVID-19 Vaccines," by Madeleine Carlisle. *Time*, April 22, 2021. https://time.com/5957032/religion-covid-19-vaccine-hesitancy-survey/ < https://tinyurl.com/34uanmbk >

81. "KFF COVID-19 Vaccine Monitor: June 2021," by Liz Hamel, et al. Kaiser Family Foundation, June 30, 2021. https://www.kff.org/coronavirus-covid-19/poll-finding/kff-covid-19-vaccine-monitor-june-2021/ < https://tinyurl.com/6sm46rs >

82. "'Wasting my breath': Southern faith leaders wary of promoting vaccines," by Dan Goldberg. *Politico*, July 3, 2021. https://www.politico.com/news/2021/07/03/southern-pastors-vaccines-497898 < https://tinyurl.com/p9rv33w7 >

83. "Most Americans Who Go to Religious Services Say They Would Trust Their Clergy's Advice on COVID-19 Vaccines." Pew Research Center, October 15, 2021. https://www.pewforum.org/2021/10/15/most-americans-who-go-to-religious-services-say-they-would-trust-their-clergys-advice-on-covid-19-vaccines/ < https://tinyurl.com/3ewujddj >

84. "Without Covid-19 jab, 'reinfection may occur every 16 months'," by Linda Geddes. *The Guardian*, October 19, 2021. https://www.theguardian.com/world/2021/oct/19/without-covid-19-jab-reinfection-may-occur-every-16-months-say-scientists < https://tinyurl.com/rwza5xjw >

85. "2 New Mexico megachurches fined over packed Christmas Eve services," by Bill Hutchinson. ABC News, December 29, 2020. https://abcnews.go.com/US/mexico-megachurches-fined-packed-christmas-eve-services/story?id=74948010 < https://tinyurl.com/y3upbxr4 >

12

Christianity's Morbid Preoccupation with Sex

As the caterpillar chooses the fairest leaves
To lay her eggs on, so the priest lays his curse
On the fairest joys.
—William Blake, "Proverbs of Hell" (from *The Marriage of Heaven and Hell*)

The goal of sexual repression is that of producing an individual who is adjusted to the authoritarian order and will submit to it in spite of all misery and degradation.
—Wilhelm Reich, *The Mass Psychology of Fascism*

While attitudes toward sex varied considerably in the ancient world, the sex negativity that characterizes Judeo-Christianity was far from universal. As one example of a contrary attitude, historian Reay Tannahill notes that "Rome had to begin legislating against celibacy as far back as 403 B.C., partly because of the unsettling effect of continuous war [which made population replenishment a concern]."[1]

That all changed in the centuries following Christianity's ascension as Europe's undisputed moral arbiter. Since its inception, Christianity has had an exceptionally unhealthy fixation on sex, to the exclusion of almost everything else (except power, money, and inflicting pain). This stems from the numerous "thou shalt nots" relating to sex, and the calumnies heaped upon it, in the Bible. To quote only a few of the many passages maligning sex and warning against it:

Dearly beloved, I beseech you as strangers and pilgrims, abstain from fleshly lusts, which war against the soul. —1 Peter 2:11

Now the works of the flesh are manifest, which are these; Adultery, fornication, uncleanliness, lasciviousness. —Galatians 5:19

For to be carnally minded is death; but to be spiritually minded is life and peace. —Romans 8:6

The church fathers echoed these views:

We Christians regard a stain upon our chastity as more dreadful than any punishment, or even death itself. —Tertullian, *Apologeticus*

The children of the flesh can never be compared to the glory of holy virginity. —St. Augustine, *De Virginitate* ("On Holy Virginity")

Nothing so much casts down the mind of man from its citadel as do the blandishments of women, and that physical contact without which a wife cannot be possessed. —St. Augustine, *Soliloquies*

Nothing is so much to be shunned as sex relations.
—St. Augustine, *Soliloquies*

And lest we forget:

It is time to cut down the forest of marriage with the ax of virginity.
—St. Jerome, Epistle 123

Jerome managed to top even that with this "different strokes for different folks" personal note:

Of all the Roman ladies, only one had the power to tempt me, and that one was Paula. She mourned and she fasted. She was squalid with dirt; her eyes were dim from weeping . . . The Psalms were her only songs; the gospel her only speech; continence her one indulgence; fasting her staple of life.
—Epistle 45

All of this sickness, all of this prudishness and calumny, stems from Christianity's most basic scriptures, including the Ten Commandments. That the Ten Commandments (enumerated in Exodus 20 and, in somewhat different form, in Exodus 34 and Deuteronomy 5) forbid coveting one's neighbor's wife, but do not even mention, let alone forbid, slavery, rape, incest, torture, or cruelty—all of which were abundantly common at the time the Commandments were written—speaks volumes about their writers' preoccupation with sex (and women as property), as well as the moral blindness of the Judeo-Christian deity, which supposedly inspired the Commandments.

Over three millennia after the Ten Commandments were written, Christian leaders still endlessly echo the anti-sexual morality espoused in them and in the rest of the Bible. To cite but two sex-negative statements from relatively recent popes:

> When Christianity is rejected, marriage inevitably sinks into the slavery of man's vile passions.
> —Pope Leo XIII, *Arcanum divinae sapientiae* (1880, "On Christian Marriage")

> You cannot belong to Christ unless you crucify all self-indulgent passions and desires.
> —Pope Benedict XVI (as Cardinal Joseph Ratzinger, prior to ascending to the papacy), "Pastoral Letter on the Care of Homosexual Persons" (1986)

Today, judging from the pronouncements of many Christian leaders, one would think that morality consists solely of what one does (more precisely, what one *doesn't* do) in the bedroom. For a completely bonkers example of this, let's turn to a prominent televangelist and former GOP presidential candidate who has posited that tolerance of homosexuality is the cause of hurricanes:

> If you wanted to get America destroyed, if you were a malevolent, evil force and you said, 'How can I turn God against America? What can I do to get God mad at the people of America to cause this great land to vomit out the people?' Well, I'd pick five things. I'd begin to have incest. I'd begin to commit adultery wherever possible, all over the country, and sexuality. I'd begin to have them offering up and killing their babies. I'd get them having homosexual relations, and then I'd have them having sex with animals.
> —Rev. Pat Robertson, quoted in *The San Francisco Examiner*, September 7, 1986

The Catholic Church, though less flamboyant than Robertson and other evangelicals, is the prime example of sex negativity, with its moral pronouncements rarely going beyond the matters of birth control and abortion, and with its moral emphasis seemingly entirely on those matters (though this has softened a bit under Pope Francis).

Also note that the official Catholic view of sex, that it's for the purpose of procreation only, reduces human sexual relations to those of brood animals. Many of the church fathers and many later popes were quite explicit about this, with the most influential among the fathers, Augustine, stating in his work *De Adulter Coniugas* ("On Conjugal Adultery"), "Intercourse with even a lawful wife is unlawful and wicked if the conception of offspring be prevented."

Thus it's no surprise that in the Western world the Catholic Church has been the driving force behind efforts to prohibit access to birth control devices and information about them to *everyone*, not just Catholics. That effort still continues. Joseph Scheidler of the Pro-Life Action League says, "I would like to outlaw contraception . . . contraception is *disgusting*—people using each other for pleasure."[2] Horrors! Consenting adults giving each other pleasure? What is the world coming to?

The Catholic Church is far from alone in its sick obsession with sex. Evangelicals and Mormons are equally guilty. To cite but one Christian sex-negative comment, Phyllis Schlafly, founder of the religious-right Eagle Forum, said in 1992, "Nothing about contraception should be taught in schools. There is no question that it will encourage sexual activity."[3] Notice that Schlafly decried sex ed solely because it supposedly "encourage[s] sexual activity." (It doesn't—it just reduces the STD and teen-pregnancy rates.) Here, she let the cat out of the bag: she revealed that her (and other Christians') primary concern isn't with women's health, but in suppressing sex. Since, as Schlafly knew, and her co-religionists surely know, "pro-life" policies lead directly to unwanted pregnancies and unwanted babies, it's a good bet that Schlafly's kindred spirits want to punish sexually active women by forcing them to bear those unwanted babies. (As further evidence of this, anti-choice extremists are even trying to outlaw the safe, effective "morning after pill" which prevents implantion of a zygote in the uterus.)

(Of course, anti-choice zealots are also punishing the unwanted babies. Unwanted children routinely have worse life outcomes than wanted children; with more than 90% of women who have unwanted children choosing to keep them, this isn't a small problem. Researcher Diana Green Foster, who leads the nationwide Turnaway Study at the University of California at San Francisco, and has published articles on the topic in the *Journal of Pediatrics*[4] and *JAMA Pediatrics*,[5] reports that "children whose mothers were denied abortions [in contrast to] those who received them [had] a greater chance of living below the poverty level"; unwanted children were also behind wanted children in development; and "Women [denied abortions were] also much more likely to report poor maternal bonding—feeling trapped as a mother, resenting their baby, or longing for the 'old days' before they had the baby—with the child born after abortion denial than with the next child born following a wanted abortion.")[6]

If you want to see horrendous physical expression of the authoritarian, misogynistic, sex-negative attitude of Catholic "pro-lifers," look no further than what until recently was "the most Catholic country in Europe," Ireland, in the years 1922–1998. There, 14 Catholic Church-run "mother and baby homes" and four "homes" run by the then-Catholic-dominated state, inflicted severe emotional abuse upon tens of thousands of unmarried pregnant women (to whom the church and the state it overshadowed denied access to contraception and abortion),* and also, according to some victims, physical abuse as well. This all happened under terrible physical conditions, as evidenced by the sky high infant mortality rate in the "homes." The Irish government's Commission of Investigation into Mother and Baby Homes and Certain Related Matters reported in January 2021 that of 57,000 babies born in the 18 "homes" it investigated, 9,000 had died—a 16% mortality rate. The worst instance occurred at the Bressborough "home" where the infant mortality rate in 1944 was 82%: 900 dead infants.[7] At another "home," in Tuam, County Galway, 796 infants and children were buried at the site,[8] with "significant quantities of human remains" found "in a disused septic tank."[9]

One victim of this system, Philomena Lee, "said that she was 'deprived' of her liberty, independence and autonomy, and was 'subject to the tyranny of the nuns,' who told [her and the other] women daily that they were to atone for their sins by 'working for our keep and surrendering our children to the nuns for forced adoption.'" Lee added that while she was in labor nuns "told her that her 'pain was a punishment for [her] promiscuity.'"[10] The nuns contributed to that pain by denying their charges analgesics during labor, with their charges including girls as young as 12.[11]

Putting the matter succinctly, Roderic O'Gorman, Ireland's Minister for Children, Equality, Disability, Integration and Youth Affairs, stated: "The report makes clear that for decades, Ireland had a stifling, oppressive and brutally misogynistic culture, where a pervasive stigmatization of unmarried mothers and their children robbed those individuals of their agency

---

* The Irish government, over strong opposition from the Catholic Church, finally legalized possession and distribution of contraceptives in 1985. In December 2018, Ireland also legalized abortion.

and sometimes their future." Human rights campaigner Susan Lohan added, "state and church worked in concert to ensure that women—unmarried mothers and girls who were deemed to be a threat to the moral tone of the country"—were "incarcerated behind these very high walls to ensure that they would not impact or offend public morality."[12]

The abuse in the Irish system was undoubtedly even more widespread, and the number of deaths higher, than the Commission reported, as it surveyed only 18 of the 180 sites in the system.[13]

We'll treat the Christian attempt to deny women the right to control their own bodies in a later chapter. For now, suffice it to say that "pro-lifers" are doing their best to eliminate contraception, sex education, and women's right to choose, while at the same time insisting that they "respect" and are "defending" women.

Christianity produces sexual misery

> It is good for a man not to touch a woman. —1 Thessalonians 7:1

> If it is good not to touch a woman, it is bad to touch a woman.
> —St. Jerome, Epistle 48

In addition to the misery produced by Christian intrusions into the sex lives of non-Christians, Christianity produces a great deal of misery among its own adherents through its insistence that sex, except the very narrow variety it sanctions, is evil, against God's law. Christianity proscribes sex between unmarried people, sex outside of marriage, sex within marriage if contraception is used (in Catholicism), homosexual relations, bestiality, masturbation, and even "impure" thoughts. Indulging in such things can and will, in the conventional Christian view, lead straight to hell.*

Given that human beings are by nature highly sexual beings, and that their urges very often do not fit into the only officially sanctioned Christian form of sexual relations, monogamous, heterosexual marriage, it's in-

---

* One indication of the Christian obsession with sex is the repeated mention of bestiality in medieval ecclesiastical writings. Former Catholic priest and professor of church history Joseph McCabe cites one 8th-century penitential (list of sins and punishments) as stating: "If a cleric has fornicated with a quadruped let him do penance for, if he is a simple cleric, two years, if a deacon, three years, if a priest, seven years, if a bishop, ten years." As McCabe remarked nearly a century ago, all of this leads one to wonder how common this practice was in the medieval church.

evitable that those who attempt to follow Christian morals in this area are often miserable, as their strongest urges run smack dab into the wall of religious belief. This is inevitable in Christian adolescents and unmarried young people in that the only "pure" way for them to behave is celibately—in the strict Christian view, even masturbation is prohibited. (Philip Roth well described the dilemma of the religiously/sexually repressed young in *Portnoy's Complaint* as "being torn between desires that are repugnant to my conscience and a conscience repugnant to my desires.") Thus the years of adolescence and young adulthood for many Christians are poisoned by "sinful" urges, unfulfilled longings, and intense guilt (after the urges become too much to bear and are acted upon).

An example of how this plays out in the lives of Christian young people was provided by writer Samantha Boesch, who was raised in evangelical "purity culture." Like many other sexually repressed teens and young adults, she was curious about sex, and turned to online porn to satisfy her curiosity. But that came with a price: "I felt excitement every time I watched it, but that rush was immediately followed by the shame of knowing that I was committing sexual sin. . . . I attempted to quiet my mind and prayed to God for forgiveness." After months of struggle, Boesch says "[I was] hyper-aware of the shame in my life and all around me. It was palpable. I would sit in church services, Bible studies and SAA [Sex Addicts Anonymous] meetings, trying to drown out my anger with prayers to God." After nearly a decade of torment, which started in high school, she dropped out of both SAA and her church, whose members had recommended that she attend that 12-step group. "I finally realized that my whole life had been made up of other people's decisions—decisions based on fear, misinformation and attempts to control [me]."[14]

For those young believers who fulfill their natural desires, Christianity delivers admonishments, dire warnings, and condemnation. As the Reverend John Furniss put it in his "charming," officially approved Catholic children's book, *Tracts for Spiritual Reading*:

> Did you ever see two deadly vipers fly at each other? Their eyes burn with rage. They shoot out their poisoned stings. They struggle to give each other the death-blow. They struggle till they have torn the flesh and blood from each other. You may see the like of this in hell. See that young man and young woman—how changed they are! They loved each other so much on earth, that for this they broke the laws of God and man. But now they fight each other like two vipers, and so they will fight to all eternity.

So, in the Catholic view, that's the sort of thing that awaits teenagers and young adults who have sex outside of marriage. (Furniss might have gotten a bit carried away; the conventional Catholic view is that such sinners merely have to face an eternity of agony in a lake of fire.)

Even after Christian young people receive a license from church and state to have sex, they often discover that the sexual release promised by marriage is not all that it's cracked up to be. One gathers that in marriages between those who have followed Christian rules up until marriage—that is, no sex at all (and often no sex education)—sexual ineptitude and lack of fulfillment are all too common. One Christian author writes that while only 65% of straight women report "having an orgasm every or almost every time they have sex, Christian women fared even worse, orgasming just 48 percent of the time."[15] (Figures from other sources are more or less in line with this figure. Because the 65% figure for all women includes Christian women, who drag down the average, the situation for nonrelgious women is somewhat better than the 65% figure indicates.)

The evangelical writer just quoted, Sheila Wray Gregoire, also cites two common "purity culture" beliefs as being destructive to women's sexual satisfaction: "High school girls who believe they must be sexual gatekeepers grow up to be less sexually satisfied in marriage,"[16] and "Women report worse sex if they believe lust is a universal, constant battle for men."[17] These beliefs are common in "purity culture," and though the author doesn't mention it, they're also common in almost all conservative Christian churches, including the Catholic Church.

Even when Christian married people do have good sexual relations, the problems do not end. Sexual attractions ebb and flow, and new attractions inevitably arise. In conventional Christian relationships, one is not allowed to act on these new attractions. One is often not even permitted to admit that they exist. As a friend put it years ago, "with traditional [Christian] morality, you have to choose between being unfaithful to yourself or to another."

The dilemma is even worse for gay teens and young adults in that Christianity *never* offers them release from their unrequited urges. They are simply condemned to lifelong celibacy. If they indulge their natural desires, they become "sodomites" subject not only to earthly persecution under religion-inspired laws, but to being barbecued forever in the pit. Given the internalized homophobia Christian teachings inspire, not to mention the very real discrimination gay people face, it's not surprising that a great many homosexually oriented Christians choose to live a lie and feign heterosexual marriage. In most cases, this leads to lifelong personal torture and gross unfairness to their spouses, who deserve someone who desires them sexually. But such internalized homophobia can have even more tragic consequences.

A prime example is Marshall Applewhite, "John Do," the guru of the Heaven's Gate religious cult, whose members committed mass suicide in 1997. Applewhite grew up in the South in a repressive Christian family. Horrified by his homosexual urges, he began to think of sexuality itself as evil, and eventually underwent castration to curb his sexual urges. Several of his followers took his anti-sexual teachings to heart and likewise underwent castration before, at Applewhite's direction, killing themselves.

One strongly suspects that Applewhite, given his upbringing, was aware of and took to heart Christ's words in Matthew 19:12: "For there are some eunuchs which were so born from their mother's womb: and there are some eunuchs, which were made eunuchs of men: and there be some eunuchs which have made themselves eunuchs for the kingdom of heaven's sake. He that is able to receive it, let him receive it."

Applewhite might also have been emulating church father Origen (184–253), who followed that inspiring biblical advice in order to curb his own sexual desires.

While Applewhite's (and Origen's) religion-inspired behavior was extreme, the level of sexual misbehavior and hypocrisy displayed by Christian clergymen and politicians is almost impossible to overstate. It's mute testimony to Christianity's impossible-to-meet moral demands and the misery they produce, and also to the fact that the sexuality of repressed Christians often leaks out in incredibly unhealthy ways. The Catholic Church's ongoing pedophilia scandal is exhibit A. A church that preaches abstinence for the unmarried, celibacy for clergy, and sex within marriage only for procreative purposes, has harbored thousands of pedophiles, has shielded them from prosecution, and has made it a routine practice to shuffle them from parish to parish, thus providing them with one fresh set of victims after another.

Even the recent pope, Benedict XVI (Joseph Ratzinger), apparently engaged in this unsavory activity. According to a report prepared for the Archdiocese of Munich, while he was Archbishop of Munich, between 1977 and 1982, Benedict shielded four pedophile priests.[18]

Protestants have nothing to brag about regarding sexual conduct, either. Exemplary Protestant hypocrites include the Rev. Ted Haggerd, whose meth-and-male-hooker scandal occurred while he was spiritual advisor to George W. Bush; the Rev. Jimmy "I have sinned!" Swaggart, whose involvement with female hookers led to his defrocking by the Assemblies of God; homophobic Republican senator Larry "Wide Stance" Crane, who was arrested for soliciting sex in an airport bathroom; Rev. Jim Bakker, who was involved in orgies with members of both sexes—though he went to jail for financial fraud involving his Heritage USA Christian theme park; "family values" Republican senator David "Diaper Man" Vitter, who was re-elected *after* his hooker scandal came to light; and the Reverend Jerry Falwell, Jr. (whose motto could well be "I like to watch"), who lost his post as head of Liberty University after a sex scandal involving him, his wife, and Giancarlo Granda, a pool boy—according to Granda, the Rev watched (and, one suspects, wanked) while he and Falwell's wife had sex.*

All of this hypocritical, sordid behavior points to one thing: Christian sexual morality produces so much misery that even its most ardent advocates often find Christian morals impossible to follow.

Endnotes

1. *Sex in History, revised & updated*, by Reay Tannahill. Scarborough House, 1992, p. 127.

2. "Quotes from the American Taliban." University of California at San Diego. http://adultthought.ucsd.edu/Culture_War/The_American_Taliban.html < https://tinyurl.com/j7k3k >

3. "Guide Charts Path for Sex Education," by Carol Lawson. *New York Times*, October 17, 1991. https://www.nytimes.com/1991/10/17/garden/guide-charts-path-for-sex-education.html < https://tinyurl.com/y537j9l4 >

4. "When women are denied an abortion, their children fare worse than peers," by Diana Greene Foster Dec. 5, 2018. *Stat News*, December 5, 2018. https://www.statnews.com/2018/12/05/how-abortion-denial-affects-children-well-being/ < https://tinyurl.com/e6ucs4up >

5. "Effects of Carrying an Unwanted Pregnancy to Term on Women's Existing Children," by Diana Greene Foster, et al. *Pediatrics*/NIH National Library of Medicine, October 30, 2018. https://pubmed.ncbi.nlm.nih.gov/30389101/ < https://tinyurl.com/r95vmx4t >

6. "Comparison of Health, Development, Maternal Bonding, and Poverty Among Children Born After Denial of Abortion vs After Pregnancies Subsequent to an Abortion," by Diana Green Foster, et al. *JAMA Pediatrics*/NIH National Library of Medicine, November 1, 2018. https://pubmed.ncbi.nlm.nih.gov/30193363/ < https://tinyurl.com/vk5b8vkn >

7. "Ireland's 'brutally misogynistic culture' saw the death of 9,000 children in mother and baby homes, report finds," by Kara Fox. CNN, January 12, 2021. https://edition.cnn.com/2021/01/12/europe/ireland-mother-baby-homes-final-report-intl/index.html < https://tinyurl.com/y3uanemu >

8. "Claim of 800 children's remains buried at Irish home for unwed mothers." *The Guardian*, June 3,

* Falwell admits to knowing of the affair, but vehemently denies watching.

2014. https://www.theguardian.com/world/2014/jun/04/claim-of-800-childrens-bodies-buried-at-irish-home-for-unwed-mothers < https://tinyurl.com/yyvxwcf9 >

9. "Irish church and state apologise for callous mother and baby homes," by Rory Carroll. *The Guardian*, January 13, 2021. https://www.theguardian.com/world/2021/jan/13/irish-church-and-state-apologise-for-callous-mother-and-baby-home-institutions < https://tinyurl.com/yyj5oqj6 >

10. "Irish PM issues state apology for mother and baby homes abuses." *Al Jazeera*, January 13, 2021. https://www.aljazeera.com/news/2021/1/13/irish-pm-issues-state-apology-for-mother-and-baby-homes-abuses < https://tinyurl.com/y4b6zj64 >

11. Fox, op. cit.

12. Ibid.

13. Ibid.

14. "My Church Told Me I Needed Sex Addicts Anonymous. Here's What Happened When I Went," by Samantha Boesch. *Huffington Post/Yahoo! News*, June 1, 2001. https://www.yahoo.com/huffpost/sex-addiction-evangelicals-religion-130000061.html?utm_source=fark&utm_medium=website&utm_content=link&ICID=ref_fark < https://tinyurl.com/c72wed2 >

15. "'I Didn't Want to Deny My Husband His Marital Rights': For Many Evangelical Women, Sex Comes With Pain and Anxiety," by Sarah Stankorb. *Jezebel*, July 28, 2021. https://jezebel.com/i-didnt-want-to-deny-my-husband-his-martial-rights-for-1847361950 < https://tinyurl.com/dn3abafu >

16. *The Great Sex Rescue: The Lies You've Been Taught and How to Recover What God Intended*, by Sheila Wray Gregoire. Grand Rapids, MI: Baker Books, 2021, p. 66.

17. Ibid., p. 85.

18. "Ex-Pope Benedict failed to act against abusive priests in Germany, report finds," by Claudio Lavanga, A.M. Pohlers, and Associated Press. NBC News, January 20, 2022. https://www.nbcnews.com/news/world/pope-benedict-failed-act-abusive-priests-munich-church-report-finds-rcna12858 < https://tinyurl.com/49m85rb6 >

13

Christianity's Narrow, Legalistic View of Morality

MORAL, adj. In the conventional Judeo-Christian sense, anything tending to increase human misery, as in 'moral conduct' and 'moral standards.'
—*The American Heretic's Dictionary*

Everything not prohibited is permitted.
—the Lotus Principle (English common law)

Christians have certainly taken the Lotus Principle to heart. They at least pretend to obey the dictates of the Bible (and those of the priests, popes, and preachers they follow), while acting as if anything not specifically prohibited, no matter how sleazy, unethical, or outright monstrous, is perfectly fine, precisely because it is not prohibited by what they consider the only moral code, that expounded in the Bible.

They often pretend to keep the Bible's commands punctiliously (an utter impossibility). To underline the sacredness of those commands, they'll insist on the unitary nature of the Bible, and will occasionally cite Jesus's words in Matthew 5:18: "For verily I say unto you, Till heaven and earth pass, one jot or one tittle shall in no wise pass from the law, till all be fulfilled." (Do Christians actually pay attention to all of those jots and tittles? Of course not. As mentioned earlier, all Christians, of necessity, are "cafeteria Christians." They only keep those biblical commands they choose to keep, especially those whose observance is open to public view.)

The words of Jesus in Matthew 5:18 sum up Christian morality: follow the law as prescribed in the Bible.

But what a law!

Here are the most prominent commands and prohibitions in the Bible, the Ten Commandments. (This very common list is an abbreviated form of the commands in Exodus 20—we'll ignore the other two versions of the commandments in Deuteronomy 5 and Exodus 34, which is specifically cited in verse 28 as "the Ten Commandments," though the list contains more than ten of them—as the Exodus 20 version is by far the most commonly cited list.)

1. I am the Lord thy God, thou shalt not have any strange gods before Me.
2. Thou shalt not take the name of the Lord thy God in vain."
3. Thou shalt not make any graven image.
4. Keep holy the Sabbath day."
5. Honour thy father and mother.
6. Thou shalt not kill.
7. Thou shalt not commit adultery.
8. Thou shalt not steal.
9. Thou shalt not bear false witness against thy neighbor.
10. Thou shalt not covet thy neighbor's wife. Thou shalt not covet thy neighbor's goods.

This is a rather minimal set of moral precepts.

The first three commandments, presumably considered the most important by their author, speak only to the pettiness of that author.

The fourth seems reasonable except that it implies wasting time on religious rites, and is it important enough to deserve being in a short list of fundamental moral precepts?

The fifth commandment also seems reasonable, but should it be a blanket command, and does it really merit being an essential part of a brief moral code?

The sixth is more than reasonable and should be a basic part of any code of morals—thus, it's a pity that the Old Testament God repeatedly commanded its followers to violate it, both in individual and social matters.

The seventh commandment makes sense to some, but again, should it be a fundamental part of a moral code? Aren't there other things a bit more important?

The eighth is also reasonable and should be part of any code of morals. Thus it's a pity that Christian churches routinely violate it by avoiding taxes while enjoying public services (garbage collection, fire protection, street repairs, etc., etc.) that everyone else is forced to pay for. In essence, the Christian legislators who created the tax exemptions for their churches legalized theft—by the religious from the nonreligious—and Christians are more than happy to benefit from that theft.

The ninth commandment should also be a part of any code of morals. Again, it's a pity that Christians and Christian churches routinely violate it by bearing false witness. Currently, the two most prominent false accusations are that there's a "gay agenda" that gay people are trying to "impose" on Christians, and that all gay men are pedophiles.

The tenth commandment is both strange and redundant. Adultery is proscribed by the seventh commandment and stealing by the eighth, so why include the thought crimes in the tenth commandment unless part of the author's purpose was to dictate the thoughts as well as the actions of believers?

Going beyond the Ten Commandments, let's see some of the other things the Bible prohibits or condemns:

Working on the sabbath (death penalty)
(Exodus 31:14–15, Exodus 35:1–2, Numbers 15:32–36)
Worshiping other gods or idols (death penalty)
(Deuteronomy 13:6–9, Deuteronomy 17:2–5, Colossians 3:5)
Cursing one's parents (death penalty)
(Deuteronomy 17:24)
Rebelliousness (death penalty)
(Deuteronomy 21:18–21)
Witchcraft and consorting with spirits (death penalty)
(Exodus 22:18, Leviticus 20:27)
Blasphemy (death penalty)
(Leviticus 24:14–16)
Stealing and selling slaves (death penalty)
(Exodus 21:16)
Not keeping the sabbath (death penalty)
(Exodus 33:14)
Eating shellfish (abomination)
(Leviticus 11:10–12)
Being a lynching victim
(Deuteronomy 21:23, Galatians 3:13)
Wearing mixed fabrics
(Leviticus 19:19, Deuteronomy 22:11)

And, of course, sacrificing a blemished ox (abomination)
(Deuteronomy 17:1)

Almost everything else that the Bible prohibits or condemns not having to do with sex is equally trivial or nonsensical.

But where the authors of the Bible really get hot and bothered is in their condemnation of sex. The Bible explicitly prohibits or condemns the following:

Adultery (abomination and death penalty)
(abomination: Ezekiel 23:36–37, Leviticus 18:20, 27)
(death penalty: Leviticus 20:10, Deuteronomy 22:22, Ezekiel 23:45–47)
Fornication (death penalty)
(Leviticus 21:9, Ezekiel 16:35–40)
Cross dressing (abomination)
(Deuteronomy 22:5)
Homosexual acts (abomination and death penalty)
(abomination: Leviticus 18:22, Leviticus 20:13)
(death penalty: Leviticus 20:13)
Sex with an "unclean" woman (abomination)
(Leviticus 18:19, 27)
Being a rape victim but not crying out (death penalty)
(Deuteronomy 22:23–24)
Inability to prove (female) virginity (death penalty)
(Deuteronomy 22:13–21)
Sex with wife and mother-in-law (death penalty)
(Leviticus 20:14)
Bestiality (death penalty and abomination)
(abomination: Leviticus 18:23, 27)
(death penalty: Exodus 22:19, Leviticus 20:15)

All of this begs the question, what *doesn't* the Bible prohibit?

Slavery. The Bible nowhere condemns it, and in many places the Bible condones it and even includes instructions on how to (mis)treat slaves. In one passage (Exodus 21:20–21) it explicitly treats slaves as property.

Cruelty. The Bible nowhere condemns it, and large parts of the Old Testament glory in it. For example, "Happy shall he be, that taketh and dasheth thy little ones against the stones" (Psalms 137:9), which refers to the longed-for murder of Babylonian infants during the Babylonian captivity).

Torture. The Bible not only doesn't forbid torture anywhere in its nearly 800,000 words, it commands it: many passages order believers to torture transgressors to death by burning them alive or by stoning them to death (e.g., Leviticus 20:14, 20:27, 21:9). As well, the Almighty is more than a bit of a sadist even to those who toe its line, as witnessed by its horrific treatment of Job and its mental torture of Abraham.

Racism. There is not a single word in the Bible condemning it.

Rape. Not only does the Bible fail to forbid rape, but God commands child rape. In Numbers 31:17–18, God not only orders that particularly horrific form of sexual abuse, but also mass murder.

Physical aggression. Nowhere does the Bible condemn physical aggression. Rather, it commands it, over and over.

Coercion. The Bible nowhere condemns coercion. And again, as it applies to individuals, the Bible commands it, over and over. As well, the relationship of God to its "chosen people" is coercive almost in its entirety, and what is slavery (which is repeatedly condoned in the Bible) if not the ultimate form of coercion?

Mass murder. God explicitly and repeatedly commands it (against the Hittites, Canaanites, and other victims of the "chosen people" in the "promised land"), and sometimes in shockingly brutal fashion.

All of this helps to explain why so many Christians behave so abominably toward their fellow human beings. They've learned from the Bible, their moral guide, and from their priests and preachers, that as long as they observe some of the injunctions in that guide, especially those relating to sex, they'll be "saved." Beyond that, they believe they have *carte blanche* to do anything they want, no matter how cruel or vile. (Here, one can't help but think of the Christian slavers in the trans-Atlantic slave trade in the 16th through 19th centuries, the mass murder and near-continual atrocities involved in the conquest of the Americas and Africa, and the torturers and torture implements employed by the Christian churches for centuries during the medieval and Renaissance periods.)

In response, Christian apologists would point out that there are passages in the New Testament, especially those purporting to be the words of Jesus, prescribing kindness and tolerance. What they don't point out is that in Matthew 5:18 Jesus specifically endorsed as "the law" all of the terrible things cited above, and that he never denounced the horrors of slavery or torture. That there are some good things in the Bible doesn't excuse the many awful things in it, nor its many grave moral omissions.

It's not hard to come up with a much better list of moral precepts than the Ten Commandments. In fact, The Satanic Temple (whose members have been described as "atheism's shock troops," though "atheism's jujitsu masters" is probably more accurate)* has done so with its Seven Fundamental Tenets:

1. One should strive to act with compassion and empathy toward all creatures in accordance with reason.
2. The struggle for justice is an ongoing and necessary pursuit that should prevail over laws and institutions.
3. One's body is inviolable, subject to one's own will alone.
4. The freedoms of others should be respected, including the freedom to offend. To willfully and unjustly encroach upon the freedoms of another is to forgo one's own.
5. Beliefs should conform to one's best scientific understanding of the world. One should take care never to distort scientific facts to fit one's beliefs.
6. People are fallible. If one makes a mistake, one should do one's best to rectify it and resolve any harm that might have been caused.
7. Every tenet is a guiding principle designed to inspire nobility in action and thought. The spirit of compassion, wisdom, and justice should always prevail over the written or spoken word.

You decide. Which is a better moral guide, the Ten Commandments or the Seven Fundamental Tenets?**

---

* The Satanic Temple has an ongoing campaign of demanding in court the same privileges that Christians have arrogated to themselves. For example, when Christians put up a Ten Commandments monument on the Arkansas Capitol grounds, the Satanists sued, demanding that they be allowed to put up a statue of Baphomet. At this writing, the case is still pending.

** Copyright © 2013 by the Satanic Temple, Inc. Used by permission.

14

Christianity Reduces Morality to an Individual Matter

> The Christian faith, from the beginning, is self-sacrifice, the sacrifice of all freedom, all pride, all self-confidence of spirit; it is at the same time subjection, self-derision, and self-mutilation.
> —Friedrich Nietzsche, *Beyond Good and Evil*

Historically, Christianity placed all responsibility, all blame on the individual for both personal and social ills. By and large, even today most Christians steadfastly refuse to acknowledge the socio-economic factors that encourage destructive, anti-social acts. It seems that for every Martin Luther King, Jr. who challenges social evils, there are a hundred Jerry Falwells who fight to preserve them. Why? The root cause can be found in the New Testament, which rejects social and political activism, and urges acceptance of the status quo: "Render unto Caesar." This order to submit is very plain in passages such as:

> Let every soul be subject unto the higher powers. For there is no power but of God: the powers that be are ordained of God. Whosoever therefore resisteth the power, resisteth the ordinance of God: and they that resist shall receive to themselves damnation. —Romans 13:1–2

> Submit yourselves to every ordinance of man for the Lord's sake: whether it be to the king, as supreme; Or unto governors, . . . —1 Peter 2:13–14

> Let as many servants [slaves] as are under the yoke count their own masters worthy of all honour, that the name of God and his doctrine be not blasphemed. —1 Timothy 6:1

In other words, do nothing to challenge your masters. Just shut up, take it, and *like it*, or you'll go to hell. Other passages reinforcing this message of submission include Colossians 3:22; Ephesians 6:5; Titus 2:9–10; and 1 Peter 2:18.

Such passages led to the "faith not works" doctrine, with its emphasis on individual salvation, which is most prominent in Calvinism, and posits that faith is all that's necessary for salvation. This is still an article of faith in many conservative Christian churches, including, in slightly modified form, the Catholic Church, which holds that a rapist/serial killer, if he makes a "good confession" or a "genuine act of contrition" immediately before death, will go to heaven, while those who lived exemplary lives helping others will go to hell if they were "in a state of mortal sin" because of unconfessed "impure thoughts" or other trivial sins when they died.

Several centuries after the New Testament was written, Christians were still reducing morality to a personal matter. A prime example is Pope Gregory the Great's (540–604) list of the Seven Deadly Sins, which is still often cited by Christians, and which Thomas Aquinas saw fit to write about extensively over six centuries after Gregory devised the list:

1. Lust
2. Gluttony
3. Greed
4. Sloth
5. Wrath
6. Envy
7. Pride

Most of these are bad things—though there's a lot to be said for lust, gluttony, and sloth—but notice that there's no mention of cruelty or hypocrisy, two of the most common human failings, in this oft-referenced list of personal shortcomings. Note also that these are all individual sins, with only two, greed and wrath, involving possible harm to other people. And note that Gregory doesn't present this list of faults as simply "some deadly sins" or "a few deadly sins." Rather, he presents this as a definitive list: *The* Seven Deadly Sins. This list, and the manner in which it's presented, are one of the clearest indications of Christian moral myopia.

As regards Christian morals, not much has changed since the time of Aquinas except in reaction to the rise of science and secularism, which have somewhat moderated Christian barbarism. The emphasis on individual responsibility and individual salvation is still a prominent feature of Christianity, and it appears in many forms, some quite surprising. A good example of this is Alcoholics Anonymous (AA).

Two of the most widespread myths about Alcoholics Anonymous are that AA is "spiritual, not religious" and that it has existed as a nonsectarian independent organization from the day in 1935 that Bill Wilson met AA's other co-founder, Dr. Bob Smith, in Akron, Ohio. When they met, Smith and Wilson were both members of a politically conservative Protestant, pietist-oriented evangelical group called the Oxford Group Movement (OGM), or more simply the Oxford Groups. (The Oxford Groups later morphed into the decidedly oddball and equally right-wing Moral Re-Armament and its painfully cleancut youth group, Up With People.)

The Oxford Group Movement—which had nothing to do with Oxford University, nor the city of Oxford, England; the OGM merely traded on the name—was founded in the 1920s by the Reverend Frank N. D. Buchman, notable for his lavish lifestyle, his right-wing views, and his virulent prudery and homophobia (despite, or perhaps because of, his almost certainly being a closeted gay).

In 1936, Buchman said in an interview in the *New York World-Telegram*, "Thank heaven for a man like Adolf Hitler" and pined for "a God-controlled democracy," a "theocracy," or "a God-controlled fascist dictatorship";[1] and, following the 1936 Berlin Olympics, where he met him, Buchman referred to Gestapo head Heinrich Himmler as "a great lad."[2]

AA's co-founders, Smith and Wilson, both conservative Republicans, evidently found all of this attractive—or at least not overly bothersome—as they were enthusiastic Oxford Group members and continued to be so for years after Buchman's "thank heaven for a man like Adolf Hitler" remarks in 1936. Those remarks would have been hard for Wilson to ignore, as he lived in New York City, was a fervent Oxford Groups member, and the comments appeared in a lengthy interview in an at-the-time-daily New York newspaper, the *New York World-Telegram*.*

---

* AA bills itself as a program built on honesty, but its official, "conference approved" biography of Bill Wilson, *Pass It On*, treats the Buchman interview in an utterly dishonest manner. The dishonesty includes patching together, without ellipses, fragments separated by hundreds of words as if they were unitary statements, while omitting inconvenient words

(continued next page)

Convinced that Oxford Group principles were the key to overcoming alcohol abuse (and all other problems in life), Wilson and Smith devoted themselves to carrying the Oxford Group message to other alcoholics. What they called the "alcoholic squadron of the Akron Oxford Group" remained as part of the Oxford Group Movement until 1939, and the group Bill Wilson founded in New York remained part of the Oxford Group Movement until late 1937, over a year after Frank Buchman's "Thank heaven for a man like Adolf Hitler" remarks. (Those remarks had nothing to do with why AA split from the Oxford Groups. Wilson and other AA members were concerned that the Catholic hierarchy would bar Catholics from joining AA as long as it remained part of a Protestant evangelical group.)

One can clearly see AA's OGM-derived emphasis on individual responsibility for alcohol abuse—entirely ignoring the economic and social factors contributing to it—in its famous 12 steps, which are a codification of OGM principles:

1. We admitted we were powerless over alcohol—that our lives had be come unmanageable.
2. Came to believe that a power greater than ourselves could restore us to sanity.
3. Made a decision to turn our will and our lives over to the care of God as we understood Him.
4. Made a searching and fearless moral inventory of ourselves.
5. Admitted to God, to ourselves, and to another human being the exact nature of our wrongs.
6. Were entirely ready to have God remove all these defects of character.
7. Humbly asked Him to remove our shortcomings.
8. Made a list of all persons we had harmed, and became willing to make amends to them all.
9. Made direct amends to such people wherever possible, except when to do so would injure them or others.
10. Continued to take personal inventory, and when we were wrong, promptly admitted it.
11. Sought through prayer and meditation to improve our conscious contact with God as we understood Him, praying only for knowledge of His will for us and the power to carry that out.
12. Having had a spiritual awakening as the result of these steps, we tried to carry this message to alcoholics, and to practice these principles in all our affairs.

(cont'd) within the fragments in order to make the patchwork read more smoothly and to put the best possible face on Buchman's fascist-friendly views. For further information on this dishonesty, see *Alcoholics Anonymous: Cult or Cure?, 2nd ed,*, pp. 23–24.

AA's religious nature—if prayers to God aren't religious, what is?—could hardly be plainer, as are its blindness to the socioeconomic factors that contribute to alcohol abuse and its heavy emphasis on individual responsibility and repentance.*

There are many other examples of Christians turning their backs on the social nature of problems, problems such as poverty and homelessness. The Christian response to these issues consists almost entirely of charity (organizations such as the Salvation Army and rescue missions); here, as in so many other areas, Christianity places responsibility on individual victims, not the political/economic system that produces them. (This isn't to say that the Salvation Army and rescue missions don't help the individuals they serve—they do—just that organized Christianity has until relatively recently been almost entirely unconcerned with social improvement, other than trying to impede it, and that even now only a small minority of Christians concern themselves with changing the social and economic structures that produce the present miseries.)

Barring organized Christianity's attempts to control the behavior (especially the sexual behavior) of individuals through governmental coercion, as well as the ongoing attempt to turn the United States into a theocracy (not to achieve social or economic betterment or "religious freedom," but to impose Christian morals on everyone), Christianity's emphasis today remains almost entirely on individual responsibility and repentance, and providing excuses for inaction on social issues ("For ye have the poor always with you; . . ." —Matthew 26:11; see also Mark 14:7 and John 12:8).

---

* Unsurprisingly, AA isn't an effective means of dealing with alcohol abuse or alcohol dependence. According to an internal analysis of AA's self-conducted surveys, "Comments on AA's Triennial Surveys," only one in twenty who "walk through the door" are still attending AA a year after that initial "walk." This 5% continued-attendance rate is no better than the rate of spontaneous remission, and in fact falls toward the lower end of that estimated rate. As well, continuing to "walk through the door" does not equate to staying sober: it's fairly common for AA members to repeatedly relapse and repeatedly return to AA, or, somewhat less commonly, to hide their drinking while continuing to attend meetings. So, that 5% continued attendance rate is worse than it looks. For more information on AA's lack of efficacy, see *Alcoholics Anonymous: Cult or Cure?, 2nd ed.*, pp. 86–104.

Christianity absolves transgressors of responsibility—but at a price

> Man is *not* to look outwards, he is to look inwards into himself, he is not to look prudently and cautiously into things as a learner, he is not to look at all, he is to *suffer* . . . And he is to suffer so as to need the priest always . . . *A savior is needed.* —Friedrich Nietzsche, *The Anti-Christ*

> Our churches by common consent . . . teach that men cannot be justified before God by their own strength, merits, or works, but are freely justified for Christ's sake, through faith, when they believe that they are received into favor, and that their sins are forgiven for Christ's sake, who, by His death, has made satisfaction for our sins.
> —Article IV, Augsburg Confession (1530, the foundational statement of Lutheranism)

At first glance, the title of this section seems to contradict the point of this chapter, that Christianity reduces morality to an individual matter. But it isn't contradictory. Christianity's exceedingly narrow view of morality focuses almost exclusively on harmless individual sexual acts and other trifles, while it does almost nothing to address truly harmful acts. When Christians violate the Bible's few commands against real harms, organized Christianity lets them off the hook.

Christianity does this in two ways. The first and most obvious is the sacrament of confession, which for Catholics and Orthodox is an expression of the Christian belief that humans are inherently sinful and can only be redeemed via God's grace purchased by Christ's suffering and death. (Nietzsche, in *The Anti-Christ*, accurately called this suffering and death "the *sacrifice for guilt*, and just in its most repugnant and barbarous form—the sacrifice of the innocent for the sins of the guilty!" He added, "What horrifying heathenism!")

The sacrament of confession is also the ultimate get-out-of-jail-free card. Catholic believers can confess to *anything*, including rape and murder, and be forgiven by a priest if they genuinely repent. (That many Catholics do not genuinely repent seems of no importance to them nor to the church: as long as they go through the motions—and keep supporting the Church—they're home free.) This sacrament is a license for the religious to commit evil. And commit it they do. Religiously observant mafia "made men" are only an extreme example of this.

In contrast, those who die while not in a "state of grace," because they failed to confess some petty offense, such as having "impure thoughts" or eating meat during Lent, will suffer eternal torment.

Why would Catholicism give even the worst criminals such an easy pass to heaven while condemning the good to eternal torment? Because the sacrament of confession inculcates dependence of the faithful on the church; it keeps all of them, the good and the bad, dependent upon the church for salvation, for passage to its imaginary heaven. As Nietzsche put it in *The Anti-Christ*: ". . . all the affairs of life are so regulated that the priest is *everywhere indispensable*; at all natural events of life, at birth, at marriage, in sickness, in death . . . the holy parasite appears . . ."

With Protestantism, things are even more straightforward: belief is all that's necessary for salvation. Romans 3:28 states, "Therefore we conclude that a man is justified by faith without the deeds of the law." Martin Luther adds, "It is faith—without good works and prior to good works—that takes us to heaven. We come to God through faith alone."

There are other statements from Protestant Christians (including some by Luther) that urge good works as well as faith, but the basic tenet is that faith in itself is enough for a ticket to heaven. Add that belief (plus Catholic confession) to the Bible's many passages that command believers to commit evil (a reasonable definition being acts that hurt people, other animals, and other parts of nature), and you have a recipe for atrocities, as generation after generation of Christian slavers, torturers, war mongers, and mass murderers have shown.

Another way Christianity lets evildoers off the hook is via the Bible's grossly inadequate moral code, its remarkably short list of prohibited harmful acts and its concomitant remarkably long list of prohibited trivialities. Anything not prohibited is permitted, and believers are blameless for destructive acts that aren't specifically proscribed. A remarkably large number of believers, both Catholic and Protestant, have taken advantage of that license to do evil, and a great many are still doing so.

And as long as evildoers make "good confessions" before death or (in the case of Protestants) simply have faith, they have a ticket straight to heaven.

Endnotes

1. *Alcoholics Anonymous: Cult or Cure? 2nd Edition*, by Charles Bufe. Tucson: See Sharp Press, 1998, p. 23.
2. *The Mystery of Moral Re-Armament*, by Tom Driberg. New York: Alfred A. Knopf, 1965, pp. 64–65.

15

Christianity Accepts Real Evils While Condemning Imaginary Evils

Christian theology has taught men that they should submit with unintelligent resignation to the worst real evils of life and waste their time in consideration of imaginary evils in the 'life to come.'
—E. Haldeman-Julius, *The Meaning of Atheism*

Christians, especially clerics, have always been skillful apologists for the status quo and all the evils that go with it. Christianity diverts attention from real problems by focusing attention on imaginary problems, on individual sexual issues, and when confronted with social evils such as poverty glibly dismisses them with platitudes such as "For ye have the poor always with you; . . ." (Matthew 26:11) At best, as regards poverty and other social problems, Christian churches, which own vast wealth, are exempt from taxation, and likely receive well over $100 billion in collection plate donations every year in the U.S. alone, deliver a few grossly inadequate palliative measures to address some problems, and often deliver nothing to address others.

As an example of the Christian attitude toward ongoing evils, consider the Christian attitude toward war and militarism. Organized Christianity, with the exception of a few small sects such as the Quakers, has never opposed these things. Unsurprisingly, that official tolerance (and sometimes enthusiasm) for these evils is mirrored in the attitudes of individual Christians: when confronted with the age-old problems of war and militarism, most Christians shrug and say, "That's human nature. It's always been that way, and it always will." One strongly suspects that 200 years ago their ancestors would have said exactly the same thing about slavery.

This regressive, conservative tendency, this support of the status quo and indifference to the suffering of others, has been present from Christianity's very start, and is still very much here. Recall Mother Teresa's statement, "I think it is very beautiful for the poor people to accept their lot . . . I think the world is being much helped by the suffering of the poor people."

Going back to the source, the Bible is quite explicit in its instructions to accept the status quo, as in Ephesians 6:5, "Servants [slaves], be obedient to them that are your masters, according to the flesh, with fear and trembling, in singleness of your heart, as unto Christ," and in Romans 13:1, which admonishes that "every soul be subject unto the higher powers" and that "the powers that be are ordained of God."

Today, with the exception of a relatively few liberal churchgoers and churches, Christians ignore the real evils plaguing our society—poverty; homelessness; hunger; militarism; maldistribution of wealth and income; poor or nonexistent healthcare; ecological devastation; overpopulation; racism; homophobia; misogyny; laws against victimless crimes; mass incarceration; an unequal, often inadequate educational system; etc., etc., etc.—unless they're actively working to *worsen* those evils in the name of Christian morality and "family values."

To fully appreciate the social irresponsibility of most Christians and most Christian sects, consider the overwhelming misery of much of the world's population and the astounding wealth and income of the Christian churches. Let's start with the world's oldest, largest, and richest Christian church, the Roman Catholic Church.

From its humble beginnings, over the centuries that Church amassed vast wealth. One indication of how wealthy it had already become by the Renaissance period is that when Henry VIII dissolved the over 800 Catholic monasteries in England in the 1530s and 1540s, the monasteries (not the Catholic Church as a whole, just the monasteries) owned over a quarter of the country's cultivated land, not to mention the myriad large, expensive buildings on that land.[1]

Today, it's very difficult to estimate the total wealth of the Catholic Church, but consider that worldwide it owns 276,000 square miles of land (176 million acres), which is slightly larger than the State of Texas.[2] Valuing this land at only $100 per acre would yield over $17 billion in wealth; valuing it at the still very low figure of $1000 per acre would yield $176 billion in wealth—and this is just for the land; it doesn't include the structures and improvements upon it. And in July 2021, *Deutsche Welle*, citing figures from the Administration of the Patrimony of the Holy See, reported that the Vatican alone (not the Catholic Church as a whole) owns over 5,000 properties worldwide, with most in Western Europe, including properties "in London, Paris, Geneva, and Lausanne—many as investments in posh districts."[3]

Beyond that, according to Gerald Posner in *God's Bankers*, the $92 million Mussolini paid the Vatican in 1929 as compensation for loss of the Papal States had grown to $655 million by the time of the book's publication in 2015. A further indication of Catholic wealth was provided by the Jesuits in 2020 when they announced that they were divesting themselves of fossil fuel investments whose worth totaled $517.5 million[4]—and this was the value of a single segment of a single Catholic religious order's portfolio.

Some guesses as to the total wealth of the Catholic Church run in the $10 to $15 billion range, though that seems extremely low given its vast land holdings and that according to CNN Money the Vatican Bank alone has assets of $8 billion;[5] the $10 to $15 billion figure also seems far too low in light of the fact that the Vatican claimed, as of 2013, that it has 1.2 billion members, hundreds of millions of whom undoubtedly contribute to it.[6] One strongly suspects that the $10 to $15 billion estimate of Catholic Church wealth is too low by at least a factor of ten, with that factor probably being closer to a hundred, and perhaps even higher than that.[7] In other words, the wealth of the Catholic Church almost certainly runs into the hundreds of billions, and quite possibly into the trillions.

One indication of this is that a 2018 *Sydney Morning Herald* investigation of Church finances revealed that "all the entities related to the Catholic Church in Australia had wealth of about $30 billion" (Australian, equivalent to about $23 billion U.S.),[8] and this in a country with a population of only 25 million. Extrapolating this, the corresponding figure for the United States (which has a comparable standard of living and a similar proportion of Catholics) would be $300 billion. But that's at best a rough estimate.

As with so many other things regarding Christian churches, it's difficult to find accurate information as regards wealth and income, but also to a lesser extent membership; it'd help tremendously if more churches were transparent about all this, but many of them are not, so for the most part we're left with making estimates that could be considerably off. For example, the billion-plus worldwide Catholic membership figure is suspect, because the Church has been hemorrhaging members for decades, at least in the industrialized world, and tends to claim all baptized persons as members. In Michigan, for instance, membership in the Catholic Church apparently dropped by close to 50% in the 2000–2018 period, as judged by Church-supplied figures: the number of Catholic baptisms, first communions, and weddings all dropped by roughly half in that time; in 2018, only Catholic funerals approached the number of such funerals in 2000.[9]

Still, if all of the Church's claimed membership of 1.2 billion contributed only $10 per week to it, that would still amount to an annual income from collection plate donations alone of $625 billion, and if only 20% of its claimed members donated that amount it would still come to $125 billion annually, which quite possibly is a low estimate.

As regards the U.S., if American Catholic giving were in line with the average 2.5% of income given to churches by Americans,[10] whose median income is $31,000, and that current U.S. Catholic membership is roughly 51 million,[11] that would work out to an annual Catholic donation income of approximately $40 billion in the U.S. (American Catholics make up only about 4% of the world's Catholics, and most of the rest live in Latin America, where their average financial support of the Church is undoubtedly much lower, so the figures for the U.S. can't be extrapolated for total worldwide donation income.)

However, the self-effacingly titled Church of Jesus Christ of Latter-day Saints (LDS, Mormons), with only about 16 million members worldwide, very probably puts the Catholics (and Protestants) to shame, at least in proportional terms.

Back in the 1980s, when LDS membership was under seven million, authors Steven Haifeh and Gregory White Smith cited estimates of LDS wealth at $15 to $50 billion.[12] Some estimates of the Church's current wealth exceed $100 billion, and even that's probably too low, perhaps considerably so. According to *Business Insider*, citing SEC filings, the Church's investment arm, Ensign Peak Advisers, alone has $100 billion in assets.[13]

Over half of Mormons live in the U.S., about 9.3 million according to the Church's own figures as of 2018, and if even one in five is working and paying tithes on the U.S. median annual income of $31,000, that works out to a tax-exempt Church tithing income of approximately $5.7 billion per year in the U.S. (The LDS Church pressures its members to tithe 10% of their gross income, and a good majority appear to do so, so I used the 10%-of-income tithing rate to calculate the $5.7 billion figure.)

As for the Protestants, there are about 141 million in the U.S., with the average contribution being about $15 weekly.[14] That indicates annual collection-plate donations to American Protestant churches of approximately $110 billion per year. This estimate is in close alignment with Baptist Church figures. Lifeway Research, in a report prepared for the Southern Baptist Convention, stated that in 2020 Baptist Church donation income was $11.5 billion, and that there were just over 14 million Baptists, almost exactly 10% of the American Protestant population. Extrapolating the Baptist figures yields an annual donation income estimate of $115 billion for all Protestant churches. Lifeway also reported that the Baptists spent $193 million on "National Cooperative Program Giving," a charitable giving rate of 1.68% of donation income. In contrast, the Baptists spent over five times as much on "mission expenditures," over $1 billion.[15]

Not even taking dividends, rents, interest, capital gains, tuition, and other sources of revenue into account, donation-plate income alone is almost certainly well over $100 billion annually in the U.S. for the Catholic, Protestant, and LDS churches combined. Given the secrecy with which most churches treat their finances, that estimate could be considerably off, and is probably too low.

Just how easy it is for churches to pile up the loot—while taking advantage of property, income, capital gains, and sales tax exemptions and, often, their members' low-paid or unpaid labor—can be seen in the wealth of the Church of Scientology, a church with a worldwide membership probably in the low tens of thousands, and perhaps as low as 15,000.[16] The Church claims millions of members in the U.S., but this is belied by Census Bureau statistics which show that the number of Scientologists is so low that the Church is not even listed in the Census Bureau's figures on denominational membership.[17] It's entirely possible that the largest Protestant megachurches have more members than the entire Church of Scientology.

In 2014, *Business Insider* estimated the total wealth of this tiny church at $1.2 billion.[18] That estimate is on the low side. Other estimates run to far more, which is impressive for a church founded in 1953 and which in its heyday in the 1980s and 1990s (prior to relentless exposure on the Internet) probably never had more than a hundred thousand members.

As evidence of the Scientologists' wealth, *The Sydney Morning Herald* reports that the Australian branch of the Church, with only an estimated 1,700 members, had assets of over $172 million (Australian) in 2019, equivalent to approximately $130 million U.S.; *The Herald* also reported that in the UK the Church had approximately 2,400 members and assets worth $150 million (Australian), equivalent to roughly $115 million U.S.[19] The puny Church of Scientology acquired its billion(s) in under seven decades, and the vastly larger Christian churches have had a head start on them of anywhere from a few hundred years to nearly two millennia.

So, what good works are the wealthy and ultra-wealthy Christian churches doing with their money? Hard figures on what percentage of their income Christian churches devote to charitable activities are hard to come by, primarily because relatively few churches reveal their finances, but estimates are typically in the 2% to 3% range,[20*] with, as mentioned above, a self-reported 1.68% rate by the Southern Baptists. (One reason such figures are hard to determine is that churches are almost entirely unaccountable, to anyone, financially. To cite but one example of this lack of accountability, churches are under no obligation to file income tax returns—so they don't.)

The figure for charitable giving might be somewhat higher as regards the Catholic Church—by far the richest Christian church—but not tremendously so, given that local, state, and federal funding accounts for 62% of the financial support for the largest American Catholic charitable organization, Catholic Charities.[21]

Even given the relatively paltry nature of their charitable giving, it's good to remember that Christian charities almost universally deal only with the effects of poverty and other social problems, not their causes.

With that in mind, let's look at the catalog of social ills listed a few paragraphs back and see how the Christian churches are addressing these problems.

Poverty. A large majority of churches do nothing to address the root causes of poverty, and many support politicians who help to ensure its continued existence.

Homelessness. Christian charities (Salvation Army, rescue missions, etc.) provide temporary housing in many places. There are also probably a few scattered projects to provide long-term housing for the homeless, but they're at best a drop in the bucket, and again the churches do nothing to address the root causes of homelessness.

Hunger. Churches support food banks and soup kitchens in many areas, which of course is praiseworthy. As for root causes, again the churches do nothing.

---

* This refers to income, not wealth, which the churches continue to amass year after year. In addition, the 2% to 3% figure might be at least slightly too high, as witnessed by the Baptists' lower figure, and the fact that some churches count "pastoral services" as a form of charitable giving.

Militarism. While there are anti-militarist Christians, organized Christianity is overwhelmingly neutral on the matter or supportive of militarism. This is especially true of evangelicals, whose end-times beliefs spur enthusiastic support for U.S. military adventurism in the Middle East, with many evangelicals hoping for a war that will bring on the end times, and fervently supporting extreme-right, militaristic American and Israeli politicians so as to hasten that desired end. The millions of deaths and untold suffering such a war would bring with it? Not a problem for these "pro-life" Christians who *want* that death and suffering.

Unequal distribution of wealth and income. The vast majority of churches are doing nothing to address this problem.

Lack of universal healthcare. Again, the vast majority of churches are doing nothing to address the causes of this problem that costs tens of thousands of lives annually in the U.S. (A 2009 study by the Harvard Medical School put the number at 45,000 unnecessary deaths per year.)[22]

Ecological despoliation and the climate crisis. Yet again, organized Christianity is doing next to nothing to address this extremely serious problem.

Overpopulation. This is a primary cause of many of the preceding problems, especially environmental degradation, yet organized Christianity actively works to worsen this root-cause problem. This is especially so with the Catholic Church, some evangelicals (e.g., the "Quiverfull" movement), and the nominally Christian LDS Church, all of which encourage irresponsible, mindless breeding, oppose abortion, and in some cases even oppose contraception.

Misogyny. Christianity itself is a prime cause of this problem. (More broadly, patriarchal religions, including Islam, religious Judaism, and Hinduism, are prime causes.)

Racism. The record of the Christian churches is very mixed. Here in the U.S., for example, during the 1950s and 1960s, black evangelicals were at the forefront of the civil rights movement, while white evangelicals were, overall, its most fervent foes (which is understandable given that there's not a single word in the Bible condemning racism, while there are numerous verses condoning slavery).

Homophobia. Christianity itself is a prime cause of this problem in the U.S. and the rest of the Western world.

Laws against victimless crimes. In the U.S., Christian moralism and cruelty are *the* prime causes.

An inadequate, unequal education system. The churches have done nothing to address this problem, but on the contrary have been working to undermine public school science and history curricula, and have also been working to siphon off public funds into their indoctrination-factory charter and parochial schools.

By and large, the ultra-rich Christian churches do nothing to address the very real evils afflicting all of us, and where they do take action, they often work to worsen those evils.

Endnotes

1. “Dissolution of the Monasteries,” by Ben Johnson. Historic-UK. https://www.historic-uk.com/HistoryUK/HistoryofEngland/Dissolution-of-the-Monasteries/ < https://tinyurl.com/46kkrv79 >

2. “The World’s 15 Biggest Landowners,” by Thornton McEnery. *Business Insider*, March 18, 2011. https://www.businessinsider.com/worlds-biggest-landowners-2011-3#3-pope-benedict-13 < https://tinyurl.com/y22debus >

3. “Vatican details worldwide property holdings for first time.” *DeutscheWelle*. https://www.dw.com/en/vatican-details-worldwide-property-holdings-for-first-time/a-58627354 < https://tinyurl.com/ypmsdm2v >

4. “42 faith groups in 14 countries announce divestment from fossil fuels,” by Brian Roewe. Earthbeat: Stories of climate crisis, faith, and action, May 17, 2020. https://www.ncronline.org/news/earthbeat/42-faith-groups-14-countries-announce-divestment-fossil-fuels < https://tinyurl.com/4pke92t6 >

5. “Vatican Inc.: 5 facts about the business of the Catholic Church,” by Ahiza Garcia. CNN Money, September 9, 2015. https://money.cnn.com/2015/09/24/news/pope-francis-visit-catholic-church/index.html < https://tinyurl.com/yyo6s6y7 >

6. “How many Roman Catholics are there in the world?,” BBC News, March 14, 2013. https://www.bbc.com/news/world-21443313 < https://tinyurl.com/y5myz326 >

7. “Wealth of Roman Catholic Church impossible to calculate,” by Kristopher Morrison, *National Post*, May 9, 2013. https://nationalpost.com/news/wealth-of-roman-catholic-church-impossible-to-calculate

8. “Scientology shifts millions to Australia, books multimillion-dollar profits,” by Ben Schneiders. *Sydnet Morning Herald*, April 1, 2021. https://www.smh.com.au/national/scientology-shifts-millions-to-safe-haven-australia-and-books-multi-million-dollar-profits-20210325-p57e18.html < https://tinyurl.com/w4n3yt5a >

9. “Michigan residents leaving the Catholic Church as many turn away from religion,” by Julie Mack. *Mlive*, April 29, 2019. https://www.mlive.com/news/2019/04/michigan-residents-leaving-the-catholic-church-as-many-turn-away-from-religion.html < https://tinyurl.com/y4zssbdb >

10. “Church And Religious Charitable Giving Statistics.” Nonprofit Source. https://nonprofitssource.com/online-giving-statistics/church-giving/ < https://tinyurl.com/yxmkj57r >

11. “7 facts about American Catholics,” by David Masci and Gregory A. Smith, Pew Research Center, October 10, 2018. https://www.pewresearch.org/fact-tank/2018/10/10/7-facts-about-american-catholics/ < https://tinyurl.com/y5hxzcmr >

12. *The Mormon Murders: A True Story of Greed, Forgery, Deceit, and Death*, by Steven Naifeh and Gregory White Smith. New York: Weidenfeld & Nicolson, 1988, p. 22.

13. "The Mormon Church's secretive $100 billion fund revealed huge stakes in Apple, Google, and Microsoft. Here are its 10 biggest holdings," by Theron Mohamed. *Markets Insider*, February 19, 2020. https://markets.businessinsider.com/news/stocks/mormon-church-billions-investment-fund-top-stocks-ensign-apple-google-2020-2-1028920228 < https://tinyurl.com/y3fvg4n8 >

14. Nonprofit Source, op. cit.

15. "Southern Baptist decline continues, denomination has lost more than 2 million members since 2006," by Bob Smietana. Religion News Service, May 21, 2021. https://religionnews.com/2021/05/21/southern-baptist-decline-continues-denomination-has-lost-more-than-2-million-members-since-2006/ < https://tinyurl.com/22rtn9eb >

16. "Scientology admits that it numbers 'tens of thousands' not millions, as we've been saying," by Tony Ortega. The Underground Bunker, April 28, 2020. https://tonyortega.org/2020/04/28/scientology-admits-that-it-numbers-tens-of-thousands-not-millions-as-weve-been-saying/ < https://tinyurl.com/y6qznyj7 >

17. "Statistical Abstract of the United States: 2011 Table 74. Population in Group Quarters by State: 2000 to 2009." Census Bureau. https://www2.census.gov/library/publications/2010/compendia/statab/130ed/tables/11s0075.pdf < https://tinyurl.com/y3x25gy9 >

18. "Church Of Scientology Worth More Than $1.2 Billion, According To New Tax Docs." *Business Insider*, April 10, 2014. https://www.businessinsider.com/church-of-scientology-worth-more-than-12-billion-according-to-new-tax-documents-2014-4 < https://tinyurl.com/y5r8c5lm >

19. Schneiders, op. cit.

20. "Are Churches More Like Charities or Country Clubs?" Galileo Unchained, May 14, 2012. https://galileounchained.com/2012/05/14/are-churches-more-like-charities-or-country-clubs/

21. "Earthly concerns." *The Economist*, August 18, 2012. https://www.economist.com/briefing/2012/08/18/earthly-concerns < https://tinyurl.com/y5fwzooe >

22. "New study finds 45,000 deaths annually linked to lack of health coverage," by David Cecere. *The Harvard Gazette*, September 17, 2009. https://news.harvard.edu/gazette/story/2009/09/new-study-finds-45000-deaths-annually-linked-to-lack-of-health-coverage/ < https://tinyurl.com/y3kmh26j >

16

Christianity Degrades and Devalues the Natural World

> In Christianity, neither morality nor religion is in contact with any point of reality. Nothing but imaginary *causes* (God, soul, ego, spirit, free will—or even 'unfree will'); nothing but imaginary *effects* (sin, salvation, grace, punishment, forgiveness of sin). . . . This purely *fictitious world* is, greatly to its disadvantage, distinguished from the dream world in that while the latter reflects reality, the former falsifies, depreciates, and negates it. When once the concept of 'nature' was devised as a concept antithetical to 'God,' 'natural' had to be the word for 'reprehensible'; that whole fictitious world has its root in *hatred* of the natural . . .
>
> —Friedrich Nietzsche, *The Anti-Christ*

In addition to its morbid preoccupation with sex, Christianity creates social myopia through its emphasis on the supposed afterlife, encouraging Christians not to be concerned with "the things of this world" (except, of course, their neighbors' sexual practices). In the conventional Christian view, life in this "vale of tears" is not important—what matters is preparing for the *next* life. It follows from this that the "vale of tears" itself is quite unimportant—it's merely the backdrop to the testing of the faithful.

The Christian belief in the unimportance of happiness and wellbeing in this world is well illustrated in a statement by St. Alphonsus, as quoted in Reverend Furniss's *Tracts for Spiritual Reading*:

> It would be a great advantage to suffer during all our lives all the torments of the martyrs in exchange for one moment of heaven. Sufferings in this world are a sign that God loves us and intends to save us. . . . The best penance we can do is to receive the sickness, because it is God's will.

Former Anglican priest and later Catholic Cardinal John Newman put it like this in his *Difficulties of Anglicans*:

> The [Catholic] church holds that it were better for sun and moon to drop from heaven, for the earth to fail, and for all the many millions who are upon it to die of starvation in extremest agony, so far as temporal affliction goes, than that one soul, I will not say should be lost, but should commit one single venial sin . . .

Combine this attitude—that the world we live in isn't important, nor is human suffering—with the words of Genesis 1:28, "And God blessed them, and God said unto them, Be fruitful, and multiply, and replenish the earth, and subdue it: and have dominion over the fish of the sea, and over the fowl of the air, and over every living thing that moveth upon the earth," and you have a recipe for disaster. That disaster's proximate cause is capitalism's profit-at-any-price-to-others motive, but the Christian "vale of tears" and "dominion" beliefs provide ideological justification for it.

Since time immemorial, believers, spurred on by the profit motive, have used Genesis 1:28 as justification for grossly mistreating animals and despoiling the earth. And despoil it they have. There's an ongoing human-caused mass extinction with in all likelihood thousands, possibly tens of thousands, of species going extinct every year. The UN's Intergovernmental Science-Policy Platform on Biodiversity and Ecosystem Services reports that there are "1,000,000 species threatened with extinction" including "more than 40% of amphibian species . . . and more than a third of marine mammals."[1] Meanwhile, the World Wildlife Federation's 2020 survey of over 4,000 vertebrate species showed that "the population sizes of mammals, birds, fish, amphibians and reptiles have seen an alarming average drop of 68% since 1970."[2]

And with every species that disappears, the environment grows more unstable, with increasingly disastrous results.

To cite but one result in the United States, the near eradication of wolves and the decimation of other top predators has led to an explosion of deer across the country. This has greatly contributed to the spread of Lyme Disease-bearing ticks, a spread which is being aggravated by global warming. At present, the disease has spread to every state in the country, with the vast bulk of cases being in the New England and Mid-Atlantic states plus Wisconsin and Minnesota,[3] with 30,000 confirmed cases annually. But this is just the tip of the iceberg: the CDC cites estimates that there are actually 240,000 to 444,000 infections of this debilitating disease every year in the U.S.[4]

The same thing is happening in Europe. According to National Geographic, "the ticks that carry Lyme disease, once largely limited to the south, are finding new hosts as far north as Sweden. Some winters aren't cold enough to kill the young nymphs, . . . A similar issue has struck a region near Russia's Ural Mountains, which has seen a 23-fold increase in tick-borne encephalitis in 20 years. Temperature changes have lengthened the tick season by half . . ."[5]

Another result of climate disruption is the global warming-induced steady creep northward of debilitating and deadly tropical diseases. The best known of these are Zika, Yellow Fever, and malaria, which have been spreading in the southern tier of the United States; but there are also lesser known diseases and disease vectors spreading north, including "the sandflies that host parasites that cause leishmaniasis, some varieties of which cause skin lesions or spleen and liver damage, [and which] are showing up in north Texas."[6]

But the spreading diseases aren't limited to land. "Among the most well documented of these new threats is the spread of ocean-traveling Vibrio bacteria that can sicken or kill unsuspecting swimmers or shellfish eaters, even though these bacteria need warm water to survive. There are more than 80 species of Vibrio, at least a dozen of which are pathenogenic to fish and humans, including the bacteria that causes cholera, . . ."[7]

These examples only scratch the surface.

There are major uncertainties about both the number of species on Earth and the number of species going extinct annually—largely because of the huge number of insect species, vast numbers of which have never been catalogued—but what is certain is that the human-caused extinction rate, while hard to calculate, is almost certainly at least a hundred to a thousand times higher than the natural extinction rate,[8] it's likely that there are at least a million species threatened with extinction,[9] and the results of species extinction and global warming are already disastrous.

In the year 1500, worldwide human population was about half a billion. It took three centuries to reach a billion. From that billion in 1800, it increased to about 1.7 billion in 1900. By 2000, it had more than tripled to over 6 billion, and at present it's over 7 billion and still rising.

That means ever-increasing human intrusion into the previously wild places on our finite planet, and with that intrusion massive habitat loss, the prime driver of extinction, along with ever increasing human-caused global warming. It also means ever more zoonotic diseases (animal diseases that can infect humans), due to consumption of wild animals for meat and other types of close contact. Historically, these zoonotic diseases included smallpox, tuberculosis, measles, leprosy, herpes, chlamydia, and cholera. More recent animal-vector diseases include SARS, MERS, ebola, and HIV—and very probably Covid-19. It's almost certain that more such disease outbreaks will arise, perhaps at an accelerating pace, with increasing human population and intrusion into previously wild areas, and increasing contact with the remaining wild animals, especially "contact" via consumption of "bushmeat." This is such a problem that the NIH states, "Zoonotic diseases are the main contributor to emerging infectious diseases (EIDs) and present a major threat to global public health."[10]

One contributing factor to the climate change-induced spread of tropical diseases is that fossil fuel entities, especially ExxonMobil and the Koch brothers, have been funding disinformation campaigns about global warming for decades.[11] In 1957, in a study conducted for the American Petroleum Institute, physicist Edward Teller ("father of the H-bomb") warned of the "greenhouse effect" caused by excess CO_2 created by the burning of fossil fuels.[12] As early as 1977, Exxon executives knew, based on Exxon's own research, that climate change was real, human caused, and largely due to the burning of fossil fuels. Their own scientists warned Exxon (in a bullet-pointed summary) that "CO_2 release [is the] most likely source of inadvertent climate modification" and that "Doubling CO_2 could result [in an] increase [in] average global temperature [of] 1 degree C to 5 degrees C (10 degrees at the poles)."[13] Not even those ominous warnings were enough for Exxon to do anything to combat this deadly threat. Instead, safeguarding its profits, Exxon did nothing to combat climate change and instead chose to lie about it—for decades.[14]

Exxon is still doing it. In July 2021, Britain's Channel 4 broadcast a video of Exxon lobbyist Keith McCoy telling Greenpeace activists, posing as corporate headhunters, that Exxon would continue to "aggressively fight against some of the science," and that it was working with "shadow groups" to do so.[15] The outcome of the petroleum industry's decades-long disinformation campaign? According to R.E. Dunlap and A.M. McCright, authors of *The Oxford Handbook of Climate Change and Society*, "It is reasonable to conclude that climate change denial campaigns in the US have played a crucial role in blocking domestic legislation and contributing to the US becoming an impediment to international policy making."[16]

You might think that all of the horrifying things listed above—many of which have been well known since the 1970s and even earlier—would have set off the alarm bells, that the environmental crisis and its cover-up by fossil fuels companies and their hired lackeys would have moved the "moral authorities" to action decades ago. But you'd be wrong.

The churches by and large did and said next to nothing until the second decade of the 21st century. It wasn't until 2015 that Pope Francis issued the first papal encyclical on the environmental crisis, *Laudato Si* ("On care of our common home"). And it wasn't until roughly the same time that some of the vastly wealthy Christian churches began to divest themselves of fossil fuels investments, and then in a relatively paltry and piecemeal fashion, with the Jesuits promising to divest only in 2020.[17]

As regards our exploding population, consequent habitat loss, species extinction, and the spread of zoonotic diseases, the churches have been even worse.

The Catholic hierarchy has always been open about encouraging endless population growth, about its desire to fill the world to overflowing with people no matter what the consequences. As Pope Pius XI put it in *Casti Connubii* ("Of Chaste Wedlock," 1930): "Since the conjugal act is designed primarily by nature for the begetting of children, those who in exercising it deliberately frustrate its natural power and purpose sin against nature and commit an act which is shameful and inherently vicious."

(Some might cite, with considerable reason, capitalism—and its profit motive-driven economic predecessors—as the root cause of ecological despoliation, but it's undeniable that Christianity has provided a religious rationale for the deliberate and seemingly endless degradation of Mother Earth in the pursuit of profit. It's also undeniable that the Catholic Church, some of the other Christian sects, and the nominally Christian Mormons encourage endless population growth with consequent endless environmental degradation.)

Let's consider for a moment three additional examples of the wanton damage inflicted upon nature by profit motive-driven Christians. Here, in what's now the United States, Christian colonizers cut down 99% of the native forests, and they deliberately destroyed entire species, such as the Carolina Parakeet, the only native parrot species whose habitat was entirely in the U.S. (They also destroyed the Thick-Billed Parrot population native to southeast Arizona, though a small population remains in the mountains of northern Mexico.) And they deliberately drove many other species, including the buffalo, to near extinction. Among other atrocities, they shot innumerable bison from railroad cars for "sport," and left the carcasses rotting on the plains. That a few buffalo survived wasn't due to lack of effort on the part of the slaughterers.

What did the Christian clergy say about this cruel, wanton, and massive destruction? Nothing, other than to *encourage* the self-identified Christian chosen people to exercise "dominion" in this new "promised land." There might have been a few clerical voices raised against the ongoing carnage, but if there were any—none come to mind—they were about as audible as a whisper in a thunderstorm. What is certain is that the largest and most powerful Christian sect, the Roman Catholic Church, said nothing about this evil, this rampant environmental destruction, until the 21st century. The various popes, in their encyclicals, instead attacked the evils of free speech, freedom of conscience, and family planning.*

Well past the midpoint of the twentieth century, organized Christianity was silent on the ecological crisis. When the environmental movement arose in the 1960s, it wasn't led by the Christian churches or by those whose Christian faith led them to take part in it. Far from it. Environmental leaders by and large came from the scientific community, the secular left, and the counterculture. Rank and file environmentalists came largely from the last of those three groups. This still holds true, though present-day rank and file environmentalists include large numbers of everyday people from the working and middle classes, some members of the well off who have a conscience, and some liberal churchgoers.

Today, ongoing and looming environmental disasters are omnipresent, overwhelming, and ever more extreme: habitat loss; accelerating species extinction; catastrophic global warming and its attendant sea level rise, droughts, crop failures, cataclysmic wild fires, more severe and more frequent hurricanes, and torrential rains and flooding, just to name the most prominent.

To cite one close-to-home example, Southern Arizona is among the worst hit parts of the United States as regards both temperature increase and drought. The drought has been with us since the late 1990s, and in

---

* To be fair, Pope Leo XIII in his 1891 encyclical, *Rerum Novarum* ("Of New Things"), went beyond such matters and recognized the need to address "the misery and wretchedness pressing so unjustly on the working class"; Pope Leo didn't get too carried away, though, as he offered no concrete steps to eradicate that "misery and wretchedness," and in the same encyclical he rejected socialism and upheld the right to private property.

2020 both Phoenix and Tucson recorded their hottest summers ever, with the average high temperature in Phoenix in August 2020 being an astounding 110.7 degrees F (43.7 C),[18] and with 2020 being the driest year ever in Tucson since records were first kept in the late 19th century: in 2020, only 4.17" of rain fell, over seven inches below the average of 11.59" in the years 2001–2010.[19] (That average itself is lower than the 12-plus-inches-per-year average in the decades prior to 2001; and during the last decade, 2011–2020, average rainfall came in at only 10.63".)

The extreme weather trend continued in 2021, with the cataclysmic "deep freeze" event in mid-February that covered much of Canada, almost the entire U.S. between the Rockies and the Appalachians, and even extended into northern Mexico. That single event caused $20 billion in damage and hundreds of deaths in Texas alone.[20,21] The proximate cause of all those deaths was power outages due to lack of preparedness by Texas's privately owned utilities, and weak regulation of them by the state.

The cause of the "deep freeze" itself? The global warming-caused weakening and destabilization of the polar vortex; the vortex destabilization in turn destabilized the jet stream, allowing it to dip much farther south than was normal in years past. An article in *Science* put it this way: "Despite the rapid warming that is the cardinal signature of global climate change, especially in the Arctic, where temperatures are rising much more than elsewhere in the world, the United States and other regions of the Northern Hemisphere have experienced a conspicuous and increasingly frequent number of episodes of extremely cold winter weather over the past four decades."[22] A BBC report adds, "The scientists [who conducted the study] believe this vortex stretching process led to the deadly Texas cold wave in February this year [2021]."[23]

Because of that destabilization, it's all but certain that such weather disasters will become more frequent in coming decades, as will other effects of global warming. Four months after the "deep freeze" event, North America endured its hottest June ever. Less than a month after that, parts of western Europe experienced torrential rains and the worst flooding in centuries, causing tens of billions in damage, the displacement of tens of thousands of people from their homes, and hundreds of deaths. German Chancellor Angela Merkel said of the flooding, which caused over $35 billion damage in Germany, "It is shocking—I can almost say that the German language doesn't have words for the devastation."[24]

To make matters worse, the BBC, citing data from the World Meteorologic Organization, states that there's been a major increase in the number of extreme weather events over the last half century, reporting 11,000 such events in the years from 1970 on. The report states, "Over two million people died as a result of these hazards, with economic losses amounting to $3.64 trillion."[25] What's even worse is that the number and cost of these catastrophic events has been drastically increasing in recent years: "Reported losses in the decade between 2010–2019 were around $383m [million] per day, a seven-fold increase on the $49m per day between 1970–1979."[26]

To make matters still worse, the effects of climate change—which are already causing misery in hot, drought-prone places such as Arizona, and even more so in low-lying island and coastal nations—over the next century are largely predictable, already well underway, and increasingly destructive: the flooding of low-lying coastal regions and small island countries resulting, ultimately, in the displacement of hundred of millions of people; climate-change refugees attempting to flee *en masse* to first world countries; widespread drought and increasing desertification resulting in decreased food production and consequent hunger and famine; the continuing mass extinction of species, further destabilizing the environment; conflicts over increasingly scarce resources, especially fresh water; massive, catastrophic wildfires; increasing numbers and severity of hurricanes; and, as mentioned above, the gradual northward creep of tropical diseases (dengue, malaria, West Nile virus, chikungunya virus, and others).[27] These interconnected disasters have already led to untold misery, two million deaths, and in all probability will lead to many millions more deaths.

Yet a great many Christians, especially "pro-life" Christians, appear entirely unconcerned with the ongoing and accelerating environmental catastrophe, with all its attendant suffering and death. A great many of them simply deny reality, deny that the climate disaster is real, and still focus their moral outrage on gay and reproductive rights. They're so concerned with denying others basic human freedoms that they not only turn a blind eye to ecological destruction, but many of them encourage and engage in it.

Yes, some religious folk and even some churches now acknowledge the severity of the environmental crisis, and some of them are working to mitigate the damage. But, they seem to be in a distinct minority. As usual, science and secular humanists lead, and religions and religious believers lag.

Worse, there are a great many Christian faithful, especially among evangelicals, who still hold to the old vale-of-tears and Dominionist beliefs. Some of them, such as Ronald Reagan's Secretary of the Interior, James Watt (and seemingly all of the members of the Bush and Trump administrations), have actively encouraged environmental devastation. James Watt actually said, “We don’t have to protect the environment, the Second Coming is at hand.”[28] During his time in office, Watt enabled the strip mining and clear cutting of the American West, reasoning that ecological degradation didn’t matter because the rapture was imminent.

More recently, the prominent evangelical pastor John MacArthur, of the Grace Community Church in Los Angeles, topped Watt. MacArthur put it like this: “God intended us to use this planet to fill this planet for the benefit of man. Never was intended to be a permanent planet. It is a disposable planet.”[29]

Several decades after James Watt’s appalling statement, and over a decade after MacArthur’s, the rapture still hasn’t arrived. But that appears not to make a whit of difference to the “pro-life” Christians who cheered on the Reagan, Bush, and Trump administrations’ massive assaults on the environment. As always, they placed, and continue to place, imposition of their perverted morality above the health, happiness, rights, and lives of others, and above the health and beauty of the natural world.

It’s a good bet they’ll continue to do so.

Endnotes

1. “UN Report: Nature’s Dangerous Decline ‘Unprecedented’; Species Extinction Rates ‘Accelerating.’” United Nations Intergovernmental Science-Policy Platform on Biodiversity and Ecosystem Services. https://www.un.org/sustainabledevelopment/blog/2019/05/nature-decline-unprecedented-report/ < https://tinyurl.com/y63bngac >

2. “Living Planet Report 2020.” World Wildlife Federation. https://livingplanet.panda.org/en-us/ < https://tinyurl.com/y5yavlma >

3. “Lyme Disease Data Tables: Historical Data.” Center for Disease Control and Prevention. https://www.cdc.gov/lyme/stats/tables.html < https://tinyurl.com/y2gvc6yx >

4. “How Many People Get Lyme Disease?,” Center for Disease Control and Prevention. https://www.cdc.gov/lyme/stats/humancases.html < https://tinyurl.com/y967yad9 >

5. “Postcards from the sixth mass extinction event,” by John P. Rafferty. Brittanica. https://www.britannica.com/topic/Postcards-from-the-6th-Mass-Extinction-2153898#ref1274124 < https://tinyurl.com/y55f434w >

6. “Climate Change Pushing Tropical Diseases Toward Arctic,” by Craig Welch, *National Geographic*, June 14, 2017. https://www.nationalgeographic.com/news/2017/06/vibrio-zika-west-nile-malaria-diseases-spreading-climate-change/ < https://tinyurl.com/yyx4lvlm >

7. Ibid.

8. “Human Induced Extinction.” Brittanica. https://www.britannica.com/science/human-induced-extinction < https://tinyurl.com/y3osh8b9 >

9. Op., cit. United Nations Intergovernmental Science-Policy Platform on Biodiversity and Ecosystem Services.

10. "Bushmeat and Emerging Infectious Diseases: Lessons from Africa," by Francesco M. Angelici, et al. US National Library of Medicine, National Institutes of Health. https://www.ncbi.nlm.nih.gov/pmc/articles/PMC7123567/ < https://tinyurl.com/45kyfsk4 >

11. "Unreliable Sources: How the News Media Help the Koch Brothers and ExxonMobil Spread Climate Disinformation." Union of Concerned Scientists, May 13, 2013. https://www.ucsusa.org/resources/how-news-media-help-koch-brothers-and-exxonmobil < https://tinyurl.com/y55ysdvh >

12. "Assessing ExxonMobil's climate change communications," by Geoffrey Supran, PhD. European Union, March 19, 2019. https://www.europarl.europa.eu/cmsdata/162144/Presentation%20Geoffrey%20Supran.pdf < https://tinyurl.com/2622e2vm >

13. Ibid.

14. "Exxon Knew about Climate Change almost 40 years ago," by Shannon Hall. *Scientific American*, October 26, 2015. https://www.scientificamerican.com/article/exxon-knew-about-climate-change-almost-40-years-ago/ < https://tinyurl.com/y5da6pxu >

15. "Climate scientists take swipe at Exxon Mobil, industry in leaked report," by Zach Coleman and Karl Mathiesen. *Politico*, July 2, 2021. https://www.politico.com/news/2021/07/02/climate-scientists-exxon-mobile-report-497805 < https://tinyurl.com/48asruxv >

16. Supran, op. cit.

17. "42 faith groups in 14 countries announce divestment from fossil fuels," by Brian Roewe. Earthbeat: Stories of climate crisis, faith, and action, May 17, 2020. https://www.ncronline.org/news/earthbeat/42-faith-groups-14-countries-announce-divestment-fossil-fuels < https://tinyurl.com/4pke92t6 >

18. "Melting weather records in August, Phoenix sees hottest summer on record," by Julia Musto. Fox News, September 2, 2020. https://www.foxnews.com/us/phoenix-hottest-summer-on-record-arizona < https://tinyurl.com/yxfctds3 >

19. "We're parched: 2020 brought Tucson's driest year on record," by Tony Davis. Tucson.com/*Arizona Daily Star*, April 16, 2021. https://tucson.com/news/local/were-parched-2020-brought-tucsons-driest-year-on-record/article_1cdf0f08-14f2-528a-839b-d388810353cd.html < https://tinyurl.com/56ru4xp4 >

20. "June 2021 was the hottest June on record for U.S." National Oceanic and Atmospheric Administration, July 9, 2021. https://www.noaa.gov/news/june-2021-was-hottest-june-on-record-for-us < https://tinyurl.com/3fa96f85 >

21. "Texas Winter Storm Death Toll Could Be Much Higher Than The State's Count, BuzzFeed Data Review Found," by Alejandro Martínez-Cabrera. Houston Public Media, May 27, 2021. https://www.houstonpublicmedia.org/articles/news/energy-environment/2021/05/27/399291/texas-winter-storm-death-toll-could-be-much-higher-than-the-states-count-buzzfeed-data-review-found/ < https://tinyurl.com/26tjbdjc >

22. "Linking Arctic variability and change with extreme winter weather in the United States," by Judah Cohen, et al. *Science*, Vol 373, Issue 6559, pp. 1116-112, September 3, 2021. https://www.science.org/doi/10.1126/science.abi9167 < https://tinyurl.com/asu9hvuw >

23. "Climate change: Arctic warming linked to colder winters," by Matt McGrath. BBC News, September 2, 2021. https://www.bbc.com/news/science-environment-58425526 < https://tinyurl.com/5ftxxpav >

24. "Enormous scale of destruction is revealed as water subsides after historic western Europe flooding," by Ivana Kottasová. CNN, July 18, 2021. https://www.cnn.com/2021/07/18/europe/western-europe-floods-sunday-intl/index.html < https://tinyurl.com/4bxtccw4 >

25. "Climate change: Big increase in weather disasters over the past five decades," by Matt McGrath. BBC News, September 1, 2021. https://www.bbc.com/news/science-environment-58396975 < https://tinyurl.com/mdr97kep >

26. Ibid.

27. "Global expansion and redistribution of Aedes-borne virus transmission risk with climate change," by Sadie J. Ryan et al. *PLOS Neglected Tropical Diseases*. https://journals.plos.org/plosntds/article?id=10.1371/journal.pntd.0007213 < https://tinyurl.com/y5yus5fg >

28. “Quotes from the American Taliban.” University of California at San Diego. http://adultthought.ucsd.edu/Culture_War/The_American_Taliban.html < https://tinyurl.com/j7k3k >

29. “The End of the Universe, Part 2,” by James MacArthur. Grace to You, September 21, 2008. https://www.gty.org/library/sermons-library/90-361/the-end-of-the-universe-part-2 < https://tinyurl.com/jzp4uthy >

17

The Christian Chosen People Mentality and its Deadly Consequences

One must not be misled: 'judge not,' they say, but send everything to hell which stands in their way. In making God judge, they themselves judge; in glorifying God, they glorify themselves.
—Friedrich Nietzsche, *The Anti-Christ*

It's only natural that those who believe (or play act at believing) that they have a direct line to the Almighty would feel superior to others. This is so obvious that it needs little elaboration. A brief look at religious terminology confirms it. Christians have often called themselves "God's people," "the chosen people," "the elect," "the righteous," "the saved," while nonbelievers have been labeled "heathens," "infidels," "pagans," and "atheistic Communists." This sets up a two-tiered division of humanity in which "God's people" feel superior to everyone else.

Extreme-right, Reconstrucionist Christian Gary North spells this out:

> It occurs to me: Was Moses arrogant and unbiblical when he instructed the Israelites to kill every Canaanite in the land . . . ? Was he an 'elitist' or (horror of horrors) a racist? No; he was a God-fearing man who sought to obey God, who commanded them to kill them all. It sounds like a 'superior attitude' to me. Of course, Christians have been given no comparable military command in New Testament times, but I am trying to deal with the attitude of superiority—a superiority based on our possession of the law of God. That attitude is something Christians must have when dealing with all pagans. God has given us the tools of dominion.
> —Gary North, *The Sinai Strategy*[1]

This superior attitude, and its accompanying arrogant, self-aggrandizing terminology, is rooted in the Old Testament, in which there are a great many references to the Israelites being "the chosen people." Deuteronomy 7:6 states the matter most baldly, making the two-tiered division of humanity explicit: "For thou art an holy people unto the LORD thy God: the LORD thy God hath chosen thee to be a special people unto himself, above all people that are upon the face of the earth." (The wording of Deuteronomy 14:2 is virtually identical, a near-exact repetition, which points to the fact that the LORD could have used a good copy editor.)

One of the earliest instances of Christians appropriating the "chosen people" identity occurred in church father Tertullian's (155–220) *Adversus Judaeos* ("Against the Jews"), in which Tertullian argued that the Jews had abandoned their status as the chosen people by refusing to accept Christ, and therefore Christians, who had accepted Christ, were the new chosen people (to which one can only say, "how convenient").

Since those ancient times, and the first claims of special status, Christians have wholeheartedly appropriated and embraced the "chosen people" label. As an illustration of this, I ran a Google search for "chosen people Bible verses," and the first result was a page on a Christian web site, openbible.info, "100 Bible Verses About Being a Chosen People." All of the other results on that first page were from Christian groups, with the sole exception of an entry all the way at the bottom by brittanica.com.

This brings up the question of how the chosen people should deal with their ("nonchosen") inferiors? The Bible supplies plenty of advice. The following passages from Deuteronomy and Numbers are among the most explicit:

> When the Lord thy God shall bring thee into the land whither thou goest to possess it, and hath cast out many nations before thee, the Hittites, and the Girgashites, and the Amorites, and the Canaanites, and the Perizzites, and the Hivites, and the Jebusites, seven nations greater and mightier than thou; And when the Lord thy God shall deliver them before thee; thou shalt smite them, and utterly destroy them; thou shalt make no covenant with them, nor shew mercy unto them: . . . But thus shall ye deal with them; ye shall destroy their altars, and break down their images, and cut down their groves, and burn their graven images with fire. For thou art an holy people unto the Lord thy God: the Lord thy God hath chosen thee to be a special people unto himself, above all people that are upon the face of the earth.
> —Deuteronomy 7:1–2, 5–6

> And Moses spake unto the people, saying, Arm some of yourselves unto the war, and let them go against the Midianites . . . And they warred against the Midianites, as the Lord commanded Moses; and they slew all the males. . . . And the children of Israel took all the women of Midian captives, and their little ones, and took the spoil of all their cattle, and all their flocks, and all their goods. And they burnt all their cities wherein they dwelt, and all their goodly castles, with fire. And they took all the spoil, and all the prey, both of men and of beasts. And they brought the captives, and the prey, and the spoil, unto Moses . . . And Moses said unto them, Have ye saved all the women alive? . . . Now therefore kill every male among the little ones, and kill every woman that hath known man by lying with him. But all the women children, that have not known a man by lying with him, keep alive for yourselves. —Numbers 31:3–18.

Other passages, such as 1 Samuel 15:3 and Deuteronomy 20:13–14, are on par with the above.

How these divine injunctions have played out is amply demonstrated in the following sections and in the next chapter: these divine commands have led directly to wars of conquest, mass murder, rape, torture, and enslavement.

Wars of Conquest

For the sake of brevity, we'll mostly bypass the centuries-long crusades and the long and bloody internecine religious wars between Catholics and Protestants in Europe following the Reformation, in which atrocities and mass murder were common. Here, we'll restrict ourselves to citing a single instance from the English Civil War. Christian writer and historian Philip Jenkins describes one massacre:

> . . . each faction labeled its (Christian) opponents as Amalekites [yet more enemies of God's chosen people] fit only for slaughter (see 1 Samuel 15:3). . . . after Scottish Protestants defeated an Irish Royalist [Catholic] army in 1646, their clergy advisers ordered a complete massacre of prisoners. Scots soldiers drowned eighty women and children, while again and again were the conquerors told [by the clergy] that the curses which befell those who spared the enemies of God would fall upon him who suffered one Amalekite (Catholic) to escape.[2]

As bad as this is, what Christian conquerors did to native peoples in the Americas, Africa, Australia, and Asia was worse.

Conquest in the Americas

Given their divine pedigree and the "inspired" commands that guided them, is it any wonder that the chosen people of the Old Testament were so arrogant and acted so brutally against "inferior" peoples (mass murder of the Canaanites, Hittites, Amorites, et al.)? Is it any wonder that their spiritual successors, Europe's and America's self-identified Christian chosen people, felt totally justified in enslaving and slaughtering those they considered their inferiors? There are many atrocious examples of such enslavement and slaughter from almost all continents, but for the sake of brevity we'll confine ourselves to events in the Americas.

Let's consider some of the statements and actions of Christian conqueror, colonizer *par excellence*, and trader in African slaves, Christopher Columbus. The Mormon writer Glen W. Chapman, in his piece, "Christopher Columbus: A Spiritual Giant," reports a statement by Columbus showing that he believed his mission was God ordained: "God made me the messenger of the new heaven and new earth of which he spoke in the Apocalypse of St. John after having spoken of it through the mouth of Isaiah; and he showed me the spot where to find it."[3]

How did this delusion of grandeur play out in practice? During his voyages of "discovery," Columbus routinely planted a cross on newly "discovered" islands, and then read a statement, the *Requerimiento* (Requirement) to the natives in Spanish, a language they didn't understand. It read in part:

> I certify to you that, with the help of God, we shall powerfully enter into your country and shall make war against you in all ways and manners that we can, and shall subject you to the yoke and obedience of the Church and of Their Highnesses [Ferdinand and Isabella]. We shall take you and your wives and your children and shall make slaves ot them, and as such shall sell and dispose of them as Their Highnesses may command. And we shall take your goods, and shall do you all the mischief and damage that we can, as to vassals who do not obey and refuse to receive their lord and resist and contradict them.[4]

Following the reading of the *Requerimiento*, Columbus's men would then shackle and force into slavery the natives present, though according to historian John Stannard they sometimes just threw them in irons and got around to reading the *Requerimiento* later.[5] They did this on island after island: Hispaniola (now the Dominican Republic and Haiti), Jamaica, Cuba, Puerto Rico, as they raped, murdered, stole, enslaved, and tortured their way across the Caribbean. "Wherever the marauding . . . heavily armed Spanish forces went out on patrol, accompanied by ferocious armored dogs trained to kill and disembowel, they preyed on the local communities . . . forcing them to supply food, women and slaves . . ."[6] On Hispaniola, though it beggars belief, things became even worse during Columbus's illness in 1494, when his "troops went wild, stealing, raping, torturing, killing natives, trying to force them to divulge the whereabouts of the imagined treasure-houses of gold."[7]

The torture inflicted by the Spanish Christians included the cutting off of the hands of natives who didn't deliver gold to the conquerors. (This was also, in the late 19th and early 20th centuries, a practice of the Belgian Catholics who had conquered the Congo, who severed the hands of enslaved natives when they didn't deliver the rubber demanded of them on the Belgians' plantations.)[8]

The savagery of Columbus's Christian conquerors rivaled that of the Nazis or ISIS. Spanish bishop Bartolomé de las Casas, an eyewitness, says in his *History of the Indies*:

> The Spanish found pleasure in inventing all kinds of odd cruelties, the more cruel the better, with which to spill human blood. They built a long gibbet, low enough for the toes to touch the ground and prevent strangling, and hanged thirteen [natives] at a time in honor of Christ Our Savior and the twelve Apostles. When the Indians were thus still alive and hanging, the Spaniards tested their strength and their blades against them, rippling them open with one blow and exposing entrails, and there were those who did worse. Then, straw was wrapped around their torn bodies and they were burned alive. One man caught two children around two years old, pierced their throats with a dagger, then hurled them down a precipice.[9]

To make matters worse, the Christian conquerors were physically as well as morally diseased—they carried with them smallpox, influenza, measles, dysentery, syphilis, and a host of other illnesses to which the natives had never been exposed and to which they had no immunity. As a result, the native populations in conquered lands plummeted. Estimates of the percentage of indigenous peoples murdered or killed by disease typically run to well over 90% throughout the Americas, with most killed by infection. On Hispaniola, for instance, the native population fell from over half-a-million to a few tens of thousands in less than a quarter-century after the coming of Columbus,[10] with the total number of victims in the Caribbean being about eight million. Stannard states that at least 94% of the population of what is now Peru, a minimum of 8.5 million people, were killed, primarily by disease, in the roughly 50 years following the arrival of the conquistadors. Historian Chris Mato Nunpa estimates that the number of natives within what is now the continental United States fell from roughly 16 million at the time of Columbus to only 237,000 by the time of the U.S. census in 1900.[11]

This isn't terribly surprising given the attitude of the Spanish toward those they conquered. Stannard reports, "One favorite sport of the conquistadors was 'dogging.' Traveling as they did with packs of armored wolfhounds or mastiffs that were raised on a diet of human flesh and were trained to disembowel Indians, the Spanish used the dogs to terrorize slaves and to entertain the troops."[12] He then goes on to quote David Grier Varner's *Dogs of the Conquest*: "A properly fleshed dog could pursue a 'savage' as zealously and effectively as a deer or a boar. . . . To many of the conquerors, the Indian was merely another savage animal, and the dogs were trained to pursue and rip apart their human quarry with the same zest as they felt when hunting wild beasts."

Conquest in the British Colonies and United States

In the Protestant north, in what was to become the United States, things were no better. Within a short time after their landing, the colonizers embarked on campaigns of theft, deceit, rape, and murder. This was to be expected. The colonizers regarded themselves as the new chosen people, the indigenous people as analogous to the Canaanites, and the entirety of the Americas as the new promised land, as their promised "inheritance." So, the native inhabitants and their lands were fair game. As Deuteronomy 7:1–2 puts it, "When the Lord thy God shall bring thee into the land whither thou goest to possess it, and hath cast out many nations before thee, the Hittites, and the Girgashites, and the Amorites, and the Canaanites, . . . And when the Lord thy God shall deliver them before thee; thou shalt smite them, and utterly destroy them; thou shalt make no covenant with them, nor shew mercy unto them: . . ."

From the very beginning, the better armed colonizers betrayed and murdered native peoples. Following the Fort Mystic massacre in the 1637 Pequot War, the burning of a fortified Pequot town and the shooting of survivors, the commander of the responsible Connecticut (Puritan) troops, John Mason, said, "And indeed such a dreadful Terror did the Almighty let fall upon their Spirits, that they would fly from us into the very Flames, where many of them perished. . . . Thus did the Lord judge among the Heathen, filling the Place with dead bodies."[13] John Underhill, one of the others responsible for the town-burning/massacre of approximately 800 Pequot on the Mystic River, put the matter like this: "Sometimes the Scripture declareth women and children must perish with their parents," adding that the victims' helplessness "did not make their deaths any less a delight to God."[14]

The Fort Mystic atrocity was only one of several similar massacres perpetrated by Underhill.[15] To justify his brutal killing of thousands of indigenous people, Underhill cited the Old Testament:

> ...It may be demanded, Why should you be so furious (as some have said) should not Christians have more mercy and compassion? But I would refer you to David's war, when a people is grown to such a height of blood, and sin against God and man, and all confederates in the action, there he hath no respect to persons, but harrows them, and saws them, and puts them to the sword, and the most terriblest death that may be: sometimes the Scripture declareth women and children must perish with their parents; some time the case alters: but we will not dispute it now. We had sufficient light from the word of God for our proceedings...[16]

John Mason, who had termed the Pequot atrocity "the just Judgment of God,"[17] was echoed by the famous Puritan minister, slave owner, and author of witch-hunting manuals, Cotton Mather, who stated, in his 1702 book, *Magnalia Christi Americana: The Ecclesiastical History of New England from Its First Planting in 1620, until the Year of Our Lord 1698,** "In a little more than one hour, five or six hundreds of these barbarians were dismissed from a world that was burdened with them."[18]

Stannard and Mato Nunpa cite many similar incidents and many similar statements by the Christian conquerors, expressions of heartfelt thanks

---

* The title of Mather's book is not only odd—with the title in Latin and the subtitle in English—but also typically verbose: the title of his 1693 witch-hunting manual was *The Wonders of the Invisible World Being an Account of the Tryals of Several Witches Lately Executed in New-England And of several remarkable Curiosities therein Occurring.* The book was published in the wake of the 1692 Salem witch hunts, in which close to 200 people were imprisoned, 19 were executed, and one, Giles Corey, was tortured to death, slowly crushed and smothered, for refusing to confess. The Salem witch-hysteria was not an isolated incident, though it was likely the largest North American outbreak of such madness and murder in the colonial period.

to the Almighty for its help in committing mass murder and industrial-scale theft. Even when the colonizers didn't specifically cite Bible passages justifying their crimes, or cite the help of God in perpetrating those crimes, their underlying racist, genocidal attitudes sprang from the same source—the Bible. (Please remember that these crimes occurred when the white population in the colonies was almost 100% Christian.)

One incident in 1763, the siege of Fort Pitt (now Pittsburgh), provides another illustration of the Christian attitude toward natives. While the fort was under siege, its commander, Captain Simeon Ecuyer, on June 24 gave the besieging natives smallpox-infested blankets. One of the other officers at the fort, William Trent, said of the incident, "We gave them two blankets and a handkerchief out of the smallpox hospital. I hope it will have the desired effect." A few days later, the commander of the British forces in the area, Lord Jeffrey Amherst, after hearing of Ecuyer's treacherous biological-warfare attack, asked, "Could it not be contrived to send the smallpox among the disaffected tribes of Indians? We must on this occasion use every stratagem in our power to reduce them."[19]

Once the United States achieved independence, the massacres, expulsions, and land theft continued as they had in colonial times. A statement by one of the worst of the conquering criminals illustrates how well the new, self-identified chosen people applied the biblical injunctions to commit murder in order to seize the new promised land. U.S. Army Colonel John Chivington was a Methodist minister with a church in Denver, and the commanding officer at the infamous Sand Creek Massacre in Colorado in 1864, a massacre involving the murder of hundreds of Cheyenne and Arapaho, mostly women, children, babies, and old men. The Reverend Chivington later said: "Damn any man who sympathizes with Indians! . . . I have come to kill Indians, and believe it is right and honorable to use any means under God's heaven to kill Indians . . . Kill and scalp all, big and little; nits make lice!"[20*]

The slaughter and theft continued unabated until the 1890s, when the last indigenous resistance in the U.S. was crushed. In the end, America's Christian conquerors, the new self-identified chosen people, stole nearly all of the land in the continental U.S., made and broke over 400 treaties,

---

* As others have pointed out, the "nits" and "lice" analogy is exactly the same as that used by the Nazis three-quarters of a century later to justify extermination of Jewish children—which indicates the short conceptual distance between the "chosen people" and "master race" concepts.

and massacred, through direct violence and through pestilence, millions of people, resulting in a native population drop of well over 90% from the arrival of the first Christian settlers, the new chosen people in the new promised land.

As the physical slaughter was abating, cultural genocide supplanted it. A key element of that genocide was the establishment of over 500 "Indian schools" across the U.S. and Canada starting in the 19th century. Given that such schools persisted for well over 150 years, it's certain that at minimum hundreds of thousands of indigenous children attended them, with the total perhaps being even higher—especially given that for most of the time of the schools' existence, the governments of both the U.S. and Canada had the legal authority to separate children from their parents in order to force them into the schools.[21] The Canadian Broadcasting Corporation reports that there were approximately 150 such schools in Canada,[22] and historian Samantha Williams lists over 350 such schools in the United States.[23] Reuters reports that the schools in Canada were "run by the government and church groups—the majority of them Catholic—the schools' stated aim was to assimilate indigenous children."[24] The same held in the United States, though in the U.S. Protestants were more often in charge of the schools.

The goal of these schools was, in fact, "complete assimilation"[25]—in other words, to separate children from their families and communities in order to achieve absorption into white culture in dress, language (English only, with punishment for using their own languages), economics (belief in private property, economic competition, and inequality, in contrast to the traditional native belief in communal property), politics (acceptance of coercive, hierarchical government), and, above all, replacement of traditional native spiritual beliefs with Christianity.[26]

As one of the most influential of the Indian school founders, Civil War veteran Richard Henry Pratt, founder and longtime headmaster of the Carlisle Indian Industrial School in Pennsylvania (founded 1879), put it, "A great general has said that the only good Indian is a dead one . . . In a sense, I agree with the sentiment, but only in this: that all the Indian there is in the race should be dead. Kill the Indian in him, and save the man."[27]

But all too often the schools killed both the Indian and the man. More accurately, they killed the Indian and the child, through crowded, unsanitary conditions which allowed diseases such as tuberculosis to run rampant, inadequate healthcare for sick children, physical neglect, poor nutrition, and, quite possibly, occasional outright murder. As well, as you might suspect, there was also "rampant sexual and physical abuse . . . in residential schools."[28] The situation at the schools was so bad that the (Canadian) National Centre for Truth and Reconciliation (NCTR) called it "cultural genocide," citing malnutrition, rape, physical abuse, and other horrors.[29]

As an example of the results of such abuse, an investigation by the Tk'emlúps te Secwépemc First Nation (which would commonly be called a "tribe" in the U.S.) discovered the remains of 215 children in unmarked graves at the Kamloops Indian Residential School in Kamloops, British Colombia in 2021; like many other such Indian schools, the Kamloops school was modeled directly upon Richard Henry Pratt's Carlisle Indian Industrial School, which leads one to suspect that the 215 dead children at Kamloops were hardly an anomaly. Tk'emlúps te Secwépemc Kukpi (Chief) Rosanne Casimir states: "To our knowledge, these missing children are undocumented deaths . . . some were as young as three years old." The Catholic Church ran the school during the time of these undocumented deaths, between 1890 and 1969.[30]

There are many reasons these deaths have not previously come to light, including the secretive behavior of the Christian churches that ran the schools: "Mary Ellen Turpel-Lafond, director of the Indian Residential School History and Dialogue Centre at the University of British Columbia states that there are 'massive ongoing problems' with historical records, including those 'held by certain Catholic entities that . . . will not release [their records].'" The NCTR reports that there are death records for 4,100 of the estimated 150,000 children who attended the Canadian schools, but "the true total is likely much higher."[31] Unfortunately, that seems to be so. The Associated Press reports that the total number of children buried in unmarked graves at the Canadian Indian schools could be up to 6,000,[32] and it seems likely that that number is also too low. Other estimates are in the 10,000 to 15,000 range. Indigenous archeologist Kisha Supernant, who is working to uncover the graves, says, "No investigation is anywhere near being complete. We have barely scratched the surface . . ."[33]

In June 2021, the Cowessess First Nation and the Federation of Sovereign Indigenous First Nations reported that "hundreds of unmarked graves" had been discovered at the Marieval Indian Residential School, with CNN reporting that there were "at least 750 unmarked graves" at the school, and *Politico* reporting there were 751.[34,35] These were individual graves, not mass graves, from which headstones had been removed, which seems to indicate a cover up to hide the number of victims.[36] Later in the same month, another investigation revealed 182 unmarked graves at the St. Eugene's Mission School outside of Cranbrook, BC.[37]

Then in July, the Penalakut Tribe in British Columbia announced that it had found another 160 unmarked graves at the Kuper Island Residential School on one of the islands off the BC coast. Survivors reported that conditions were so bad at the island school that they referred to it as "Canada's Alcatraz." They also reported that "some children died after taking to the water in whatever they could find to try to escape the abuse they suffered at the school."[38] Such attempted escapes, and probable resultant deaths, were common at other schools, though it's nearly impossible to estimate the total number of children who died while escaping.

The combined total of child-victims in unmarked graves at the Canadian residential schools could quite possibly be far higher than the 6,000 estimate in the AP report on Marieval, or even the 10,000 to 15,000 estimate, given that the total number of such schools in Canada was approximately 150, and that the well over a thousand dead in unmarked graves discovered in the spring and early summer of 2021 came from only the four schools cited here.

The discovered gravesite total continued to climb over the remainder of the summer, with the estimated total standing at over 1,500 by September. Survivors report that in at least some cases surviving children were forced to dig the graves of those who died, and that "often, parents were not notified at all" of the deaths; the children were simply dumped in unmarked graves. And they suffered all this for "inappropriate education, often only up to lower grades, that focused mainly on prayer and manual labour in agriculture, light industry such as woodworking, and domestic work such as laundry work and sewing."[39]

To get an idea of the horrors these indigenous children suffered, consider the experience of one of the victims of the Indian residential schools, Roberta Hill, who at age 6, in 1957 was taken from her family and forced to attend the Anglican-run Mohawk Institute Residential School in Ontario. As happened with all of the children at the school, when Hill arrived she was stripped of her name and assigned a number, "34" in Hill's case.

The victimized children at the Institute suffered the same physical, emotional, and sexual abuse as children in the other Christian-run residential schools. At Mohawk, the students called the place the "mush hole," referring to "the porridge-like food, often contaminated with maggots, that students were forced to eat up to three times a day, while staff ate roast beef and vegetables in the same dining hall."[40]

The horrors didn't end there. Hill states that she was repeatedly sexually assaulted by the school's headmaster, an Anglican minister, starting when she was 7 or 8.[41] Another victim of the residential school system, former chief George Guerin, of the Musqueam First Nation, who was forced to attend the Kuper Island school, recalls:

> Sister Marie Baptiste had a supply of sticks as long and thick as pool cues. When she heard me speak my language, she'd lift up her hands and bring the stick down on me. I've still got bumps and scars on my hands. I have to wear special gloves because the cold weather really hurts my hands. I tried very hard not to cry when I was being beaten and I can still just turn off my feelings.... And I'm lucky. Many of the men my age, they either didn't make it, committed suicide or died violent deaths, or alcohol got them. And it wasn't just my generation. My grandmother, who's in her late nineties, to this day it's too painful for her to talk about what happened to her at the school.[42]

In a BBC report, a student-victim of the Pine Creek Residential School in Manitoba described his own experiences being bullied, beaten, forbidden from using his own language, and forcibly indoctrinated. Because of the abuse, he developed a bed-wetting problem, which the nun running the dormitory handled in a shocking manner: "[She] rubbed my face in my own urine."[43] She treated him, literally, like a dog.

How did the Catholic Church react to these horrifying revelations? Richard Gagnon, Archbishop of Winnipeg and President of the Canadian Conference of Catholic Bishops, said that he's become "a lightning rod" and has been "bombarded" by the media. He said that it's "not a simple question," and went on to say that there's been "a lot of blame, a lot of accusations, a lot of exaggerations, a lot of false ideas. And so I say in my heart. 'You know something? There's a persecution happening here. There's a persecution happening here.'" He added that he didn't know if the "persecution" of the Church was due to "ignorance" or "ill will," and went on to say, "And we look at this and say, you know, 'We're all sinners.' Remember what Jesus said, you know, 'Before you tell your brother to take that speck out of his eye, you've got a log in your own eye.'"[44,45]*

The type of callousness and contempt toward indigenous peoples displayed by Archbishop Gagnon and those who ran the Indian schools was,

---

* One can see the archbishop's point. Who among us hasn't emotionally, physically, and sexually abused tens of thousands of kids? Who hasn't killed thousands of them through disease, malnutrition, medical neglect, filthy conditions, and physical abuse? And who hasn't buried thousands of kids in unmarked graves?

and to a great extent still is, common the world over. Perhaps the best illustration of the Christian conquerors' attitudes toward native peoples was the celebrated speech by Senator Albert Beveridge on January 9, 1900 on the floor of the U.S. Senate, in which he lauded the U.S. seizure of the Philippines. A taste of the justification for that seizure, and the accompanying condescension, abuse, and arrogance, can be found in Beveridge's description of the Filipino people:

> They are a barbarous race, modified by three centuries of contact with a decadent race [the Spanish]. The Filipino is the South Sea Malay, put through a process of three hundred years of superstition in religion [Catholicism], dishonesty in dealing, disorder in habits of industry, and cruelty, caprice, and corruption in government. It is barely possible that a thousand men in all the archipelago are capable of self-government in the Anglo-Saxon sense.

He followed that with additional slanderous comments about the Filipinos, and went on to cite religious justification for the bloody war of conquest that delivered the Philippines into American hands:

> We will not renounce our part in the mission of our race, trustee, under God, of the civilization of the world. And we will move forward to our work . . . with gratitude for a task worthy of our strength, and thanksgiving to Almighty God that He has marked us as His chosen people, henceforth to lead in the regeneration of the world . . . Mr. President, this question is deeper than any question of party politics; deeper than any question of isolated policy of our country even; deeper even than any question of constitutional power. It is elemental. It is racial. God has not been preparing the English speaking and Teutonic Peoples for a thousand years for nothing but vain and idle self-contemplation and self-admiration. No! He has made us the master organizers of the world to establish systems where chaos reigns. He has given us the spirit of progress to overwhelm the forces of reaction throughout the earth. He has made us adept in government that we may administer government among savage and senile peoples.
>
> Were it not for such a force as this the world would relapse into barbarism and night. And of all our races, He has marked the American people to finally lead in the regeneration of the world. This is the divine mission of America, and it holds for us all the profit, all the glory, all the happiness possible for man . . .
>
> Blind indeed is he who sees not the hand of God in events so vast, so harmonious, so benign.

In his glorious, God-ordained, "harmonious" and "benign" war of conquest, the Phillipines-American War (1899–1902), some 20,000 Filipino guerrillas died as did (mostly of disease and hunger) up to 200,000 Filipino civilians, while American casualties ran to under 5,000, with most of those succumbing to disease.[46]

That many competing sects and religions make the same claim, that their adherents are the chosen people, seems not to matter at all to the members of the other sects that claim the exact same thing. It's too convenient a claim to give up. That claim gives license to commit murder, rape, theft, and enslavement—and to feel righteous about it.

Endnotes

1. *The Sinai Strategy: Economics and the Ten Commandments*, by Gary North. Tyler, TX: Institute for Christian Economics, 1986, pp. 59–60.

2. *Laying Down the Sword: Why we can't ignore the Bible's violent verses*, by Philip Jenkins. New York: HarperCollins, 2011, pp. 11–12.

3. "Christopher Columbus: A Spiritual Giant," by Glen W. Chapman. Yumpu, November 2001. https://www.yumpu.com/en/document/read/32343281/christopher-columbus-a-spiritual-giant-chapmanresearch < https://tinyurl.com/yxcyc4ta >

4. Quoted by David Stannard in *American Holocaust: The Conquest of the New World*. New York: Oxford University Press, 1992, p.66.

5. Ibid.

6. Ibid., p. 69.

7. Ibid.

8. "The horrific consequences of rubber's toxic past," by Tim Harford. BBC News, July 23, 2019. https://www.bbc.com/news/business-48533964 < https://tinyurl.com/y62mnc5u >

9. Quoted by Stannard, op. cit., p. 72.

10. "Hispaniola." Yale University Genocide Studies Program. https://gsp.yale.edu/case-studies/colonial-genocides-project/hispaniola < https://tinyurl.com/y6tuycvn >

11. *The Great Evil: Christianity, the Bible, and the Native American Genocide*, by Chris Mato Nunpa. Tucson: See Sharp Press, 2020, p. 60.

12. Stannard, op. cit., p. 83.

13. Quoted by Stannard, pp. 113–114.

14. Quoted by Mato Nunpa, op. cit., p. 73.

15. "John Underhill—Religious Maniac and Mass Murderer," by Leighton "Blue Sky" Delgado. Matouwak Research Center. http://www.montaukwarrior.info/?page_id=277 < https://tinyurl.com/13on9nr6 >

16. Ibid.

17. Quoted by Stannard, p. 114.

18. Ibid.

19. "Smallpox in the Blankets," by John Koster. Historynet. https://www.historynet.com/smallpox-in-the-blankets.htm < https://tinyurl.com/y7t8zghy >

20. Quoted by Mato Nunpa, op. cit., p. 102.

21. "Death by Civilization," by Marie Annette Pember. *The Atlantic*, March 2019. https://www.theatlantic.com/education/archive/2019/03/traumatic-legacy-indian-boarding-schools/584293/ < https://tinyurl.com/4zcvserd >

22 "Remains of 215 children found buried at former B.C. residential school, First Nation says." CBC News, May 27, 2001. https://www.cbc.ca/news/canada/british-columbia/tk-eml%C3%BAps-te-secw%C3%A9pemc-215-children-former-kamloops-indian-residential-school-1.6043778 < https://tinyurl.com/3ynf5s48 >

23. "Native American Boarding Schools: Some Basic Facts and Statistics," by Samantha Williams. https://www.samanthamwilliams.com/blog/native-american-boarding-schools-some-basic-facts-and-statistics < https://tinyurl.com/2x7fpvjj >

24. "Canada's Trudeau blasts Catholic Church for ignoring role in indigenous schools," by Anna Mehler Peperny and Steve Scherer. Reuters, June 4. 2021. https://www.reuters.com/world/canadas-trudeau-blasts-catholic-church-ignoring-role-indigenous-schools-2021-06-04/ < https://tinyurl.com/jd385275 >

25. "History and Culture, Boarding Schools." Northern Plains Reservation Aid. http://www.nativepartnership.org/site/PageServer?pagename=airc_hist_boardingschools < https://tinyurl.com/sz9b6ru3 >

26. Pember, op. cit.

27. "Kill the Indian, and Save the Man: Capt. Richard H. Pratt on the Education of Native Americans." *History Matters*, George Mason University. http://historymatters.gmu.edu/d/4929 < https://tinyurl.com/cxyp5vxe >

28. CBC News, op. cit.

29. Peperney and Scherer, op. cit.

30. CBC News, op. cit.

31. Ibid.

32. "Unmarked graves found at another Indigenous school in Canada." Associated Press, June 24, 2021. https://apnews.com/article/canada-e094163e28b8a9c2e41c836b5c913312 < https://tinyurl.com/nc2khxu6 >

33. "Kids' Graves Exposed the Horror of Canada's Residential Schools. Outrage Isn't Enough," by Anya Zoledziowski. *Vice*, September 30, 2021. https://www.vice.com/en/article/n7baw7/indigenous-children-graves-horror-residential-schools < https://tinyurl.com/62u9aj5d >

34. "More than 700 unmarked graves found at a former residential school in Canada, officials say," by Paula Newton and Nicole Chávez. CNN, June 24, 2021. https://edition.cnn.com/2021/06/24/americas/canada-unmarked-graves-discovered/index.html < https://tinyurl.com/n9yx2j9a >

35. "Trudeau: 'Canadians are horrified and ashamed,'" by Nick Taylot-Vaisey. *Politico*, June 25, 2021. https://www.politico.com/news/2021/06/25/trudeau-canada-indigenous-history-496307 < https://tinyurl.com/2jx3chjb >

36. "An Overview of the Indian Residential School System." Union of Ontario Indians. http://www.anishinabek.ca/wp-content/uploads/2016/07/An-Overview-of-the-IRS-System-Booklet.pdf < https://tinyurl.com/yyxn2jv7 >

37. "Canada: 182 unmarked graves found at another residential school." *Al Jazeera*, June 30, 2021. https://www.aljazeera.com/news/2021/6/30/canada-182-unmarked-graves-found-at-another-residential-school < https://tinyurl.com/49rrh9mw >

38. "More unmarked graves discovered in British Columbia at a former indigenous residential school known as 'Canada's Alcatraz,'" by Paula Newton. CNN, July 13, 2021. https://edition.cnn.com/2021/07/13/americas/canada-unmarked-indigenous-graves/index.html < https://tinyurl.com/n44djmd9 >

39. "The Residential School System," by Erin Hanson, et al. Indigenousfoundations. https://indigenousfoundations.arts.ubc.ca/the_residential_school_system/ < https://tinyurl.com/nc2khxu6 >

40. Zoledziowski, op. cit.

41. Ibid.

42. “Remains of more than 1,000 Indigenous children found at former residential schools in Canada,” by Mindy Weisberger. *LiveScience*, July 13, 2021. https://www.livescience.com/childrens-graves-residential-schools-canada.html < https://tinyurl.com/r2ymwxnx >

43. “Canada: Hundreds of unmarked graves found at residential school: More on residential schools in Canada.” BBC News, June 24, 2021. https://www.bbc.com/news/world-us-canada-57592243 < https://tinyurl.com/6b2nmf4v >

44. “June 27, 2021: Thirteenth Sunday of Ordinary Time.” Youtube. https://www.youtube.com/watch?v=uwVxUwdl8aI&t=4194s < https://tinyurl.com/dtaeujrb >

45. “Archbishop fuels more anger by saying the church is being persecuted over residential schools,” by Tavia Grant. *The Globe and Mail*, July 2, 2021. https://www.theglobeandmail.com/canada/article-archbishop-fuels-more-anger-by-saying-the-church-is-being-persecuted/ < https://tinyurl.com/wj9jk623 >

46. “The Philippine-American War, 1899–1902.” U.S. Department of State. https://history.state.gov/milestones/1899–1913/war < tinyurl.com/86zv2ea8 >

18

Christianity's All Too Comfortable Relationship to Slavery

> And if a man smite his servant [slave], or his maid with a rod, and he die under his hand; he shall surely be punished. Notwithstanding, if he continue for a day or two, he shall not be punished; for he is his money.
> —Exodus 21:20–21

From its very beginnings, from its roots in the Old Testament, Christianity (and before it religious Judaism) has condoned slavery. There is not a single word in the Bible that condemns it, let alone prohibits it. Instead, the Bible accepts slavery as a given, and several passages provide God's chosen people with handy hints on how to treat (and mistreat) slaves. (The King James Version translators used the euphemisms "servant," "bondman," and "bondmaid" in place of the more accurate "slave.")

In addition to Exodus 21:20–21, relevant Old Testament passages include:

> If thou buy an Hebrew servant, six years he shall serve: and in the seventh he shall go out free for nothing. If he came in by himself, he shall go out by himself: if he were married, then his wife shall go out with him. If his master have given him a wife, and she have born him sons or daughters; the wife and her children shall be her master's, and he shall go out by himself. And if the servant shall plainly say, I love my master, my wife, and my children; I will not go out free: Then his master shall bring him unto the judges; he shall also bring him to the door, or unto the door post; and his master shall bore his ear through with an aul; and he shall serve him for ever. —Exodus 21:2–6

> Both thy bondmen, and thy bondmaids, which thou shalt have, shall be of the heathen that are round about you; of them shall ye buy bondmen and bondmaids. Moreover of the children of the strangers that do sojourn among you, of them shall ye buy, and of their families that are with you, which they begat in your land: and they shall be your possession. And ye shall take them as an inheritance for your children after you, to inherit them for a possession; they shall be your bondmen for ever: but over your brethren the children of Israel, ye shall not rule one over another with rigour. —Leviticus 25:44–46

The New Testament is every bit as explicit in its acceptance of slavery, and goes considerably beyond the Old Testament by urging slaves to both accept their lot and to embrace it:

> Servants, be subject to your masters with all fear; not only to the good and gentle, but also to the froward. For this is thankworthy, if a man for conscience toward God endure grief, suffering wrongfully. For what glory is it, if, when ye be buffeted for your faults, ye shall take it patiently? but if, when ye do well, and suffer for it, ye take it patiently, this is acceptable with God. For even hereunto were ye called: because Christ also suffered for us, leaving us an example, that ye should follow his steps: Who did no sin, neither was guile found in his mouth: Who, when he was reviled, reviled not again; when he suffered, he threatened not; but committed himself to him that judgeth righteously:
> —1 Peter 2:18–23

> Servants, obey in all things your masters according to the flesh; not with eyeservice, as menpleasers, but in singleness of heart, fearing God.
> —Colossians 3:22

Other New Testament passages say essentially the same thing: that "servants" (slaves) should obey their owners with "singleness of heart," and at times, as in 1 Peter 2:18–23, add that this obedience should be unconditional, no matter how awful the master. Other relevant passages include Titus 2:9–10, Ephesians 6:5, and 1 Timothy 6:1. The closest the Bible comes to condemning slavery in any of its passages is in the Old Testament in Exodus 21:16: "He that stealeth a man and selleth him, or if he be found in his hand, he shall surely be put to death," which is a condemnation of stealing slaves, not of slavery itself.

The early church fathers also endorsed the institution of slavery. As early as the beginning of the second century, Bishop Ignatius of Antioch advised the bishop of Smyrna that Christian slaves should use their beliefs to help them be better slaves, and that church funds shouldn't be used to purchase the freedom of slaves.[1] Later church fathers were just as explicit, with Ambrose, bishop of Milan, opining in the fourth century that the suffering in slavery was a spiritual good: "The lower the station in life, the more exalted the virtue."[2] St. Augustine, in *De Civitate Dei* ("The City of God"), expressed his approval of slavery like this: "That one man should be put in bonds by another—this happens only by the judgment of God."

The better part of a thousand years later, Thomas Aquinas, widely considered the most important Catholic theologian, stated in his masterwork, *Summa Theologica:*

> A son, as such, belongs to his father, and a slave, as such, belongs to his master; yet each, considered as a man, is something having separate existence and distinct from others. Hence in so far as each of them is a man, there is justice towards them in a way: and for this reason too there are certain laws regulating the relations of father to his son, and of a master to his slave; but in so far as each is something belonging to another, the perfect idea of 'right' or 'just' is wanting to them.

To make matters even plainer, he goes on to endorse coercive violence against both children and slaves:

> . . . since the child is subject to the power of the parent, and the slave to the power of his master, a parent can lawfully strike his child, and a master his slave that instruction may be enforced by correction . . .[3]

Following the early ratifications of slavery, Christian-dominated Europe sank into the Dark Ages, and church teachings on slavery, as evidenced by Aquinas's remarks, didn't change a whit for the following thousand years. No pope ever condemned the loathsome institution, which persisted in Christendom for over 1,500 years after the first Christian emperor, Constantine. That emperor, in fact, worsened the conditions of slaves by letting parents sell their children into slavery and by issuing a decree mandating the death penalty for any free Christian woman who had sex with a slave.[4] (Constantine issued no matching decree for free Christian men.)

In the middle of the fifth century, Pope Leo I (aka Pope Leo the Great) forbade slaves from being Christian clerics, banning it "lest the sacred ministry be polluted by the vileness of their association."[5] Indeed, century after century, the church kept large numbers of slaves and, increasingly serfs, with serfdom gradually replacing outright slavery in Europe from about the ninth century on.

In the year 1455, near the beginning of the "age of discovery," while the entire Christian world was still Catholic, at least in Central and Western Europe (with the East being largely Orthodox), Pope Nicholas V issued the encyclical *Romanus Pontifex* ("the Roman Pontiff"), in which he stated:

> [Catholic monarchs should] invade, search out, capture, vanquish and subdue all Saracens [Muslims] and pagans whatsoever, and other enemies of Christ wheresoever placed, and . . . to reduce their persons to perpetual slavery, and to apply and appropriate . . . possessions and goods, and to convert them to their use and profit . . .

Unsurprisingly, Christian conquerors proceeded to zealously implement this inspired decree. They not only enslaved the native peoples they conquered in the Americas and Africa, but Christian merchants and sailors built and conducted a massive slave trade that persisted for centuries. From the beginnings of the trans-Atlantic slave trade in the 16th century to its end in the late 19th century, European Christian slavers, especially Portuguese and Spanish slavers, transported an estimated 10 to 12 million Africans to the Americas, with about an eighth of their victims dying en route—sometimes up to 30% on individual voyages—because of the horrendous conditions on board the slave ships, ships with names such as Madre de Deus (Mother of God), King David, Providencia (Providence), and Jesus of Lubeck. (While most slave ships didn't bear religious names, the names of these ships indicate the widespread, indeed almost universal, acceptance of slavery by Christians until well into the 19th century.)

The Catholic Church provided the justification for the centuries-long atrocities visited upon their perceived inferiors by Christian slavers. Because the enslaved indigenous people in the New World were dying in droves shortly after the "discovery" of the Americas—due to mass murder by the Spanish and the spread of previously unknown diseases such as influenza, measles, dysentery, and smallpox—in the early 16th century Spanish bishop Bartolomé de las Casas suggested that the Spanish crown import enslaved Africans in place of indigenous slaves. Joseph McCabe states:

> The Spanish authorities, who liked the suggestion, consulted the Catholic hierarchy; . . . On the one hand, they replied, with perfect truth, that the Church had never condemned slavery. On the other hand, they discovered the most useful truth that this would enable the Church to baptize and convert immense numbers of the blacks, who showed no eagerness for baptism and conversion, and that this eternal gain to the African outweighed all the

> paltry human advantages of freedom in his native home. So the [trans-Atlantic slave] trade began.[6]

The attitude of the Church authorities toward all this was, overall, approval, approval which continued over the centuries following Columbus. Even though the Roman Inquisition condemned slavery in 1686, the popes and the Church bureaucracy continued to condone it and engage in it well into the modern period. As one example, the Vatican still used slaves on its galleys in the Mediterranean up until the time of the French Revolution of 1789, over a century after the Inquisition condemned slavery.[7]

As another example, in his massive *Christianity: The First Three Thousand Years*, author Diarmaid MacCulloch, a Christian writer, notes that at Luanda (in the then-Portuguese colony of Angola), a slave-shipping port, "the clergy's main role in the city became to baptize them [slaves] before their departure; right up to the 1870s, the Portuguese Bishop of Loanda [sic] was accustomed to being enthroned in a marble chair at the dockside, presiding over the rite [baptism] before captives were dispatched across the Atlantic"[8] (to Brazil, which abolished slavery only in 1888).

While the bulk of the slave trade was controlled and conducted by Catholics, Protestants were hardly blameless. In 1663, the British king Charles I granted a charter to The Company of Royal Adventurers of England Relating to Trade in Africa (later the Royal African Company) giving it control of the British slave trade. (Conveniently enough, Charles and his brother James, the Duke of York, later King James II, were among those who set up and controlled the company.) In addition to subjecting their victims to the horrors of the slave ships, and then a lifetime of slavery, the British traffickers subjected them to an additional, painful indignity: many of the kidnapped, shackled Africans were branded with the letters DY, the letters standing for Duke of York.[9]

Once the survivors of the slave ships were delivered to the New World, other Christians, both Catholic and Protestant, bought the enslaved Africans and proceeded to rape, torture, murder, humiliate, and work them to death. Organized Christianity was not silent on this horror. It actively encouraged it and engaged in it. From the friars who enslaved Native Americans in the Southwest and Mexico to the Protestant preachers who defended slavery from the pulpit in Virginia, the Carolinas, and Georgia, the record of Christianity as regards slavery is very extensive and very shameful, if largely unacknowledged.

(Those who point out that many of the abolitionists were Christians, including John Brown, should remember that almost all white Americans were Christians at the time, and that the abolitionists were a small minority well hated by many of their fellow Christians. While some Northern congregations came to oppose the "peculiar institution" as the Civil War approached, Southern congregations almost unanimously supported that "institution.")

The Christians who defended slavery and engaged in it were amply supported by the Bible, in which slavery is accepted as a given, as simply a part of the social landscape. Christian slave owners, and the preachers who provided them with moral guidance, were well acquainted with the above-quoted pro-slavery biblical passages and undoubtedly found great comfort in them.

Prior to the Civil War, prominent Philadelphia Presbyterian minister and abolitionist Albert Barnes said of Christian support for slavery, "it is probable that slavery could not be sustained in this land if it were not for the countenance, direct and indirect, of the churches."[10] Barnes wasn't alone in his assessment. Theodore Parker, a leading abolitionist and Unitarian minister stated, "If the whole American Church had dropped through the continent and disappeared altogether, the anti-slavery cause would have been further on."[11]

As if to illustrate Parker's point, in 1853 another pre-Civil War clergyman, the Reverend Robert N. Anderson, in his "Letter to West Hanford Presbytery," said:

> Now dear Christian brethren . . . if there be any stray goat of a minister among you, tainted with the blood-hound principles of abolitionism, let him be ferreted out, silenced, excommunicated, and left to the public to dispose of him in other respects. Your affectionate brother in the Lord.[12]

Putting the matter more baldly, though less venomously, the Reverend J.C. Postell said,:

> So far from being a moral evil, slavery is a merciful visitation . . . It is the Lord's doing and it is marvelous in our eyes; . . . It is by divine appointment.[13]

A great many Protestant clergymen evidently agreed, as evidenced by the Resolution of the General Conference of the American Methodist Church in May 1838:

> The delegates of the annual conference are decidedly opposed to modern Abolitionism, and wholly disclaim any right, wish or intention to interfere

> in the civil and political relation between master and slave as it exists in the slave-holding states of the nation.[14]*

In 1844, due to growing dissension over the issue, the southern Methodists split from their northern brethren to form the Methodist Episcopal Church, South.

Likewise, in 1845, the Baptists in the South split from the northern Baptists over the issue of slavery and formed the Southern Baptist Convention, which supported the "peculiar institution." The Convention didn't apologize for its support of slavery (and subsequently Jim Crow laws and segregation) until 1995.

The nominally Christian Mormons (who also engaged in slavery) were in accord with the 19th-century Southern Baptists. In Section 104 of their "inspired" *Doctrines and Covenants*, the Mormons state:

> . . . we do not believe it right to interfere with bond servants [slaves] . . . nor to meddle with or influence them in the least, to cause them to be dissatisfied with their situations in this life, thereby jeopardizing the lives of men; such interference we believe to be unlawful and unjust[!], and dangerous to the peace of every government allowing human beings to be held in servitude.

This was completely in line with the Book of Mormon's famous passage on skin color: ". . . wherefore as they were white, and exceedingly fair and delightsome, that they might not be enticing unto my people the Lord God did cause a skin of blackness to come upon them." (2 Nephi 5:20–21)

As to why so many Christians supported slavery, there's a simple answer beyond scriptural support of it: money. There were approximately 4,000,000 slaves in the United States at the time of the Civil War, and they were overwhelmingly owned by Christians, including Christian churches. Joseph McCabe, in *Christianity and Slavery*, estimates that "the Baptists owned 225,000 and the Methodists 250,000 slaves."[15] Hard figures on slave ownership by churches are difficult to come by, so this century-old estimate should be taken with a grain of salt. However, it's certain that slave ownership was common among both individual Christians and Chris-

---

* The year the Methodist resolution passed, 1838, provided an example of another facet of Christian acceptance of slavery: ownership of slaves by religious institutions. In June of that year, the Jesuits who founded, administered, and owned Georgetown University, sold 232 enslaved Africans to pay the university's debts. The Jesuits could have sold some of the land the university owned. Instead, they chose to sell hundreds of human beings.

tian churches. As an indication of how common slave ownership was, the Southern Baptist Theological Seminary, the Southern Baptist Convention's oldest seminary, issued a report in 2018 that revealed that all of the seminary's founders were slave owners, between them owning dozens of slaves.[16]

Even today, some hard-line Christian Dominionists (taking the label from Genesis 1:28), still support the reintroduction of slavery. R.J. Rushdoony, a founder of the Christian Reconstructionist movement, a Holocaust denier, and a highly influential Dominionist writer, stated as recently as 1973, in his massive *The Institutes of Biblical Law*, a book that was split into three volumes and is still in print, both as a set of pricey hardbacks and as e-books:

> The [biblical] Law here is humane and also unsentimental. It recognizes that some people are by nature slaves and will always be so. It both requires that they be dealt with in a godly manner and also that the slave recognizes his position and accepts it with grace.[17]

Finally, as regards the aftermath of slavery, it's pertinent that the religious right arose in the South, the most religion-soaked part of the country. It appeared in the 1960s and 1970s as a reaction against school desegregation after *Brown v. Board of Education*. As Sarah Posner details at length in *Unholy: Why Evangelicals Worship at the Altar of Donald Trump,* religious bodies established Christian "segregation academies" across the South in the wake of Brown, and were outraged after they lost their IRS tax-exempt status because of their discriminatory practices (as did far-right Bob Jones University). As Posner notes, *that* was the spur to the rise of the religious right, not *Roe v. Wade*.[18]

As further evidence of this—and as surprising as it might seem today—the Southern Baptist Convention was solidly pro-choice throughout the entirety of the 1970s. A 1973 article published by the Convention's official news service, *Baptist Press*, makes this plain. The article, by W. Barry Garrett, then head of the *Press's* Washington bureau, appeared immediately after *Roe V. Wade* and declared that the decision had "advanced the cause of religious liberty, human equality and justice."[19]

The claim that *Roe v. Wade* triggered creation of the religious right is a convenient fiction, and it's utterly dishonest. The decision to pivot to opposition to abortion was entirely opportunistic: prior to their pivot, fundamentalists had tended to regard abortion as a purely Catholic issue. The founders of the religious right (Jerry Falwell, Paul Weyrich, Ralph Reed,

Donald Wildmon, Ed Dobson, et al.) were seeking an emotional issue with which to manipulate their followers into electing extreme-right politicians, politicians who would be beholden to them and would support religious privilege (such as income and property tax exemptions for their schools)—and if those politicians were racist, so much the better.

As an example of the racism of the religious figures who established and supported the "segregation academies," and created the religious right, Baptist preacher Jerry Falwell, founder of the Moral Majority, called the Civil Rights Act of 1964 a "terrible violation of human and property rights"; he circulated literature smearing Martin Luther King and called him "the most notorious liar in the country"; and in 1968 he invited arch-segregationist presidential candidate George Wallace to address his congregation from the pulpit of his church, the Thomas Road Baptist Church in Lynchburg, Virginia.*

Another religious right founder, Sam Francis, put the matter of slavery (and its woeful after effects) even more baldly than Falwell. Francis said that the Enlightenment was the reason for rejection of slavery, that the Enlightenment resulted in "a bastardized form of Christian ethics that condemns slavery."[20] (Not incidentally, this is a *de facto* admission that science and secular humanism have blunted Christian savagery.)

So much for Christian morality and the good it supposedly does. So much for the assertion that Christianity opposed slavery and led the fight against it.

As a final note regarding slavery, the murderous racism left in its wake, and the supposed beneficial effects of Christianity upon morals, compare two maps: one showing the extent of the Bible Belt (the most religious part of the U.S., thus supposedly the most moral part of the country) and the other showing the locations of the almost 5,000 lynchings in the 19th and 20th centuries in the United States. The maps are virtually identical.[21,22]

---

* National Opinion Research Center figures reveal that *all* white American Christian groups, especially evangelicals, are more racist than nonreligious whites: 50% of white evangelicals oppose or strongly oppose a close relative marrying a black person, as do 34% of religious moderates, 42% of religious liberals, and 22% of nonreligious whites.[23] Public Religion Research Institute (PRRI) figures confirm that Christians are more biased than the unaffiliated. Robert P. Jones, CEO and founder of the Institute, reports that *all* American white Christian groups support the building of Trump's border wall, with 58% supporting it, and the only groups opposing it being unaffiliated white people and black Protestants, both showing only 28% support.[24] PRRI also reports that "in the United States today, the more racist attitudes a person holds, the more likely he or she is to identify as a white Christian."[25]

Endnotes

1. *Christianity: The First Three Thousand Years*, by Diarmaid MacCulloch. New York: Penguin, 2009, p. 116.

2. Ibid.

3. "Philosophers Justifying Slavery." BBC. http://www.bbc.co.uk/ethics/slavery/ethics/philosophers_1.shtml < https://tinyurl.com/ktm585v >

4. *Christianity and Slavery*, by Joseph McCabe. Tucson: See Sharp Press, 1997, p. 15.

5. Ibid., p. 16.

6. Ibid., p. 30.

7. MacCulloch, op. cit., p. 711.

8. Ibid., p. 710.

9. "Britain's involvement with New World slavery and the transatlantic slave trade," by Abdul Mohamud and Robin Whitburn. British Library. https://www.bl.uk/restoration-18th-century-literature/articles/britains-involvement-with-new-world-slavery-and-the-transatlantic-slave-trade < https://tinyurl.com/y2wwpk8d >

10. *The Church and Slavery*, by Albert Barnes. New York: Negroes University Press (originally published in Philadelphia in 1857). Quoted in "Religious Schism as a Prelude to the American Civil War: Methodists, Baptists, and Slavery," by Allen Carden. *Andrews University Seminary Studies*, Spring 1986, Vol. 24, No. 1, p. 20. https://www.andrews.edu/library/car/cardigital/Periodicals/AUSS/1986-1/1986-1-03.pdf < https://tinyurl.com/mn2c9kw3 >

11. McCabe, op. cit., p. 30.

12. Quoted by Kirby Page in *Jesus or Christianity: A Study in Contrasts*. New York: R.R. Smith, 1931.

13. Ibid.

14. Quoted in *The American Churches, the Bulwarks of Slavery*, by An American. Newburyport: Charles Whipple, 1842. https://www.loc.gov/resource/rbaapc.02800/?sp=1&st=text < https://tinyurl.com/u8w3kk45 >

15. McCabe, op. cit., p. 32.

16. "Report on Racism and Slavery in the History of the Southern Baptist Theological Seminary." Southern Baptist Theological Seminary, 2018. https://sbts-wordpress-uploads.s3.amazonaws.com/sbts/uploads/2018/12/Racism-and-the-Legacy-of-Slavery-Report-v3.pdf < https://tinyurl.com/ua9xhtx7 >

17. *The Institutes of Biblical Law*, by R.J. Rushdoony. Presbyterian and Reformed Publishing Co., 1973, p. 251.

18. *Unholy: Why White Evangelicals Worship at the Altar of Donald Trump*, by Sarah Posner. New York: Random House, 2020, pp. 100–124.

19. "How Southern Baptists became pro-life," by David Roach. *Baptist Press*, January 16, 2015. https://www.baptistpress.com/resource-library/news/how-southern-baptists-became-pro-life/ < https://tinyurl.com/dp7e7rxu >

20. Posner, op. cit., p. 107.

21. "What States Make Up the 'Bible Belt'?" Quora. https://www.quora.com/what-states-make-up-the-Bible-Belt < https://tinyurl.com/y56do73a >

22. "Racial Terror Lynchings." Lynching in America. https://lynchinginamerica.eji.org/explore < https://tinyurl.com/y77qzc5g >

23. *What You Don't Know About Religion (but should)*, by Ryan Cragun. Durham, NC: Pitchstone Publishing, 2012, pp. 120–121.

24. *White Too Long: The Legacy of White Supremacy in American Christianity*, by Robert P. Jones. New York: Simon & Schuster, 2021, pp. 164.

25. Ibid,, p. 170.

19

Christian Misogyny

Unto the woman he said, I will greatly multiply thy sorrow and thy conception; in sorrow thou shalt bring forth children; and thy desire shall be to thy husband, and he shall rule over thee.
—Genesis 3:16

How then can man be justified with God? or how can he be clean that is born of a woman?
—Job 25:4

There are many other misogynistic passages in the Old Testament, for example:

> . . . If a woman have conceived seed, and born a man child: then she shall be unclean seven days; according to the days of the separation for her infirmity shall she be unclean. And in the eighth day the flesh of his foreskin shall be circumcised. And she shall then continue in the blood of her purifying three and thirty days; she shall touch no hallowed thing, nor come into the sanctuary, until the days of her purifying be fulfilled. But if she bear a maid child, then she shall be unclean two weeks, as in her separation: and she shall continue in the blood of her purifying threescore and six days.
> —Leviticus 12:2–5

Indeed, the entire Old Testament takes male domination and female submission as a given, and treats women as both property and as somehow unclean. (See Appendix A for many additional misogynistic passages.)

The New Testament is nearly as bad:

> But I would have you know, that the head of every man is Christ; and the head of the woman is the man; and the head of Christ is God. . . . Neither was the man created for the woman; but the woman for the man.
> —1 Corinthians 11:3, 9

> Wives, submit yourselves unto your own husbands, as unto the Lord. For the husband is the head of the wife, even as Christ is the head of the church: and he is the saviour of the body. —Ephesians 5:22–23

> These [redeemed] are they which were not defiled with women.
> —Revelation 14:4

While misogyny and the subjugation of women almost certainly date to antiquity, to the first societies based on private property and the desire of property-owning men to know that their heirs were in fact theirs, misogyny worsened with the ascension of Christianity. Misogyny is embedded in its foundational writings; indeed, misogynistic biblical passages are so common that it's difficult to know which to cite. In passage after passage, in both the Old and New Testaments, women are commanded to accept an inferior role and to be ashamed of themselves for the simple fact that they are women.*

The early church fathers extended the misogynistic themes in the Bible with a vengeance. Tertullian (155–240), one of the first of them, wrote:

> The judgment upon your sex endures even today; and with it inevitably endures your position at the bar of justice. [Woman] you are the gateway to hell. —*De Cultu Feminarum* ("On Women's Dress")

He went on:

> In pain shall you bring forth children, woman, and you shall turn to your husband and he shall rule over you. And do you not know that you are Eve? God's sentence hangs still over all your sex and His punishment weighs down upon you. You are the devil's gateway; you are she who first violated the forbidden tree and broke the law of God. It was you who coaxed your way around him whom the devil had not the force to attack. With what ease you shattered that image of God: Man! Because of the death you merited, even the Son of God had to die. . . . Woman, you are the gate to hell.

---

* Other relevant Old Testament passages include Numbers 5:20–22 and Leviticus 15:17–33; other relevant New Testament passages include Colossians 3:18; 1 Peter 3:7; 1 Corinthians 14:34; and 1 Timothy 2:11–12 and 5:5–6.

The Catholic Journal, in a piece titled "The Catholic Church and Women," by Vincent Ruggiero, quotes another early church father, St. Clement of Alexandria (150–215), as saying "A woman should cover her head with shame at the thought that she is a woman."[1]

The views of the later church fathers didn't moderate at all. St. John Chrysostom (347–407), in his "Homilies on the Gospel of Matthew," said, "Woman is a foe to friendship, an inescapable punishment, a necessary evil . . . Among all savage beasts none is found so harmful as woman";[2] St. Jerome (347–420), echoing Tertullian, said, "Woman is the gate of the devil, the road to iniquity, the sting of the scorpion, in a word, a dangerous species";[3] and Pope Gregory the Great said, "Woman is slow in understanding, and her unstable and naive mind renders her by way of natural weakness to the necessity of a strong hand in her husband."[4] One can find similarly misogynistic—though sometimes less acidic—statements in the writings of many other church fathers and theologians, including St. Ambrose, St. Anthony, Thomas Aquinas, St. Augustine, and St. Gregory of Nazianzus, who termed woman "a foe to friendship, an inescapable punishment, a necessary evil."

As you might expect, the lot of women grew worse after Christianity's adoption as the Roman Empire's state religion in 312 following Constantine's conversion. In pre-Christian Rome, in both the republican and imperial periods, women had the right to divorce and to own and inherit property. Women could also own property in Sparta, though not in Athens. In both Greece and Rome, though, the other rights of women were severely restricted, with, for instance, women being denied the right to vote in both Athens and the Roman Republic.

This already bad situation worsened during the centuries following Constantine's conversion.

By the time of the aptly named Dark Ages in Europe, women were little more than chattel; they had lost the right to divorce, and upon marriage they permanently lost any property they owned to their husbands.

In the thirteenth century, well over a thousand years after the advent of Christianity, St. Thomas Aquinas could still write:

> As regards the individual nature, woman is defective and misbegotten, for the active power of the male seed tends to the production of a perfect likeness in the masculine sex; while the production of a woman comes from defect in the active force or from some material indisposition, or even from some external influence. —*Summa Theologica*

The misogynistic bias in Christian scripture, the writings of the church fathers, theologians, pope after pope, and innumerable preachers has long been translated into misogyny in practice. Throughout almost the entire time that Christianity held Europe and America in its lock grip, women were all but slaves—they had essentially no political rights, their right to own property was severely restricted, and they were oft times subjected to shockingly brutal treatment.

Perhaps the clearest illustration of the status of women in the ages when Christianity was at its most powerful was the witch-burning hysteria in the Middle Ages and Renaissance. Christians all across Europe engaged in a centuries-long orgy of torture and murder at the direct behest and under the direction of the highest church authorities. The watchword of the time was Exodus 22:18, "Thou shalt not suffer a witch to live," and at minimum tens of thousands of women were brutally murdered as a result of this divine injunction and the papal bulls and decrees amplifying it (e.g., the *Spondent Pariter* decree [colloquially, "The Same As"], by John XXII, and *Summis Desiderantes* ["Desiring with Supreme Ardor"], by Innocent VIII).

The early Protestants were no better in their attitudes toward women, which largely mirrored those of their Catholic brethren. Like their Catholic counterparts, they preached female inferiority and advocated female subordination. (Not incidentally, they also believed that witchcraft was a diabolical threat, and both tortured and murdered supposed witches.)

In 1566, Martin Luther, stated:

> Women . . . have but small and narrow chests, and broad hips, to the end that they should remain at home, sit still, keep house, and bear and bring up children. —*Table Talk*

John Knox, the founder of Presbyterianism, went even further in his colorfully titled *The First Blast of the Trumpet Against the Monstrous Regiment of Women* (1558):

> Nature doth paint them [women] further to be weak, frail, impatient, feeble and foolish; and experience hath declared them to be unconstant, variable, cruel, and lacking the spirit of counsel.[5]

As regards women being kept in their place, Knox stated in the same screed:

> To promote a woman to bear rule, superiority, dominion, or empire above any realm, nation, or city, is repugnant to Nature; contumely to God, a thing most contrarious to His revealed will and approved ordinance; and finally, it is the subversion of good order, of all equity and justice.

In regard to divorce, the situation improved marginally with Henry VIII's rupture with Rome over his desire to rid himself of Catherine of Aragon and marry Anne Boleyn, which he did (via an annulment he, as head of the Church of England, gave himself) before ordering Boleyn's murder three years later. The Church of England in the years following Henry was in lockstep with the Catholic Church on divorce, which had forbade it from the start. Even in the 19th and 20th centuries, the Catholic Church fought a rearguard action against the right to divorce, doing its best to restrict the grounds for it for *everyone*, not just Catholics.

As for the Protestants, they were as retrograde as the Catholics as regards both divorce and women's ownership of property. The early feminist Elizabeth Cady Stanton, in *History of Woman Suffrage*, describes the situation in Boston in 1850:

> Woman could not hold any property, either earned or inherited. If unmarried, she was obliged to place it in the hands of a trustee, to whose will she was subject. If she contemplated marriage, and desired to call her property her own, she was forced by law to make a contract with her intended husband by which she gave up all title or claim to it. A woman, either married or unmarried, could hold no office of trust or power. She was not recognized as a citizen . . . She was not a unit, but a zero, in the sum of civilization.
>
> The status of a married woman was little better than that of a domestic servant. By the English Common Law her husband was her lord and master. He had the sole custody of her minor children. . . . He could by will deprive her of every part of his property, and also of what had been hers before marriage. . . . She did not own a rag of her clothing. She had no personal rights and could hardly call her soul her own.[6]

One can only shudder at the horrors suffered by generation upon generation of women, deprived of property (which deprived them of both independence and means of escape), and totally at the mercy of their husbands, no matter how brutal and abusive—all thanks to Christianity's emphasis on the "sacredness" and "indissolubility" of marriage, and the perennial Christian desire to enshrine Christian morals into civil and criminal law.

Well into the 20th century, the Catholic Church was still doubling down on its contempt for women. In 1930, Pope Pius XI's encyclical *Casti Connubii* ("Chaste Wedlock") reaffirmed male domination and female subordination: "Married life presupposes the power of the husband over the wife and children, and subjection and obedience of the wife to the husband."

As you'd expect, this misogynistic attitude has been mirrored within church structures. Given the misogynistic nature of the Bible, the church fathers, the popes, and the founders of Protestantism, it's not surprising that women have almost always held subservient positions in Christian churches and denominations. There appear to have been no female clergy in any Christian denomination of note from the fourth century until the 20th century, with the exceptions of the Shakers and Christian Scientists (both founded by women), and probably a few women posing as men in other denominations. Even today, many Christian sects, most prominently the Catholic Church, continue to resist ordaining female clerics.

Many of those leading the fight for women's rights had no illusions about the misogynistic nature of Christianity. These women included Mary Wollstonecraft, Victoria Woodhull, Elizabeth Cady Stanton, and Margaret Sanger, whose slogan, "No God. No master," remains relevant to this day.

Unfortunately, even today many religious figures are not as enlightened:

> I know this is painful for the ladies to hear, but if you get married, you have accepted the headship of a man, your husband. Christ is the head of the household and the husband is the head of the wife, and that's the way it is, period. —Rev. Pat Robertson[7]

> I listen to feminists and all these radical gals. These women just need a man in the house. That's all they need. Most of the feminists need a man to tell them what time of day it is and to lead them home. And they blew it and they're mad at all men. Feminists hate men. They're sexist. They hate men; that's their problem. —Rev. Jerry Falwell, Sr.[8]

A lot of religious-right women are no more aware than their men, as illustrated by the words of former Kansas state senator Kay O'Connor: "I'm an old-fashioned woman. Men should take care of women, and if men were taking care of women today, we wouldn't have to vote."[9]

This type of benighted attitude, this Christian legacy, is what women still face in the 21st century. Given the long record of Christian misogyny, it's ironic that women still tend to be more religious than men—and that there is no definitive, or even commonly agreed upon, reason for it.

Endnotes

1. "The Catholic Church and Women," by Vincent Ruggiero. *Catholic Journal*, December 19, 2019. https://www.catholicjournal.us/2019/12/19/the-catholic-church-and-women < https://tinyurl.com/y6zcd685 >

2. Ibid.

3. Ibid.

4. Ibid.

5. *The Works of John Knox*, Woodrow Society, Vol. 4, p. 374. https://babel.hathitrust.org/cgi/pt?id=uc1.$b463076&view=1up&seq=11 < https://tinyurl.com/y9hunmau >

6. *History of Woman Suffrage*, Vol. 2, p. 290. Quoted by Joseph McCabe in *Judeo-Christian Degradation of Woman*. Tucson: See Sharp Press, 1998, p. 8.

7. "imdb 700 Club quotes." IMDb. http://www.imdb.com/title/tt0149408/quotes < https://tinyurl.com/25sb77 >

8. "Controversial comments by Jerry Falwell: 1979–2006." Religious Tolerance. http://www.religioustolerance.org/falwell.htm < https://tinyurl.com/y3e5rqn2 >

9. "Quotes from the American Taliban." University of California at San Diego. http://adultthought.ucsd.edu/Culture_War/The_American_Taliban.html < https://tinyurl.com/j7k3k >

20

Christian Opposition to Reproductive Rights

. . . in divine matrimony man receives by divine institution the faculty to use his wife for the begetting of children.
—Thomas Aquinas, *Summa Theologica*

Almost certainly, the most salient current example of Christian misogyny is the attempt by Catholics, evangelicals, and Mormons to restrict reproductive rights, to deprive women of control over their own reproductive functions—in essence to restrict their choices in the most fundamental way possible. They want to restrict women to their traditional submissive roles as stay-at-home wives and mothers, with no independent sources of income, little or no control over the number of kids they have, and hence no way out no matter how bad their home situations.

The 19th-century German slogan *Kirche Kuche Kinder* ("Church, Kitchen, Kids") neatly encompasses this traditional prescription for the role of women. Conservative Christians, by and large, regret the decline of that traditional role. As far-right Catholic Pat Buchanan lamented in his 2002 book, *Death of the West*, "Who is going to convert American women to wanting what their mothers and grandmothers wanted and prayed for: a good man, a home in the suburbs, and a passel of kids. Sounds almost quaint."

Yes it does. Thank god.

Christian opposition to women's reproductive rights dates back almost to the beginnings of Christianity. Even though contraception is forbidden nowhere in the Bible, with the possible exception of the sin of Onan (see Genesis 38:9), which is open to three interpretations with the sin consisting of masturbation, *coitus interruptus*, or disobedience to religious law. Nonetheless, early clerics widely opposed contraception because they regarded pleasurable sex as inherently sinful, even within marriage, and thought that contraception encouraged sinfulness—adultery, fornication, and prostitution. Formal pronouncements against contraception and abortion by church leaders were, however, few and far between, though both were condemned and treated as serious sins in at least some penitentials (lists of sins and punishments) during the Middle Ages.[1]

Effraenatam ("With No Restraint"), by Pope Sixtus V, the first papal bull outlawing both contraception and abortion, wasn't issued until 1588. In it, he equated both with homicide, and demanded the imposition of civil and church penalties for those guilty of either offense. "However, both church and civil authorities refused to enforce his orders, and laypeople virtually ignored them."[2] The following pope, Gregory XIV, "revoked the decisions of *Effraenatam* and reinstated the original punishment of excommunication for procured abortion only after the animation or ensoulment of [when the soul, whatever that might be, is somehow implanted in] the fetus."[3] Prior to that, because the fetus didn't have a soul, it wasn't human, and so abortion *couldn't* be murder. (Revealingly, the Church held that ensoulment took place 40 days after conception for male fetuses, but 80 days after conception for female fetuses.)*

While the Catholic Church continued to oppose both contraception and abortion over the coming centuries, the next major pronouncement on those matters wasn't until Pius XI's 1930 encyclical *Casti Connubii* ("Chaste Wedlock"), which condemned both practices. It was followed by Paul VI's 1968 encyclical *Humanae Vitae* ("Human Life"), which reaffirmed the Church's traditional position on contraception. Since then, the Church has held unwaveringly to its opposition to both contraception and abortion.

In contrast, the Protestant churches, which had been in lock step with the Vatican on these issues until well into the 20th century, finally broke ranks with the Catholic Church in 1930, when the Lambeth Conference,

---

* The ensoulment doctrine is an almost perfect example in miniature of Christian theological beliefs. The process involves a nebulous, never-shown-to-exist entity (God) performing a nebulous, never-shown-to-exist process (ensoulment) that installs a nebulous, never-shown-to-exist substance (the soul) in a fetus (which at least does exist). As if this fog of unverifiable assertions wasn't enough, the church, apparently just for the hell of it, threw in some misogyny.

reluctantly and with apparent distaste, relaxed the Anglicans' opposition to birth control in the Conference's Resolution 15. It stated in part, "in those cases where there is such a clearly felt moral obligation to limit or avoid parenthood, and where there is a morally sound reason for avoiding complete abstinence, the Conference agrees that other methods may be used."[4] Since then, a large majority of Protestant churches in both the UK and US have accepted the use of contraception, though their positions on the right to abortion vary widely, with the more conservative churches tending to loudly and stridently oppose it.

On this side of the Atlantic, in 1873 the United States Congress, acceding to pressure from Christian moral reformers (concerned as always with reforming the morals of *others*), passed the Comstock Act, which criminalized the sale, and even possession, of "articles of immoral use," i.e., contraceptives, including but not limited to condoms, spermicides, cervical caps, and contraceptive sponges. The Act also criminalized the importation of birth control devices, and even criminalized the *description* of such devices and their use.[5] In the following years, many states followed suit and passed similar laws ("the Comstock laws").

An organized movement against these laws began on the eve of World War I, led by women such as Margaret Sanger and Emma Goldman. Sanger was indicted in 1914 for writing and distributing the book *Family Limitation*, and fled to England, fearing imprisonment would put an end to her activism. Her husband continued to distribute birth control information in her absence, and he was indicted and imprisoned for 30 days as a result.

After Sanger returned from Europe in 1916, she and other women opened the first birth control clinic in the United States, the Brownsville Clinic in New York City, which was an immediate but short-term success. The New York police quickly shut down the facility and dragged Sanger from the premises. She was subsequently indicted and imprisoned, as was her sister, Ethel Byrne, though she continued the struggle for reproductive rights after she was released.

It would be a long struggle. The Comstock laws weren't struck down by the Supreme Court until 1965 in *Griswold v. Connecticut*, a decision which applied only to married people. The Court didn't strike down laws against contraceptive possession by single people until 1972. Following that victory, the Supreme Court delivered another in the form of *Roe v. Wade* in 1973, which established the right to abortion.

Having lost the fight to prohibit possession and distribution of contraceptives, the Catholic Church shifted its focus to prohibiting abortion.

There is not a single word on abortion in the nearly 800,000 words of the Bible, but that didn't deter the Catholics. By the 1980s, right-wing evangelicals had joined them, and since then Catholics, evangelicals, and Mormons have managed to pass one restrictive law after another, making abortion very difficult to obtain in many states, especially for poor women.

Because *Roe* declared abortion a fundamental individual right, Christian opponents of abortion have had to come up with inventive ways to justify their efforts to restrict that right. Since they can't flatly state that they intend to restrict (prior to eliminating) this Supreme Court-affirmed right for religious reasons, they invariably cite transparently phony, hypocritical rationales for their restrictive measures.

One of the most frequently cited spurious grounds for restricting abortion rights is "concern" for the health of women. This is outright, obvious bullshit. It's been well established for decades that legal abortion is far safer than childbirth. The National Institutes of Health placed the mortality rate for abortion at .6 per 100,000 and the mortality rate for live births at 8.8 per 100,000 as of 2012—in other words, live birth was approximately 15 times as dangerous as having an abortion at that time.[6] But the maternal mortality rate in the United States has been rising since the year 2000, and the mortality rate from abortion has been falling. As of 2020, the maternal mortality rate stood at 17.2 deaths per 100,000 births, by far the highest in any industrialized country—twice as high as in any of the other nations surveyed, and ten times higher than the rates in New Zealand and Norway.[7] As for abortion, CDC figures indicate that in 2018 the mortality rate from legal abortion stood at .3 per 100,000—in other words, exactly two women died that year in the entire country from abortion complications.[8] So, as of the end of the second decade of the 21st century, the ratio of per capita deaths from childbirth vs. deaths from abortion in the United States was 57 to 1.

Given that there are roughly 600,000 abortions annually in the U.S., this means that if abortion was outlawed and the pregnant women who wanted legal abortions were forced to give birth, over 100 of them would die, in comparison with the two or so who would have died from abortion complications. In other words, if "pro-life" policies were instituted nationwide, over 100 women would die annually from preventable deaths caused by involuntary pregnancy.

But the total would probably be higher than that, because some pregnant women would turn to back alley abortions and die as a result. One indication of this is that hundreds, sometimes thousands, of women died annually from such abortions in the pre-*Roe* era. In 1930, for instance, the cause of death of 2,700 American women was listed as abortion,[9] though the true total was probably much higher, as it's highly likely that the cause of death of thousands of other women was mislabeled, ascribed to other causes, in order to avoid scandal. The number of deaths from illegal abortions fell sharply following the introduction of antibiotics in the mid-1940s, but the facts remain that illegal abortion is much more hazardous than legal abortion, and that legal abortion is far safer than childbirth.

Opponents of reproductive rights are well aware of all this—they have to be, the medical and scientific literature is almost unanimous on the matter—yet these self-appointed guardians of women (who, of course, can't be trusted to make their own decisions) routinely lie through their teeth, while posing as purer-than-the-driven-snow moralists who are altruistically safeguarding women and their health. Just how cynical that claim is was laid bare by a bill introduced in the Tennessee legislature in 2021 that would allow "a man who gets a woman pregnant to request an injunction barring her from having an abortion."[10] The bill not only gives men veto power over women's reproductive decisions, but gives that right to rapists: there is no exception in case of rape, nor in case of incest. Almost as bad, "Proof of parenthood requires only that the petitioner acknowledges paternity. A DNA test is not required."[11] So, any man who claimed paternity could block a woman from having an abortion. (Not incidentally, Tennessee is one of the most "pro-life" states in the country, having the highest percentage of evangelicals of any state, 52% of the population.)[12]

Anti-choice, authoritarian Christian activists in groups such as Operation Rescue have for decades also routinely harassed women arriving at abortion clinics, and have stalked and harassed abortion providers, sometimes at their own homes. Some Christian activists have gone further and turned to outright terrorism, murdering doctors and bombing clinics. Since the late 1970s, Christian anti-choice terrorism in the United States has resulted in at least 11 murders, countless harassment and stalking incidents, over 40 arson and bombing attacks, and over 90 attempted bombings and attempted arson attacks.[13]

The war on reproductive rights continues in virtually every other country where there are large numbers of evangelicals and conservative Catholics. Throughout Latin America, regimes do the church's bidding and actively suppress reproductive rights. In a number of particularly reprehensible incidents, women have been jailed for *years*, sometimes decades, for having miscarriages in countries with draconian anti-choice laws.

Countries with such laws include El Salvador, the Dominican Republic, Haiti, Honduras, Nicaragua, and Suriname, all of which completely ban abortion, no matter what the circumstances—not even to save the life of a pregnant woman. The situation in many other Catholic- (and increasingly evangelical-) dominated Latin American countries isn't much better, with abortion outlawed in Venezuela, Guatemala, and Paraguay except to save the life of the woman, in a few others, including Brazil, in case of rape, and in Chile in case of rape or to save the life of a woman. In the entire region, abortion is fully legal only in Cuba, Guyana, French Guiana, Uruguay, and Argentina.

The effects of Christianity-inspired anti-choice laws upon individual women are often devastating. To cite but two examples, in El Salvador, a country with a total abortion ban, Teodora del Carmen Vásquez was freed in 2018 after serving more than a decade of a 30-year sentence for "aggravated homicide"—having a miscarriage; the only reason she was freed was that the Salvadoran supreme court ruled there was insufficient evidence of homicide (in other words, insufficient evidence that she had induced her miscarriage) and commuted her sentence.[14] Another Salvadoran woman freed in 2018, Maria Figueroa Marroquín, suffered more than 15 years imprisonment for a similar "crime."[15] As of 2018, in El Salvador, human rights campaigners had managed to free a total of five women who'd had miscarriages and were imprisoned for homicide, but another 24 remained in prison.

The country's hard line anti-choice position remains in place. In 2020 and the first five months of 2021, another 10 women were charged with homicide for having miscarriages. And in May 2021, another woman, Sara Rogel, was freed after serving 10 years of a 30-year sentence, in part because the judge stated that she "doesn't represent a danger to society." The state is appealing the decision freeing her.[16]

How badly were these women treated? Almost all of them were "poor, and many . . . lacked access to prenatal care. Some have said they were handcuffed to their hospital beds and then taken straight to prison." And some of them "were shunned and beaten" by their presumably religious fellow prisoners.[17]

As badly as Catholic Latin American regimes treat women, they treat girls even worse. Amnesty International reports that in Paraguay, another country with a stringent anti-choice law, over 1,000 girls *14 years old and under* were forced to give birth in 2019 and 2020, which is hazardous to their health: "Girls under the age of 15 are four times more likely to die from pregnancy-related complications [than girls and women 15 and over]."[18] Given their ages, it's certain that all of these abused girls were victims of incest and/or rape. And conservative Catholics and evangelicals are just fine with forcing them to give birth.

But it gets even more sickening—even in countries that permit abortion.

In one particularly egregious case in 2019, in Tucamán Province in northwest Argentina, Catholic healthcare officials and providers, and the Catholic Church, pressured an 11-year-old rape victim to carry her pregnancy to term. They pressured her even though the girl and her mother stated repeatedly that they wanted her to have an abortion. Among other things, the hospital she went to stalled for almost a month after the girl and her mother first requested the procedure. As well, the presumably Catholic head of Tucumán's healthcare system tried to bribe her family into forcing the girl to go through the dangerous procedure (for an 11-year-old who still had some of her baby teeth) of giving birth, offering them both a house and a scholarship for the pregnant girl. In addition, the presumably Catholic nurses at the hospital lied to the girl, telling her that they were giving her a vitamin shot, when in fact it was a corticoid shot designed to quicken the development of the fetus's lungs. And the hospital's chaplain admonished the girl that she would carry a "burden of conscience" if she had an abortion; he also lied to the girl's mother, telling her that an abortion would endanger the girl's life. Finally, after nearly a month of stalling by healthcare providers, the doctor treating the now-23-weeks-pregnant girl performed a "micro" C-section to terminate the pregnancy.[19]

To put the maggot-ridden cherry atop this nauseating sundae, Tucumán's archishop, Carlos Alberto Sánchez, publicly shamed the girl, using her full name, as part of his and the Catholic Church's anti-choice jihad.[20]

So much for Christian respect for women's health and wellbeing. So much for Christian respect for women and girls.

Endnotes

1. "Quotes from the American Taliban." University of California at San Diego. http://adultthought.ucsd.edu/Culture_War/The_American_Taliban.html < https://tinyurl.com/j7k3k >

2. "Effraenatam (1588), by Pope Sixtus V," by Katherine Brind'Amour. The Embryo Project Encyclopedia. https://embryo.asu.edu/pages/effraenatam-1588-pope-sixtus-v < https://tinyurl.com/yyyxvgyz >

3. Ibid.

4. “The Lambeth Conference Resolutions Archive from 1930.” Anglican Communion Office, 2005. https://www.anglicancommunion.org/media/127734/1930.pdf < https://tinyurl.com/y4uaej2l >

5. “Legal History of Contraceptives.” *Jurist*, January 28, 2014. https://www.jurist.org/archives/feature/legal-history-of-contraceptives-in-the-us/ < https://tinyurl.com/y2yehmyb >

6. “The comparative safety of legal induced abortion and childbirth in the United States,” by Elizabeth G. Raymond and David Grimes. NIH National Library of Medicine. https://pubmed.ncbi.nlm.nih.gov/22270271/ < https://tinyurl.com/yxo8lqsp >

7. “US Ranks Worst in Maternal Care, Mortality Compared With 10 Other Developed Nations,” by Gianna Melillo. *American Journal of Managed Care*, December 3, 2020. https://www.ajmc.com/view/us-ranks-worst-in-maternal-care-mortality-compared-with-10-other-developed-nations < https://tinyurl.com/2hfsbmpa >

8. “Abortion Surveillance—United States, 2018,” by Katherin Kortsmit, et al. Centers for Disease Control and Prevention, Morbidity and Mortality Weekly Report, November 27, 2020. https://www.cdc.gov/mmwr/volumes/69/ss/ss6907a1.htm < https://tinyurl.com/ejfxcr2z >

9. “Lessons from Before Roe: Will Past be Prologue?,” by Rachel Benson Gold. Gutenmacher Institute, March 1, 2003. https://www.guttmacher.org/gpr/2003/03/lessons-roe-will-past-be-prologue < https://tinyurl.com/3cz75p9t >

10. “Tennessee Lawmakers Introduce Bill To Allow Fathers To Veto Abortions,” by Melissa Jeltsen. *Huffington Post*, February 11,2021. https://www.huffpost.com/entry/tennessee-lawmakers-introduce-bill-allow-fathers-veto-abortions_n_6025ae58c5b6f88289fa797a?guccounter=1&guce_referrer=aHR0cHM6Ly9mcmllbmRseWF0aGVpc3QucGF0aGVvcy5jb20v&guce_referrer_sig=AQAAALxeiqwRyFxhFSZnSM9qOTeAzJ-EhJddqDrJinCWPEzoJe10DobGzRwH2EameFCtS2RIbqnT5cwm2l5Uyez6Vd-ToT9gkZ-O1NS6JebLmuE9aVF3dyzSnpgEFRts6whjxIFf5dj8QSE2xAeo4I_t872GUWMPQrpm86sA-jV1FRndnx < https://tinyurl.com/3wn8x3yv >

11. Ibid.

12. “The Most Evangelical States in America,” by Joseph Gedeon. *24/7 Wallst*, September 22, 2017. https://247wallst.com/special-report/2017/09/22/the-most-states-in-america/11/ < https://tinyurl.com/4orhbvso >

13. “Abortion Clinic Violence,” by Liam Stack. *New York Times*, November 29, 2015. https://www.nytimes.com/interactive/2015/11/29/us/30abortion-clinic-violence.html < https://tinyurl.com/y2jsld42 >

14. “They Were Jailed for Miscarriages,” by Elizabeth Malkin. *New York Times*, April 9, 2018. https://www.nytimes.com/2018/04/09/world/americas/el-salvador-abortion.html < https://tinyurl.com/y9ycbk77 >

15. Ibid.

16. “Un juez ordena la libertad de una mujer condenada a 30 años tras un aborto involuntario en El Salvador,” by Carlos Salinas Maldonado. *El País*, May 31, 2021. https://elpais.com/sociedad/2021-05-31/un-juez-ordena-la-libertad-de-una-mujer-condenada-a-30-anos-tras-un-aborto-involuntario-en-el-salvador.html < https://tinyurl.com/tjeck46 >

17. “She Was Sent To Prison For Losing Her Baby. Now She Wants To Clear Her Name,” by Karla Zabludovsky. *BuzzFeedNews*, July 13, 2021. https://www.buzzfeednews.com/article/karlazabludovsky/el-salvador-abortion-laws-imprisoned-freed < https://tinyurl.com/h4xc87ds >

18. “Sexual violence and abortion restrictions in Paraguay are fueling an epidemic of childhood pregnancy: Amnesty,” by Kara Fox. CNN, December 1, 2021. https://edition.cnn.com/2021/12/01/americas/paraguay-pregnancy-child-abuse-sexual-violence-intl/index.html < https://tinyurl.com/yckwk8cz >

19. “How Doctors And The Church Conspired To Stop An 11-Year-Old Girl From Having An Abortion After She Was Raped,” by Karla Zabludovsky. *BuzzFeedNews*, April 13, 2019. https://www.buzzfeednews.com/article/karlazabludovsky/argentina-lucia-catholic-church-abortion < https://tinyurl.com/7fmk4b4v >

20. Ibid.

21

Christian Homophobia

Homosexuals want their depraved 'values' to become our children's values. Homosexuals expect society to embrace their immoral way of life. Worse yet, they are looking for new recruits!
—Beverly LaHaye, Concerned Women for America

Christianity from its beginnings has been markedly homophobic. The biblical basis for this homophobia lies in Genesis, in the story of Sodom and Gomorrah, and in Leviticus. Leviticus 18:22 reads: "Thou shalt not lie with mankind, as with womankind: it is abomination," and Leviticus 20:13 reads: "If a man lie with mankind as he lieth with a woman, both of them have committed an abomination: they shall surely be put to death; their blood shall be upon them."

While the passages in Leviticus on homosexuality seem remarkably harsh, Leviticus also proscribes a great many other things, declares still others abominations, and prescribes the death penalty for still others, some of them shockingly picayune. Leviticus 17:10–13 prohibits the eating of blood sausage; Leviticus 11:6–7 prohibits the eating of "unclean" hares and swine; Leviticus 11:10 declares shellfish abominations; Leviticus 20:9 prescribes the death penalty for cursing one's father or mother; Leviticus 20:10 prescribes the death penalty for adultery; Leviticus 20:14 prescribes the penalty of being burnt alive for marrying one's wife's mother; and Leviticus 20:15 declares, "And if a man lie with a beast, he shall surely be put to death: and ye shall slay the beast," which seems rather unfair to the poor, abused beast. (One suspects that contemporary American Christians have never attempted to pass laws enforcing Leviticus 20:15, because if passed and enforced such laws would decimate both the Bible Belt and the cattle industry.)

The only other Old Testament passage of note, which bears only tangentially on homosexuality, is Deuteronomy 22:5, which anathematizes transvestism: "The woman shall not wear that which pertaineth unto a man, neither shall a man put on a woman's garment: for all that do so are abomination unto the Lord thy God."

The New Testament also condemns homosexuality, notably in Romans 1:26–27: ". . . God gave them up unto vile affections: for even their women did change the natural use into that which is against nature: And likewise also the men, leaving the natural use of the woman, burned in their lust one toward another . . ."

Early church fathers echoed the condemnations of homosexual activity in Leviticus and Romans. St. John Chrysostom (347–430), in his Homily on Romans, said, "All these affections then were vile, but chiefly the mad lust after males; . . ."[1] His contemporary, St. Augustine (354–430) said, referring to the same verses, "Sins against nature, therefore, like the sin of Sodom, are abominable and deserve punishment whenever and wherever they are committed."[2] Pope Gregory III (690–741) went further, saying that homosexuality was "a vice so abominable in the sight of God that the cities in which its practitioners dwelt were appointed for destruction by fire and brimstone."[3] Half a millennium later, theologian Thomas Aquinas (1225–1274), speaking again of Romans 1:26–27, echoed his forebears: "For if the sins of the flesh are commonly censurable because they lead man to that which is bestial in him, much more so is the sin against nature, by which man debases himself lower than even his animal nature."[4]

Given such hostility, it's not surprising that following the adoption of Christianity as the state religion of Rome in the fourth century, penalties for homosexual behavior became quite harsh, with passive male partners being subject to the penalty of being burned alive. By the sixth century, under the Code of Justinian, both participants in gay male sex were subject to the death penalty. These barbaric sanctions remained in place in Christian lands for well over a thousand years, with burning alive being the normal form of execution.

Other penalties were almost worse. James McDonald, an expert on medieval and church history, states that in the thirteenth century "Alfonso X [1221–1284] of Castile [Spain] favoured castration followed by hanging upside down until dead, but at the end of the fifteenth century Ferdinand and Isabella changed this to the more traditional burning."[5] Alfonso wasn't alone. Historian Reay Tannahill, in *Sex In History*, reveals that the cringe-inducing penalty of castration was in force in Spain as early as the end of the seventh century; she also quotes the Council of Toledo, which decreed that "if any one of those males who commit this vile practice against nature with other males is a bishop, a priest, or a deacon, he shall be degraded from his order and shall remain in permanent exile . . ."[6] Even associating with such sinners was a crime, with those guilty subject to the penalties of "a hundred lashes, a shaven head, and banishment . . ."[7]

Shortly after Alfonxo X was imposing his gruesome penalties in Castile, one member of the British royalty caught having homosexual relations supposedly suffered an even more grisly fate: Edward II's (1284–1327) alleged penalty was being held down while a red hot poker was jammed through his rectum and intestines. There's some dispute about how Edward was killed, but there's no dispute that he was killed.

He was hardly alone in meeting a horrific end, though the penalties levied against gay people were often less stringent, as can be seen in medieval penitentials, lists of sins and punishments. One seventh-century penitential cited by Tannahill has an ascending list of sins and punishments, ranging from "simple kissing" by males under the age of 20, which merited "six special fasts," up to fellatio, which merited "a penance of four years, for habitual offenders, seven years," and sodomy, which brought "seven years penance."[8] Though inconsistently applied (except in ultra-religious Spain where it was more commonly enforced), the penalty of being burnt alive for having gay sex was in force all over Europe through the medieval and Renaissance periods, and as Tannahill reveals was carried out as late as 1725 in France.[9]

In the Spanish colonies in the New World, things were no better, with burning being the normal form of execution. The 1583 Third Provincial Council of Lima (Peru) admonished native converts:

> If there is one among you who commits sodomy, sinning with another man, or with a boy, or with a beast, let [it] be known that, because of that, fire and brimstone burned the cities of Sodom and Gomorrah and left them in ashes. Let it be known that it carries the death penalty under the just laws of our Spanish kings . . .[10*]

---

* Note that the Council blamed homosexuality for the destruction of Sodom and Gomorrah. This is an age-old Christian trope. Pat Robertson provided a recent example of it: "I don't think I'd be waving those [rainbow] flags in God's face if I were you. This is not a message of hate; this is a message of redemption. But a condition like this will bring about

(continued next page)

In England, parliament passed a law in 1533, the Buggery Act, mandating the death penalty for "the detestable and abominable vice of buggery." After being repealed shortly after it was passed, the law was reinstated in 1563 and remained in force unmodified until 1861, when parliament changed the punishment to life in prison.[11]

In the English colonies, things were just as bad. In 1641, the Bay Colony (Massachusetts) passed a law that was simply an exact transcription of Leviticus 20:13,[12] and in 1672 Connecticut also passed a law making explicit the connection of Christianity to criminalization of homosexuality. The law's preamble read in part, "the Serious Consideration of the Necessity of the Establishment of wholesome LAWES, for the Regulating of each Body Politik; Hath enclined us mainly in Obedience unto JEHOVAH the Great Law-giver: Who hath been pleased to set down a *Divine Platforme*, not only of the *Morall*, but also of *Judicial lawes*, suitable for the people of *Israel*."[13]

But in Pennsylvania, due to Quaker influence, the death penalty for homosexuality was abolished in 1682 and replaced with a punishment of six months imprisonment. This remained the lightest penalty ever put into law in America until 1961. However, the relatively mild approach in Pennsylvania was short lived. In 1700, the Pennsylvania legislature passed a law mandating castration for married men convicted of sodomy and a separate law mandating the death penalty for slaves guilty of the "vice." In 1718, under British pressure, Pennsylvania reinstituted the death penalty.[14]

The colonials didn't restrict their zeal for the death penalty to gay people, though; they passed laws mandating capital punishment for other offenses, including many of the victimless death-penalty crimes specified in the Old Testament. (See Chapter 14 for a list.) Historian James McDonald states that all of the colonies passed laws mandating capital punishment for witchcraft, sodomy, blasphemy, bestiality, adultery, and disrespecting one's parents. As regards homosexual acts (sodomy), McDonald notes, "In most colonies, no special provision was originally made for homosexual rape nor for the rape of children. . . . victims were also subject to the death penalty, presumably because the Bible made no provision for them to be excused as innocent victims."[15]

The death penalty for sodomy was rarely enforced, though laws mandating capital punishment for it remained on the books throughout the

---

(cont'd) terrorist bombs, it'll bring earthquakes, tornadoes, and possibly a meteor."[16] Another Robertson statement makes his contempt for gay people even clearer: "Homosexuality is an abomination. Many of those people involved with Adolf Hitler were Satanists, many of them were homosexuals. The two things seem to go together."[17]

colonial period and after the American Revolution, with reduced penalties once the colonies had achieved independence. Unfortunately, British colonial laws (modeled on section 377 of the Indian Penal Code, itself modeled on Britain's 16th-century Buggery Act)[18] remain in place in many former British colonies, with those countries making up over half of the 69 nations in which homosexuality is still illegal. Ironically, section 377 is no longer in force in India, which legalized homosexuality in 2018, though the laws it inspired remain in effect in many other countries, including Malaysia, Singapore, Bangladesh, Myanmar, and Sri Lanka.[(19)]

But the most notorious former colony that still outlaws homosexuality is Uganda, where American evangelicals, some connected with the Christian pray-away-the-gay "conversion therapy" movement, have been working with their Ugandan counterparts to reintroduce the death penalty for same-sex relations, a considerable step up from the already draconian penalty of 10 years imprisonment.[20,21]

In their campaign in Uganda, beginning in 2009, the evangelicals, both American and Ugandan, trotted out the Christian right's standard charges—that the "gay agenda" is anti-family and anti-Christian, that gays want to "recruit" children, that they molest children, and that homosexuality is as bad as bestiality. In 2010, a Ugandan newspaper, *Rolling Stone* (*not* the American music/politics magazine), published the names, photos, and addresses of 100 of Uganda's "top" gays and lesbians, along with a banner headline reading "Kill Them: They Are After Our Kids." In 2011, one of those "top" gays, David Kato, was beaten to death with a hammer in Kampala, Uganda's capital.[22,23]

Three of the others named by *Rolling Stone* sued the paper, and were awarded the equivalent of 400 British pounds in compensation as well as an order forbidding the paper from publishing any more such articles. Shortly after that, in December 2013, the Ugandan legislature passed a bill that in its original form mandated the death penalty for "aggravated homosexuality," a penalty that was reduced to life imprisonment in the bill's final form; the bill also included a provision imposing five years imprisonment for anyone renting an apartment to a gay person and failing to report it to the authorities,[24] the probable effect of which was to leave at least some gay people homeless. The nation's high court subsequently struck down the law, but since then anti-gay violence has continued in Uganda, with the gay rights organization Sexual Minorities Uganda (with the unfortunate acronym SMUG, which the group uses) reporting that four gay people were murdered in Uganda in the July–October 2019 period, a time when the Ugandan government was threatening to reintroduce the "kill the gays" bill, and Ugandan Minister for Ethics and Integrity (sic), Simon Lokodo, blamed gay people for "massive recruitment" of children and young people.[25]

A similar attempt to persecute gay people took place in Ghana, with the introduction of the ironically named "Promotion of Proper Human Sexual Rights and Ghanaian Family Values Bill" in 2021. This "rights" bill provides penalties of six months to a year in jail for public displays of same-sex affection, three to five years in jail for simply *identifying* as LGBT, and five to ten years in jail for distributing LGBT materials or providing space for or funding LGBT groups or events. The bill, however, gives gay people a way to avoid jail time: proven-ineffective "conversion therapy." Without a hint of irony or historical awareness, Emmanuel Kwasi Bedzrah, one of the MPs sponsoring the bill, insisted that "We love them, we are asking them not to do it." ("Asking" because "we love them"? Really?) Bedrazh also stated that homsexuality is "against our traditions," which makes sense only if "our traditions" refers to the homophobic, punitive Anglican religious traditions imposed on Ghana by the British in the 19th century.[26]

Back in the U.S., laws against gay relations (still on the books in every state through the mid-20th century) were rarely enforced up until the time of the Comstock laws in the 1870s, when the states began to more vigorously, if still sporadically, enforce them. In the increasingly urbanized United States, police harassment on the street, employment discrimination, housing discrimination, raids on gay bars, etc., remained routine through most of the 20th century; but in the post-World War II period things began to change. In 1961, Illinois became the first state to repeal its anti-sodomy law, and in the 1970s, in the wake of the Stonewall riots in 1969, 20 more states repealed their anti-sodomy statutes. Others followed suit in the 1980s through the early 2000s, either through repeal of the laws in state legislatures or through state high courts striking them down. Finally, in 2003 the Supreme Court, in *Lawrence v. Texas*, struck down anti-sodomy laws nationwide as unconstitutional.

Since then, the religious right, along with its accomplices in the Republican Party, has continued its anti-LGBT+ rampage, primarily focusing on giving religious bigots the "freedom" to discriminate against gay people. The Republicans use Christian anti-gay bigotry to manipulate the bigots into supporting Republican candidates through the use of wedge issues, such as "defense of marriage" legislation (as if allowing gay people to marry is somehow a threat to other marriages); even after the 2015 Supreme

Court ruling that legalized gay marriage, the "defense of marriage" trope continues to be a perennial favorite of the religious right, though it seems to be running out of steam. A more recent and still very useful (to Republicans) wedge issue is the promotion and passing of "bathroom bills" that deny trans people the right to use appropriate public restrooms. In essence, religious-right Republican politicians are pandering to homophobes in exchange for their votes.

Today, legions of anti-gay Christians continue to whine endlessly about "gay recruiters," "the gay agenda," and being "persecuted" by gays. The anti-mask, anti-social distancing, anti-vaccination Reverend Gary Locke, of the Global Vision Bible Church in Mount Juliet, Tennessee, provides an example. Alleging that gay marriage is a smokescreen for pedophiles, Locke, quotes imaginary gay people: "'If you just gave us same-sex marriage, we would leave you alone.' [Let me] tell you something. . . . It has always been about the children, it wasn't about same-sex marriage! It's always been about these pedophiles!"[27] (Notice that Locke not only accuses gay people of being pedophiles, he also whines about imaginary persecution by gays. One might well ask for examples of exactly how, when, and where gay people won't "leave you alone.") Of course, this charge, that all gay people, especially gay males, are pedophiles, is false. The American Psychological Association states that, as a great many scientific studies have shown, "homosexual men are not more likely to sexually abuse children than heterosexual men are."[28]

The ever-indignant Tony Perkins of the Family Research Council provides still another example of rhetoric that's both homophobic and self-pitying—a perfect example of the Christian Persecution Complex: "Just a few decades ago, these activists said all they wanted was recognition, autonomy, coexistence. Now, a few years after *Obergefell* [*v. Hodges*, the Supreme Court decision that guaranteed the right to gay marriage] . . . Pride is the new religion, and everyone must bow a knee to their sexual gods or face the left's fiery furnace."[29] To ask the obvious, what "fiery furnace"? And who's forcing anyone to "bow a knee" other than Christian (and Muslim) parents inflicting that indignity on their own children? Perkins remains oblivious to such questions, and instead continues to whinge on about "surviving the rainbow onslaught" and "escaping the left's forced sexual revolution."[30] (Ummmm . . . "forced"? Sounds kinky. Please tell us—we're all ears—what the gay minions of Satan are "forcing" you to do, Tony.)

In contrast to the imaginary depredations of gays, and the imaginary persecution of Christians by gay people, hundreds, probably thousands, of LGBT+ people have been murdered in the United States in hate crimes over the years, and many such killings (especially of trans people) still occur annually. As evidence that the number of victims is well into the thousands, Human Rights Watch, which tracks anti-gay violence, reports that in under a decade, in the years 2013–2021, over 250 trans people were murdered in the U.S.[33]—and this doesn't even include gay, lesbian, and bi victims of gay bashings.

Christian homophobes can find justification for such violence in the Bible and the anti-gay rhetoric of Republican politicians—and, of course, in the hate-filled sermons issuing from all too many pulpits in this country. If history is any indication, such homophobic sermons will continue to be issued for many years to come, as will the gay bashings and murders they inspire.

But perhaps the worst, or at least most widespread, suffering currently inflicted by Christians on gay people is the epidemic of homelessness and suicide among LGBT+ teens. Virtually no such teens become homeless voluntarily; virtually none of them decide, "I'll leave home, live on the streets or in an abandoned building, with no source of income other than begging, stealing, or peddling my ass. Yeah, sounds great! I'm outta here!" That just doesn't happen. Rather, moralistic Christian parents turn their backs on their children, driving them from their homes and into oft-times dire situations.

While gay teenagers make up only about 5% of teens (in line with general population figures), they make up about 40% of homeless teens, with roughly 320,000 to 400,000 gay teens being homeless as of 2014.[31]* Gay teens also attempt suicide more often than their straight counterparts, probably two to three times as often, though it's difficult to give an accurate estimate because families of suicidal gay youths, and often the youths themselves, feel shame and attempt to hide the homophobic aspects of suicides and suicide attempts.

As a concrete example of what parental homophobia looks like, writer Alex Morris cites the case of "Jackie," an Idaho teen who came out to her devout Catholic mother: "'You can't hate me after I say this,' she pleaded

* The CDC reports that as of 2019 gay or bi male teenagers comprised 5.5% of the nation's male teens, while the figure for gay or bi female teens was 16.8%;[32] other figures show that trans teens make up about .5% of teenagers. Even assuming that the higher percentage for female teens reported in 2019 is correct, and that homeless male youths outnumber homeless female youths by a ratio of 3:2,[34] LGBT+ teens still suffer homelessness at a rate at least four times that of their straight counterparts.

when . . . her mom picked up the phone. 'Oh, my God, you're pregnant . . . Are you in jail? Did you get expelled? Are you in trouble? What happened? What did you do?' Suddenly her mom's silence matched Jackie's own. 'Oh, my God, . . . 'Are you gay?' 'Yeah,' Jackie forced herself to say. After what felt like an eternity, her mom finally responded. 'I don't know what we could have done for God to have given us a fag as a child.'"

Following that conversation, Jackie's parents immediately cut her off financially and refused to speak with her, delegating the task of reading her out of the family to her brother. She recounts part of what he said: "Mom and Dad don't want to talk to you . . . All your cards are going to be shut off, and Mom and Dad want you to take the car and drop it off at this specific location. Your phone's going to last for this much longer. They don't want you coming to the house, and you're not to contact them. You're not going to get any money from them. Nothing. And if you don't return the car, they're going to report it stolen."[35]

This is how deep homophobia runs in Christianity: it leads many Christian parents to reject their own children simply because of who they are, or, to put it in Christian terms, many Christian parents reject their own children because of "the way God made them."*

Endnotes

1. "Dishonorable Passions," by Fr. John Peck. The Orthodox Church of Tomorrow. https://frjohnpeck.com/dishonorable-passions/ < https://tinyurl.com/y2rfh8m9 >

2. Ibid.

3. Quoted by Reay Tannahill in *Sex in History, revised & expanded*. Scarborough Publishers, 1992, p. 153.

---

* As bad as this is, there are other instances of religious parents turning their backs on their children that are even worse. In his enlightening *What You Don't Know About Religion (but should)*, Ryan Cragun, a professor of sociology at the University of Tampa, relates the story of "Bronn," a fellow participant in an academic conference on religion. Bronn's family were Christian Scientists, and when at age ten he became ill with an abscessed tooth, they let him suffer for days while they read the Bible to him. Bronn grew worse, and a non-Christian Scientist relative contacted a doctor; surprisingly, Bronn's parents allowed the doctor to examine him. The doctor told them he'd be dead within a day if he wasn't hospitalized immediately. His parents left the decision up to Bronn. When he decided that he would go to the hospital, they disowned him. They told him—a ten-year-old boy who was suffering horribly and was near death because of their negligence—that they wouldn't allow him to return home after going to the hospital. The anti-science, anti-medical treatment dogma of their ironically named church was more important to them than their suffering child.[36]

4. Peck, op. cit.

5. "Homosexuality and Christianity," by James McDonald. *Bad News About Christianity.* http://www.badnewsaboutchristianity.com/gff_homosexuality.htm < https://tinyurl.com/y39dtmz6 >

6. Tannahill, op. cit., p. 157.

7. Ibid.

8. Ibid., p. 158–159.

9. Ibid., p. 377.

10. Ibid., p. 300.

11. "Homosexuals and the Death Penalty in Colonial America," by Louis Crompton. *Journal of Homosexuality*, Vol. 1(3), 1976, pp. 277–278. https://digitalcommons.unl.edu/cgi/viewcontent.cgi?article=1061&context=englishfacpubs < https://tinyurl.com/y4dtsv8j >

12. Ibid., p. 279.

13. Ibid., p. 278.

14. Ibid., p. 282–283.

15. McDonald, op. cit.

16. "imdb 700 Club quotes." IMDb. http://www.imdb.com/title/tt0149408/quotes < https://tinyurl.com/25sb77 >

17. Quoted in "PFLAG, Pat Robertson Censorship Fight," by John De Salvio. *Albion Monitor*, January 12, 1996. http://albionmonitor.com/1-12-96/pflagrobertson.html < https://tinyurl.com/3jr96dtd >

18. "This Alien Legacy: The Origins of 'Sodomy' Laws in British Colonialism." Human Rights Watch, December 17, 2008. https://www.hrw.org/report/2008/12/17/alien-legacy/origins-sodomy-laws-british-colonialism < https://tinyurl.com/yxh4flcv >

19. "377: The British colonial law that left an anti-LGBTQ legacy in Asia," by Tessa Wong. BBC News, June 29, 2021. https://www.bbc.com/news/world-asia-57606847 < https://tinyurl.com/ynm78exd >

20. "Meet the American Pastor Behind Uganda's Anti-Gay Crackdown." *Mother Jones,* March 2014. https://www.motherjones.com/politics/2014/03/scott-lively-anti-gay-law-uganda/ < https://tinyurl.com/szjvjbw >

21. "Uganda's New Anti-Homosexuality Law Was Inspired by American Activists," by Abby Ohlheiser. *The Atlantic*, December 20, 2013. https://www.theatlantic.com/international/archive/2013/12/uganda-passes-law-punishes-homosexuality-life-imprisonment/356365/ < https://tinyurl.com/y4b-g9u2s >

22. "Ugandan Gay Rights Advocate David Kato Killed." Business and Human Rights Resource Center, January 27, 2011. https://www.business-humanrights.org/en/latest-news/uganda-gay-rights-activist-david-kato-killed/ < https://tinyurl.com/y4p7mxll >

23. "Homosexuals' lawsuit to prevent newspaper inciting violence." Business and Human Rights Resource Center. https://www.business-humanrights.org/en/latest-news/homosexuals-lawsuit-to-prevent-newspaper-inciting-violence-re-uganda/ < https://tinyurl.com/yygvckaa >

24. "Uganda Passes Anti-Gay Bill That Includes Life In Prison." National Public Radio, December 20, 2013. https://www.npr.org/sections/parallels/2013/12/20/255825383/uganda-passes-anti-gay-bill-that-includes-life-in-prison < https://tinyurl.com/y6jv7p2a >

25. "Amid Kill the Gays Bill Uproar, LGBT+Q Activist is Killed," by Tim Fitzsimons. NBC News, October 19, 2019. https://www.nbcnews.com/feature/nbc-out/amid-kill-gays-bill-uproar-ugandan-LGBTq-activist-killed-n1067336 < https://tinyurl.com/y2sqgsvy >

26. "How a US group with links to the far-right may have influenced a crackdown on Ghana's LGBTQ community," by David McKenzie and Nimi Princewill. CNN, October 8, 2021. https://edition.cnn.com/2021/10/08/africa/ghana-LGBTq-crackdown-intl-cmd/index.html < https://tinyurl.com/y8sdxbr3 >

27. "Christian Hate Preacher: 'Pride Month Has Always Been About These Pedophiles,'" by Heman Mehta. *Friendly Atheist*, June 13, 2021. https://friendlyatheist.patheos.com/2021/06/13/christian-hate-preacher-pride-month-has-always-been-about-these-pedophiles/ < https://tinyurl.com/tm-d8at4e >

28. "Tony Perkins Offers Tips on 'Surviving the Rainbow Onslaught' During Pride Month," by Kyle Mantyla. Right Wing Watch, June 14, 2021. https://www.rightwingwatch.org/post/tony-perkins-offers-tips-on-surviving-the-rainbow-onslaught-during-pride-month/ < https://tinyurl.com/6d6yk6hh >

29. Ibid.

30. "10 Myths About Gay Men and Lesbians." Southern Poverty Law Center. https://www.splcenter.org/sites/default/files/d6_legacy_files/downloads/publication/IR140_10_Myths_whitepaper.pdf < https://tinyurl.com/sr9bx94s >

31. "The Forsaken: A Rising Number of Homeless Gay Teens Are Being Cast Out by Religious Families," by Alex Morris. *Rolling Stone*, September 3, 2014. https://www.rollingstone.com/culture/culture-news/the-forsaken-a-rising-number-of-homeless-gay-teens-are-being-cast-out-by-religious-families-46746/ < https://tinyurl.com/y58yb4mh >

32. "Number and percentage of students, by sexual identity." Centers for Disease Control. https://www.cdc.gov/healthyyouth/data/yrbs/2019_tables/students_by_sexual_identity.htm < https://tinyurl.com/3wbk86ns >

33. "Marking the Deadliest Year on Record, Human Rights Campaign Announces Release of Annual Report on Violence Against Transgender and Gender Non-Conforming People," by Laurel Powell. Human Rights Watch, November 17, 2021. https://www.hrc.org/press-releases/marking-the-deadliest-year-on-record-human-rights-campaign-announces-release-of-annual-report-on-violence-against-transgender-and-gender-non-conforming-people?utm_source=fark&utm_medium=website&utm_content=link&ICID=ref_fark < https://tinyurl.com/58vrk2c2 >

34. "The 2020 Annual Homeless Assessment Report (AHAR) to Congress." U.S. Department of Housing and Urban Development. https://www.huduser.gov/portal/sites/default/files/pdf/2020-AHAR-Part-1.pdf < https://tinyurl.com/3wvs46za >

35. Morris, op. cit.

36. *What You Don't Know About Religion (but should)*, by Ryan Cragun. Durham, NC: Pitchstone Publishing, 2013, p. 86.

22

Christian Antisemitism

The Jews are a frightened people. Nineteen centuries of Christian love have broken down their nerves.
—Israel Zangwill

If I had to baptize a Jew, I would take him to the bridge of the Elbe, hang a stone around his neck and push him over with the words, 'I baptize thee in the name of Abraham.'
—Martin Luther, *On The Jews and Their Lies*[1]

What exactly is the root source of Christian antisemitism? A look at the New Testament is instructive:

> I know that ye [Pharisees] are Abraham's seed; but ye seek to kill me, because my word hath no place in you. . . . Ye are of your father the devil, and the lusts of your father ye will do. He was a murderer from the beginning, and abode not in the truth, because there is no truth in him. . . . He that is of God heareth God's words: ye therefore hear them not, because ye are not of God."
> —John 8:37, 44, 47 (Jesus speaking)

> Ye stiffnecked and uncircumcised in heart and ears, ye do always resist the Holy Ghost: as your fathers did, so do ye. Which of the prophets have not your fathers persecuted? and they have slain them which shewed before of the coming of the Just One; of whom ye have been now the betrayers and murderers: . . .
> —Acts 7:51–52 (St. Stephen speaking to a synagogue council prior to his execution)

Such passages are the source of the "deicide charge," the libel that all Jews, past and present, are somehow guilty of murdering Jesus.*

Another passage added fuel to the fire:

> And therefore did the Jews persecute Jesus, and sought to slay him, because he had done these things [healed an invalid] on the sabbath day. But Jesus answered them, My Father worketh hitherto, and I work. Therefore the Jews sought the more to kill him, because he not only had broken the sabbath, but said also that God was his Father, making himself equal with God.
> —John 5:16–18

But the passage that in all likelihood contributed most to the deicide charge (and almost two millennia of persecution and pogroms) is from Matthew:

> [T]he chief priests and elders persuaded the multitude that they should ask Barabbas, and destroy Jesus. The governor answered and said unto them, Whether of the twain will ye that I release unto you? They said, Barabbas. Pilate saith unto them, What shall I do then with Jesus which is called Christ? They all say unto him, Let him be crucified. And the governor said, Why, what evil hath he done? But they cried out the more, saying, Let him be crucified. When Pilate saw that he could prevail nothing, but that rather a tumult was made, he took water, and washed his hands before the multitude, saying, I am innocent of the blood of this just person: see ye to it. Then answered all the people, and said, His blood be on us, and on our children.
> —Matthew 27:20–25

These passages set the tone. They were the impetus for the horrors inflicted upon the Jewish people over the next two thousand years in Christian Europe, and to a lesser extent the rest of the world.

Antisemitism in organized Christianity goes back to at least the second century CE. In 167, Melito, the Christian bishop of Sardis, Turkey preached a sermon titled "Homily on the Passover" (aka "Easter Homily"), in which he said the Jews had "murdered God" by crucifying Jesus; this was one

---

* Neither the loathsome, irrational concept of collective guilt—holding individuals responsible for acts they didn't commit, simply because they're members of a target group—nor the perhaps even crazier concept of holding members of a target group responsible for acts that happened before they were born, seem to bother Christians at all, as witnessed by the murderous antisemitism they've visited upon Jews century after century, based on the utterly irrational deicide charge.

of the first recorded instances of the deicide charge following the writing of the gospels,[2] a charge which has been repeated almost continually for nearly two thousand years, and which is still having deadly effect.

Antisemitism in Christian-controlled lands (as opposed to antisemitism in organized Christianity) dates back to the conversion of the Roman emperor Constantine in 312. Once he converted, Constantine abused Jews in both word and deed, inserting antisemitism directly into Roman law. In a letter following the First Nicene Council in 325, he attacked the "detestable Jewish crowd," saying that Jews were guilty of "enormous sin" (presumably deicide).[3] In 329, he institutionalized those views by banning mixed marriages between Jews and Christians, and declared the death penalty for Christians who converted to Judaism.

This set the stage for what was to come.

While anti-Jewish atrocities took place sporadically all over Europe from the start of the Dark Ages on, they reached an early peak in the years prior to the millennium and then again during the crusades, when crusaders committed crimes *en masse* against Jews, especially in Germany, on their marches to the Holy Land. (Not all of the crusaders reached it; a fair number contented themselves with committing atrocities in Europe.) Historian Robert Wistrich states that the first crusade resulted in "massacres [of Jews] hitherto unprecedented in the history of Christian-Jewish relations. . . . Between a quarter and a third of the Jewish population in Germany and Northern France (about 10,000 people) were killed in the first six months of 1096 alone."[4]

The atrocity at Mainz in 1096 provides an enlightening example. Albert of Aix, a Christian chronicler, describes the massacre: "Breaking the bolts and doors, they killed the Jews, about seven hundred in number, who in vain resisted the force and attack of so many thousands. They killed the women, also, and with their swords pierced tender children of whatever age and sex . . ."[5] There were similar atrocities all over the Rhineland, with the number of victims uncertain due to poor record keeping, but numbering in the thousands at minimum, with the total likely in the 10,000 to 20,000 range.

Following these early atrocities, a new defamatory charge surfaced in the 12th and 13th centuries, the "blood libel" (aka "ritual murder charge"), which baselessly accused Jews of murdering Christian children in order to use their blood in Jewish ceremonies, such as the making of matzo balls for Passover. Many falsely accused Jews were murdered as a result, first in England and then across Europe.

In 1298, a new wave of pogroms swept southern Germany, the Rintfleisch pogroms, which took place in approximately 150 villages; the number of victims was likely in the 20,000 range.

These pogroms were inspired at least in part by another charge against Jews, the "usury" charge. The Bible contains several condemnations of usury, but the church interpreted those passages as prohibiting Christians from lending money to each other at *any* interest rate, no matter how low.

During the Middle Ages, Jews were banned from practicing a great many professions (and from owning land), with banking and money lending being one of the relatively few jobs open to them.* So, they provided this essential service, in large part due to their very restricted employment alternatives. Thus arose the stereotype of greedy Jews taking financial advantage of Christians, as memorably and slanderously portrayed in Shakespeare's "The Merchant of Venice."

In the 14th century, another entirely baseless charge, that Jews were responsible for the Black Death by poisoning wells, led to further persecution and murder on a mass scale during the plague outbreak, which lasted in Europe from the early 1330s to the early 1350s. Former priest Luke Timothy Johnson states in his lecture "The Great Plague," in his series, "The History of Christianity," that thousands of Jews were murdered and that 150 small Jewish settlements and 60 large Jewish centers in cities were destroyed across Europe, including the large communities in Cologne and Mainz, which were "wiped out" in 1349. Johnson estimates that in Strasbourg alone 2,000 Jews were murdered in the same year.

In the centuries immediately preceding the plague, various popes and theologians added fuel to the always smoldering fire of Christian antisemitism. For example, in the early 13th century, Pope Innocent III wrote:

> The Jews, like Cain, are doomed to wander the earth as fugitives and vagabonds, and their faces are covered with shame.
> —Letter to Count de Nevers,[6] 1208

Thomas Aquinas's words are even more horrifying. They also give us a glimpse of how antisemitism was being codified in secular laws (inasmuch as anything could be secular in the Christian Europe of the time):

---

* These restrictions were so pervasive and so detailed that Jewish musicians were even prohibited from playing certain types of instruments, with the earliest Jewish (Klezmer) bands restricted to strings and woodwinds, which in part explains the unique sound of Klezmer music.

> Since the Jews are according to the law sentenced to perpetual slavery for their sins, the rulers of the countries in which they are found may seize their property, provided that they do not deprive them of the necessities of life.
> —Letter to the Duchess of Brabant, circa 1271 (also known as Letter to Margaret of Flanders)[7]

Massacres continued in various European countries until well into the twentieth century,[8] with Jewish people being despised by a great many of their Christian neighbors everywhere in Europe. This festering antisemitism became even worse around the beginning of "the age of discovery."

While not all medieval and Renaissance popes were murderously antagonistic toward Jews—Eugenius IV (pope, 1431–1447) was an apparent exception—in 1555, in the papal bull *Cum nimis absurdum* ("With Complete Absurdity"), Pope Pius IV ordered the expulsion of Jews from the Papal States:

> Since it is absurd and utterly inconvenient that the Jews, who through their own fault were condemned by God to eternal slavery . . . We order that each and every Jew of both sexes in our temporal dominion, and in all the cities, lands, places and baronies subject to them shall depart completely out of the confines thereof within the space of three months after these letters shall have been made public.[9]

As bad as the persecution had been in the Middle Ages and early Renaissance periods, it became worse with the unleashing of the Inquisition upon Spain's Jews in the late 15th and early 16th centuries. The toll was staggering. In 1492, Ferdinand and Isabella decreed that those who wouldn't convert to Catholicism were to be expelled. Approximately 100,000 to 200,000 Jews (estimates vary) were forced to flee their homes, and tens of thousands more, perhaps up to 100,000, submitted to forced religious conversion. They quickly became favorite targets of the Inquisition.

Henry Charles Lea, in *A History of the Inquisition of the Middle Ages*, reveals the brutality of the treatment they suffered:

> Two hundred wretches crowded the filthy gaol and it was requisite to forbid the rest of the Conversos [Jews intimidated into converting to Christianity] from leaving the city [Jaen, Spain] without a license. With Diego's assistance [Diego de Algeciras, a petty criminal and kept perjurer] and the free use of torture, on both accused and witnesses, it was not difficult to obtain whatever evidence was desired. The notary of the tribunal, Antonio de Barcena, was especially successful in this. On one occasion, he locked a young girl of fifteen in a room, stripped her naked and scourged her until she consented

> to bear testimony against her mother. A prisoner was carried in a chair to the auto da fe with his feet burnt to the bone; he and his wife were burnt alive . . . The cells in which the unfortunates were confined in heavy chains were narrow, dark, humid, filthy and overrun with vermin, while their sequestrated property was squandered by the officials, so that they nearly starved in prison while their helpless children starved outside.

As for those expelled, historian David Stannard notes:

> On the very day that Columbus finally set forth on his journey that would shake the world, the port of the city he sailed from [Cadiz] was filled with ships that were deporting Jews from Spain. By the time the expulsion was complete, between 120,000 and 150,000 Jews had been driven from their homes, their valuables, often meager, having first been confiscated and then they were cast out to sea.[10]

Stannard then quotes a witness to the expulsions:

> It was pitiful to see the sufferings. Many were consumed by hunger, especially nursing mothers and their babies. Half-dead mothers held dying children in their arms. . . . I can hardly say how cruelly and greedily they were treated by those who transported them. Many were drowned by the avarice of the sailors, and those who were unable to pay their passage sold their children.[11]

The expulsion from Spain in 1492 was not an isolated event; Portugal followed suit in 1496. Expulsions, however, had begun in earnest eight centuries earlier, with Spain's Jews suffering under an earlier convert-or-die order in the seventh century; other early persecutions included expulsion of Jews from France in 1182, England in 1290, and Hungary in 1360. Many other European countries and regions followed suit in expelling (and stealing from) their Jews, including Lithuania, parts of what is now Germany, and parts of what is now Italy. (Neither Germany nor Italy became unified nation states until the late 19th century.)

To add insult to injury, in 1555's *Cum Nimis Absurdum* ("With Complete Absurdity"), Innocent III ordered the establishment of a ghetto in Rome, stating that while Jews "persisted in their errors they are made to feel and see that they are slaves and the Christians free men." Ghettos were also established in almost all other European Catholic countries (at least those with significant Jewish populations), including the Papal States, Germany, Italy, France, Spain, Austria, Poland, and Hungary. Pogroms continued during the following centuries in Christian Europe, ending only with the

Holocaust. (The word "pogrom" was apparently first used in the 19th century, but the massacres in previous centuries certainly fit the definition.)

Things weren't much better in Protestant countries; Protestant leaders and their followers were just as antisemitic as their Catholic brethren. A few excerpts from Martin Luther's work, *The Jews and Their Lies*,[12] illustrate just how vicious the Protestants could be:

> Moreover, they [Jewish people] are nothing but thieves and robbers who daily eat no morsel and wear no thread of clothing which they have not stolen and pilfered from us by means of their accursed usury. Thus they live from day to day, together with wife and child, by theft and robbery, as arch-thieves and robbers, in the most impenitent security.
>
> [W]e let them get rich on our sweat and blood, while we remain poor and they suck the marrow from our bones.
>
> Therefore be on your guard against the Jews, knowing that wherever they have their synagogues, nothing is found but a den of devils in which sheer self-glory, conceit, lies, blasphemy, and defaming of God and men are practiced most maliciously . . .
>
> If we wish to wash our hands of the Jews' blasphemy and not share in their guilt, we have to part company with them. They must be driven from our country.

Luther, in the land where the Holocaust took place four centuries after he wrote, went on to advocate that Christians burn synagogues and destroy Jewish homes:

> First to set fire to their synagogues or schools and to bury and cover with dirt whatever will not burn, so that no man will ever again see a stone or cinder of them. This is to be done in honor of our Lord and of Christendom, so that God might see that we are Christians, and do not condone or knowingly tolerate such public lying, cursing, and blaspheming of his Son and of his Christians. For whatever we tolerated in the past unknowingly—and I myself was unaware of it—will be pardoned by God. But if we, now that we are informed, were to protect and shield such a house for the Jews, existing right before our very nose, in which they lie about, blaspheme, curse, vilify, and defame Christ and us (as was heard above), it would be the same as if we were doing all this and even worse ourselves, as we very well know.
>
> Second, I advise that their houses also be razed and destroyed. For they pursue in them the same aims as in their synagogues. Instead they might be

> lodged under a roof or in a barn, like the gypsies. This will bring home to them that they are not masters in our country, as they boast, but that they are living in exile and in captivity, as they incessantly wail and lament about us before God.

While garden variety antisemitism (with consequent pogroms) continued to fester in the European Christian nations in the centuries following Luther, it occasionally surfaced in spectacular form, as in the 1890s Dreyfus Affair (which became a *cause celebre* in France's left because of the blatant injustice), in which a French Jewish military officer, Alfred Dreyfus, was falsely accused and convicted of treason by Catholic antisemites, who suppressed exculpating evidence and protected the probable perpetrator; Dreyfus was condemned to Devil's Island as a result.[13] The French Catholic hierarchy and France's political right "declared the Dreyfus case to be a conspiracy of Jews and Freemasons designed to damage the prestige of the army and thereby destroy France."[14] (The lingering Catholic antisemitism exemplified by the Dreyfus Affair almost certainly helps to explain why the Vichy [Nazi puppet] government under Marshall Petain so willingly rounded up France's Jews and sent them to Nazi concentration camps during World War II.)

Commencing in the late 19th century and continuing into the 20th century there was a new wave of pogroms in religiously devout Poland and Russia. In Russia and the Ukraine, the monarchist, ultra-nationalist Black Hundreds terrorist group carried out massacres all across the region. This brutality was fueled in part by the widely circulated and entirely spurious "The Protocols of the Learned Elders of Zion" (more commonly called "The Protocols of the Elders of Zion"). It's a mishmash of previously published antisemitic concoctions and forgeries, and is often attributed to the czarist secret police; it was revealed as a fraud by the *London Times* in 1921. The "Protocols" presented as fact the blood libel (Jews kidnapping and murdering Christian children and using their blood in ceremonies) as well as other antisemitic tropes, such as that a Jewish cabal was intent on taking over the world.[15] Today, even though they have been thoroughly debunked for over a century, the "Protocols" are still widely circulated by antisemites.

In the wake of World War I, the Russian Whites (extreme-right czarists) carried out atrocious pogroms during the civil war that followed the Russian Revolution; in England, the notorious antisemite Oswald Mosley's British Union of Fascists arose in the 1930s and staged marches in cities across the country including London, especially in its immigrant and working class East End, where it fought pitched street battles with the area's Jewish residents and anarchists, communists, and other leftists. In Germany, the Nazis arose in the 1920s, seized power in 1933, and immediately began persecuting Germany's Jews, a persecution that culminated in the Holocaust. (As mentioned in the chapter on Christian authoritarianism, the Germans who fought for the Reich and carried out the Holocaust were almost all at least nominal Christians, as were virtually all of the troops from conquered lands and other fascist states that fought on the Eastern Front.)

In the United States, following World War I, industrialist Henry Ford, who had been raised Episcopalian, was the leading antisemite. Ford's newspaper, *The Dearborn Independent* (Michigan), which at one point had a circulation of close to a million, printed a series of grossly antisemitic articles which were later published in book form as *The International Jew*. It was distributed in the millions in both the United States and, in translation, Germany. Ford also paid for the printing of half-a-million copies of "The Protocols of the Elders of Zion," and only disavowed it in 1927. Hitler, who had been raised Catholic, so admired Ford that he kept Ford's photo on his wall in Munich at the time of the Beer Hall Putsch in 1923, and even praised Ford in *Mein Kampf*: "It is Jews who govern the stock exchange forces of the American Union. Every year makes them more and more the controlling masters of the producers in a nation of one hundred and twenty millions; only a single great man, Ford, to their fury, still maintains full independence."[16] The admiration continued during Hitler's time in office. In 1938, Hitler awarded Henry Ford the Nazis' highest award for non-Germans, the Grand Cross of the German Eagle. This occurred at a time when the murderous brutality and antisemitism of the Nazis were already abundantly clear—and Ford accepted the award.

Besides Ford, there were many other prominent antisemites in the United States. During the 1920s, the avowedly Christian, antisemitic Ku Klux Klan arose in its second wave, with a nationwide membership that reached at least three million and perhaps as many as eight million—and this in a country with a population at the time of only about 115 million. In the 1930s, other fascistic, antisemitic groups arose in America, notably the German-American Bund, an openly Nazi organization. Prominent American antisemites of the era included aviator Charles Lindbergh and Disciples of Christ minister Gerald L.K. Smith, founder of the magazine *The Cross and The Flag*. There were also overtly fascist thug groups with thousands of members, most prominently the Silver Shirts (Silver Legion of America) modeled on Mussolini's blackshirts; that group was founded by fascist writer William Pelley, the Christian Party candidate in the 1936 presidential election. In 1942, Pelley was convicted of sedition and sentenced to 15 years in prison, though he only served about half that.

The most influential antisemite, though, was Father Charles Coughlin, the fascist "radio priest" whose nationwide broadcast had a weekly audience in the millions throughout the 1930s, and whose magazine, *Social Justice*, published a version of "The Protocols of the Elders of Zion" in 1938. In the same year he encouraged the formation of the Christian Front, a fascist thug group similar to today's "patriotic" alt-right vigilante/"militia" groups; and still in 1938, following the atrocities of *Kristallnacht*, "Coughlin defended the state-sponsored violence of the Nazi regime, arguing that *Kristallnacht* was justified as retaliation for Jewish persecution of Christians."[17]

None of this apparently bothered the Catholic hierarchy, which isn't surprising. In the 1930s the Catholic hierarchy had a cozy relationship with Mussolini in Italy, was peacefully co-existing with Hitler in Germany, and openly supported Francisco Franco's fascists during the Spanish Civil War (1936–1939). (See Chapter 8 on Christian authoritarianism for more on the relationship of Christianity to fascist regimes and the Holocaust.)

Following World War II, fascism and antisemitism went into decline. In the U.S., the first post-war, prominent openly fascist group was would-be fuehrer George Lincoln Rockwell's American Nazi Party, which he founded in 1959, but which never achieved a significant following—in part, probably, because their main activity seemed to be parading around in ridiculous uniforms (as parodied in the *Blues Brothers* movie). In 1967, a former member assassinated Rockwell, and the American Nazi Party all but disappeared.

As for specifically Christian antisemitism, the Ku Klux Klan—which self-identifies as Christian, whose symbol was and is a burning cross, and which features the singing of "The Old Rugged Cross" at its cross burning ceremonies—entered its third wave in the 1950s as a reaction against the civil rights movement. Its members were responsible for numerous murders, beatings, and bombings, including the savage beatings of Freedom Riders on bus trips through the South, the murders of civil rights workers Michael Schwerner, Andrew Goodman, and James Chaney in Mississippi in 1964, and the Birmingham church bombing in 1963, which killed four children.

The next wave of Christian antisemitism appeared toward the close of the 1970s with KKK Grand Dragon (appointed by David Duke) and ordained Christian Identity minister Tom Metzger. In 1980, Metzger broke away from Duke's group, and in 1982 founded his own separate hate group, which he named White Aryan Resistance (WAR), a name which still holds. Like Rockwell before him, Metzger and WAR maintained friendly relations with the Nation of Islam ("Black Muslims") because of their mutual antisemitism and racial separatism. He also maintained friendly relations with racist skinheads, indeed was a primary influence on them, and in 1988, along with his son John, organized the first racist hate-rock festival. In the same year, three members of WAR murdered Mulugeta Seraw, an Ethiopian student, in Portland, Oregon, beating Seraw to death with a baseball bat. One of the three turned state's evidence, and the other two were convicted of murder. Seraw's survivors sued Metzger and WAR, and in 1990 won a $12.5 million verdict, which destroyed Metzger and WAR financially. Metzger died in 2020, but WAR lives on, mostly in name, as a vehicle for Metzger's racist and antisemitic propaganda.

The other significant Christian antisemitic hate groups that arose in the 1970s and 1980s were the Posse Comitatus and Richard Butler's Church of Jesus Christ Christian, which he established in northern Idaho. Both were Christian Identity groups. Posse Comitatus was largely based in white rural areas, in states such as Kansas and Nebraska, and was a forerunner of today's extreme-right "militia" groups. A statement by the Posse's founder, ex-army officer and ordained Episcopalian priest, William Potter Gale, exemplifies the group's political approach: "We're gonna cleanse our land ... and we're gonna do it with a sword . . . You're damn right I'm teaching violence . . . It's about time somebody is telling you to get violent, whitey."[18] But Butler's church, with its national outreach and permanent site, was arguably the more important of the two groups.

Butler was a lifelong antisemite, whose racist career began in 1961 when he joined the Anglo-Saxon Christian Church, whose pastor, Methodist minister Wesley Swift, had been a KKK organizer. The following year, Swift appointed Butler as director of his Christian Defense League, and Butler shortly became an ordained Christian Identity minister. In 1974, he left his job as an aerospace engineer at Lockheed and moved to Hayden Lake in northern Idaho, where he established his Church of Jesus Christ Christian and its associated political arm, Aryan Nations, with the aim of establishing a white homeland in the Pacific Northwest (a longtime goal of white nationalists, dating back to the 19th century). Butler quickly turned his barbed wire-ringed compound into a major gathering place for white racists and antisemites of all stripes, but especially Christian Identity racists.

In the early 1980s, several Aryan Nations members formed the Christian Identity terrorist group The Order, with Bob Matthews as its head. In 1983–1984 it pulled off a string of armored car robberies, bombings, and murders, including that of Jewish talk show host Alan Berg in Denver in 1984. One member of the group, Tom Martinez, found all this too much, and became an FBI informant. In the winter of 1984/spring of 1985, most of the group was arrested, Matthews was killed in a shootout, and one of The Order's members, David Tate, committed its final murder, that of a Missouri state trooper. Tate fled to the fortified Christian-Identity Covenant, Sword and Arm of the Lord (CSA) compound on the Missouri/Arkansas border, where Tate, two other Order members, and several CSA members were arrested.[19]

The following year, CSA founder and leader James Ellison and five of his followers pled guilty to federal weapons charges, with all receiving lengthy prison sentences. Other CSA members were later convicted on bombing and arson charges, and sent to prison, with one, Richard Snell, being executed in 1995 for the first-degree murder of a Jewish pawnbroker in Fulton, Arkansas following a CSA attempted bombing of a natural gas pipeline; Snell was also found guilty in a separate trial of the first-degree murder of an Arkansas policeman.

In 1998, drunk guards at Richard Butler's compound shot at and beat two Native Americans on the road next to the compound. With the help of the Southern Poverty Law Center, they sued, and in 2000 were awarded a judgment of $6.3 million, which forced Butler and Aryan Nations into bankruptcy. They lost the compound as a result, which badly crippled Butler's Church of Jesus Christ Christian and Aryan Nations. Splinter groups live on, but they're a shadow of what Butler built.

Following the Oklahoma City bombing and the revulsion it provoked, Christian racist/antisemitic groups went into decline. But the election of Barack Obama spurred them to new fury, and with the election of the overtly racist Donald Trump they slithered out from under their rocks, encouraged by the new president's actions and words, especially his words after the Unite the Right rally in Charlottesville, Virginia in 2017, in which torch bearing white supremacists and neo-Nazis marched and chanted, "Jews will not replace us!," and also murdered a counter-protester. In the wake of the neo-Nazi march and the murder, Trump said that some of the racists and neo-Nazis were "very fine people."

Antisemitic attacks increased after Trump's election, and especially after Charlottesville. The worst incident was the massacre at the Tree of Life Synagogue in Pittsburgh in October 2018, carried out by far-right high school dropout David Bowers, who killed 11 people. Bowers used the following self-descriptive words on the Gab social media site: "Jews are the children of Satan (John 8:44). The Lord Jesus Christ [has] come in the flesh."

Throughout his entire time in office, Trump's encouragement of white racists and antisemites continued. He even defended 17-year-old killer Kyle Rittenhouse, who shot three anti-racism protesters with an assault rifle in Kenosha, Wisconsin, after traveling there from Illinois during demonstrations spurred by the police shooting of an unarmed black man, Jacob Blake; the cops shot Blake seven times in the back, leaving him paralyzed.

Trump's encouragement of racist, violent, antisemitic thugs culminated in the coup attempt of January 6, 2021, which Trump and his accomplices instigated through their endless demonizing of Trump's opponents and their completely baseless assertion that the election (which Trump lost by over 7,000,000 votes) was stolen from him.* Not incidentally, many of the Trumpists who stormed the Capitol were Christian QAnon members; some were bused in by their churches; some waved crosses, and carried signs and flags with Christian symbols and slogans, including "Jesus fish" symbols (painted, of course, in red, white, and blue); other signs proclaimed "Jesus Saves" and "Jesus 2020"; and one later-arrested antisemitic goon wore a "Camp Auschwitz" shirt while rioting inside the Capitol. Prior to assaulting that seat of government, fully costumed, neo-fascist Proud Boys knelt in the street praying to Jesus, asking for His help in the coming coup attempt. (Unfortunately for them, He's evidently not a fan of fascist scum or violent coup attempts, so He didn't show up.)

It's virtually certain that, even with Trump out of power, racist and antisemitic attacks will continue. It's also virtually certain that the extreme-right, racist, antisemitic, and largely evangelical QAnon conspiracy group—which posits that Trump is fighting a cannibalistic pedophile ring involving Hillary Clinton, Barack Obama, George Soros, Tom Hanks, and the "deep state"—will also continue, as it has considerable support among white evangelicals, other conservative Christians, and Mormons, and is promoted endlessly in the right-wing echo chamber.

---

* The Trumpists filed over 60 lawsuits challenging election procedures, losing all but one of them. The single suit they won, in Pennsylvania, allowed their election observers to watch the counting of ballots from six feet away rather than the twenty feet away allowed prior to the lawsuit.

Of course, mainline Protestant groups find all of this appalling, but I have yet to hear a single one of them say that any of the current antisemitic murderous craziness has anything to do with, let alone is a direct result of, nearly two thousand years of Christian antisemitism, beginning with the passages in the New Testament blaming Jews for the death of Christ.

White evangelicals, while they might tut-tut about the murders committed by violent racists and antisemites, seem not to have a huge problem with the racist, antisemitic, extreme-right Christian Identity, Dominionist, Reconstructionist, and QAnon movements. There are three primary reasons for this. The first is that white evangelicals are by far the most racist and antisemitic religious group in the United States, bar none.* The second is that like the overtly racist, antisemitic groups they seem to love (and definitely tolerate), they also love the thoroughly racist, authoritarian Donald Trump, who they consider to be doing the Lord's work. The third is that the aim of white evangelicals is quite similar to the aim of the Christian Identity and Dominionist movements: turning the United States into a "Christian nation," that is, into a theocracy in which Christian morals are imposed by force on everyone, in which extreme-right Christians control all branches of government in perpetuity, and in which all non-Christians, including Jews, perhaps especially Jews, are second-class citizens.

As for the Catholic Church, in 1964 Pope Paul VI finally apologized for the deicide charge (that the Jews were and are responsible for killing Christ), which was at the root of over 1,500 years of pogroms, mass murders, discrimination against, theft from, and expulsions of Jews from Christian lands. In 1998, Pope John Paul II apologized for the Church's inaction during the Holocaust; and in 2000, he apologized for the centuries upon centuries of pogroms, murders, discrimination, theft, and expulsions.

Better late than never.

Barely.

---

* In addition to abundant anecdotal and observational evidence, there's also scientific evidence of this. One piece of it is that the National Opinion Research Center's General Social Survey, 1972–2010 reported that 50% of white evangelicals oppose or strongly oppose a close relative marrying a black person, with the figure for religious moderates being 34%, religious liberals 42%, and the nonreligious 22%. The corresponding figures for those opposing or strongly opposing a close relative marrying a Jewish person were 22% for evangelicals, 12% for religious moderates, 13% for religious liberals, and 6% for the nonreligious.[20]

Endnotes

1. *On the Jews and Their Lies*, by Martin Luther. https://www.prchiz.pl/storage/app/media/pliki/Luther_On_Jews.pdf (full text) < https://tinyurl.com/y5pqz8uk >

2. "Melito, Bishop of Sardis. Easter Homily: The First Charge of Deicide against Jews." Center for Online Jewish Studies. http://cojs.org/melito-_bishop_of_sardis-_easter_homily-_the_first_charge_of_deicide_against_jews/ < https://tinyurl.com/y6qkd43s >

3. "Decoding Nicea: the Appendixes, Constantine's Letter to the Churches." Christian History for Every Man. https://www.christian-history.org/ibwl-appendices-for-web.html#CouncilLetter < https://tinyurl.com/y4vdu5sl >

4. *Antisemitism: The Longest Hatred*, by Robert Wistrich. New York: Pantheon, 1991, p. 23.

5. Quoted by Susan Jacoby in "The First Victims of the First Crusade," *New York Times*, February 13, 2015. https://www.nytimes/2015/02/13/opinion/sunday/the-first-victims-of-the-first-crusade.html < https://tinyurl.com/y2a86woz >

6. "Pope Innocent III, On the Jews and Forced Baptisms." Council of Centers on Jewish-Christian Relations. https://www.ccjr.us/dialogika-resources/primary-texts-from-the-history-of-the-relationship/pope-innocent-iii-on-the-jews-and-forced-baptisms-1199-and-1201 < https://tinyurl.com/y6gae3sn >

7. "Letter to Margaret of Flanders." Thomistica. https://thomistica.net/letter-to-margaret-of-flanders < https://tinyurl.com/y2q2p9lf >

8. "Persecution Perpetuated: The medieval origins of anti-Semitic violence in Nazi Germany," by Nico Voigtlaender and Hans-Joachim Voth. National Bureau of Economic Research, June 2011. https://www.nber.org/papers/w17113.pdf < https://tinyurl.com/y4kn4ls4 >

9. "*Cum Nimis Absurdum*," by Pope Paul IV. Council of Centers on Jewish-Christian Relations. https://www.ccjr.us/dialogika-resources/primary-texts-from-the-history-of-the-relationship/paul-iv < https://tinyurl.com/y8crsmt2 >

10. *American Holocaust: The Conquest of the New World*, by David Stannard. New York: Oxford University Press, 1992, p. 62.

11. Ibid.

12. Luther, op. cit.

13. *A Convenient Hatred: The History of Antisemitism*, by Phyllis Goldstein. Facing History and Ourselves, 2012, pp. 209–215.

14. "Antisemitism: Alfred Dreyfus & 'The Affair.'" Jewish Virtual Library. https://www.jewishvirtuallibrary.org/alfred-dreyfus-and-ldquo-the-affair-rdquo < https://tinyurl.com/y4rfgd3m >

15. "Protocols of the Elders of Zion." Jewish Virtual Library. https://www.jewishvirtuallibrary.org/the-ldquo-protocols-of-the-elders-of-zion-rdquo < https://tinyurl.com/y66tcxw4 >

16. "Ford and the Fuehrer," by Ken Silverstein. *The Nation*, January 6, 2000. https://www.thenation.com/article/archive/ford-and-fuhrer/ < https://tinyurl.com/y9zsrtrm >

17. "Charles Coughlin." Holocaust Encyclopedia, Holcoaust Museum. https://encyclopedia.ushmm.org/content/en/article/charles-e-coughlin < https://tinyurl.com/y3z4lbnk >

18. "Right-Wing Extremism Has Been Taking Root In Rural Kansas For Decades," by Jim McLean. KCUR 89.3, July 5, 2021. https://www.kcur.org/news/2021-07-02/right-wing-extremism-has-been-taking-root-in-rural-kansas-for-decades < https://tinyurl.com/zvjsxr9t >

19. *Brotherhood of Murder*, by Thomas Martinez with John Gunther. New York: McGraw-Hill, 1988, pp. 198–200.

20. *What You Don't Know About Religion (but should)*, by Ryan Cragun. Durham, NC: Pitchstone-Publishing, 2012, pp. 120–121.

23

The Bible is Cruel, Disorganized and Irrational

> Historical investigations have revealed to us the origin and growth of the Bible. We know that by this name we designate a collection of writings as radically unlike in origin, character and contents, as if the Niebelungen Lied, Mirabeau's speeches, Heine's love poems and a manual of zoology had been printed and mixed promiscuously, and then bound into one volume. . . .
>
> We find collected in this book the superstitious beliefs of the ancient inhabitants of Palestine, with indistinct echoes of Indian and Persian fables, mistaken imitations of Egyptian theories and customs, historical chronicles as dry as they are unreliable, and miscellaneous poems, amatory, human and Jewish-national, which are rarely distinguished by beauties of the highest order, but frequently by superfluity of expression, coarseness, [and] bad taste . . .
>
> As a literary monument the Bible is of much later origin than the Vedas; as a work of literary value it is surpassed by everything written in the last two thousand years by authors even of the second rank, and to compare it seriously with the productions of Homer, Sophocles, Dante, Shakespeare or Goethe would require a fanaticized mind that had entirely lost its power of judgment. Its conception of the universe is childish, and its morality revolting. —Max Nordau, *Conventional Lies of Our Civilization*

Previous chapters covered the Bible's cruelty and hatefulness: the divine commands to the chosen people to commit theft, rape, enslavement, and mass murder; the commands to murder individuals and to torture them to death (via burning alive and stoning); and the commands to beat and murder children. But there's more.

There's the outright sadism in the Bible toward the faithful, as exemplified by the treatment of Abraham (tormented by the divine order to murder his son as a show of faith) and Job (tormented endlessly, like some poor animal abused by a sadistic owner).

There are many passages urging believers to submit to authority, both religious and secular, including the authority of slave master over slave.

The Bible's misogynistic passages are almost endless.

It has many perverse passages degrading sex.

It contains many unfulfilled prophecies, notably those that predict the end of the world during readers' (very early Christians') lifetimes, which was prophesied in many passages.

It's rife with inconsistencies and flat out contradictions.

It's remarkably parochial. For instance, its divinely inspired authors were quite familiar with animals native to the Middle East, but completely unfamiliar with those beyond their native lands. As author James McDonald notes, "locusts are covered exceptionally well, but penguins are badly underrepresented."[1]

It contains a number of repetitive, near-identical passages.

It doesn't prohibit, or even condemn, evils such as slavery and torture, while at the same time it bans trifles such as cursing and working on the sabbath, and in many cases orders horrific punishments for those who transgress those absurd prohibitions.

It promotes destructive superstitious beliefs: it treats demons, sorcerers, witches, and witchcraft as real, and as real threats, and it orders that witches and sorcerers be murdered.

It's antisemitic (New Testament).

Its literary quality is inconsistent. There are beautiful passages in some books (e.g., Psalms), but other passages read about as well as a page torn from a badly translated crockpot instruction manual (e.g., the genealogical passages in Exodus, Psalms, Chronicles, etc.).

One book is outright, bat-shit crazy (Revelation).

And a fair number of the Bible's passages are just plain crude.

The following verses illustrate these things. For the sake of brevity, I've only included one or two passages per category. (Some of these appeared in previous chapters. While there are similar passages pertaining to many of the following things, these are the clearest examples, so I've once again cited them. For many similar passages, see Appendix A and the previous chapters.)

Cruelty and Hatefulness

> O daughter of Babylon, who art to be destroyed; happy shall he be, that rewardeth thee as thou hast served us. Happy shall he be, that taketh and dasheth thy little ones against the stones. —Psalms 137:8–9

This verse (and the entire chapter) deals with the Babylonian captivity and the joy the chosen people would feel beating infants to death by smashing them against rocks.

Murder of Individuals

> Ye shall keep the sabbath therefore; for it is holy unto you: every one that defileth it shall surely be put to death: for whosoever doeth any work there in, that soul shall be cut off from among his people. Six days may work be done; but in the seventh is the sabbath of rest, holy to the Lord: whosoever doeth any work in the sabbath day, he shall surely be put to death.
> —Exodus 31:14–15

There are many other such commands in the Bible. It orders the murder of individuals for a number of reasons beyond working on the sabbath, with the Good Book commanding the killing of people for the crimes of adultery, fornication, homosexuality, being a rape victim (yes, being) but not crying out,* bestiality, witchcraft, blasphemy, rebelliousness, and being unable to prove (female) virginity.

Mass Murder

> And the Lord spake unto Moses, saying, . . . Arm some of yourselves unto the war, and let them go against the Midianites . . . Of every tribe a thousand, throughout all the tribes of Israel, shall ye send to the war. . . . And Moses sent them to the war, a thousand of every tribe . . . And they warred against

---

* At least some Christians appear to still be on board with this in the spirit, if not the letter, of this biblical law. A child sex-abuse lawsuit filed in 2021 against Grace Baptist Church in Lansingburgh, New York stated that the church's pastor, Larry Hallock, sexually abused a girl in his congregation "on a daily basis" from the time she was 15 to the time she was 17. The suit further stated that the alleged victim informed the church leadership of the abuse several times, but "the church leadership did nothing," and said that "because plaintiff didn't 'cry for help' she was culpable for the abuse perpetrated upon her.")[2]

> the Midianites, as the Lord commanded Moses; and they slew all the males. . . . And the children of Israel took all the women of Midian captives, and their little ones, and took the spoil of all their cattle, and all their flocks, and all their goods. And they burnt all their cities wherein they dwelt, and all their goodly castles, with fire. And they took all the spoil, and all the prey, both of men and of beasts. And they brought the captives, and the prey, and the spoil, unto Moses . . . And Moses was wroth with the officers of the host, with the captains over thousands, and captains over hundreds, which came from the battle. And Moses said unto them, Have ye saved all the women alive? . . . Now therefore kill every male among the little ones, and kill every woman that hath known man by lying with him. But all the women children, that have not known a man by lying with him, keep alive for yourselves.
> —Numbers 31:1–18

There are many similar passages in the Old Testament that show God ordering mass murder. This particular passage is a "twofer," with Jehovah ordering not only mass murder but also child rape.

Authoritarianism

> Let every soul be subject unto the higher powers. For there is no power but of God: the powers that be are ordained of God. Whosoever therefore resisteth the power, resisteth the ordinance of God: and they that resist shall receive to themselves damnation. —Romans 13:1–2

There are many similar passages in the New Testament.

Blasphemy (opposition to free speech)

> Bring forth him that hath cursed without the camp; and let all that heard him lay their hands upon his head, and let all the congregation stone him. And thou shalt speak unto the children of Israel, saying, Whosoever curseth his God shall bear his sin. And he that blasphemeth the name of the Lord, he shall surely be put to death, and all the congregation shall certainly stone him: as well the stranger, as he that is born in the land, when he blasphemeth the name of the Lord, shall be put to death. —Leviticus 24:14–16

There are a number of other passages anathematizing blasphemers, passages which led to Christianity's nearly two-millennia-long crusade against free speech, and which led to the torture and murder of many dissenters during the ages when Christianity was at its most powerful.

Slavery

> And if a man smite his servant [slave], or his maid, with a rod, and he die under his hand; he shall be surely punished. Notwithstanding, if he continue a day or two, he shall not be punished: for he is his money.
> —Exodus 20:20–21

> Servants, be obedient to them that are your masters according to the flesh, with fear and trembling, in singleness of your heart, as unto Christ; Not with eyeservice, as menpleasers; but as the servants of Christ, doing the will of God from the heart; . . . —Ephesians 6:5–6

Slavery was pervasive at the time the Bible was written, and this is reflected in its pages: its authors treat slavery as a given. Nowhere in the Bible's nearly 800,000 words is there a single sentence condemning slavery, let alone prohibiting it. The Old Testament largely confines itself to telling the chosen people how to treat and mistreat slaves, while the focus of the New Testament is on encouraging slaves to accept their lot and to remain docile.

Misogyny

> But if thou hast gone aside to another instead of thy husband, and if thou be defiled, and some man have lain with thee beside thine husband: Then the priest shall charge the woman with an oath of cursing, and the priest shall say unto the woman, The Lord make thee a curse and an oath among thy people, when the Lord doth make thy thigh [a euphemism for genitals] to rot, and thy belly to swell; And this water that causeth the curse shall go into thy bowels, to make thy belly to swell, and thy thigh to rot: And the woman shall say, Amen, amen. —Numbers 5:20–22

> Let the woman learn in silence with all subjection. But I suffer not a woman to teach, nor to usurp authority over the man, but to be in silence.
> —1 Timothy 2:11–12

There are many similar misogynistic passages in both the Old and New Testaments. The primary concern in the Old Testament is the control of women's reproductive functions, while in the New Testament the main concern is with maintaining female subservience.

Degradation of Sex

It is good for a man not to touch a woman.
—1 Corinthians 7:1

There are a number of other passages that denigrate sex in the New Testament, many of them in the Pauline texts.

Failed Prophecies

And he said unto them, Verily I say unto you, That there be some of them that stand here, which shall not taste of death, till they have seen the kingdom of God come with power. —Mark 9:1 (J.C. speaking)

There are a number of other passages in the New Testament that indicate its writers thought they were in the end times. These verses prophesy the imminent return of Christ, the end of the world, and the bodily assumption of the faithful into heaven—all within readers' lifetimes. Given how explicit these verses are, it's very difficult to see them as anything other than spectacularly failed prophecies. (See Appendix A for another dozen such prophecies.)

Contradictions

If I bear witness of myself, my witness is not true.
—John 5:31 (J.C. speaking)

I am one that bear witness of myself, . . . —John 8:18 (J.C. speaking)

There are a significant number of other direct contradictions in the Bible, with many of them involving the words of Jesus, some within the same books. (Again, see Appendix A for more examples.)

Redundant Passages

For thou art an holy people unto the Lord thy God: the Lord thy God hath chosen thee to be a special people unto himself, above all people that are upon the face of the earth. —Deuteronomy 7:6

> For thou art an holy people unto the Lord thy God, and the Lord hath chosen thee to be a peculiar people unto himself, above all the nations that are upon the earth. —Deuteronomy 14:2

There are other such redundant passages in the Old Testament. For instance, Exodus 34:26 is a word-for-word copy of Exodus 23:19, but for a single letter in a single word ("unto" and "into"); likewise, Joshua 15:15–19 is almost identical to Judges 1:11–15; and Psalms 14 and 53 are very similar, with parts of Psalm 53 being exact repetitions of portions of Psalm 14. For additional redundant passages, see Chapter 24, Appendix A, and John David Conner's *All That's Wrong with the Bible.*

Moral Omissions

The Bible nowhere condemns slavery or torture, not even in the Ten Commandments, Judeo-Christianity's basic moral code, while at the same time the Commandments condemn trivialities such as cursing and not keeping the sabbath. This in itself should be enough to make it obvious that the "divinely inspired" writers of the Bible were anything but; it should also suffice to show that those authors were Iron Age, slave-holding semi-barbarians who invented a brutal god in their own image.

Antisemitism

> [T]he chief priests and elders persuaded the multitude that they should ask Barabbas, and destroy Jesus. The governor answered and said unto them, Whether of the twain will ye that I release unto you? They said, Barabbas. Pilate saith unto them, What shall I do then with Jesus which is called Christ? They all say unto him, Let him be crucified. And the governor said, Why, what evil hath he done? But they cried out the more, saying, Let him be crucified. When Pilate saw that he could prevail nothing, but that rather a tumult was made, he took water, and washed his hands before the multitude, saying, I am innocent of the blood of this just person: see ye to it. Then answered all the people, and said, His blood be on us, and on our children. —Matthew 27:20–25

Antisemitism is, of course, absent from the Old Testament. But the New Testament laid the foundation for the better part of two millennia of horrors visited upon the Jewish people once Christianity became formally organized and entwined with the state.

Uneven Literary Quality

> And these are the names of the sons of Levi according to their generations; Gershon, and Kohath, and Merari: and the years of the life of Levi were an hundred thirty and seven years. The sons of Gershon; Libni, and Shimi, according to their families. And the sons of Kohath; Amram, and Izhar, and Hebron, and Uzziel: and the years of the life of Kohath were an hundred thirty and three years. And the sons of Merari; Mahali and Mushi: these are the families of Levi according to their generations. And Amram took him Jochebed his father's sister to wife; and she bare him Aaron and Moses: and the years of the life of Amram were an hundred and thirty and seven years. And the sons of Izhar; Korah, and Nepheg, and Zichri. And the sons of Uzziel; Mishael, and Elzaphan, and Zithri. . . . —Exodus 6:16–22

And on it goes. There are similar lengthy genealogical passages in Genesis, Kings, Psalms, 1 Chronicles, 2 Samuel, Ezra, Isaiah, and Matthew.

As Max Nordau says, it would require a "fanaticized mind that had entirely lost its power of judgment" to compare such passages with anything "written in the last two thousand years by authors even of the second rank."

The Book of Revelation is Bat-Shit Crazy

> And I stood upon the sand of the sea, and saw a beast rise up out of the sea, having seven heads and ten horns, and upon his horns ten crowns, and upon his heads the name of blasphemy. And the beast which I saw was like unto a leopard, and his feet were as the feet of a bear, and his mouth as the mouth of a lion: and the dragon gave him his power, and his seat, and great authority. —Revelation 13:1–2

The rest of Revelation is every bit as nuts as this passage, if sometimes less florid. If you doubt this, read the entire book or just the remainder of chapter 13 (which I'd have loved to include here, but didn't because it would have taken up too much space).

Just Plain Crudity

> Behold, I will corrupt your seed, and spread dung upon your faces, even the dung of your solemn feasts; . . . —Malachi 2:3

As the title of an old atheist pamphlet so accurately put it, the Bible truly is a "spiritual guide to gracious living."

There are well over 100 passages in Appendix A that provide additional examples of the above. If you have doubts about any of this, please look at those passages, and please read the Bible, cover to cover if you can stand it. Nothing will drive an open minded person away from Christianity faster than that.

As Mark Twain said:

> The mind that becomes soiled in youth can never again be washed clean. I know this by my own experience, & to this day I cherish an unappeased bitterness against the unfaithful guardians of my young life, who not only permitted but compelled me to read an unexpurgated Bible through before I was 15 years old. None can do that and ever draw a clean sweet breath again on this side of the grave.
>
> —Letter to Asa Don Dickerson, November 21, 1905

Endnotes

1. *Beyond Belief: Two Thousand Years of Bad Faith in the Christian Church*, by James McDonald. New York: Penguin, 2011, p. 17.

2. "Lawsuit: Troy church ignored youth pastor's abuse, claimed child 'led him on,'" by Robin Gavin. *Albany Times Union*, August 26, 2021. https://www.timesunion.com/news/article/Lawsuit-Troy-church-ignored-youth-pastor-s-16414034.php < https://tinyurl.com/4p4pwhfe >

24

The Bible Is Not a Reliable Guide to Christ's Words

SCRIPTURES, The sacred books of our holy religion, as distinguished from the false and profane writings on which all other faiths are based.
—Ambrose Bierce, *The Devil's Dictionary*

Christians insist that they're following the words of Jesus, but they're not. They only *think* they're following his words: most Christians are unfamiliar with the Bible,* and all of them are relying on a singularly unreliable source. (We briefly covered the myriad forgeries, alterations, interpolations, misattributions, suppression of inconvenient documents, etc. in both scripture and other church documents in Chapter 2 on Christian dishonesty, so we'll concentrate here on the Bible itself, especially the New Testament.)**

---

* A 2010 Pew survey reported that atheists were more knowledgeable about religion than members of any religious group, although Jews and Mormons were close: "On average, Americans correctly answer 16 of the 32 religious knowledge questions on the survey. Atheists and agnostics average 20.9 correct answers. Jews and Mormons do about as well, averaging 20.5 and 20.3 correct answers, respectively. Protestants as a whole average 16 correct answers; Catholics as a whole, 14.7."[1] The survey also revealed that over half of American Protestants (53%) don't know that Martin Luther was the founder of Protestantism, and 43% of them can't name the four books comprising the gospels. As for the Catholics, 45% of them don't know that "their tradition teaches that sacramental bread and wine [literally] become Christ's body and blood."[2,3]

** There are also many inconsistencies in the Old Testament. Citing but three examples, in the accounts of the Israelites' mass-murder and land-stealing campaigns, historian James

(continued on next page)

The unreliability of the Bible as regards the words of Jesus is most obvious in the following passages, in which Jesus directly contradicts himself in the same books.

I and my Father are one. —John 10:30

I go unto the Father: for my Father is greater than I. —John 14:28

If I bear witness of myself, my witness is not true. —John 5:31

I am one that bear witness of myself, . . . —John 8:18

Think not that I am come to send peace on earth. I came not to send peace, but a sword. —Matthew 10:34

" . . Put up again thy sword into his place: for all they that take the sword shall perish with the sword. —Matthew 26:52

In addition, Jesus directly contradicts passages in both the Old and New Testaments, including the Fifth Commandment:

Honour thy father and thy mother. —Exodus 20:12

If any man come to me, and hate not his father and mother, and wife, and children, and brethren, and sisters, year, and his own life also, he cannot be my disciple. —Luke 14:26

(cont'd) McDonald notes: "'The Edomites rebelled (2 Kings 8:22) after every male of that race had been killed (1 Kings 11:16). The Midianites were even more impressive. With all their males killed and females captured (Numbers 31:7–9) they somehow managed to defeat the Israelites (Judges 6:1-5). The Amalekites, having been utterly destroyed by Saul (1 Samuel 7–20), rose up against David, who left neither man nor woman alive amongst them (1 Samuel 27:9), after which they attacked him yet again (1 Samuel 30:1–17)." For additional examples, see McDonald's well documented and entertaining *Beyond Belief: Two thousand years of bad faith in the Christian Church* and Steve Wells' *The Skeptic's Annotated Bible.*

Other contradictory passages include:

For verily I say unto you, Till heaven and earth pass, one jot or one tittle shall in no wise pass from the law, till all be fulfilled.
—Matthew 5:18 (J.C. speaking)

Christ hath redeemed us from the curse of the law, . . .
—Galatians 3:13 (St. Paul speaking)

And if any mischief follow, then thou shalt give life for life, Eye for eye, tooth for tooth, hand for hand, foot for foot, Burning for burning, wound for wound, stripe for stripe. —Exodus 21:23–25

But I say unto you, That ye resist not evil: but whosoever shall smite thee on thy right cheek, turn to him the other also. —Matthew 5:39 (J.C. speaking)

A good man leaveth an inheritance to his children's children. —Proverbs 13:22

Sell that ye have and give alms; . . . —Luke 12:33 (J.C. speaking)

If a man have a stubborn and rebellious son, which will not obey the voice of his father, or the voice of his mother, and that, when they have chastened him, will not hearken unto them: Then shall his father and his mother lay hold on him, and bring him out unto the elders of his city, and unto the gate of his place; And they shall say unto the elders of his city, This our son is stubborn and rebellious, he will not obey our voice; he is a glutton, and a drunkard. And all the men of his city shall stone him with stones, that he die: so shalt thou put evil away from among you; and all Israel shall hear, and fear. —Deuteronomy 21:18–21

But whoso shall offend one of these little ones which believe in me, it were better for him that a millstone were hanged about his neck, and that he were drowned in the depth of the sea. —Luke 17:2 (J.C. speaking)

In the house of the righteous is much treasure: . . . —Proverbs 15:6

Lay not up for yourselves treasures upon the earth . . .
—Matthew 6:19 (J.C. speaking)

> Blessed is the man that feareth the Lord, that delighteth greatly in his commandments. . . . Wealth and riches shall be in his house: . . . —Psalms 112:1–3

> And again I say unto you, It is easier for a camel to go through the eye of a needle, than for a rich man to enter into the kingdom of God.
> —Matthew 19:24 (J.C. speaking)

Christians routinely attempt to explain away the above and other contradictions involving the words of Jesus in one of two ways. In the first, they claim that the contradictions are the result of mistranslation, which begs the question, if the contradictory statements in this supposedly inerrant book are mistranslated, why should we trust any other passage to be correctly translated?

The second way in which Christians attempt to explain away contradictions is by saying that the New Testament supersedes the Old Testament, so the Old Testament passages no longer apply. This common belief was probably first expressed by the apostle Paul, who wrote, in Galatians 3:13, "Christ hath redeemed us from the curse of the law, . . ."

That's all well and good, but many Christians consider both testaments to be the inerrant Word of God, and Jesus explicitly endorsed everything in the Old Testament in Matthew 5:18: "For verily I say unto you, Till heaven and earth pass, one jot or one tittle shall in no wise pass from the law, till all be fulfilled."

Hence there are irreconcilable contradictions in both the New and Old Testaments involving the words of Christ.

There are also many conflicting accounts in the Bible of events in Christ's life, including important ones. To cite probably the best known, scholars generally agree that Christ was born between 7 BCE and 3 BCE in Nazareth. This doesn't square with the accounts in Luke and Matthew. These accounts relate that Christ's family was forced to go to Bethlehem, because of a census of the entire Roman Empire ordered by Augustus Caesar at the time of Christ's birth. (Luke 2:1–3)

This makes no sense at all. First, because Caesar never issued such an order—if he did, only the author(s) of Luke noticed it. Second, because Roman censuses were conducted for the purpose of property taxation, it would have been nonsensical to order subjects to move away from their properties for a census. (Luke 2:1 states, regarding the nonexistent census supposedly ordered by Augustus Caesar at the time of Christ's birth, "there went out a decree from Caesar Augustus that all the world should be taxed," confirming that taxation was the reason for the supposed census.) Third, while a regional census did take place in Judea in 6 CE (nine to 13 years after Jesus's birth), it didn't affect Galilee, so there would have been no reason for Christ's family to uproot themselves from their home in Nazareth to travel to Bethlehem, even if the census had taken place at the time of Christ's birth. In addition, Luke 2:2 states that the census took place "when Cyrenius was governor of Syria," but he was governor from 6 CE to 12 CE; in other words, according to this passage in Luke, the regional census took place at least nine years after Christ's birth, and perhaps when he was a young adult.

Why would the authors of the gospels create the fiction that Christ was born in Bethlehem rather than Nazareth? Because there's no mention whatsoever of Nazareth in the Old Testament, while there's a prophecy in Micah 5:2 that the messiah would hail from Bethlehem: "But thou, Bethlehem Ephratah, though thou be little among the thousands of Judah, yet out of thee shall he come forth unto me that is to be ruler in Israel; whose goings forth have been from of old, from everlasting."

(One reason that the Church got away with the sham that Christ was born in Bethlehem for well over a millennium is that the vast bulk of the populace was illiterate, and that until well into the Renaissance period the Church discouraged the laity from reading the Bible. Even today, the Catholic Church still, arguably, discourages such reading; at the very minimum, it does nothing to encourage it.)*

If the gospels are this far off in their accounts of Christ's birth, why would they be any more accurate in reporting Christ's words?

On a related matter, another supposed miraculous event involving Christ, Gibbon's comments in *The Decline and Fall of the Roman Empire* regarding the Crucifixion (see Luke 23:44–45, Mark 15:33, and Matthew 27:45) are telling:

> But how shall we excuse the supine inattentiveness of the Pagan and philosophic world to those evidences which were presented by the hand of Om-

---

* While attending Catholic grade school and high school, I don't recall ever hearing a single Bible verse read aloud by any of my teachers. My classmates and I were definitely not encouraged to read the Bible; the schools I attended gave us Baltimore Catechisms to read and memorize, not Bibles. That might have been for the best. While Catholic catechisms are authoritarian, dogmatic, and filled with absurd assertions that induce guilt, shame, and unquestioning obedience, at least they aren't filled with murderous, sadistic commands.

> nipotence . . . ? Under the reign of Tiberius, the whole earth, or at least a celebrated province of the Roman empire [Judea], was involved in a preternatural darkness of three hours [at the crucifixion of J.C.]. Even this miraculous event . . . passed without notice in an age of science and history . . . during the lifetime of Seneca and the elder Pliny, who must have experienced the immediate effects, or received the earliest intelligence of the prodigy. Each of these philosophers, in a laborious work, has recorded all the great phenomena of Nature, earthquakes, meteors, comets, and eclipses, which his indefatigable curiosity could collect. Both the one and the other had omitted to mention the greatest phenomenon to which the mortal eye has been witness since the creation of the globe.

Then there's the matter of when the gospels were written. Mark, the oldest of the gospels, was written 30 to 40 years after Christ's death, at a time when written historical records were rare, the vast bulk of the population was illiterate, and the average age of death was around 35. Worse, the authors of the gospels, with the possible exception of the author(s) of Mark, very probably never met Jesus; with John, which was the last gospel to appear, probably a good six decades after Christ's death, there's no chance of that whatsoever. So, the authors of the gospels had no choice but to rely heavily upon oral tradition. That's analogous to a contemporary author writing a biography of Ronald Reagan decades after Reagan's death, while having scant access to research materials, no opportunity to cross check those materials for accuracy, never having seen Reagan in the flesh or on television, and relying on (at best) a few witnesses getting up in years.

But it gets worse. As author John David Conner states: "[W]e have no original manuscripts of any kind, *not a single scrap of a single verse of a single book of the Bible*. In fact, most manuscripts we have are from several centuries after the originals were likely composed . . . For instance, the oldest surviving copy of MT [Masoretic Text] the most authoritative source of the Hebrew OT [Old Testament] dates from the ninth century CE, well over 1,200 years after most of its contents were originally written" (italics in original).[4] To complicate things even further, ancient Hebrew was written in all caps, without vowels, without punctuation, without spaces between words, and, as in Latin, letters used in place of number symbols. As historian James McDonald notes, "This provided plenty of scope for misunderstandings, especially as the tense had to be guessed from the context."[5]

Beyond that, the Bible was written in three different languages, Hebrew, Aramaic, and Koine (common) Greek. (Add in Coptic if you include the Gospel of Thomas, though it was probably translated from Hebrew, or possibly Greek or Aramaic, with the original text long since vanished.) Given that the New Testament was written in Greek, the original writers had to translate the words of Christ from Aramaic (his native tongue), or from Hebrew translations of Christ's Aramaic, to Greek. (If they were even Christ's words—remember that the authors of the gospels were working largely from oral tradition decades after the death of Christ, or from older versions of the writings that comprise the gospels, with some of those versions varying considerably from each other, and others having disappeared entirely.) Regarding the poor quality of the Greek in the New Testament, Nietzsche, who was a philologist as well as a philosopher, noted in *Beyond Good and Evil*, "It is a curious thing that God learned Greek when he wished to turn author—and that he did not learn it better."

Following the original Greek versions of the gospels, later translators had to take the Greek New Testament text and translate it into *their* languages. All of these translators were in essence playing a centuries-long game of "telephone." So, it's no surprise that there are dozens of different versions of the Bible in English alone (with every fresh set of translators evidently thinking that they could do a better job than their predecessors). As an illustration of the plethora of varying translations, as of 2020 the Bible reference site biblegateway.com featured 55 different English-language versions. But that's paltry when you consider that the Bible, over the centuries, has been translated into over 1,500 languages.[6]

As well as having myriad competing translations, Christians can't even agree on what books constitute the Bible. Do you include the Apocrypha? The recently discovered (1945) Gospel of Thomas? (There were many competing scriptural documents, some likely genuine, that were excluded from the original canons.)

To further complicate matters, many of the sayings attributed to Jesus in Luke and Matthew do not appear in Mark, the earliest gospel. This has led Bible scholars to speculate that there was a "Q" document ("Quelle," "source" in German) that contained the sayings, a document which has apparently vanished. The Gospel of Thomas consists entirely of sayings attributed to Christ, about a third of which do not appear in the other gospels; this has fueled further speculation about the existence of a "Q" document.

Beyond that, as writer and analyst G. Richard Bozarth points out, the gospels are not even a reliable guide to the nature of Jesus: "In Mark, he's a normal human being promoted to adopted Son of God and Messiah. In Matthew and Luke, he's the biological Son of God just like other pagan sons of the various gods and goddesses . . . In John, Jesus is the second oldest and second most powerful supernatural entity, created before the angels and the universe, and is thus clearly using the Jesus body simply as an avatar."[7]

In sum, the gospels (and the supposed words of Jesus) have been amended, translated, and re-translated so often that it's difficult to gauge the accuracy of current versions, even aside from the matter of the accuracy of texts written decades after the death of their subject, and written with few written reference materials.

As well, biblical scholars are largely agreed that a number of interpolations were added to the gospels by later writers during the early Christian period. For instance, Mark 16:9–20 is clearly an interpolation, as it does not appear in the earliest versions of Mark. As a note in the New International Version of the Bible puts it, "The most reliable early manuscripts and other ancient witnesses do not have Mark 16:9–20."*

Even beyond that, all versions of the Bible prior to Gutenberg's Bible (printed in Latin in 1454) were hand copied, with errors likely creeping in.

The end result? Contradiction and inconsistency. As James McDonald notes, there are over 5,000 early New Testament manuscripts, and none of them agree exactly with any of the others.

All of this is such a problem that the Jesus Seminar, a colloquium of over 200 Protestant gospel scholars, mostly employed at religious colleges and seminaries, undertook in 1985 a multi-year investigation into the historicity of the statements and deeds attributed to Jesus in the New Testament. Their conclusion in *The Five Gospels: What Did Jesus Really Say?* (they included the Gospel of Thomas, hence "five gospels") was that only 18% of the statements and 16% of the deeds attributed to Jesus have a high likelihood of being historically accurate.[8]

So, in a very real sense, Christians are not followers of Jesus Christ. Rather, they are followers of those who, decades or centuries after his death, put words in his mouth.

---

* James McDonald lists many other interpolations in *Beyond Belief: Two thousand years of bad faith in the Christian Church*, as does John David Conner in *All That's Wrong with the Bible.*

Endnotes

1. "New Pew Forum on Religion & Public Life Survey Explores Religious Knowledge in the U.S." Pew Forum, September 28, 2010. https://www.pewforum.org/2010/09/28/new-pew-forum-on-religion-public-life-survey-explores-religious-knowledge-in-the-us/ < https://tinyurl.com/c8jdv8cy >

2. "In US, atheists know religion better than believers. Is that bad?," by G. Jeffrey MacDonald. *Christian Science Monitor*, September 28, 2010. https://www.csmonitor.com/USA/Society/2010/0928/In-US-atheists-know-religion-better-than-believers.-Is-that-bad < https://tinyurl.com/pfufdd8 >

3. Pew Forum, op. cit.

4. *All That's Wrong with the Bible: Contradictions, Absurdities, and More (2nd ed.)*, by John David Conner. CreateSpace, 2017, p. 12.

5. *Beyond Belief: Two thousand years of bad faith in the Christian Church*, by James McDonald. Reading, England: Garnet Publications, 2011, p. 20.

6. *The History of Christianity: From the Disciples to the Dawn of the Reformation*, by Luke Timothy Johnson. The Learning Company, 2021, course number 6610.

7. Personal correspondence, October 8, 2020.

8. "The Jesus Seminar." Westar Institute. https://www.westarinstitute.org/projects/the-jesus-seminar/ < https://tinyurl.com/4d7zvbvv >

Appendix A

Some Enlightening Bible Verses

> If you take the cruel passages, the verses that inculcate eternal hatred, verses that writhe and hiss like serpents, you can make a creed that would shock the heart of a hyena. It may be that no book contains better passages than the New Testament, but certainly no book contains worse. Below the blossom of love you find the thorn of hatred; on the lips that kiss, you find the poison of the cobra. The Bible is not a moral guide.
>
> —Robert Ingersoll, "What Would You Substitute for the Bible as a Moral Guide?"

The following passages are taken in large part from what historian Chris Mato Nunpa (*The Great Evil: Christianity, the Bible, and the Native America Genocide*) calls the "hidden Bible"—the cruel, horrific verses that are so shocking they're impossible to justify, especially the verses commanding mass murder and individual murder, often in horribly brutal fashion. Hence a large majority of Christians and Christian churches studiously avoid them.

Other passages in this appendix illustrate the authoritarian, misogynistic, homophobic, petty, arbitrary, contradictory nature of far too much of Christian scripture. If, for instance, you need to find verses showing the Bible's misogyny, you'll find them here. Unfulfilled prophecies? You'll find several passages that clearly show that Christ and his disciples believed they were in the end times, verses which are very difficult for Christian apologists to explain away.

As for the source of the verses, all of the passages used in this book are from the King James Version, which was rife with euphemisms, including "servant" in place of "slave." The King James Version uses euphemisms for many other things, with sexual euphemisms being especially common. Bible critic K.J. Aaron states, "In the Bible, euphemisms for the sexual organs include such terms as 'secrets' (Deuteronomy 25:11), 'stones'

(Deuteronomy 23:1), 'loins' (Genesis 46:26), 'thigh' (Genesis 24:2), 'privy member' (Deuteronomy 23:1), 'fountain' (Leviticus 20:18), and 'the place of the breaking forth of children' (Hosea 13:13)." Once you realize this, many biblical passages become even more disturbing than they appear at first glance.

Finally, there is some unavoidable duplication of passages here, as many of the verses in this appendix could fit well into two or even three categories. I've done my best to reduce the duplication by reserving it for only the most important passages, but a small amount is still there, nonetheless.

Readers needing to find passages on a particular matter would be well advised to look not only through the most relevant section(s), but also through related sections and subsections for additional verses. Many of them will be in various parts of the "Murderous Commands" sections, which were included to show the wide-ranging nature of the Almighty's thirst for blood.

Please dive in and—though this is undoubtedly the wrong word—enjoy.

Contradictions

There are a great many contradictions and inconsistencies in the Bible, in both the Old and New Testaments. For instance, there are several inconsistencies regarding the life and death of Jesus in the four gospels. Here, however, we'll list only the most direct contradictions, including some within the same books.

These contradictions are so blatant that they're impossible to explain away, at least adequately: Christian apologists often insist that these contradictions are the result of mistranslation. However, if all of these direct contradictions are the result of mistranslation, how do we know that any other translated passage is accurate? In short, we don't—and neither do the Christian apologists.

Contradictions Involving the Words of Jesus

(All passages from the gospels are attributed to Jesus)

"Think not that I am come to send peace on earth. I came not to send peace, but a sword." —Matthew 10:34

". . . Put up again thy sword into his place: for all they that take the sword shall perish with the sword. " —Matthew 26:52

"I and my Father are one." —John 10:30

"I go unto the Father: for my Father is greater than I." —John 14:28

"If I bear witness of myself, my witness is not true." —John 5:31

"I am one that bear witness of myself, . . ." —John 8:18

These are the most direct contradictions in the New Testament involving the words of Jesus. Christ, however, also directly contradicts passages in the Old Testament, including the Fifth Commandment:

"Honour they father and thy mother." —Exodus 20:12

"If any man come to me, and hate not his father and mother, and wife, and children, and brethren, and sisters, year, and his own life also, he cannot be my disciple." —Luke 14:26

"And if any mischief follow, then thou shalt give life for life, Eye for eye, tooth for tooth, hand for hand, foot for foot, Burning for burning, wound for wound, stripe for stripe." —Exodus 21:23–25

"But I say unto you, That ye resist not evil: but whosoever shall smite thee on thy right cheek, turn to him the other also. " —Matthew 5:39

"If a man have a stubborn and rebellious son, which will not obey the voice of his father, or the voice of his mother, and that, when they have chastened him, will not hearken unto them: Then shall his father and his mother lay hold on him, and bring him out unto the elders of his city, and unto the gate of his place; And they shall say unto the elders of his city, This our son is stubborn and rebellious, he will not obey our voice; he is a glutton, and a drunkard. And all the men of his city shall stone him with stones, that he die: so shalt thou put evil away from among you; and all Israel shall hear, and fear." —Deuteronomy 21:18–21

"But whoso shall offend one of these little ones which believe in me, it were better for him that a millstone were hanged about his neck, and that he were drowned in the depth of the sea." —Luke 17:2

"A good man leaveth an inheritance to his children's children." —Proverbs 13:22

"Sell that ye have and give alms; . . ." —Luke 12:33

"In the house of the righteous is much treasure: . . ." —Proverbs 15:6

"Lay not up for yourselves treasures upon the earth . . ." —Matthew 6:19

"Blessed is the man that feareth the Lord, that delighteth greatly in his commandments. . . . Wealth and riches shall be in his house: . . ." —Psalms 112:1–3

"And again I say unto you, It is easier for a camel to go through the eye of a needle, than for a rich man to enter into the kingdom of God. " —Matthew 19:24

Other Biblical Contradictions

The contradictions listed here barely scratch the surface. For much lengthier lists of contradictions see James McDonald's *Beyond Belief: Two thousand years of bad faith in the Christian Church,* John David Conner's *All That's Wrong with the Bible,* and G. Richard Bozarth's upcoming *The Hidden Gospels.*

"Let no man say when he is tempted, I am tempted of God: for God cannot be tempted with evil, neither tempteth he any man:" —James 1:13

"And it came to pass after these things, that God did tempt Abraham, . . ."
—Genesis 22:1

". . . The son shall not bear the iniquity of the father, neither shall the father bear the iniquity of the son: the righteousness of the righteous shall be upon him, and the wickedness of the wicked shall be upon him. " —Ezekiel 18:20

". . . I the Lord thy God am a jealous God, visiting the iniquity of the fathers upon the children unto the third and fourth generation of them that hate me;"
—Exodus 20:5

"... I am merciful, saith the Lord, and I will not keep anger for ever."
—Jeremiah 3:12

"Ye have kindled a fire in mine anger, which shall burn forever. Thus saith the Lord." —Jeremiah 17:4

"Happy is the man that findeth wisdom, and the man that getteth understanding." —Proverbs 3:13

"For in much wisdom is much grief; and he that increaseth knowledge increaseth sorrow ..." —Ecclesiastes 1:18

" One generation passeth away, and another generation cometh: but the earth abideth for ever."—Ecclesiastes 1:4

"But the day of the Lord will come as a thief in the night; in the which the heavens shall pass away with a great noise, and the elements shall melt with fervent heat, the earth also and the works that are therein shall be burned up."
—II Peter 3:10

And last but not least:

"I have seen God face to face, and my life is preserved." —Genesis 32:30

"No man hath seen God at any time."
—John 1:18

"And I [God] will take away mine hand, and thou shalt see my back parts ..."
—Exodus 33:23

Christian apologists typically attempt to explain away such contradictions by claiming that the fault lies in the translation, and that there were no contradictions in the original text. It's difficult to see how this could be, given how direct many biblical contradictions are; but even if these Christian apologetics held water, it would follow that every part of the Bible should be as suspect as the contradictory sections, thus reinforcing the point of the previous chapter: the Bible is not a reliable guide to Christ's words.

The End of the World

(An Unfulfilled Prophecy)

"Verily, verily, I say unto you, The hour is coming, and now is, when the dead shall hear the voice of the Son of God: and they that hear shall live." —John 5:25 (J.C. speaking)

"And there shall be signs in the sun, and in the moon, and in the stars; and upon the earth distress of nations, with perplexity; the sea and the waves roaring; Men's hearts failing them for fear, and for looking after those things which are coming on the earth: for the powers of heaven shall be shaken. And then shall they see the Son of man coming in a cloud with power and great glory. And when these things begin to come to pass, then look up, and lift up your heads; for your redemption draweth nigh. . . .when ye see these things come to pass, know ye that the kingdom of God is nigh at hand. Verily I say unto you, This generation shall not pass away, till all be fulfilled." —Luke 21:25–32 (J.C. speaking)

"Immediately after the tribulation of those days shall the sun be darkened, and the moon shall not give her light, and the stars shall fall from heaven, and the powers of the heavens shall be shaken: And then shall appear the sign of the Son of man in heaven: . . . and they shall see the Son of man coming in the clouds of heaven with power and great glory. . . . when ye shall see all these things, know that it is near, even at the doors. Verily I say unto you, This generation shall not pass, till all these things be fulfilled." —Matthew 24:29–34 (J.C. speaking)

"But in those days, after that tribulation, the sun shall be darkened, and the moon shall not give her light, And the stars of heaven shall fall, and the powers that are in heaven shall be shaken. And then shall they see the Son of man coming in the clouds with great power and glory. . . . Verily I say unto you, that this generation shall not pass, till all these things be done." —Mark 13:24–26, 31 (J.C. speaking)

"And he said unto them, Verily I say unto you, That there be some of them that stand here, which shall not taste of death, till they have seen the kingdom of God come with power. " —Mark 9:1 (J.C. speaking)

"Verily I say unto you, There be some standing here, which shall not taste of death, till they see the Son of man coming in his kingdom. "
—Matthew 16:28 (J.C. Speaking)

"But I tell you of a truth, there be some standing here, which shall not taste of death, till they see the kingdom of God." —Luke 9:27 (J.C. speaking)

"Verily I say unto you, This generation shall not pass away, till all be fulfilled." —Luke 21:32 (J.C. speaking)

"Little children, it is the last time: and as ye have heard that antichrist shall come, even now are there many antichrists; whereby we know that it is the last time." —1 John 2:18 (J.C. speaking)

"But the end of all things is at hand: be ye therefore sober, and watch unto prayer." —1 Peter 4:7

Slavery and Submission

All verses quoted in this book are from the King James Version. Please bear in mind that the King James translators used a great many euphemisms, including "servant," "bondman," and "bondmaid" in place of "slave." With that in mind, many passages are even darker than they appear at first glance.

"And if a man smite his servant, or his maid, with a rod, and he die under his hand; he shall be surely punished. Notwithstanding, if he continue a day or two, he shall not be punished: for he is his money." —Exodus 20:20–21

"If thou buy an Hebrew servant, six years he shall serve: and in the seventh he shall go out free for nothing. If he came in by himself, he shall go out by himself: if he were married, then his wife shall go out with him. If his master have given him a wife, and she have born him sons or daughters; the wife and her children shall be her master's, and he shall go out by himself. And if the servant shall plainly say, I love my master, my wife, and my children; I will not go out free: Then his master shall bring him unto the judges; he shall also bring him to the door, or unto the door post; and his master shall bore his ear through with an aul; and he shall serve him for ever." —Exodus 21:2–6

"And whosoever lieth carnally with a woman, that is a bondmaid, betrothed to an husband, and not at all redeemed, nor freedom given her; she shall be scourged; they shall not be put to death, because she was not free." —Leviticus 19:20

"Both thy bondmen, and thy bondmaids, which thou shalt have, shall be of the heathen that are round about you; of them shall ye buy bondmen and bondmaids. Moreover of the children of the strangers that do sojourn among you, of them shall ye buy, and of their families that are with you, which they begat in your land: and they shall be your possession. And ye shall take them as an inheritance for your children after you, to inherit them for a possession; they shall be your bondmen for ever: . . ." —Leviticus 25:44–46

"Submit yourselves to every ordinance of man for the Lord's sake: whether it be to the king, as supreme; Or unto governors, as unto them that are sent by him for the punishment of evildoers, and for the praise of them that do well. For so is the will of God, . . ." —1 Peter 2:13–15

"Servants, be subject to your masters with all fear; not only to the good and gentle, but also to the froward." —1 Peter 2:18

"Let as many servants as are under the yoke count their own masters worthy of all honour, that the name of God and his doctrine be not blasphemed."
—1 Timothy 6:1

"Exhort servants to be obedient unto their own masters, and to please them well in all things; not answering again; Not purloining, but shewing all good fidelity; that they may adorn the doctrine of God our Saviour in all things."
—Titus 2:9–10

"Servants, be obedient to them that are your masters according to the flesh, with fear and trembling, in singleness of your heart, as unto Christ; Not with eyeservice, as menpleasers; but as the servants of Christ, doing the will of God from the heart;" —Ephesians 6:5–6

"Servants, obey in all things your masters according to the flesh; not with eyeservice, as menpleasers; but in singleness of heart, fearing God;" —Colossians 3:22

"Let every soul be subject unto the higher powers. For there is no power but of God: the powers that be are ordained of God. Whosoever therefore resisteth the power, resisteth the ordinance of God: and they that resist shall receive to themselves damnation." —Romans 13:1–2

Sex

"It is good for a man not to touch a woman." —1 Corinthians 7:1

"Dearly beloved, I beseech you as strangers and pilgrims, abstain from fleshly lusts, which war against the soul; . . ." —1 Peter 2:11

"For I would that all men were even as I myself. But every man hath his proper gift of God, one after this manner, and another after that. I say therefore to the unmarried and widows, it is good for them if they abide even as I. But if they cannot contain, let them marry: for it is better to marry than to burn."
—1 Corinthians 7:7–9

"For there are some eunuchs, which were so born from their mother's womb: and there are some eunuchs, which were made eunuchs of men: and there be eunuchs, which have made themselves eunuchs for the kingdom of heaven's sake. He that is able to receive it, let him receive it." —Matthew 19:12 (J.C. Speaking)

"And the man that committeth adultery with another man's wife, even he that committeth adultery with his neighbour's wife, the adulterer and the adulteress shall surely be put to death." —Leviticus 20:10

(see also Deuteronomy 22:22 and Ezekiel 23:45–47 in the "Murderous Commands" Adultery subsection)

"And if a man also lie with mankind, as he lieth with a woman, both of them have committed an abomination; they shall surely be put to death; their blood shall be upon them." —Leviticus 20:13

"And if a man lie with a beast, he shall surely be put to death: and ye shall slay the beast." —Leviticus 20:15

(see also Exodus 22:19 in the "Murderous Commands" Bestiality subsection)

"And if a woman approach unto any beast, and lie down thereto, thou shalt kill the woman, and the beast: they shall surely be put to death; their blood shall be upon them." —Leviticus 20:16

"Now the works of the flesh are manifest, which are these; Adultery, fornication, uncleanness, lasciviousness." —Galatians 5:19

"And the daughter of any priest, if she profane herself by playing the whore, she profaneth her father: she shall be burnt with fire [to death]." —Leviticus 21:9

Misogyny

"Unto the woman he said, I will greatly multiply thy sorrow and thy conception; in sorrow thou shalt bring forth children; and thy desire shall be to thy husband, and he shall rule over thee." —Genesis 3:16

". . . If a woman have conceived seed, and born a man child: then she shall be unclean seven days; according to the days of the separation for her infirmity shall she be unclean. And in the eighth day the flesh of his foreskin shall be circumcised. And she shall then continue in the blood of her purifying three and thirty days; she shall touch no hallowed thing, nor come into the sanctuary, until the days of her purifying be fulfilled. But if she bear a maid child, then she shall be unclean two weeks, as in her separation: and she shall continue in the blood of her purifying threescore and six days." —Leviticus 12:2–5

"And every garment, and every skin, whereon is the seed of copulation, shall be washed with water, and be unclean until the even. The woman also with whom man shall lie with seed of copulation, they shall both bathe themselves in water, and be unclean until the even. And if a woman have an issue, and her issue in her flesh be blood, she shall be put apart seven days: and whosoever toucheth her shall be unclean until the even. And every thing that she lieth upon in her separation shall be unclean: every thing also that she sitteth upon shall be unclean. And whosoever toucheth her bed shall wash his clothes, and bathe himself in water, and be unclean until the even. And whosoever toucheth any thing that she sat upon shall wash his clothes, and bathe himself in water, and be unclean until the even. And if it be on her bed, or on any thing whereon she sitteth, when he toucheth it, he shall be unclean until the even. And if any man lie with her at all, and her flowers be upon him, he shall be unclean seven days; and all the bed whereon he lieth shall be unclean. And if a woman have an issue of her blood many days out of the time of her separation, or if it run beyond the time of her separation; all the days of the issue of her uncleanness shall be as the days of her separation: she shall be unclean. Every bed whereon she lieth all the days of her issue shall be unto her as the bed of her separation: and whatsoever she sitteth upon shall be unclean, as the uncleanness of her separation. And whosoever toucheth those things shall be unclean, and shall wash his clothes, and bathe himself in water, and be unclean until the even. . . . This is the law of him that hath an issue, and of him whose seed goeth from him, and is defiled therewith; And of her that is sick of her flowers, and of him that hath an issue, of the man, and of the woman, and of him that lieth with her that is unclean." —Leviticus 15:17–27, 32–33

"And whosoever lieth carnally with a woman, that is a bondmaid, betrothed to an husband, and not at all redeemed, nor freedom given her; she shall be scourged; they shall not be put to death, because she was not free." —Leviticus 19:20

"If any man take a wife, and go in unto her, and hate her, . . . and say, I took this woman, and when I came to her, I found her not a maid: . . . if this thing be true, and the tokens of virginity be not found for the damsel: Then they shall bring out the damsel to the door of her father's house, and the men of her city shall stone her with stones that she die: . . ." —Deuteronomy 22:13–21

"But if thou hast gone aside to another instead of thy husband, and if thou be defiled, and some man have lain with thee beside thine husband: Then the priest shall charge the woman with an oath of cursing, and the priest shall say unto the woman, The Lord make thee a curse and an oath among thy people, when the Lord doth make thy thigh [a euphemism for genitals] to rot, and thy belly to swell; And this water that causeth the curse shall go into thy bowels, to make thy belly to swell, and thy thigh to rot: And the woman shall say, Amen, amen." —Numbers 5:20–22

"How then can man be justified with God? or how can he be clean that is born of a woman?" —Job 25:4

"Wives, submit yourselves unto your own husbands, as unto the Lord. For the husband is the head of the wife, even as Christ is the head of the church:"
—Ephesians 5:22–23

"Wives, submit yourselves unto your own husbands, as it is fit in the Lord."
—Colossians 3:18

""But I would have you know, that the head of every man is Christ: and the head of the woman is the man." —1 Corinthians 11:3

"Neither was the man created for the woman, but the woman for the man."
—1 Corinthians 11:9

"Let your women keep silence in the churches: for it is not permitted unto them to speak; but they are commanded to be under obedience as also saith the law."
—1 Corinthians 14:34

"Let the woman learn in silence with all subjection. But I suffer not a woman to teach, nor to usurp authority over the man, but to be in silence."
—1 Timothy 2:11–12

"Now she that is a widow indeed, and desolate, trusteth in God, and continueth in supplications and prayers night and day. But she that liveth in pleasure is dead while she liveth." —I Timothy 5:5–6

"Likewise, ye husbands, dwell with them according to knowledge, giving honour unto the wife, as unto the weaker vessel, and as being heirs together of the grace of life; that your prayers be not hindered." —1 Peter 3:7

"These [redeemed] are they which were not defiled with women . . ."
—Revelation 14:4

Redundant Passages

"For thou art an holy people unto the Lord thy God: the Lord thy God hath chosen thee to be a special people unto himself, above all people that are upon the face of the earth." —Deuteronomy 7:6

"For thou art an holy people unto the Lord thy God, and the Lord hath chosen thee to be a peculiar people unto himself, above all the nations that are upon the earth." —Deuteronomy 14:2

"The first of the firstfruits of thy land thou shalt bring into the house of the Lord thy God. Thou shalt not seethe a kid in his mother's milk." —Exodus 23:19

"The first of the firstfruits of thy land thou shalt bring unto the house of the Lord thy God. Thou shalt not seethe a kid in his mother's milk." —Exodus 34:26

"And he went up thence to the inhabitants of Debir: and the name of Debir before was Kirjathsepher. And Caleb said, He that smiteth Kirjathsepher, and taketh it, to him will I give Achsah my daughter to wife. And Othniel the son of Kenaz, the brother of Caleb, took it: and he gave him Achsah his daughter to wife. And it came to pass, as she came unto him, that she moved him to ask of her father a field: and she lighted off her ass; and Caleb said unto her, What wouldest thou? Who answered, Give me a blessing; for thou hast given me a south land; give me also springs of water. And he gave her the upper springs, and the nether springs."
—Joshua 15:15–19

"And from thence he went against the inhabitants of Debir: and the name of Debir before was Kirjathsepher: And Caleb said, He that smiteth Kirjathsepher, and taketh it, to him will I give Achsah my daughter to wife. And Othniel the son of Kenaz, Caleb's younger brother, took it: and he gave him Achsah his daughter to wife. And it came to pass, when she came to him, that she moved him to ask of her father a field: and she lighted from off her ass; and Caleb said unto her, What wilt thou? And she said unto him, Give me a blessing: for thou hast given me a south land; give me also springs of water. And Caleb gave her the upper springs and the nether springs." —Judges 1:11–15

"And it shall come to pass in the last days, that the mountain of the Lord's house shall be established in the top of the mountains, and shall be exalted above the hills; and all nations shall flow unto it. And many people shall go and say, Come ye, and let us go up to the mountain of the Lord, to the house of the God of Jacob; and he will teach us of his ways, and we will walk in his paths: for out of Zion shall go forth the law, and the word of the Lord from Jerusalem. And he shall judge among the nations, and shall rebuke many people: and they shall beat their swords into plowshares, and their spears into pruninghooks: nation shall not lift up sword against nation, neither shall they learn war any more." —Isaiah 2:2–4

"But in the last days it shall come to pass, that the mountain of the house of the Lord shall be established in the top of the mountains, and it shall be exalted above the hills; and people shall flow unto it. And many nations shall come, and say, Come, and let us go up to the mountain of the Lord, and to the house of the God of Jacob; and he will teach us of his ways, and we will walk in his paths: for the law shall go forth of Zion, and the word of the Lord from Jerusalem. And he shall judge among many people, and rebuke strong nations afar off; and they shall beat their swords into plowshares, and their spears into pruninghooks: nation shall not lift up a sword against nation, neither shall they learn war any more." —Micah 4:1–3

For additional near-identical passages, see John David Conner's *All That's Wrong with the Bible.*

Murderous Biblical Commands
(Individual Murders)

Adultery

"And the man that committeth adultery with another man's wife, even he that committeth adultery with his neighbour's wife, the adulterer and the adulteress shall surely be put to death." —Leviticus 20:10

"If a man be found lying with a woman married to an husband, then they shall both of them die, both the man that lay with the woman, and the woman; so shalt thou put away evil from Israel." —Deuteronomy 22:22

"And the righteous men, they shall judge them after the manner of adulteresses, and after the manner of women that shed blood; because they are adulteresses, and blood is in their hands. For thus saith the Lord God; I will bring up a company upon them, and will give them to be removed and spoiled. And the company shall stone them with stones, and dispatch them with their swords; they shall slay their sons and their daughters and burn up their houses with fire." —Ezekiel 23:45–47

Sex

(keeping it all in the family)

"And the man that lieth with his father's wife hath uncovered his father's nakedness: both of them shall surely be put to death; their blood shall be upon them."
—Leviticus 20:11

"And if a man lie with his daughter in law, both of them shall surely be put to death: they have wrought confusion; their blood shall be upon them."
—Leviticus 20:12

"And if a man take wife and her mother, it is wickedness; they shall be burnt with fire, both he and they; that there be no wickedness among you."
—Leviticus 20:14

Bestiality

"Whosoever lieth with a beast shall surely be put to death." —Exodus 22:19

"And if a man lie with a beast, he shall surely be put to death: and ye shall slay the beast." —Leviticus 20:15

"And if a woman approach unto any beast, and lie down thereto, thou shalt kill the woman, and the beast: they shall surely be put to death; their blood shall be upon them." —Leviticus 20:16

Blasphemy

"Bring forth him that hath cursed without the camp; and let all that heard him lay their hands upon his head, and let all the congregation stone him. And thou shalt speak unto the children of Israel, saying, Whosoever curseth his God shall bear his sin. And he that blasphemeth the name of the Lord, he shall surely be put to death, and all the congregation shall certainly stone him: as well the stranger, as he that is born in the land, when he blasphemeth the name of the Lord, shall be put to death." —Leviticus 24:14–16

Cursing thy Father or Mother

"For every one that curseth his father or his mother shall be surely put to death: he hath curse his father or his mother; his blood shall be upon him." —Leviticus 20:9

Fornication

"And the daughter of any priest, if she profane herself by playing the whore, she profaneth her father: she shall be burnt with fire." —Leviticus 21:9

Harlotry

(fornication and/or adultery)

"Wherefore, O harlot, hear the word of the Lord: Thus saith the Lord God; Because thy filthiness was poured out, and thy nakedness discovered through thy whoredom with thy lovers, and with all the idols of thy abominations, and by the blood of thy children, which thou didst give unto them; Behold, therefore I will gather all thy lovers, with whom thou has taken pleasure, and all them that thou hast loved, with all them that thou hast hated; I will even gather them round against thee, and will discover thy nakedness unto them, that they may see all thy nakedness. And I will judge thee, as women that break wedlock and shed blood are judged; and I will give thee blood in fury and jealousy. And I will also give thee into their hand, and they shall throw down thine eminent place, and shall break down thy high places: they shall strip thee also of thy clothes, and shall take thy fair jewels, and leave thee naked and bare. They shall also bring up a company against thee, and they shall stone thee with stones, and thrust thee through with their swords." —Ezekiel 16:35–40

Homosexual Acts

"And if a man also lie with mankind, as he lieth with a woman, both of them have committed an abomination; they shall surely be put to death; their blood shall be upon them." —Leviticus 20:13

". . . God gave them up unto vile affections: for even their women did change the natural use into that which is against nature: And likewise also the men, leaving the natural use of the woman, burned in their lust one toward another . . ."
— Romans 1:26–27

Rape Victim

(being one, but not crying out)

"If a damsel that is a virgin be betrothed unto an husband, and a man find her in the city, and lie with her; Then ye shall bring them both out unto the gate of that city, and ye shall stone them with stones that they die; the damsel, because she cried not, being in the city; and the man, because he hath humbled his neighbour's wife: so thou shalt put away evil from among you." —Deuteronomy 22:23–24

"If a man find a damsel that is a virgin, which is not betrothed, and lay hold on her, and lie with her, and they be found; Then the man that lay with her shall give unto the damsel's father fifty shekels of silver, and she shall be his wife; because he hath humbled her, he may not put her away all his days." —Deuteronomy 22:28–29

Rebelliousness

"If a man have a stubborn and rebellious son, which will not obey the voice of his father, or the voice of his mother, and that, when they have chastened him, will not hearken unto them: Then shall his father and his mother lay hold on him, and bring him out unto the elders of his city, and unto the gate of his place; And they shall say unto the elders of his city, This our son is stubborn and rebellious, he will not obey our voice; he is a glutton, and a drunkard. And all the men of his city shall stone him with stones, that he die; so shalt thou put evil away from among you; and all Israel shall hear and fear." —Deuteronomy 21:18–21

Virginity

(inability to prove, female)

"If any man take a wife, and go in unto her, and hate her, And give occasions of speech against her, and bring up an evil name upon her, and say, I took this woman, and when I came to her, I found her not a maid: Then shall the father of the damsel, and her mother, take and bring forth the tokens of the damsel's virginity unto the elders of the city in the gate: And the damsel's father shall say unto the elders, I gave my daughter unto this man to wife, and he hateth her; And, lo, he hath given occasions of speech against her, saying, I found not thy daughter a maid; and yet these are the tokens of my daughter's virginity. And they shall spread the cloth before the elders of the city. And the elders of that city shall take that man and chastise him; And they shall amerce him in an hundred shekels of silver, and give them unto the father of the damsel, because he hat brought up an evil name upon a virgin of Israel: and she shall be his wife; he may not put her away all his days. But if this thing be true, and the tokens of virginity be not found for the damsel: Then they shall bring out the damsel to the door of her father's house, and the men of her city shall stone her with stones that she die: because she hath wrought folly in Israel, to play the whore in her father's house: so shalt thou put evil away from among you." —Deuteronomy 22:13–21

Witchcraft and Wizardry

"Thou shalt not suffer a witch to live." —Exodus 22:18

"A man or a woman that hath a familiar spirit, or that is a wizard, shall surely be put to death: they shall stone them with stones: their blood shall be upon them."
—Leviticus 20:27

Working on the Sabbath

"And Moses gathered all the congregation of the children of Israel together, and said unto them, These are the words which the Lord hath commanded, that ye should do them. Six days shall work be done, but on the seventh day there shall be to you an holy day, a sabbath of rest to the Lord: whosoever doeth work therein shall be put to death." —Exodus 35:1–2

"Ye shall keep the sabbath therefore; for it is holy unto you: every one that defileth it shall surely be put to death: for whosoever doeth any work there in, that soul shall be cut off from among his people. Six days may work be done; but in the seventh is the sabbath of rest, holy to the Lord: whosoever doeth any work in the sabbath day, he shall surely be put to death." —Exodus 31:14–15

"And while the children of Israel were in the wilderness, they found a man that gathered sticks upon the sabbath day. And they found him gathering sticks brought him unto Moses and Aaron, and unto all the congregation. And they put him ward, because it was not declared what should be done to him. And the Lord said unto Moses, The man shall surely be put to death; and all the congregation shall stone him with stones without the camp. And all the congregation brought him without the camp, and stoned him with stones, and he died; as the Lord commanded Moses." —Numbers 15:32–36

Worshiping Other Gods

"If thy brother, the son of thy mother, or thy son, or thy daughter, or the wife of thy bosom, or thy friend, which is as thine own soul, entice thee secretly, saying, Let us go and serve other gods, which thou hast not known, thou, nor thy fathers; Namely, of the gods of the people which are round about you, nigh unto thee, or far off from thee, from the one end of the earth even unto the other end of the earth; Thou shalt not consent unto him; neither shall thine eye pity him, neither shalt thou spare, neither shalt thou conceal him; But thou shalt surely kill him; thine hand shall be first upon him to put him to death, and afterwards the hand of all the people." —Deuteronomy 13:6–9

"If there be found among you, within any of thy gates which the Lord thy God giveth thee, man or woman, that hath wrought wickedness in the sight of the Lord thy God, in transgressing his covenant, And hath gone and served other gods, and worshipped them, either the sun, or moon, or any of the host of heaven, which I have not commanded; And it be told thee, and thou hast heard of it, and enquired diligently, and, behold, it be true, and the thing certain, that such an abomination is wrought in Israel: Then shalt thou bring forth that man or that woman, which have committed that wicked thing, unto thy gates, even that man or that woman, and shalt stone them with stones, till they die." —Deuteronomy 17:2–5

Murderous Biblical Passages
(Mass Murder)

"And Israel vowed a vow unto the Lord, and said, If thou wilt indeed deliver this people into my hand, then I will utterly destroy their cities. And the Lord hearkened to the voice of Israel, and delivered up the Canaanites; and they utterly destroyed them and their cities: . . ." —Numbers 21:2–3

"And the Lord spake unto Moses, saying, . . . Arm some of yourselves unto the war, and let them go against the Midianites . . . Of every tribe a thousand, throughout all the tribes of Israel, shall ye send to the war. . . . And Moses sent them to the war, a thousand of every tribe . . . And they warred against the Midianites, as the Lord commanded Moses; and they slew all the males. . . . And the children of Israel took all the women of Midian captives, and their little ones, and took the spoil of all their cattle, and all their flocks, and all their goods. And they burnt all their cities wherein they dwelt, and all their goodly castles, with fire. And they took all the spoil, and all the prey, both of men and of beasts. And they brought the captives, and the prey, and the spoil, unto Moses . . . And Moses was wroth with the officers of the host, with the captains over thousands, and captains over hundreds, which came from the battle. And Moses said unto them, Have ye saved all the women alive? . . . Now therefore kill every male among the little ones, and kill every woman that hath known man by lying with him. But all the women children, that have not known a man by lying with him, keep alive for yourselves." —Numbers 31:1–18

"When the Lord thy God shall bring thee into the land whither thou goest to possess it, and hath cast out many nations before thee, the Hittites, and the Girgashites, and the Amorites, and the Canaanites, and the Perizzites, and the Hivites, and the Jebusites, seven nations greater and mightier than thou; And when the Lord thy God shall deliver them before thee; thou shalt smite them, and utterly destroy them; thou shalt make no covenant with them, nor shew mercy unto them:" —Deuteronomy 7:1–2

"When thou comest nigh unto a city to fight against it, then proclaim peace unto it. And it shall be, if it make thee answer of peace, and open unto thee, then it shall be, that all the people that is found therein shall be tributaries unto thee, and they shall serve thee [become slaves]. And if it will make no peace with thee, but will make war against thee, then thou shalt besiege it: And when the Lord thy God hath delivered it into thine hands, thou shalt smite every male thereof with the edge of the sword: But the women, and the little ones, and the cattle, and all that is in the city, even all the spoil thereof, shalt thou take unto thyself; and thou shalt eat the spoil of thine enemies, which the Lord thy God hath given thee. Thus shalt thou do unto all the cities which are very far off from thee, which are not of the cities of these nations. But of the cities of these people, which the Lord thy God doth give thee for an inheritance, thou shalt save alive nothing that breatheth: But thou shalt utterly destroy them; namely, the Hittites, and the Amorites, the Canaanites, and the Perizzites, the Hivites, and the Jebusites; as the Lord thy God hath commanded thee." —Deuteronomy 20:10–17

"And Joshua . . . took Hazor, and smote the king thereof with the sword: . . . And they smote all the souls that were therein with the edge of the sword, utterly destroying them: there was not any left to breathe: and he burnt Hazor with fire. And all the cities of those kings, and all the kings of them, did Joshua take, and smote them with the edge of the sword, and he utterly destroyed them, as Moses the servant of the Lord commanded. . . . And all the spoil of these cities, and the cattle, the children of Israel took for a prey unto themselves; but every man they smote with the edge of the sword, until they had destroyed them, neither left they any to breathe." —Joshua 11:10–14

"Thus saith the Lord of hosts, . . . Now go and smite Amalek, and utterly destroy all that they have, and spare them not; but slay both man and woman, infant and suckling, ox and sheep, camel and ass." —I Samuel 15:2–3

A Few Inspiring Passages

"Behold, I will corrupt your seed, and spread dung upon your faces, even the dung of your solemn feasts; . . ." —Malachi 2:3

". . . hath he not sent me to the men that sit upon the wall, that they may eat their own dung, and drink their own piss with you?" —Isaiah 36:12

"And thou shalt eat it as barley cakes, and thou shalt bake it with dung that cometh out of man, in their sight. And the Lord said, Even thus shall the children of Israel eat their defiled bread among the Gentiles, whither I will drive them. . . . Then he said unto me, Lo, I have given thee cow's dung for man's dung, and thou shalt prepare thy bread therewith." —Ezekiel 4:12–15

"O daughter of Babylon, who art to be destroyed; happy shall he be, that rewardeth thee as thou hast served us. Happy shall he be, that taketh and dasheth thy little ones against the stones." —Psalms 137:8–9

A Final Benediction

"For my love they are my adversaries: but I give myself unto prayer. And they have rewarded me evil for good, and hatred for my love. Set thou a wicked man over him: and let Satan stand at his right hand. When he shall be judged, let him be condemned: and let his prayer become sin. Let his days be few; and let another take his office. Let his children be fatherless, and his wife a widow. Let his children be continually vagabonds, and beg: let them seek their bread also out of their desolate places. Let the extortioner catch all that he hath; and let the strangers spoil his labour. Let there be none to extend mercy unto him: neither let there be any to favour his fatherless children. Let his posterity be cut off; and in the generation following let their name be blotted out." —Psalms 109:4–13

Appendix B
Some Useful Resources

It's risky to publish lists of recommended resources such as organizations, magazines and (especially) web sites and blogs, as you'll undoubtedly omit some that you absolutely *should* have included—and their directors, editors, and publishers will understandably be upset. So, I haven't done that. Instead, I've listed only those resources I consult at least occasionally, plus a few that are both prominent and/or long lived. To avoid any appearance of favoritism, the following lists are strictly alphabetized. While some of these resources, especially blogs and web sites, might have disappeared by the time you read this, those that remain will still be of value.

Atheist & Secularist Organizations

American Atheists
225 Cristiani St.
Cranford, NJ 07016
(www.atheists.org)

American Humanist Association
1821 Jefferson Place NW
Washington, DC 20036
(https://americanhumanist.org)

Americans United for Separation of Church and State
1301 L Street #200
Washington, DC 20005
(https://www.au.org)

Atheist Alliance International
216 Mt. Hermon Rd. SteE #178
Scotts Valley, CA 95066
(www.atheistalliance.org)

Black Nonbelievers
P.O. Box 133351
Atlanta, GA 30333
(www.blacknonbelievers.org)

Center for Inquiry
P.O. Box 741
Amherst, NY 14226
(https://centerforinquiry.org)

Freedom from Religion Foundation
P.O. Box 750
Madison, WI 53701
(https://ffrf.org)

Hispanic American Freethinkers
11890 Sunrise Valley Dr. #452,
Reston, VA 20191
(www.hafree.org)

The Satanic Temple
(https://thesatanictemple.com/)

Secular Student Alliance
PO Box 411477
Los Angeles, CA 90041
(https://secularstudents.org)

Magazines

American Atheist
225 Cristiani St.
Cranford, NJ 07016
(www.atheists.org)

Free Inquiry
P.O. Box 664
Amherst, NY 14226
(https://secularhumanism.org)

Freethought Today
P.O. Box 750
Madison, WI 53701
(www.freethoughttoday.com)

The Humanist
1821 Jefferson Place NW
Washington, DC 20036
(https://americanhumanist.org)

Skeptic
P.O. Box 338
Altadena, California 91001
(www.skeptic.com)

The Truth Seeker
P.O. Box 161413
San Diego, CA 92176
(thetruthseeker.net)

Web Sites & Blogs

Atheist Revolution
(https://www.atheistrev.com/)

Bible Gateway
(https://www.biblegateway.com/)

Cult News Network
(https://cultnews.net/)

Daylight Atheism
(www.patheos.com/blogs/daylightatheism/)

Fark
(www.fark.com)

Friendly Atheist
(https://onlysky.media/friendlyatheist/)

Godzooks
(www.patheos.com/blogs/godzooks/)

Raw Story
(www.rawstory.com)

Reason Advocates
(www.patheos.com/blogs/reasonadvocates/)

Secular Directory
(https://seculardirectory.org/)

Secular Woman
(http://www.secularwoman.org/)

Skeptic's Annotated Bible
(https://skepticsannotatedbible.com/)

The Thinking Atheist
(www.thethinkingatheist.com)

Secular Recovery Groups

Lifering
(https://lifering.org)

Moderation Management
(https://moderation.org)

Secular Organizations for Sobriety
(www.sossobriety.org)

SMART Recovery
(www.smartrecovery.org)

Women for Sobriety
(https://womenforsobriety.org)

Bibliography

Alumkal, Antony. *Paranoid Science: The Religious Right's War on Reality*. New York: NYU Press, 2017.

Bakunin, Mikhail. *God and the State*. New York: Dover, 1970.

Bierce, Ambrose. *The Devil's Dictionary* (volume 7 of *The Collected Works of Ambrose Bierce*). Walter Neale, 1909.

Bozarth, G. Richard. *Bible Tales for Ages 18 and Up*. Tucson: See Sharp Press, 2014.

Brody, Fawn. *No Man Knows My History*. New York: Knopf, 1945 (rev. ed. 1971).

Bufe, Charles (ed.). *Godless: 150 Years of Disbelief.* Oakland: PM Press, 2019.

—*The American Heretic's Dictionary (Revised & Expanded).* Tucson: See Sharp Press, 2016.

—*Alcoholic Anonymous: Cult or Cure?* Tucson: See Sharp Press, 1998.

—*The Heretic's Handbook of Quotations*. Tucson: See Sharp Press, 1992.

Dawkins, Richard. *The God Delusion*. Boston: Houghton Mifflin, 2006.

Dennett, Daniel. *Breaking the Spell: Religion as a Natural Phenomenon*. London, New York: Penguin, 2006.

Diggins, John P. *Mussolini and Fascism: The View from America*. Princeton, NJ: Princeton University Press, 1972.

Driberg, Tom. *The Mystery of Moral Re-Armament*. New York: Alfred A. Knopf, 1965.

Edwards, Chris. *Spiritual Snake Oil: Fads and Fallacies in Popular Culture.* Tucson: See Sharp Press, 2011.

Edwards, Chris (as S.C. Hitchcock). *Disbelief 101: A Young Person's Guide to Atheism*. Tucson: See Sharp Press, 2009.

Ellis, Albert. *The Case Against Religiosity*. New York: Institute for Rational Emotive Therapy, 1980.

Evans, Harold and Goldstein, Phyllis. *A Convenient Hatred: The History of Anti-Semitism*. Facing History and Ourselves, 2012.

Faure, Sebastien. "Twelve Proofs of the Nonexistence of God" in *Godless: 150 Years of Disbelief*, Chaz Bufe, ed. Oakland: PM Press, 2019.

Flynn, Tom. *The New Encyclopedia of Unbelief.* Buffalo: Prometheus, 2007.

Freud, Sigmund. *The Future of an Illusion*. New York: W.W. Norton, 1927.

Funk, Robert, Hoover, Roy, and the Jesus Seminar. *The Five Gospels: What Did Jesus Really Say?* New York: Macmillan, 1993.

Furniss, Rev. John. *Tracts for Spiritual Reading*. New York: P.J. Kenedy (sic), 1877.

Gibbon, Edward. *The Decline and Fall of the Roman Empire*. London: Strahan and Cadell, 1776–1789 (6 volumes). (Project Gutenberg. Free e-book, www.gutenberg.org)

Gottlieb, Scott. *Uncontrolled Spread: Why COVID-19 Crushed Us and How We Can Defeat the Next Pandemic*. New York: Harper, 2021.

Grant, John. *Corrupted Science: Fraud, Ideology, and Politics in Science (revised & expanded)*. Tucson: See Sharp Press, 2018.

Grayling, A.C. *The God Argument: The Case Against Religion and for Humanism*. New York: Bloomsbury USA, 2014.

Green, Justin. *Binky Brown Sampler* (including *Binky Brown Meets the Holy Virgin Mary*, Green's autobiographical comic about growing up Catholic in the 1950s). San Francisco: Last Gasp, 1995.

Harris, Sam. *The End of Faith. Religion, Terror, and the Future of Reason*. New York: W.W. Norton, 2004.

Harris, Sam. *Letter to a Christian Nation*. New York: Knopf, 2006.

Hassan, Steven. *The Cult of Trump: A Leading Cult Expert Explains How the President Uses Mind Control*. New York: Free Press, 2019.

Hitchens, Christopher. *God Is Not Great: How Religion Poisons Everything*. New York: Hachette, 2007.

Hitchens, Christopher. *The Missionary Position: Mother Teresa in Theory and Practice*. London: Verso, 1995.

Irish, David. *America's Taliban: In Its Own Words*. Tucson: See Sharp Press, 2003.

Jones, Robert P. *White Too Long: The Legacy of White Supremacy in American Christianity*. New York: Simon & Schuster, 2020.

Kertzer, David I. *The Pope and Mussolini: The Secret History of Pius XI and the Rise of Fascism in Europe*. New York: Random House, 2015.

Lea, Henry Charles. *A History of the Inquisition of the Middle Ages*. 1888. (Project Gutenberg, 2012. Free e-book, www.gutenberg.org)

Lecky, William Edward Hartpole. *A History of European Morals from Augustus to Charlemagne*. London: Longman, Green, and Co., 1920. (originally published 1869) (Project Gutenberg, 2012. Free e-book, www.gutenberg.org)

Lifton, Robert Jay. *Losing Reality: On Cults, Cultism, and the Mindset of Political and Religious Zealotry*. New York: New Press, 2019.

Lifton, Robert Jay. *Thought Reform and the Psychology of Totalism: A study of brainwashing in China*. Mannsville Center, CT: Martino Publishing, 2014.

Luther, Martin. *On the Jews and Their Lies*. 1543.

MacCulloch, Diarmaid. *Christianity: The First Three Thousand Years*. New York: Penguin, 2011.

MacDonald, George E. *Thumbscrew and Rack*. Tucson: See Sharp Press, 1998.

Martinez, Thomas with John Gunther. *Brotherhood of Murder: How one man's journey through fear brought The Order—the most dangerous racist gang in America—to Justice*. New York: McGraw-Hill, 1988.

Mato Nunpa, Chris. *The Great Evil: Christianity, the Bible, and the Native American Genocide*. Tucson: See Sharp Press, 2020.

McCabe, Joseph. *Christianity and Slavery*. Tucson: See Sharp Press, 1997.

—*Horrors of the Inquisition*. Tucson: See Sharp Press, 1998.

—*How Christianity Grew Out of Paganism*. Tucson: See Sharp Press, 1998.

—*Judeo-Christian Degradation of Woman*. Tucson: See Sharp Press, 1998.

—*Pagan Christs*. Tucson: See Sharp Press, 1999.

McDonald, James. *Beyond Belief: Two thousand years of bad faith in the Christian Church*. Reading, England: Garnet Press, 2012.

McWilliams, Peter. *Ain't Nobody's Business If You Do: The Absurdity of Consensual Crimes in a Free Society*. Prelude Press: West Hollywood, CA, 1996.

Mencken, H.L. *The Philosophy of Friedrich Nietzsche*. Tucson: See Sharp Press, 2003. (originally published 1908)

Nietzsche, Friedrich. *The Anti-Christ*. Tucson: See Sharp Press, 1999. (Project Gutenberg, 2006. Free e-book, www.gutenberg.org)

—*Beyond Good and Evil*. New York: Penguin, 2003. (Project Gutenberg, 2009. Free e-book, www.gutenberg.org)

—*Human, All Too Human*. New York: Penguin, 1994.

Nordau, Max. *Conventional Lies of Our Civilization*. Chicago: Laird and Lee, 1886.

—*The Interpretation of History*. New York: Willey Book Co., 1910.

Paine, Thomas. *The Age of Reason*. Paris: Barrois, 1794. (Project Gutenberg, 2010. Free e-book, www.gutenberg.org)

Pearl, Michael and Debi. *To Train Up a Child*. No Greater Joy Ministries, 1994.

Posner, Gerald. *God's Bankers: A History of Money and Power at the Vatican*. New York: Macmillan, 2015.

Posner, Sarah. *Unholy: Why White Evangelicals Worship at the Altar of Donald Trump*. New York: Random House, 2020.

Posner, Sarah. *God's Profits: Faith, Fraud, and the Republican Campaign for Values Voters*. Sausalito, CA: Polipoint Press, 2008.

Rae, Noel. *The Great Stain: Witnessing American Slavery*. New York: Overlook Press, 2018.

Reinke-Heinemann, Uta. *Eunuchs for the Kingdom of Heaven's Sake: Women, Sexuality, and the Catholic Church*. New York: Doubleday, 1990.

Reiterman, Tim with John Jacobs. *Raven: The Untold Story of the Rev. Jim Jones and His People*. New York: Penguin, 2008.

Russell, Bertrand. *Why I Am Not a Christian*. Lecture at Battersea, 1927. Multiple publishers.

Smith, George H. *Atheism: The Case Against God*. Buffalo: Prometheus, 2016.

Stannard, Dave E. *American Holocaust: The Conquest of the New World*. New York: Oxford University Press, 1992.

Stanton, Elizabeth Cady. *The History of Woman Suffrage, Vol. 1*. Andesite Press (Simon & Schuster imprint), 2015.

—*The History of Woman Suffrage, Vol. 2*. Andesite Press, 2015.

Stenger, Victor. *God: The Failed Hypothesis: How Science Shows that God Does Not Exist*. Buffalo: Prometheus, 2008.

Stenger, Victor. *God and the Folly of Faith: The Incompatibility of Science and Religion*. Buffalo: Prometheus, 2012.

Tannahill, Reay. *Sex in History*. New York: Stein and Day, 1980.

Wells, Steve. *The Skeptic's Annotated Bible*. Moscow, ID: SAB Books, 2013. (Free online version at www.skepticsannotatedbible.com)

—*Drunk with Blood: God's Killings in the Bible*. Moscow, ID: SAB Books, 2013.

—*Strange Flesh: The Bible and Homosexuality*. Moscow, ID: SAB Books, 2014.

White, Andrew Dickson. *The History of the Warfare of Science with Theology in Christendom*. Various publishers, 1896. (Project Gutenberg, 2009. Free e-book, www.gutenberg.org)

Wistrich, S.W. *A Lethal Obsession: Anti-Semitism from Antiquity to the Global Jihad*. New York: Random House, 2010.

Wright, Lawrence. *Going Clear: Scientology, Hollywood, & the Prison of Belief*. New York: Alfred A. Knopf, 2013

Index

Related See Sharp Press Books

Alcoholics Anonymous: Cult or Cure?, by Charles Bufe. This groundbreaking book covers AA's history, religious origins, religious nature, cult-like tendencies, and remarkable ineffectiveness.

"Both supporters and critics of AA could benefit from reading this factual book." —*Ottawa Citizen*

"This book is exceptionally well written. It is articulate, objective, concise, and complete . . ." —*Journal of Rational Recovery*

The American Heretic's Dictionary, by Chaz Bufe. The 21st-century successor to Ambrose Bierce's *Devil's Dictionary*. The *Heretic's Dictionary* contains over 650 definitions by Bufe, dozens of illustrations, and an appendix containing Bierce's 200 best definitions.

"Such bitterness, such negativity, such unbridled humor, wit and sarcasm." —*Mensa Bulletin*

"Sick and offensive" —*Small Press*

The Anti-Christ, by Friedrich Nietzsche (translated by H.L. Mencken). The capstone of Nietzsche's writing career: his insightful, biting, and devastating takedown of Christianity.

"Bombastic, acerbic, and coldly analytical, *The Anti-Christ* exemplfies the muscularity of thought that surrounds the Nietzsche legend . . . a profound parting shot from perhaps the most significant philosopher of the 19th century." —*Eye Magazine*

Bible Tales for Ages 18 and Up, by G. Richard Bozarth. This very funny, ribald retelling of well known Bible stories reveals what these tales, stripped of euphemisms and obfuscation, really mean. As the author notes, "These stories are more fully developed than in the Old Testament and are humorous, though some parts are appalling because Bible stories are often appalling."

Disbelief 101: A young person's guide to atheism, by S.C. Hitchcock. The best introduction to atheism for young people.

"Sure to outrage religious readers, and not just fundamentalists, this chatty, totally irreverent title . . . speaks to teen rebels of all faiths who question religious indoctrination." —*Booklist*

"Not just for young people, this book is for everyone!" —*The Moral Atheist*

Free Radicals: A novel of utopia and dystopia, by Zeke Teflon. This dark, funny, science fiction prison-planet novel features multiple settings in religious and political cults and several cult-leader characters.

"Solidly entertaining" —*Publishers Weekly*

"*Free Radicals* is among the best future-shock reads in years. . . . If we lived in the '60s and '70s—when audience-rattling paperbacks like *Naked Lunch* were cheap, plentiful and available on pharmacy spinner racks—critics would hail *Free Radicals* as a masterpiece." —*Tucson Weekly*

The Great Evil: Christianity, the Bible, and the Native American Genocide, by Christ Mato Nunpa. A depiction and denunciation of the horrors visited upon Native Americans by European and American Christians.

The Heretic's Handbook of Quotations: Cutting Comments on Burning Issues, Charles Bufe, ed. This is the quotations book for atheists, anarchists, and everyone else on the left side of the political spectrum. *The Heretic's Handbook* contains over 2,000 revealing and oft-times funny quotations on myriad topics as well as dozens of illustrations, cartoons, and other graphics.

"This book is a far-reaching collection of timeless, provocative, politically astute quotations from a wide range of people in many walks of life. It is fun, informative, and more." —*Z Magazine*

The Mormon Cult: A former missionary reveals the secrets of Mormon mind control, by Jack B. Worthy. This book is both a fascinating memoir of former-elder Worthy's misadventures as a Mormon missionary in Hong Kong and a very revealing exposé of Mormon indoctrination methods.

The Philosophy of Friedrich Nietzsche, by H.L. Mencken. A very insightful look at the foremost iconoclastic philosopher of the 19th century by the foremost iconoclastic journalist of the first half of the 20th century. Contains a lengthy introduction comparing and contrasting the lives and views of Nietzsche and Mencken.

Spiritual Snake Oil: Fads & fallacies in pop culture, by Chris Edwards. This scathing small book dissects the preachings of the most prominent New Age snake oil salesmen (and women), and also goes after advocates of oxymoronic "intellectual Christianity."

—"A whale of a read for those interested in stripping away the magical thinking of our contemporary world with incisive—sometimes brutal—wit." —*Nuvo*